Economic Crisis in Africa

African Perspectives on Development Problems and Potentials

edited by
Adebayo Adedeji and
Timothy M. Shaw

Lynne Rienner Publishers, Inc • Boulder, Colorado

Acknowledgment

Figure 5.1, Regional Organizations in Africa, reprinted with permission. © Sceptre Books Limited, London.

Published in the United States of America in 1985 by
Lynne Rienner Publishers, Inc.
948 North Street, Boulder, Colorado 80302

Library of Congress Cataloging in Publication Data
Main entry under title:

Economic Crisis in Africa

Bibliography: p.
Includes index.
1. Africa--Economic policy--Addresses, essays, lectures. 2. Africa--Economic conditions--1960- -- Addresses, essays, lectures. 3. Economic assistance--Africa--Addresses, essays, lectures. I. Adedeji, Adebayo. II. Shaw, Timothy M.
HC800.E27 1985 338.96 85-10763
ISBN 0-931477-43-3

Distributed outside of North and South America and Japan by Frances Pinter (Publishers) Ltd, 25 Floral Street, London WC2E 9DS England. UK ISBN: 0-86187-571-0

Printed and bound in the United States of America

Economic Crisis in Africa

MELILLA
Tunis
CEUTA
Algiers
TUNISIA
Rabat
MOROCCO
Benghazi
Tripoli
Cairo
El-Ayoun
ALGERIA
LIBYA
EGYPT
WESTERN SAHARA
CAPE VERDE IS.
Praia
MAURITANIA
Nouakchott
MALI
NIGER
CHAD
Khartoum
SUDAN
SENEGAL
Dakar
THE GAMBIA
Banjul
Bamako
Niamey
BURKINA FASO
Ouagadougou
DJIBOUTI
Djibouti
Ndjamena
GUINEA-BISSAU
Bissau
GUINEA
Conakry
BENIN
Porto Novo
ETHIOPIA
Freetown
SIERRA LEONE
IVORY COAST
Abidjan
GHANA
Accra
NIGERIA
Lagos
Addis Ababa
Monrovia
LIBERIA
TOGO
Lome
CAMEROON
Yaounde
CENTRAL AFRICAN REPUBLIC
Bangui
SOMALIA
EQUATORIAL GUINEA
Malabo
UGANDA
Kampala
KENYA
Mogadishu
SAO TOME E PRINCIPE
Libreville
GABON
RWANDA
Kigali
ZAIRE
Nairobi
CONGO
Brazzaville
Kinshasa
BURUNDI
Bujumbura
ZANZIBAR
Dar es Salaam
TANZANIA
SEYCHELLES IS.
Victoria
Luanda
ANGOLA
Lilongwe
MALAWI
Moroni
COMORO IS.
ZAMBIA
Lusaka
Harare
MOZAMBIQUE
Antananarivo
ZIMBABWE
NAMIBIA
MAURITIUS
BOTSWANA
MADAGASCAR
Port Louis
REUNION
Windhoek
Gaborone
Pretoria
Maputo
SWAZILAND
Mbabane
SOUTH AFRICA
LESOTHO
Maseru

Contents

Maps, Tables, and Figures

MAPS

TABLES

FIGURES

Preface

The cosponsors of the innovative November 1984 Conference on Africa's Economic Crisis and the Lagos Plan of Action[1] had agreed to organize the meeting out of which this book grew[2] long before the Western media "discovered" Ethiopia. By coincidence, however, the Halifax conference assembled as the famine was flashing onto Western television screens. The weekend we met in Nova Scotia, the United Nations General Assembly began during its 39th session a special debate on the crisis, and coordinators for emergency responses were appointed.[3] This background added salience to our agenda: the relevance of the Lagos Plan not only to the immediate disaster, but also to its longer-term causes, resolution, and elimination.

The joint conference was made possible by the generosity of both African and Canadian institutions. Aside from monies from the cosponsors--the UN Economic Commission for Africa (ECA) and Dalhousie University--the event attracted support from the Canadian International Development Agency (CIDA), the International Development Research Center (IDRC), the Commonwealth Secretariat, the Ford Foundation, various UN specialized agencies and organizations such as FAO and UNDP, the IBRD, and the IMF, who also sent representatives. And the preparation of this edited and retyped manuscript was made possible by timely assistance from the Faculty of Graduate Studies at Dalhousie and from Employment Canada for the invaluable services of Leslie J. Adamson and G. Kirk Williams, respectively.

If the conference drew attention to Africa's own position on the continent's direction, it also served to launch the Centre for African Studies at Dalhousie into "development education." The present volume is but one product of the meetings; others are a 50-minute videotape "Africans Respond to Their Continental Crisis" and a 16-page "Briefing Paper on Africa's Economic Crisis," both available from the Centre office (1444 Seymour Street, Dalhousie University, Halifax, Nova Scotia, B3H 4H6, Canada). In addition, the Centre is actively involved with other agencies in transforming the current spontaneous concern over the Ethiopian famine into more sustained and informed awareness of the causes and consequences of underdevelopment through school, community, business, service, and NGO activities.

Finally, the November conference marked a further stage in the evolution of African-Canadian relations. Canada has much to learn from as well as contribute to the African continent. We hope this collection of original papers by African scholars and policy-makers will serve to enhance the continent's development as well as ensure further and appropriate Canadian contributions.[4] All authors write in their personal capacities; none of these chapters should be taken to reflect the policies of institutions with which they are or have been associated.

Adebayo Adedeji and Timothy M. Shaw

NOTES

1. The full title of the conference was "The Lagos Plan of Action and the Final Act of Lagos and the Future of Africa's International Economic Relations: Projections and Implications for Policy-makers." A list of the conference participants is provided in the appendix to this book.

2. The present volume includes only a selection of papers and documents presented at the meeting; others are to appear in a variety of journals and collections, including a few in "Dalhousie African Working Papers."

3. On this conjuncture see Timothy M. Shaw and David Fasholé Luke, "Africa's Economic Problems and Potentials: joint ECA-Dalhousie conference," Canadian Journal of Development Studies 6 (1), 1985 (forthcoming).

4. On the implications for Canadian foreign, especially development, policy of the African crisis, see Timothy M. Shaw, "Ethiopia: beyond the famine," International Perspectives, May/June 1985.

About the Contributors

Adebayo Adedeji, Nigeria, is executive secretary of the Economic Commission for Africa, Addis Ababa, Ethiopia, and a U N undersecretary general.

Agnes Akosua Aidoo, Ghana, is with the African Training and Research Centre for Women, Addis Ababa, Ethiopia.

Julius Olu Aiyegbusi, Nigeria, is director of the ECA's Policy and Programme Coordination Office, Addis Ababa, Ethiopia.

S. K. B. Asante, Ghana, is visiting professor of African studies at the University of Florida, Gainesville, Florida.

Negussay Ayele, Ethiopia, is associate professor in the College of Social Sciences, University of Addis Ababa, Ethiopia.

Robert S. Browne, the United States, is in the African Studies and Research Program at Howard University, Washington, D.C.

Cyril Kofie Daddieh, Ghana, is in the University of Iowa's Program in Development Studies, Iowa City, Iowa.

Ibrahim H. El-Issawy, Egypt, is professor of economics in the Institute of National Planning, Cairo.

Amir Jamal, Tanzania, is minister of state for cabinet affairs, Dar es Salaam, Tanzania.

George M. Kimani, Kenya, is director of the Joint ECA/UNIDO Industry Division, ECA, Addis Ababa, Ethiopia.

G. E. A. Lardner, Sierra Leone, is former director of the ECA's Policy and Programme Coordination Office.

L. A. Odero-Ogwel, Kenya, is with the Joint ECA/FAO Agriculture Division of the ECA.

E. P. Pallangyo, Tanzania, is with the Joint ECA/FAO Agriculture Division of the ECA.

Timothy M. Shaw, Canada, is director of the Centre for African Studies and professor of political science at Dalhousie University, Halifax, Nova Scotia.

D. Babatunde Thomas, Nigeria, is director of the African Regional Centre for Technology, Dakar, Senegal.

Abbreviations

ACP	African, Caribbean and Pacific States (in Lomé Convention)
ADB	African Development Bank
AFCC	African Federation of Chambers of Commerce
ASEAN	Association of South East Asian Nations
ATRCW	African Training and Research Center for Women
BADEA	Arab Development Bank in Africa
BHN	Basic Human Needs
CEAO	West African Economic Community
CIDA	Canadian International Development Agency
CMEA	Council for Mutual Economic Assistance (COMECON)
DAC	Development Assistance Committee (OECD)
EAC	East African Community
ECA	UN Economic Commission for Africa
ECCAS	Economic Community of Central African States
ECLAC	Economic Commission for Latin America and the Caribbean
ECOSOC	United Nations Economic and Social Council
ECOWAS	Economic Community of West African States
EEC	European Economic Community
FAO	UN Food and Agricultural Organization
FLS	Front Line States (of Southern Africa)
GATT	General Agreement on Tariffs and Trade
GDP	Gross Domestic Product
GNP	Gross National Product
IGOs	Inter-Governmental Organizations
IBRD	International Bank for Reconstruction and Development (World Bank)
IDA	International Development Association (IBRD)
IFAD	International Fund for Agricultural Development
ILO	UN International Labor Organization
IMF	International Monetary Fund

LPA	Lagos Plan of Action
MNCs	Multi-National Corporations
MRU	Mano River Union
MULPOC	(ECA) Multinational Programming and Operational Center
NGOs	Non-Governmental Organizations
NIC	Newly Industrializing Countries
NIEO	New International Economic Order
OAU	Organization of African Unity
ODA	Official Development Assistance
OECD	Organization for Economic Cooperation and Development
OPEC	Organization of Petroleum Exporting Countries
PTA	Preferential Trade Area for Eastern and Southern Africa
SADCC	Southern African Development Coordination Conference
SATCC	Southern African Transport and Communications Commission (SADCC)
SDR	Special Drawing Rights
SSA	Sub-Saharan Africa
TNCs	Trans-National Corporations
UDEAC	Central African Customs and Economic Union
UN	United Nations
UNCTAD	United Nations Conference on Trade and Development
UNDP	United Nations Development Program
UNEP	United Nations Environmental Program
UNESCO	United Nations Educational, Scientific and Cultural Organization
UNIDO	United Nations Industrial Development Organization
WFP	World Food Program
WMVA	World Manufacturing Value-Added

Adebayo Adedeji and Timothy M. Shaw

Introduction: Africa's Condition and Projections for the Future

> We are aware that African countries recognise that they have the primary responsibility for their development and for addressing the present crisis....We agree that in confronting the challenge of development, national policies and measures, such as those outlined in the Lagos Plan of Action...provide a framework for national and subregional action and international support.
>
> UN "Resolution on the Critical Economic Situation in Africa"[1]

> 1984 will go down in history as Africa's worst year, economically, since the great depression. Throughout the year concern was publicly or privately expressed about the rapidly deteriorating economic situation in Africa....
>
> The cumulative effect of three factors--severe and persistent drought; an extremely unfavorable global economic environment; and dramatic increases in Africa's external debt, interest rates and debt-servicing costs--led to the escalation of the crisis in 1984.
>
> Adebayo Adedeji, "State of the Continent, 1984"[2]

> The predicament of sub-Saharan Africa is a recurring theme throughout this Report...for the region as a whole, GDP per capita fell during the 1970s. It could well do so again in the years up to 1995. Of the policy failings that contributed to slow growth in other developing countries, all can be found in more or less chronic form in many African countries. The scope for raising growth rates by improving policies is therefore greatest in Africa.
>
> IBRD *World Development Report, 1984*[3]

The image and status of Africa in the mid-1980s--one hundred years after the Berlin Conference that balkanized the "dark continent"[4]--is not very positive: the agony of Ethiopia has generated concern and emotion everywhere.[5] Yet, not only was the famine in the Horn of Africa predicted and anticipated--"when" was the only question--but further droughts in several parts of the continent have occured during the 1982-85 period and many more may be expected before the year 2000. In the aftermath of the Ethiopian, Sahelian, Southern and Eastern African emergencies, what can and might the rest of the world do to head off further catastrophies? If only the incidence and impact of droughts are in doubt, can their results yet be contained?

The African condition[6] of declining development and increasing misery had already generated a positive and creative indigenous response years before the famine of 1984. The earlier Ethiopian and Sahelian droughts combined with the global shocks of the early 1970s to produce a serious reevaluation of Africa's development performance and direction, as spelled out in chapter 1 of this volume. A series of academic and practitioner consultations from the mid-1970s onward led to the articulation and adoption of the Monrovia Strategy, which introduced the now-established notions of self-reliance and self-sustainment into continental forums and debates.[7] The mix of environmental and social concerns was based on the interaction of the intellectual, developmental, and political predispositions of participants as reflected in the Monrovia papers and positions.[8] In turn, these reflected a variety of pressures, problems, and possibilities:

1. disappointing development *performances* in most of Africa;
2. unpromising *projections* for the rest of the twentieth century based on current trends;
3. inappropriate development *policies*--modernization assumptions seemed to lead to dependence rather than development or autonomy;
4. *failure of demands* for a New International Economic Order (NIEO)--Africa was not about to be saved by a grand reordering of the global economy;
5. increasing *inequalities* between and within African states that undermined progress toward national and regional integration; and
6. growing determination of African institutions and leaders to assert their own path--their *own pedagogy and philosophy*--and resist continued extracontinental pressures.

In short, the very intensity of the crisis concentrated attention on these issues, leading to Africa's first economic summit in Lagos in April 1980.

This book constitutes an evaluation of the causes and consequences of the declarations of Africa's own development direction: the Lagos Plan of Action and the Final Act of Lagos.[9] Two decades after independence, the continent's economic future may appear to be gloomy;[10] yet, the limitations and frustrations of formal decolonization without economic change have finally produced their antithesis: collective African nationalism. Having inherited or borrowed development policy as well as political theory, Africa has now begun to revive its own economic assumptions and design its own orientations, just as it has come to reject much of its neocolonial legal and organizational legacy.[11]

The salient elements of this new nationalism of self-reliance--appropriate for a continent in crisis in a world under stress--are discussed in the following chapters; these elements combine contemporary dependencia, environmentalism, and basic human needs (BHN) with indigenous and long-standing values and priorities. The least developed continent has begun to recognize its distinctive, not entirely unattractive, position and its potential in this consensual declaration of economic independence. Africa is now in a better position to respond to intracontinental problems and extra-continental pressures; it has presented its own response to intensifying development challenges. If the rest of the international community really wants to assist, then it can consult and respect Africa's position as articulated in the Monrovia Strategy and the Lagos Plan.[12]

The Lagos Plan not only reflects academic and practitioner perspectives from a variety of disciplinary and institutional affiliations; it also constitutes a long- as well as a short-term response, one that treats Africa's social, political, economic, environmental, and intellectual systems as a whole. In response to the tenuousness of political without economic independence, the Lagos Plan seeks to transform the productive basis of Africa's political economy. In emphasizing industrial and agricultural production for continental rather than external consumption, the plan seeks to transcend inherited, balkanized bilateral linkages with assorted European metropoles; collective self-reliance is intended to supersede national dependencies. The apparent contradiction of a rich resource base and deficient economic performance is seen as the result of external demand for resources; eliminate or reduce foreign involvement, and Africa's natural resources can be processed for continental development, not European affluence. The Lagos Plan attempts to capture and mold the physical and organizational capacities of the continent for a "willed future" rather than a Hobbesian vision.[13]

In so doing, the Lagos Plan--in process as well as policy--has brought together a rich mélange of individuals, institutions, interests, and ideals. Moreover, it has indicated ways out of both current crises and continuing constraints by replacing Africa's excessive extroversion with relative introversion in order to balance an overly outward-looking inheritance. In carefully navigating between the Scylla of autarky and the Charybdis of vulnerability, the plan charts not only an acceptable course--one which leads to an attractive destination--but also allows for a safe passage in very choppy seas. Given the fundamental changes taking place in the global economy, for the African ship of state to take any other route would be hazardous if not irresponsible. The Lagos Plan attempts, then, to marry innovation with caution, change with security. It represents a mix of responses to both the new international division of labor and the new intellectual discovery of dialectic. It thus builds upon policy choices and analytical imperatives.

The abundance of continental resources available to support informed and enlightened revisionism is reflected in the contributions in the present volume of original essays by African policy-makers and academics. These innovative, indigenous authors build upon the framework provided and legitimized by the Lagos Plan to provide a range of explanations, propositions, and projections. Their range of approaches is catholic--from new technologies to old truths and from national regimes to global constraints. Yet, the underlying theme remains the relevance, in both original and revised forms, of the Lagos Plan. The political and psychological benefits of the plan are already apparent; primary among them is a new self-confidence on the part of Africans to address the crucial issues before them.[14]

In contrast to the World Bank's detractive Agenda for the continent,[15] the Lagos Plan is holistic; it treats environment as well as economics, and gender as well as infrastructure. The plan also advances psychological as well as political self-reliance. Its goals for independence are not limited to production, distribution, and accumulation, but embrace technology, training, and family as well. The World Bank is preoccupied with material recession and revival, whereas the Plan treats their metaphysical correlates also.

The potential for renovation and innovation rather than depression has been augmented as the continental crisis has intensified, because old approaches obviously have become outmoded. The new confidence is expressed not only in the Lagos Plan consensus but also in the ability of Africans to redefine development, exchange, and relationship. This was reflected in the candidness of the presentations and discussions that took place at Dalhousie and has been captured in this book. Throughout both proceedings and publication, the participants remained willing to reconsider and reorient as well as revive and restate. The ability of the UN Economic Commission on Africa (ECA) to learn from the crisis apparently surpasses the World Bank's present capacity.[16]

This volume is then the result of an exercise in radical political economy: "radical" because it goes to the roots of the problem--capitalism, colonialism, corporations, and compradors--and "political" economy because it recognizes the interrelationship between policy and production, exchange and exploitation. The politics of the Lagos Plan are treated by Adedeji, Ayele, and Jamal, while El-Issawy and Aidoo examine two of the bases of Africa's underdevelopment: uneven class and gender roles. The tension between different definitions and levels of self-reliance is addressed frankly by Aiyegbusi and Jamal while they, along with Adedeji, El-Issawy, and Kimani, discuss fluctuating levels of external assistance and the transitional if paradoxical need for extra-African involvement in the enhancement of intra-African self-reliance. El-Issawy and Kimani augment the points of Ayele, Aiyegbusi, and Jamal on the popularization of the plan by identifying possible transnational coalitions of supporters that bridge the North-South divide. The imperative of concentrating on agriculture for both food production and industrial input is noted by Pallangyo, Odero-Ogwel, and Daddieh and also mentioned by Kimani and Thomas in their discussions of the possibilities for more autonomous and appropriate industrial, technological, and distributive institutions. Both of the latter urge caution concerning new postindustrial technologies and the obsolescence of many of Africa's assumptions, arrangements, and commodities. They also emphasize the need for foreign exchange for imported inputs and parts, indicating the implications for donors as well as recipients, particularly in the short-term.

The recurrent themes of policy, poverty, resources, revenues, communications, and productivity are raised in many chapters, albeit from different perspectives and with diverse emphases. A crucial issue addressed in both the plan and this book is one of gender. If women, as the majority of Africa's population, are able to play a full and recognized role in development, then not only agriculture, industry, technology, and infrastructure will be transformed, but development itself may be redefined in the direction of basic human needs (BHN), to the benefit of all. The radical potential of the *Lagos Plan* is such that it may come to redefine the sexual as well as international and intranational divisions of labor.

In the end, Africa's quest for regeneration and renaissance will depend not only on the quality of its policies and strategies, crucial though these are as prerequisites, but also on the degree to which the *Lagos Plan of Action*'s myriad elements are adopted, implemented, revised, and transcended. The politics of the plan consist not only of its conceptualization, adoption, articulation, and popularization but also in how African and other governments and peoples perceive and receive it. It is this imponderable that will maintain interest in the plan until at least the end of the century, hopefully long after economic and personal survival are no longer in jeopardy. However, in the perspectives of the contributors to this volume and of all the participants at the ECA/Dalhousie 1984 Conference there is no cause for despair. There is indeed every possibility that out of this present crisis will emerge an increasingly self-reliant and self-contained process of development in Africa. One of the main themes which runs through the volume is that the international community has a crucial role to play in this process. Will it be able to rise to this profound challenge. This collection is intended to inform and advance such pioneering so that despair will indeed give way to development.

NOTES

1. UN, "Resolution on the Critical Economic Situation in Africa" (A/RES/39/29), 7 December 1984, pp. 3-4.
2. Adebayo Adedeji, "State of the Continent, 1984," reprinted as "Africa's Economy in 1984: Crisis upon Crisis," *West Africa* 3516 (14 January 1985): 52.
3. World Bank, *World Development Report, 1984* (Oxford: OUP for World Bank, 1984), p. 2.
4. For a recent review of precolonial white adventurers see Christopher Hibbert, *Africa Explored: Europeans in the Dark Continent, 1769-1889* (Harmondsworth: Penguin, 1984).
5. See, for example, "The African Emergency: A Continent in Crisis," *UNICEF Canada Communiqué* (Winter 1985) and "Africa: The Land is Growing Old. What Will the Children Inherit?," *UNICEF News* 120 (1984).
6. For an idiosyncratic precrisis overview see Ali A. Mazrui, *The African Condition: A Political Diagnosis* (London: Heinemann, 1980).

7. See "Africa towards the Year 2000: Final Report on the Joint OAU/ECA Symposium on the Future Development of Africa," IFDA Dossier 7 (May 1979) and OAU, "Monrovia Strategy for the Development of Africa and the Declaration of Commitment," (Addis Ababa, 1979).

8. See Ibid. and OAU, What Kind of Africa by the Year 2000? (Addis Ababa: OAU, May 1979).

9. See OAU, Lagos Plan of Action for the Economic Development of Africa, 1980-2000 (Geneva: International Institute for Labor Studies, 1981), which includes the "Final Act of Lagos" as annex one, pp. 127-128; selections appear in appendix one of Luke and Shaw, eds., Continental Crisis, pp. 155-164.

10. See the set of projections in Timothy M. Shaw, ed., Alternative Futures for Africa (Boulder: Westview, 1982).

11. See the political as well as economic reactions in Timothy M. Shaw and Olajide Aluko, eds., Africa Projected: from Recession to Renaissance by the Year 2000? (London: Macmillan; New York: St. Martins, 1985).

12. See Timothy M. Shaw, "Debates about Africa's Future: the Brandt, World Bank and Lagos Plan Blueprints," Third World Quarterly 5 (2) (April 1983): 330-344, and Timothy M. Shaw and David Fasholé Luke, "Africa's Economic Problems and Potentials," Canadian Journal of Development Studies 6 (1) (forthcoming in 1985).

13. See ECA, ECA and Africa's Development, 1983-2008: A Preliminary Perspective Study (Addis Ababa: ECA, 1983).

14. On the potential of African economic and analytic self-reliance see, inter alia Adebayo Adedeji, "Africa: Permanent Underdog?" International Perspectives (March-April 1981) and Timothy M. Shaw, "The African Crisis: Alternative Development Strategies for the Continent," Alternatives 9 (1), (1983): 111-127.

15. See World Bank, Accelerated Development in Sub-Saharan Africa: An Agenda for Action (Washington: World Bank, 1981).

16. Contrast, for instance, ECA and Africa's Development with the successor volumes to the "Berg Report," (Agenda for Action): Sub-Saharan Africa: Progress Report on Development Prospects and Programs (Washington: World Bank, 1983) and Toward Sustained Development in Sub-Saharan Africa: A Joint Program of Action (Washington: World Bank, 1984).

Part 1

Self-Reliance and Self-Sustainment

Adebayo Adedeji

1 The Monrovia Strategy and the *Lagos Plan of Action*: Five Years After

On 29 April 1980 history was made in Africa by African leaders when at their first economic summit, held in Lagos, they unanimously adopted the Lagos Plan of Action for the Economic Development of Africa, 1980-2000. In adopting this plan, the African heads of state and government acknowledged "the tremendous effort which will be required of us individually and collectively, to attain the goals we have set for ourselves."[1] They, however, expressed their confidence in the determination of African governments to overcome any obstacles that may lie in their path and the hope that the international community would provide Africa with active support in the realization of the objectives of the Plan. Indeed, the document has been described as Africa's economic Magna Carta. It is the first time in the history of the continent--and, for that matter, of the entire international community--that 50 independent states, which differ markedly in their levels of economic development, in their political ideologies, and in their social systems, have subscribed to a common set of development objectives and goals and have adopted a common development strategy. The Lagos Plan is also Africa's regional approach to the economic decolonization of the continent. It provides a long-term bias for its socio-economic restructuring and development.

Yet nearly five years after the adoption of the Plan, Africa is faced with its most serious economic crisis. The African economy, particularly since 1980, has been characterized by a persistent fall in the overall output of goods and services. The crisis has had its most devastating impact on the directly productive sectors. The fall in the outputs of food and agriculture and of mining and manufacturing sectors has been the most spectacular manifestation of the crisis. In spite of Africa's high population growth rate of about 3.0 percent per annum, food production increased by only 1.0 percent from 1980 to 1981, 3.7 percent from 1981 to 1982, and 0.2 percent between 1982 and 1983 (see table 1.1). These very low growth rates have had a most serious effect on per capita growth rates of food output, which were -2.0 percent between 1980 and 1981, 0.6 percent between 1981 and 1982 and -2.0 percent between 1982 and 1983, with an overall growth rate of -0.9 percent between 1981 and 1983. When these negative per capita growth rates are set against the persistently very high population growth rate of 3.0 percent per annum, the reason why Africa is today faced with a major food crisis becomes abundantly clear. Figure 1.1 provides a comparative index of per capita food production between 1961 and 1983 for Asia, Latin America and Africa, south of the Sahara.

Table 1.1

Growth rates of manufacturing, agriculture, food, and mining sectors in Africa (in percentages)

Period	Manufacturing	Agriculture	Food	Mining
1960-65	8.5	1.4	1.6	18.5
1965-70	7.3	3.7	3.8	16.2
1970-75	5.5	1.3	1.7	- 1.8
1975-80	6.3	1.2	2.1	4.2
1980-81	3.6	1.1	1.0	-13.2
1981-82	3.7	3.4	3.7	- 7.7
1982-83	0.4	0.4	0.2	-24.6[a]

Sources: 1. FAO, _The State of Food and Agriculture_, 1966 and 1981.

2. United Nations Industrial Development Organization, _Industry in a Changing World_ (UN, 1983), table V.2, p. 102.

3. Economic Commission for Africa.

[a]Provisional estimate.

The mining sector, which in the 1970s accounted for 9.8 percent of Africa's GDP, coming next only to agriculture in relative importance as a contributor to total output, has also suffered severe setbacks since 1980. As is shown in table 1.1, whereas in the 1960s mining's average annual rate of growth was 17.3 percent, performance between 1970 and 1975 was a negative growth of -1.8 percent and between 1975 and 1980 it was 4.2 percent. Since 1980 the situation has deteriorated considerably. Between 1980 and 1981, 1981 and 1982, and 1982 and 1983, the annual rates of growth of the mining sector were -13.2, -7.7, and -24.6 percent respectively. Yet this sector is particularly important for such countries as Botswana, the Central African Republic, Guinea, Lesotho, Liberia, Mauritania, Niger, Sierra Leone, Tanzania, Zaire, and Zambia as a major source of foreign exchange earnings, of government revenue, and of employment.

Figure 1.1

Index of Per Capita Food Production, 1961-65 to 1983
(1961-65 average = 100)

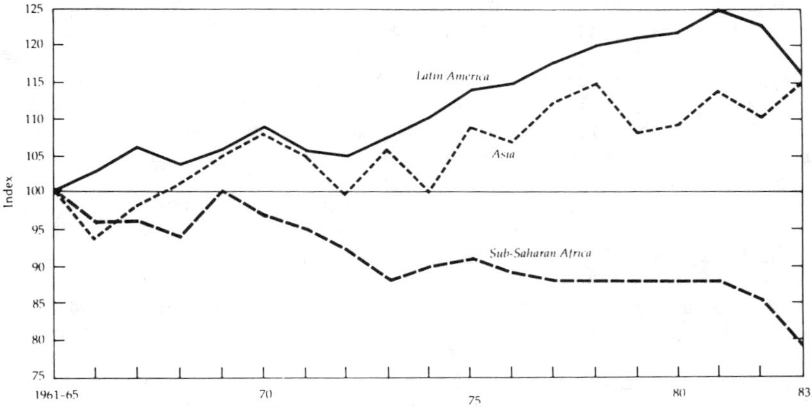

SOURCE: World Bank, Toward Sustained Development in Sub-Saharan Africa: A Joint Program of Action (Washington, D.C.: World Bank, 1984, pp. 14-15)

The industrial sector, on which great hope had been pinned for bringing about the necessary transformation of the economy to attain self-sustained growth and development, has performed equally badly since 1980. Indeed, there has been a persistent downward trend in performance since the 1960s, which has become intensified from 1980 onwards and which reached the trough of 0.4 percent in 1982-83, having been as high as 8.5 percent in 1960-65. Today, the crisis facing the manufacturing sector in Africa is no less serious than that facing the food, agriculture, and mining sectors.

As I said recently to the Conference of African Ministers of Industry at their seventh meeting held at ECA headquarters in Addis Ababa in March 1984 and later to UNIDO IV at Vienna in August 1984[2], at a time when the manufacturing sector should ameliorate Africa's present economic crisis, there is considerable excess manufacturing capacity (as high as between 60 and 100 percent in many cases) due to shortages of imported industrial raw materials and spare parts because of the lack of foreign exchange with which to pay for them. Thus, today Africa's budding industrial sector is faced with a crisis of emergency proportions similar to the one being confronted in other sectors.

Over and above the poor performance of the directly productive sectors of agriculture, mining, and manufacturing, Africa has been facing a number of other major crises: energy, balance of payments, external debt, and deteriorating climatic conditions, to mention only a few. If we include the collapse in the commodity markets, which has led to dramatic falls in the prices of Africa's major export commodities, the significant fall in the flow of aid and private foreign investment, and the high rates of interest payable on external loans from the banking system, the pervasiveness of Africa's economic crisis becomes crystal clear.

It is therefore not surprising that for many African countries the struggle is one of sheer economic survival. So serious has the situation become that the secretary-general of the United Nations (UN) decided in January 1983 to focus the attention of the international community on Africa's dire economic situation with a view to mobilizing international support to solve the crisis. Is it any wonder therefore that many concerned people and organizations--African and non-African--are asking the inevitable question: what has happened to the *Lagos Plan*? Has it suffered the fate of earlier declarations and programs of action in Africa and elsewhere? What impact, if any, has it had? And why, in any case, is Africa facing such a serious economic crisis after the hope of a better and improved future generated by the *Plan*? What went wrong? How, when and why? And what are the prospects for the future?

It is not possible to answer fully and comprehensively all these questions. Indeed, they are easier posed than answered. My objective is a modest one of providing a preliminary analytical overview of developments since April 1980 and a tentative prognostication for the future. But before doing this, I shall briefly discuss the background to the *Lagos Plan of Action*; some of the theoretical and intellectual foundations of the Monrovia Strategy and the *Lagos Plan*, as well as the main features of both documents; the criticisms, controversy, and conflict that they have generated; and the consensus that is beginning to emerge as to the appropriate path of development that Africa needs. I shall then review the recent ECA perspective study, the current economic crisis, and the responses of both Africa and the international community to the crisis. And in conclusion, I shall examine once again policy options that are available to Africa.

BACKGROUND TO THE MONROVIA STRATEGY AND THE *LAGOS PLAN*

I have narrated elsewhere in extenso what, beginning in late 1975, made the ECA lead the attack on inherited colonial and neocolonial economic policies and to assume the vanguard role in search of an alternative strategy to such policies being perpetuated by independent African countries.[3] Suffice it for me to state that it had become clear by mid-

1975 that unless there was a change in economic policy, strategy, and tactics, the African economies were in for a very long "winter." ECA's annual survey of economic and social conditions in Africa showed unmistakably, year after year, the danger signs, and the biennial reviews and appraisals of the social and economic performance of the African economies confirmed the relentless approach of the crisis. Then, in response to UN General Assembly Resolution 3508(XXX), which called upon ECA and the other four regional economic commissions to "prepare studies on the long-term trends in and forecasts of the economic development of their respective regions," the ECA undertook and published in 1977 a "preliminary assessment of long-term development trends and prospects in Africa."[4]

The annual economic surveys, the biennial reviews and appraisals, and the Preliminary Assessment all showed clearly not only that Africa's economic performance has been on the downward slide since 1971 but also that the prospects for the future were dim if the mix of public policies was to persist and if the existing international economic order, in which Africa was at the periphery of the periphery of the international community, to continue. It was the findings of these various studies that led to the conclusion that if Africa was to reverse this gloomy prognostication, "we will need to install, first, at the national level, a new economic order based on the principles of self-reliance and self-sustainment. This will require confidence in our capabilities to free our national economies from the shackles of excessive external dependence, and the institution of a new socio-economic order within our countries which maximizes not only the rate of development but also social justice and equity. Regionally, there is an urgent need for concentrating on achieving an increasing measure of collective self-reliance among African states."[5]

We had also realized in ECA, even as far back as 1975/76 when the demand for a New International Economic Order (NIEO) was loudest and most persistent among Third World countries, that Africa was the least prepared to derive optimal benefits from any such order. "In reviewing past performance in the region...and in spelling out the dynamics of self-sustaining and self-reliant economic change, what has become apparent is that the Africa region appears the least prepared of all Third World regions for the NIEO. Indeed, most national development plans...implicitly assume an increased degree of external dependence. Successive development plans fail to provide any guidance as to when policy-makers and planners foresee the beginning of the process of reduction of dependence on extra-African sources for skilled manpower...for finance...for raw materials...for capital goods and services...for technology...and for markets."[6]

Consequently, development strategies and policies concentrated on such major economic parameters as increases in the gross domestic product (GDP), massive capital formation through increases in investments and savings and foreign aid and foreign private investments, and incentives for attracting the latter with external trade as the engine of growth. These early development plans, insofar as they contained any political or ideological orientation, simply borrowed from one or the other of the existing perspectives.

The task that was therefore before the ECA in 1975 was fourfold. First, we had to challenge the conventional wisdom of the inherited theories of development and economic growth. These theories linked the rate and direction of international socio-economic change with export markets and with imports of skills, technology, and capital goods and services and modern consumer products. They also centered discussions on trade gaps, savings gaps, and investment gaps, with insufficient attention paid to indigenous factor inputs, such as national resources availability, local entrepreneurship, skilled manpower, and technology, and the domestic market.

Second, we had to analyze the impact of imitative life-styles and borrowed foreign concepts and ideologies on Africa's social and economic transformation. Instead of finding an authentic path to social and economic development, our governments and leaders seek an identity for our respective countries and societies in the images of others. As I once had occasion to say, we give the impression that we want to create little Frances, little Britains, little Americas, little USSRs and little Chinas all over Africa. "Although we pretend to be real, to be original, to be learning and to be preparing ourselves and our countries for self-reliant development processes and for an authentically African life-style, all we really have succeeded in doing is to mimic other societies and their life-styles. In doing so, we use borrowed phrases and jargons and terminologies which are foreign to our people and thus succeed in beclouding the issues before us and in confusing our people."[7]

The third ECA challenge was to undertake a cost-benefit analysis of the NIEO as far as Africa was concerned in consideration of Africa's socio-economic circumstances. That there was a need for an NIEO was not in doubt. Indeed Africa, through Algeria, had been in the forefront of the demand for such a new order. But it was clear that unless the continent successfully put its own house in order by restructuring its economy at the national, subregional, and regional levels, it would remain on the periphery of the periphery in the international economy, even if an NIEO were to come into existence. A strategy that would ensure that Africa did not remain the "lowest caste in the international (economic) hierarchy"[8] was therefore urgently required.

It continues to be our firm conviction in ECA, even in spite of the current economic crisis that Africa faces, that in the final analysis it is only the African governments and peoples themselves that can bring about a fundamental change in their relations with the international economy. As I said in my 1976 Turkeyen Third World Lectures in Guyana, Africa and indeed the whole of the Third World "will achieve this not by political shibboleths and rhetorics, not by a welter of formulations and verbiage, but by planned, long-term action-oriented strategies whose foundation will be based first, on the ushering further of a new economic order at national level; secondly, on collective self-reliance at subregional and regional levels; and, thirdly, through collective self-reliance and through the forging of unity of purpose among the entire Third World countries."[9]

Finally, we had the task of making the African governments--all of them--accept the need for a fundamental change in approach and strategy. As is generally known, no strategy or set of policy formulations can be expected to be adopted and implemented unless governments and their policy-makers and planners perceive a need for change. And challenging conventional wisdom is a potentially politically volatile undertaking: it can backfire and become counterproductive, particularly in view of the vested interests involved. What was even more difficult was the notion that we would get 50 (in 1975 there were 48) independent African countries to subscribe to the same strategy. The Monrovia Strategy for the Economic Development of Africa and the Monrovia Declaration of Commitment on Guidelines and Measures for National and Collective Self-Reliance in Social and Economic Development for the establishment of a New International

Economic Order, which were adopted by our heads of state and government in July 1979 on the recommendations of the ECA Conference of Ministers, were the culmination of four years of persistent effort. The adoption of the Lagos Plan of Action for the implementation of the Monrovia Strategy was our crowning glory. ECA's dogged determination to effect a complete turnaround in African governments' perceptions and positions had at last paid off. All our leaders had subscribed to a common set of goals and strategies. The halting of the unfavorable economic tide suddenly became a high probability.

THE INTELLECTUAL AND THEORETICAL FOUNDATIONS OF THE MONROVIA STRATEGY AND THE LAGOS PLAN

Nowhere in either the Monrovia Strategy or the Lagos Plan of Action were theoretical issues of development economics, political economy, and public policy discussed at length. Those documents simply came out with a political declaration, a development strategy, a set of priorities, sectoral programs of action, and a blueprint for regional and subregional integration. But underlying all these are fundamental principles, some of which are explicit but quite a number of which are implicit and unexpatiated. Indeed, it is to the ECA Revised Framework of Principles for the Implementation of the New International Economic Order in Africa[10] as well as to various ECA staff papers, which provided the main intellectual and theoretical foundation, that I must turn in order to explain the underlying fundamental assumptions and principles. Since elsewhere I have dealt at some length with the main features of the Revised Framework,[11] it will suffice simply to state the five main pillars on which the Monrovia Strategy and the Lagos Plan of Action were based. These are as follows:

1. the deliberate promotion of an increasing measure of national self-reliance;
2. the acceleration of internally located and relatively autonomous processes of growth and diversification and the achievement of a self-sustained development process;
3. the democratization of the development process;
4. the progressive eradication of mass poverty and unemployment and a fair and just distribution of income and the benefits of development among the populace; and,
5. the acceleration of the process of regional economic integration through cooperation.

In other words, in the Revised Framework, we argued for a complete departure from the past and the substitution of an inward-looking development strategy for the inherited externally oriented one. But even more significant is the fact that we were putting forward a strategy that does not suffer from the limitations of foreign ideologies. This new strategy also puts the development of the domestic market rather than dependence on foreign markets at the heart of Africa's development effort. It emphasizes the fundamental importance of indigenous factor inputs in development.

In the new strategy, we put the utmost emphasis on the development of indigenous factor inputs because they constitute the core of self-reliance. Without them the fate of Africa's natural resources base will continue to be left to the accidental interest of foreign companies pursuing global strategies that more often than not are determined by long-term profit considerations. The principle of self-reliance compels us to devise national, multinational, and regional programs to build up as rapidly as possible the corresponding competence required for determining the volume, quality, and quantity of our natural resources. Indigenous factor inputs are also crucial for reducing the enormous and rising cost of foreign inputs. "In Africa, we are so intensely pre-occupied with export commodity prices and commodity terms of trade that we tend to overlook the growing importance of invisibles. We gain a few cents in the price per kilo of this or that export product and a week later the unit price of imported services goes up by ten times the amount gained and we do not even notice it. We then wonder why the balance of payments will not balance, why we have so little foreign exchange to pay for imports of capital goods; why we are getting into debt and, worse still, staying in it."[12]

Indeed, it is the dearth of indigenous factor inputs that has led African countries to make such a sacred cow of foreign exchange because foreign exchange is directly convertible into foreign factor inputs as well as foreign consumer goods. Therefore, without a vigorous push to increase the supply and quality of indigenous factor inputs, Africa's over-concern with foreign exchange will continue, and this in turn will perpetuate its export-orientation and external dependence. And worse still, the mobilization of domestic financial resources will not lead to investment, since an economy can only convert domestic financial savings into domestic investment if indigenous factor inputs are available or are being created or both. Need we remind one another that investment really means the application of relevant know-how, technology, equipment, and services, etc., to the raw materials from which the increased physical output of goods and services are to come? Indeed, without far-reaching measures for enlarging the supply and improving the quality of domestic factor inputs, the achievement of an increasing measure of self-reliance will remain a will-o'-the-wisp.

We have over the years in various ECA documents spelled out what to us constitute the main elements of self-sustainment. Consequently, I shall only list some of them here. They are, first, the recognition that economic growth means increases in the physical output of goods and services; and these increases must rest primarily on the identification, evaluation, extraction, and conversion of the abundant natural resources of the continent into semifinished and finished products. And second, necessary measures must be introduced for equipping the population with the know-how required to identify, evaluate, extract, convert, and market these natural resources and their products. It has long been our firm conviction in ECA that it is the natural resources available for producing economic growth that must determine the pattern of relevant skills developed and multiplied, the selection of technologies imported, adapted, and developed locally, the type of institutional services provided, and the domestic flows of financial and material resources.

Self-sustainment also requires the integration of the rural and urban sectors of each national market and the gradual integration of the large number of national markets through economic cooperation arrangements to accommodate economies of scale. It further demands that the patterns of enclaves, semienclaves, and dysfunctional relations should be integrated.

Thus, the agriculture sector will depend on inputs from the industrial sector, on transport and communications services, on infrastructural services such as energy, etc. The industrial sector will similarly require inputs from agriculture, extractive industries, services, etc. Energy will depend on inputs from industry and provide inputs to all other sectors. In other words, sectors and subsectors will mutually interact and support each other.

In putting forward a development strategy designed to achieve an increasing measure of self-reliance and the acceleration of internally located and relatively autonomous processes of growth and diversification, ECA had, as it were, committed a heresy: we had rejected inherited theories of economic development that linked the rate and direction of internal socio-economic change in the developing world with export markets and that regarded foreign trade as the engine of growth. We had moved the discussion of engineering socio-economic change away from the usual parameters of trade gaps, savings gaps, investment gaps, growth rates in GDP, and per capita income, and instead concentrated attention on natural resource availability, local entrepreneurship, skilled manpower, technology, the domestic and intra-African markets, and the quality of life. Above all, we had put a question mark on "the much-talked-of positive link between the expansion of the economies of the advanced world and that of the Third World"[13] and shown that, in practice, it is the opposite that takes place. We have argued as forcefully as we could that the central concern of development must be individuals, not abstracts such as GDP, per capita growth rates, or investment and savings gaps. The final objective of development must be an increase in the quality of life of people without the destruction of their culture.

There are three other factors that feature prominently in our development strategy because of their importance in promoting a self-reliant and an internally located, self-sustaining process of development. These are (1) rediscovering of self-confidence; (2) mastering sovereignty over natural resources; and (3) strengthening the leadership role of government in socio-economic engineering.

Nowhere in the now extensive literature on development economics will one ever find mention of the discovery or rediscovery of self-confidence as a factor in development. Yet nothing could be more important a determinant of development and social change than this, particularly in Africa where for centuries it has been drummed into Africans' ears that they belong to an inferior race and are therefore incapable of attaining the heights that others have reached. If the slave trade dehumanized the black man for a long time, colonialism consistently undermined his self-confidence. Africans were made to believe -- and indeed for a long time did believe -- that the colonial masters were near supernatural, while Africans belonged to the lowest caste of Homo sapiens. The neocolonial development strategy, which African governments pursued after independence by extending the dependence of their economies in virtually all areas (raw materials, manpower, technology, money, finance, etc.), continued to sap whatever little self-confidence remained.

Although the achievement of political independence went some way in regenerating that self-confidence, our growing dependent economic relations soon neutralized or diffused self-confidence to the point that Africans' inability to run a modern society and sustain their political independence through the process of internally generated development became the new conventional wisdom. Africa as the economic underdog of the world combined the worse possible oddities--the largest number of least developed countries, the largest number of countries most seriously affected by the lack of development, vast numbers of people dependent on food aid and all other forms of handouts for mere existence--and Africa's new image was not inconsistent with the one that it had tried so hard to shed. The tragedy was that many highly placed Africans believed Africa could not succeed on its own.

It is for these reasons that ECA has put the recovery of self-confidence by the peoples of Africa and in their capacities to initiate and organize their own concepts, policies, and instruments at the center of our new development strategy. As I stated in the 1976 Turkeyen Lectures, "some Western economists have made take-off into self-sustaining growth dependent on a certain level of savings and investment. This is a mistake. Take-off is primarily dependent on the establishment or recovery of self-confidence in identifying, defining and solving problems of substance and relevance to socio-economic development and welfare of the mass of the people. And this self-confidence is, to a large extent, a function of mobilizing national talents and capabilities and creating the right type of environment and motivation for unleashing inventive and innovative abilities. I doubt very much if this recovery of self-confidence can be brought about in externally-oriented and excessively open economies such as we have in Africa."[14]

The steadfast support given to and the sustained loyalty received by the _Lagos Plan_ are best understood within the context of this important phenomenon--the recovery of self-confidence. Whatever may be its limitations, its defects, and deficiencies, the _Plan_ is the first undiluted effort of African governments themselves, under the aegis of the ECA secretariat, to delineate at the continental level how their economic destinies should be ordered. As such, the _Lagos Plan_ is not merely a technical treatise but also a political document that took four years of preparation to develop. The fact that a draft plan prepared for the OAU secretariat by a group of African experts was withdrawn in favor of the _Lagos Plan_, which was prepared with the help of all African governments, was a good indication that African governments were determined to assert their self-confidence. Since then, they have individually and collectively insisted on their partners-in-development respecting their perceptions of goals, strategies, and priorities and have unequivocally rejected any alternative strategy with approaches, concepts, and objectives that diverge from the plan as being in "fundamental contradiction with the political, economic and social aspirations of Africa."[15] At every conceivable opportunity, African governments have reaffirmed their commitment to the _Plan_, so strong is their attachment to it.[16]

Let me now turn to another factor ECA considered important in the _Revised Framework_ and in its various papers produced during the 1975-79 period, when what later became known as the Monrovia Strategy evolved: establishing effective control over Africa's natural resources. Regrettably, natural resources are not featured in either neoclassical economic theory nor, for that matter, in current development theory. Consequently, the link between natural resources and population--its structure, movement, and growth--has been either totally ignored or taken for granted. In our search for an alternative development strategy for Africa, we could ill-afford to follow suit, as we knew that, in some quarters, African underdevelopment was blamed on a assumed lack of a natural resource base. As the preamble to the Lagos Plan rightly asserts, "Africa's underdevelopment is not inevitable. Indeed, it is a paradox when one bears in mind the immense human and natural resources of the continent. In addition to its reservoir of human resources, our continent has 97 percent of world reserves of chrome, 85 percent of world reserves of platinum, 64 percent of world reserves of manganese, 25 percent of world reserves of uranium and 13 percent of world reserves of copper, without mentioning bauxite, nickel and lead; 20 percent of world hydro-electrical potential, 20 percent of traded oil in the world (if we exclude US and USSR), 70 percent of world cocoa production; one-third of world coffee production, 50 percent of palm produce, to mention just a few."[17]

But what is a glaring fault shared by African governments is their lack of effective control over these natural resources. Many African governments do not have any well-articulated policies for the exploitation, conservation, transformation, and marketing of their resources with a view to deriving maximum benefits from them. Effective sovereignty over natural resources in Africa therefore requires (1) increased knowledge of the nature of these resources; (2) increased capability to determine when, how, why, and by whom these resources are to be exploited and the terms and conditions of such exploitation; (3) the capability to protect such resources from unauthorized or wasteful exploitation; (4) special competence in the design and application of royalty and tax systems, in the economics and legal aspects of natural resources, and in the analysis of market information; (5) gradual assumption of responsibility by the African governments and people for all phases of natural resources exploration and development including processing and exploitation where appropriate; and (6) improvement in the competence of governments to negotiate the terms by which resources are extracted, processed and exported by the private sector, whether local or foreign.

Finally, I come to the most neglected of all factors in development economics literature: the domestic market. In the literature on development economics, the foreign international market is considered the only viable market for the primary commodities and mineral products of developing countries, as well as, in the case of the newly industrialized countries (NICS), the only market for manufactured products. National domestic markets receive scant attention. In a way this is consistent with the main externally oriented, export-dependent, and growth-generating conventional theories. But in view of our rejection of foreign trade as the engine of growth, it was only logical that the ECA should consider the domestic market as one of the major instruments for triggering and sustaining the massive, pervasive, and multidimensional processes of development strategy we were advocating.

We were quite clear in our minds that domestic markets in Africa cannot simply be left to look after themselves if they are to constitute an important element in the design of new national and regional orders. Not only are these markets weak, they are small in scope and very numerous. And combining several national markets will not automatically provide the foundation for self-sustaining development, unless the dynamics of the markets are fully understood with a view to restructuring them to meet a broad base of homogeneous demand for industrial production, to expand employment opportunities, and to reduce mass poverty.

And any focus on the domestic market inevitably requires looking at distribution of income--both between the urban and the rural sectors and between the moneyed and the subsistence sectors. Income distribution determines, particularly in market-oriented economies, the character and economic significance of the national market and the various submarkets. It determines not only what is produced but how much is produced, how it is produced, and why it is produced. And in turn, these factors determine the dynamics of markets, which impact development, economic growth, and welfare.

As for the importance of African governments participating in the development strategy that the ECA advocated, I need only quote the last paragraph of the Revised Framework, which inter alia stated that

> if substantial meaning is to be given to self-reliant, dynamic growth and diversification, governments are expected to play a larger role in the process of socio-economic transformation than they have explicitly and formally agreed to play so far. In view of the multiple objectives of socio-economic policy, governments will inevitably find themselves performing several roles. They will act as planners, instituting State-wide planning networks, linkages, plan monitoring facilities, control mechanisms, information systems and feedback effects; as entrepreneurs running state enterprises...and, as allocators of national resources through fiscal and monetary policies, incentives and disincentives.[18]

These then are the intellectual and theoretical foundations of the Monrovia Strategy and the Lagos Plan. Unconventional and unorthodox as they are, I dare anyone to challenge their appropriateness and relevance to Africa's socio-economic conditions.

CONFLICT AND EMERGING CONSENSUS REGARDING THE MONROVIA STRATEGY AND THE LAGOS PLAN

As was to be expected, the ECA, in preparing for submission to the Assembly of heads of state and government of the OAU in July 1979 what later became known as the Monrovia Strategy for the Development of Africa and the Monrovia Declaration of Commitment,[19] was guided by the principles discussed above. Similarly, in submitting the draft of the Plan of Action for the Implementation of the Monrovia Strategy for the Economic Development of Africa[20] to the first economic summit, the ECA was also guided by these basic principles, by the Monrovia Strategy, and by the Declaration of Commitment. Consequently, it did not consider it necessary to restate these principles in the Lagos Plan.

Unfortunately, most of the commentators on the Lagos Plan--the friendly critics as well as the not-so-friendly ones--do not appear to be familiar with the precursors to the plan, such as the ECA Revised Framework, the Monrovia Strategy, and the Monrovia Declaration of Commitment. Thus, when Browne and Cummings stated in their very useful little compendium entitled The Lagos Plan of Action vs. the Berg Report that the plan's "most serious flaw as a planning vehicle...is its failure to rank unambiguously its priorities, although self-sufficiency in food is clearly number one,"[21] it was evident that they could not have linked these four documents together as constituting a whole and as having been issued in a sequential order. Had they made this connection, they would have been the first to agree that, in view of the unambiguous listing in the Declaration of Commitment of the 10 priority areas to be pursued, little would have been achieved in repeating them again. As for ranking, surely there is nothing to suggest that the list does not reflect the ranking. Reading the strategy should have removed all such doubts and convinced all concerned that the setting of priorities has not "been temporarily laid aside in the interest of obtaining agreement on the overall thrust of the document."[22]

Indeed, that agreement had been obtained as far back as 1976 when the executive committee of the ECA approved the Revised Framework, an approval that was subsequently endorsed by the OAU Summit in June 1977. The Monrovia Strategy with the Declaration of Commitment was a decisive reaffirmation two years later, while the Lagos Plan spelled out in detail its implementation sector by sector. Surely, the sector by sector approach in the plan--or what Benachenhou described as the "sectorization of actions to be undertaken"[23]--would have been totally meaningless if there were no guiding principles and macroanalytical framework, strategies, and priorities. Indeed, the consistency between the Plan and its precursors is unexceptionable.

Critics who have found a number of ambiguities and errors of omission in the Plan obviously lack familiarity with this earlier document. The list of purported omissions and ambiguities is too long to be repeated here. Let me just mention two or three to illustrate my thesis that our critics have failed to inform themselves properly. They have been content to read only the Lagos Plan.

Benachenhou in his article referred to above stated (wrongly, I must add) that "nowhere in the Plan is any supervisory system over Africa's non-agricultural land and enterprises--specifically mining enterprises--identified"[24] and went on to list, inter alia, four other omissions. These are (1) the non-assessment of existing bilateral or multilateral relations of cooperation and their implications on African governments' capabilities to self-determine their domestic economic policies; (2) the failure to appraise critically intra-African cooperation policies; (3) the failure to consider issues concerning financing the plan in particular and development in general; and (4) ambiguities concerning the role of government in the development process in Africa.

There is no doubt that such criticisms have been put forward out of ignorance of the contents of the Revised Framework, the Monrovia Strategy, and the Declaration of Commitment. Benachenhou is also no doubt unfamiliar with the various publications of the ECA, particularly those issued between 1975 and 1979 on major policy matters. All these issues have been dealt with in extenso in these various documents. For example, on intra-African cooperation, we stated in the Revised Framework that, while Africa has some experience in this area, attempts at economic cooperation may have been only partially successful "... because the machinery for co-operation was too long-term or too indeterminate" or because of "the existence of concepts and models in some parts of the world" that may not be appropriate to the African context. We then went further to state that for economic cooperation arrangements to be effective, "there must be agents of production and distribution which are able and willing to exploit the opportunities which the arrangements provide. In terms of increasing self-reliance these must now more and more be interpreted to mean indigenous agents of production and distribution."[25]

On the question of financing the Plan, if critics had read the statement I made when presenting the draft of the document to the fifteenth ECA session, they would at least have framed their criticisms differently. Let me quote in extenso what I stated then:

> One of the critical questions which the Plan raises is the mobilization of financial and real resources for its implementation and here we must distinguish between financial and real resources and between domestic and external resources and take full account of the links among them. We must also bear in mind that the central issue is not simply the amount of resources concerned but the objects to which they are applied and the objectives prompting this application.
>
> In so far as the mobilization of domestic financial resources (i.e. domestic savings) is concerned I believe we need to weigh the possibilities of new methods of mobilization including life insurance, unit trusts, save-as-you-go schemes, and to give greater attention to the promotion of traditional rural and small scale savings arrangements fairly well known throughout the Region. In spite of the low income money earnings of the bulk of our people, it is surprising how much of the money incomes flow from the rural to the urban areas to finance housing, construction, and consumption.
>
> It is also astonishing what rural communities have been able to do once they accept a challenge to do-it-yourself and are shown how to do it. In effect we have to take into account the savings and investment potential of different segments of our populations. We believe that inter-country sharing of experiences will make a substantial contribution to the mobilization of savings at different income levels and within different income groups. In addition to domestic personal savings there is domestic corporate savings--i.e., mainly the profit, allocation to reserves, and re-investment policies in both the private and the public business sectors.
>
> However, the very nature of underdevelopment has created situations in which the availability of domestic financial savings is unmatched by the availability of domestic real factor inputs (particularly mixes of skilled production manpower, entreprenurial and management manpower, raw materials, R & D facilities, institutional services and, more than anything else, capabilities for converting raw materials into investment goods, i.e., the capital goods producing industries). The gap, as has often been pointed out by African financial authorities, is not so much finance as real factor inputs, including sufficiently well-trained and experienced managers and a sufficient spread of entrepreneurial technical assistance, which could be used to improve and expand supply. I do not wish to take up more time on this issue as I propose to invite not only the AACB and the African Monetary Centre but also development banks and corporations,

> etc. to assist us in examining the problems of mobilization of domestic financial resources.[26]

Of course, it was not these criticisms that fomented the controversy that surrounded the Lagos Plan. Rather it was the publication by the World Bank of Accelerated Development in Sub-Saharan Africa: an agenda for action a year or so after the adoption of the plan. The controversy arose because this World Bank report is in many ways an antithesis to the Plan. Where the Plan emphasizes self-reliance and self-sustaining development based on integrated and dynamic national, subregional, and regional markets, the Bank's Agenda puts the emphasis on the external market and on the continuation of the colonial export-oriented economies inherited at independence. While the Agenda identifies agricultural exports as the motor for African development, the Lagos Plan recognizes that the motor in each country will depend on the content and nature of its natural resource endowment. Because it fully endorses the perpetuation of an economically dependent development strategy based on export-orientation, it is quite logical for the Agenda to argue that African trade and exchange-rate policies are the reason for inadequate incentives for exports in much of Africa. The Agenda goes on to draw the mistaken conclusion that it is poor export performance rather than the worsening external economic environment (which manifested itself in the collapse of the commodity market) that is responsible for Africa's poor overall economic performance.

But even more significant, the authors of the Agenda failed to appreciate the strength of the attachment of African governments and their leaders to the Lagos Plan, which after all, as already stated, was the first indigenous effort in the recovery of self-confidence by Africans in themselves and their capabilities to initiate and organize their own concepts, policies, and strategies. The Agenda was seen, wrongly no doubt, as yet another attempt by foreigners to discourage the Africans and to abort any recovery of that self-confidence. Indeed, the Agenda was viewed as the World Bank's vision of how the global economy should be ordered. According to this vision--which is also the Western vision of the world economy--the delinkage concept advocated in the Lagos Plan was "inimical to Western interests and consequently should be ignored or ridiculed."[27] By emphasizing interdependence, the Agenda would thus ensure that Africa remains "the storehouse of natural resources necessary for the maintenance of the West's industrial power and leadership--hegemony if you wish."[28] It was felt that the West and the World Bank saw in the self-reliant development strategy and the almost inevitable delinking from the capitalist system too much orthodox Marxist thinking, which must be counteracted.

Of course, we know that the World Bank study was initiated at the request of the African governors of the bank. Therefore, it would be improper to impute motives. The World Bank in responding to this request came out with a genuine and sincere analysis and prescription based on well-established theories of development. But there is also no doubt that while the Lagos Plan is Africa-centered, the Agenda sees Africa from the perspective of the Western world. Chester A. Crocker, the U.S. Assistant Secretary of State for African Affairs, put this with admirable honesty and succinctness in a speech at the Georgetown University Center for Strategic and International Studies:

> There is a striking contrast between African and Western perspectives....The African viewpoint, particularly that of politicians, must assume a future that is economically viable and politically sustainable. It must assume industrialization and, at least, a promise of technological equality with the West (including Japan). It must encompass spiritual health and self-reliance as well as material well-being. The perspective is quite naturally African-centric.
>
> ...The Western perspective is...that of the policy-maker....Africa does not dominate his perspective, it is only one of a panoply of global concerns. Unlike the African politician, the Western bureaucrat is not compelled to assume politically viable solutions within Africa, nor does he take for granted the feasibility of rapid economic progress. Quite the contrary, he is usually more impressed by the negative, short-term implications of Africa's economic crisis, particularly its effect on political stability....
>
> These differing perspectives, African and Western, are reflected in two much-discussed documents, the "Lagos Plan of Action" and the report of the World Bank entitled "Accelerated Development in Sub-Saharan Africa: an agenda for action."[29]

As is well known, the African governments were unanimous in their rejection of the Agenda. The ECA Conference of Ministers, the institutional architects of the Lagos Plan, declared that the World Bank strategy is in fundamental contradiction with the political, economic, and social aspirations of Africa. In contrast, these ministers reaffirmed that "the goals and objectives defined by the African countries for themselves in the Monrovia Strategy and the Lagos Plan of Action remain the authentic and authoritative goals and objectives for Africa."[30]

Fortunately, since 1982 the controversy has abated; the conflict has given way to greater understanding and to the emergence of a consensus. Indeed, as subsequent World Bank reports have shown, some of the major viewpoints put forward in the Agenda have either been dropped or considerably modified. The World Bank has indeed moved closer to the ECA position on a number of fundamentals. On a number of other issues there has been a meeting of minds between the World Bank and the ECA, so much so that the bank could write in its latest, third document on Africa that "neither the essential objectives of Africa's development, nor the policy issues which need to be addressed to achieve them are in dispute, even though views on timing and priorities may differ....The emerging consensus on policy issues dwarfs any remaining areas of dissent. Delay in action taken, whether by African governments or by donors, can no longer be justified on the grounds of major disagreements in diagnosis and prescription."[31]

OPTIONS AVAILABLE TO AFRICA IN LIGHT OF THE ECA'S PERSPECTIVE STUDY

On 29 April 1983, exactly three years after the adoption of the Lagos Plan, the ECA in celebrating its Silver Jubilee Anniversary published a perspective study entitled ECA and Africa's Development 1983-2008. This, the first major ECA publication since 1980, has the principal objective of laying bare the consequences of continuing to pursue the "historical trends" scenario of the export-orientated and externally dependent development strategy and the consequences of the "normative development" scenario, as advocated in the Lagos Plan.

The ECA perspective study addressed itself to a number of fundamental questions. What will Africa be like in the year 2008--the year of ECA Golden Jubilee--in terms of its total population, the urban and rural distribution of that population, its age distribution, etc.? Second, what will these demographic phenomena mean for the people of Africa in 2008, specifically in terms of meeting their educational needs for primary, secondary, and tertiary schools and for books, stationary, laboratory equipment, school uniforms, and footwear? Third, what will an expanded population mean for the labor market--the number who will be joining, the number who can be absorbed into gainful employment, and those who will join the already large army of the unemployed and underemployed? Fourth, what are the implications of the population projections for Africa's current food crisis? With a billion mouths to feed by 2008, what does this mean in terms of the projected consumption of cereals, roots, tubers and pulses, and meat and poultry, for example? Where will Africa's food self-sufficiency ratio be and what will be its per capita level in 2008? And fifth, if today's Africa is gravely short of energy, what are the projections of demand and supply for the major sources of energy--petroleum, electricity, coal, natural gas, to mention only a few?

I now come to a host of questions relating to the industrial sector, i.e., capital goods, intermediate goods and inputs, and industrial consumer goods. In each of these subsectors, we made projections both of supply and consumption of some representative and crucial product groups. Thus in the capital goods subsector, two product groups--(1) tractors and animal traction for agricultural machinery and implements and (2) passenger cars and commercial vehicles--were chosen. In the intermediate goods subsector, three critical inputs--fertilizers, cement and iron and steel--were analyzed. And finally, in the consumer goods subsector, textiles and pharmaceuticals were chosen, as they constitute major elements of basic needs. Transport infrastructure was our seventh area of investigation, and here our projections covered all modes of transport. The final subsector included was external trade.

The projections of supply and demand for all subsectors covered were made for each of the scenarios; the historical trends scenario and the normative development scenario. Under the former, which assumes no major changes in either the domestic or external environments -- no fundamental break from Africa's unenviable economic past and present -- the picture that emerges is horrendous; Africa would in 2008 become even more economically dependent than it is at present; its economy would be more open and exposed. The region would require more food imports and more food aid to feed its teeming populations; over 90 percent of all its capital goods requirements would be imported; and critical intermediate goods, such as fertilizers and cement, would be imported. On the social side, the deterioration in the quality and quantity of social services, which has already begun, would accelerate. Access to education, health, potable water, and electricity would be available to a diminishing minority; cities would become overpopulated ghettoes; and diseases, famine, riots, and crimes would escalate. In brief, life would be short and brutish. Without doubt, under the historical trends scenario, the 1960s would seem like a golden age, and self-reliance and meaningful and effective political independence would, to the generation of 2008, sound like slogans of the past.

It is to the normative development scenario that we must perforce look for salvation--for economic survival, for the prevention of political collapse, and for a turnaround in Africa's economic fortune. But such a willed future will not be built on slogans and words alone, although they are necessary to sensitize the people about the dire consequences that await them unless they mobilize and organize themselves to bring about change. The future depends on purposeful action at all levels and on a development-oriented leadership. This indeed is what the Monrovia Declaration of Commitment is all about, and this is the raison d'être for the Monrovia Strategy and the Lagos Plan.

Table 1.2 is illustrative of the magnitude of the task that lies ahead. Outputs in the strategic sectors and subsectors have to increase at consistently high rates per annum. Imagine the task that is involved to increase cereal production at an annual average rate of 12.0 percent; root tubers and pulses at 9.5 percent; meat and poultry at 11.9 percent; electricity at 9.3 percent; and tractors, fertilizers and cement at 28.7, 9.2, and 37.7 percent, respectively. Even with all these, supply would still fall short of demand in most cases. The implications for investment, human resources development, the mobilization of the people, and the organization and management of the economy stagger the imagination. And the qualities of leadership required are better imagined than described. These are what are required by the normative development scenario. Overall, we are talking about a 7.3 percent average annual growth of GDP; an agriculture and food growth rate of 4.3 percent per annum; and an industrial output averaging 8.8 percent per annum growth.

The normative development scenario would thus impel African countries to "restructure their economies extensively in order to achieve the above targets. The dynamics of development would have to be based on the region's own resources and potential....The countries will have to establish...capital, intermediate and consumer goods industries. This means that foreign trade has to be perceived as a component of growth rather than as its sole determinant. Thus, the main thrust of the normative scenario is that Africa's future development should be conceived not in terms of how much GDP but rather in terms of how much physical goods are being produced with local expertise and domestic resources and how much change is being made to structure the economy in terms of diversification and greater vertical and horizontal sectoral integration."[32] I cannot conclude without emphasizing again that this normative development scenario is not a futuristic adventure. It is a scenario based on developing a will to survive and, what is more, to reach greater heights and become a true and effective partner in the international economy. It is the only honorable option open to Africa.

Table 1.2

Average annual growth rates in selected sectors required for normative development scenario

Sectors and Sub-Sectors	Average annual requirements 1978-1980	Projected demand in the year 2008	Required average annual growth between now and the year 2008 (in percentages)	Balance sheet difference between demand and supply after average annual growth rates
Food:				
Cereals (million tons)	74.8	22,400.0	12.0	- 33.6
Roots, tubers and pulses (million tons)	85.1	202.3	9.5	- 1.2
Meat (million tons)	4.7	13.6	11.9	
Electricity (GWH)[a]	69,985.0	1,019,639.0	9.3	
Tractors (thousands)	253.3	1,821.5	28.7	- 99.7
Passenger cars (millions)	3.3	22.7	27.5	- 2.1
Commercial vehicles (millions)	1.7	44.6	11.6	- 7.6
Fertilizers (million tons)	2,278.0	21,490.0	9.2	-2,900.0
Cement (million tons)	28.0	264.0	37.7	
Iron and Steel (million tons)	6.5	61.0	3.7	- 134.0
Textiles (million tons)	0.8	5.1	25.5	- 1.0

Sources: Compiled from tables 14 to 18 of ECA and Africa's Development 1983-2008, Addis Ababa, 1983, pp. 64-78.

[a]GWH = giga watt hours

AFRICA'S CURRENT ECONOMIC CRISIS AND ITS IMPLICATIONS FOR THE MONROVIA STRATEGY AND THE *LAGOS PLAN*

In a way, 1984 can be seen as Africa's most unfortunate year. It was the year that natural disasters and harmful weather patterns arising from drought and desertification spread to 36 of its 50 member states. It was the year that the devastating impact of the global economic recession -- with its attendant collapse of commodity prices, accompanied by unprecedented high interest rates, sharp exchange rate fluctuations, increased protectionism, chronic balance of payments deficits, mounting external debts and steady declines in real terms of official development assistance (ODA) --gave Africa, particularly Sub-Saharan Africa, its worst economic situation in modern times.

It should be abundantly clear from the preceding sections that Africa's economic and social crisis has not developed all of a sudden. As already indicated, it was the deterioration in the economic and social conditions of Africa that led the ECA in 1976 to look critically at Africa's development strategy. Since then, the commission has not ceased to raise the alarm and to draw attention to the evolving situation, as all regular readers of its annual *Survey of Economic Conditions in Africa* will testify. Indeed, at its April 1981 session--that is the session immediately following the one at which it prepared the draft of the *Lagos Plan*--the ECA held a closed meeting to consider a confidential paper that the executive secretary of the commission had submitted and that was entitled *Africa's Rapidly Escalating Crisis--Proposals for a Short-term Immediate Programme for Survival.*[33]

In that report I stated inter alia "that Africa faces a critical economic crisis and challenge, more immediate in its intensity and compelling in terms of urgent demand for solutions." I then proposed an emergency program of action in the critical areas of food and drought, energy, and the balance of payments. However, as I warned, the emergency program of action was not meant to replace or substitute the *Lagos Plan* or the international development strategy for the Third United Nations Development Decade. Indeed, the emergency program was envisaged to clear the ground and lay the necessary foundation for the successful implementation of the *Plan*. While crisis-ridden economies may have little time and resources for long-term development issues and problems, it is equally essential that, in resolving such crises, future development prospects must not be put in jeopardy.

As I have repeatedly stated, underlying Africa's persistent and drawn-out crisis is its underdevelopment and economic backwardness; its failure to achieve a clear break from its unenviable colonial economic inheritance and pursue instead a normative development path. Therefore, until a structural adjustment that will install a self-reliant and internally generating process of development can be achieved, Africa will continue to move from one crisis to another.

There are three immediate causes of the present crisis: (1) the widespread severe and persistent drought, which now affects 36 out of Africa's 50 independent countries; (2) the collapse of the commodity markets and the deteriorating international economic environment; and (3) the heavy burden of Africa's external debt. Although these are responsible for the current social and economic crisis facing the continent, they are also the result of Africa's underdevelopment, economic backwardness, and the persistence of the colonial and neocolonial mix of economic policies.

Let us take the drought and its impact on the food crisis. Colonial economic policy concentrated all attention and resources on production and marketing of export crops to the neglect of the production and marketing of food crops, which were left largely to the subsistence sector. Post-independence Africa unfortunately followed more or less the same policy. Although initially self-sufficient in food (in spite of neglect of food production), as the population grew rather fast (about 3 percent per annum), as urbanization grew even faster (at the rate of about 5 percent per annum), and given the low productivity in the food production sector, it was not surprising that Africa evolved within the last two decades as a food deficit region. As shown in figure 1.1, there has been a steady decline in per capita food production in Africa south of the Sahara since 1960-65, whereas in Latin America and Asia the reverse has been the case.

Thus, even if there was no drought, the African food crisis has been in the making since independence. Unfortunately, the drought accelerated its arrival and aggravated its intensity. Because of the neglect of food production, the resources necessary to make the agriculture sector increasingly less dependent on rainfall were never acquired. Thus Africa's food crisis is the result of a conjuncture of three different crises:

1. a technical crisis arising from the difficult nature of farming in the continent with its fragile and easily eroded soils, less reliable rainfall, and nearly nonexistent irrigation (covering only 2 percent of the arable land);

2. a development crisis stemming from the highest population growth in the world, rapid urbanization, and continuing desertification; and

3. a political crisis resulting from political upheavals in a number of countries in Africa, which have exacerbated the food shortages.

It is thus clear that while emergency food aid is not only desirable but also an imperative necessity in order to save people from hunger and starvation, the long-term solution to the crisis lies in pursuing appropriate measures designed to arrest the downward trend in per capita food production and, eventually, to restore food self-sufficiency. This requires a determined and single-minded pursuit of the goals and objectives of the strategy and the *Lagos Plan* based on the ECA normative development scenario.

In other words, whether it is to combat the consequences of the collapse of the commodity market or the mounting external debt, there is no doubt that short-term action must be taken that is consistent with long-term structural adjustment as stipulated in the Monrovia Strategy and the *Lagos Plan* and spelled out in considerable detail in *ECA and Africa's Development 1983-2008*. As I have repeated again and again, most recently in a statement on the crisis at the summer session of the UN Economic and Social Council, "it is highly important to appreciate that the emergency, short-, medium- and long-term implications and ramifications are not only interrelated but are closely intertwined. Any measures to be taken, whether at national, regional or international levels, must ensure internal consistency between the different requirements, be they short-, medium- or long-term or for emergency purposes. Otherwise we may be compounding the problems posed by the crisis."[34]

What then are the implications of the crisis for the Lagos Plan? First and foremost, it is clear that the present crisis validates both the analytical reasons for the Monrovia Strategy and the Lagos Plan and the urgency of pressing ahead with their implementation. Most analysts of the Lagos Plan have thought of it only as a perspective plan, because they have failed to study its contents in detail. If they did, they would realize that the Plan contains short-, medium- and long-term measures. Let me quote a few examples.

On food, the Lagos Plan recommends that "over the period 1980 to 1985 the objective should be to bring about immediate improvement in the food situation....Priority action should be directed to securing a substantial reduction in food wastage, attaining a markedly higher degree of food security, and bringing about a large and sustained increase in the production of food, especially cereals...."[35] On the drought, the Lagos Plan identifies the following areas of environmental concern as requiring immediate action: promotion of reafforestation programs with native trees and adaptable exotic species to be planted as wind breaks, planting of indigenous grasses for soil stabilization, exploitation of underground water for irrigation, maintenance of carrying capacity of arid lands, establishment of meteorological and hydrological monitoring stations, and enforcement of strict land management. The industrial program has three parts: long-term objectives up to the year 2000; medium-term objectives up to the year 1990; and short-term objectives up to the year 1985.

Second, the current crisis shows how prophetic we were in setting the priorities contained in the Monrovia Strategy. Food self-sufficiency and combating drought and desertification still remain Africa's top priorities. In other words, the crisis has brought into sharper focus Africa's development priorities not only for the short and medium term but also for the long term.

However, as to the implications of the crisis on the implementation of the Plan--which is my third point--I must admit that the crisis has had a devastating effect. As the World Bank stated recently, "the crisis management of recent years has resulted in widespread neglect of programs dealing with the long-term constraints on development. Schools are unable to teach effectively because of shortages of books and other materials; clinics are frequently without medicines; deforestation, overgrazing and other environmental hazards are not being checked."[36]

One of the inevitable consequences of the crisis is that the limited resources available have been directed to cope with the emergency situation. Limited resources must also be used to service the external debt. For many countries, the ratio of debt service to export earnings currently ranges from 30 to 60 percent. Thus less and less resources are available to deal with the medium- and long-term problems of development.

This then brings me to my final point--the international community's support in solving the crisis and in the implementation of the Lagos Plan. This in itself is a major issue, and comprehensive coverage is beyond the scope of this chapter. But let me make five points on the subject. First, the Lagos Plan with all its emphasis on self-reliance was realistic enough to assume that substantial external assistance in terms of loans, aid, and technical assistance would be required. In fact in some sectors (e.g., food and agriculture, and transport and communications) estimates of external resources required were made. Second, unfortunately Africa has faced stagnation in official development assistance (ODA) and a significant decrease in net capital flows since 1980. Third, the World Bank projection is that this trend will continue at least up to 1987. It is estimated that net capital flows to Sub-Saharan Africa will decline from the average of about US$10.8 billion in 1980-82 to about US$5.0 billion per annum in 1985-87, unless special measures are taken by the donor community. Fourth, in the emergency area, particularly in the provision of food aid to drought-affected countries, the response of the international community has been encouraging. Although gaps still exist between needs and pledges, the response by the donor community has on the whole been sympathetic, no doubt on purely humanitarian grounds. Thus there is emerging--and this is my fifth and final point--a new phenomenon in external assistance to Africa. On the one hand, a declining trend in medium- and long-term flow of resources and on the other hand a mildly positive response to appeals for emergency assistance--a mixture of polarization of assistance and donor fatigue. If this were to continue, the African crisis situation would continue for a long time as the continent would always be short of resources for economic rehabilitation, reconstruction, and self-sustaining development.

THE *LAGOS PLAN OF ACTION* AND AFRICA'S FUTURE PROSPECTS

It is clear from my analysis that, while the *Lagos Plan* remains as valid to Africa's development needs today as it was in 1980 when it was launched, its implementation has been rather slow, partly because of the economic crisis that has gripped Africa since then and partly because any turnaround in economic policy and strategy and any initiation and implementation of policy changes and reform are slow processes. Finally, there is, as we have just seen, the unfortunate and persistent declining trend in net capital flows to Africa, including a decline in real terms of ODA at a time when such assistance is urgently required to facilitate the turnaround in policies and strategies proposed by the *Lagos Plan* and the normative development scenario. It is no wonder that, in view of the combination of these negative factors, many analysts have come to the conclusion that Africa's, particularly Sub-Saharan Africa's, future prospects are far from bright. Indeed, Christine A. Bogdanowics-Bindert in her article entitled "Sub-Saharan Africa: An Agenda for Action" foresees "a continuation of economic stagnation and human misery, recurrent crises and stop gap measures."[37]

As is well known, we in the ECA reject such pessimistic prognostications, although as indicated in this chapter they conform to what Chester Crocker described as the Western perspective, which focuses more on the negative aspects of the African economic crisis rather than on the positive, confidence-building aspects that he called "Africa-centric." This persistent pessimism on the part of Western analysts may in a way be a reflection of their scepticism regarding the capacity and capability of Africans to sustain for long a modern state, let alone transform it economically and socially. As I said during the ECA Silver Jubilee celebrations, "such a point of view which is put across *ad nauseum* by the foreign media is directed at sapping our self-confidence. Colonialism having done its worst to destroy that self-confidence, our detractors are doing everything, both subtly and openly, to make us lose whatever remains of it. The unfortunate thing is that many Africans, and one suspects, a growing number of our people are beginning to believe such propaganda."[38]

Fortunately, we at the ECA are no longer the only ones to reject such pessimism about Africa's future. The World Bank has recently joined its considerably weighty voice with ours. In its latest report on Sub-Saharan Africa the World Bank puts its position unequivocally as follows:

> Against this disquieting background, is it possible to look with hope toward the future? The World Bank...has answered with an emphatic "yes". This optimism can be justified by recent experience both in Africa and elsewhere. For instance, the despair that is now focussed on Africa was matched by a comparable feeling about India in the early 1960s. In recent years, India, despite its terrible poverty, has emerged from despair to hope in the eyes of the world. This change has been achieved largely through sustained improvement in the government's policies and programmes, with support from donors wherever their finance, technical assistance or advice could be useful. There are many other cases around the world of the mutually reinforcing roles of good domestic programmes and appropriate external assistance.
>
> The same combination of domestic reform and donor support can be successful in Sub-Saharan Africa.[39]

In other words, Africa can invent or "will" for itself a future that will bring rising prospects of prosperity, of economic self-determination, and national and collective self-reliance and self-sustainment by the vigorous implementation of the objectives of the Monrovia Strategy and the programs and projects of the Lagos Plan. For Africa to be able to do this, it needs to develop the necessary self-confidence; and it is essential for Africa's foreign partners-in-development not to do anything to erode this self-confidence. Equally important, it is necessary for them to lend generous support--financial and technical--to Africa's effort. As the Special Memorandum by the ECA Conference of Ministers on Africa's Economic and Social Crisis, addressed to the 1984 Second Regular Session of the UN Economic and Social Council, concluded, we are convinced that given the necessary support from the international community, Africa, particularly Sub-Saharan Africa, is "capable, in the not-too-distant future of establishing at national, sub-regional and regional levels truly dynamic, self-reliant and interdependent economies, capable of functioning as effective partners in the international economic system."[40]

NOTES

1. OAU, Lagos Plan of Action for the Economic Developme Africa, 1980-2000 (Geneva: International Institute for Labor Studies p. 9.

2. Statements by the Executive Secretary of ECA at the forn opening of the Seventh meeting of the Conference of African Ministe Industry held at ECA headquarters, Addis Ababa, Ethiopia from 26 to 28 March 1984 and at the fourth General Conference of UNIDO on 6 August 1984.

3. Adebayo Adedeji, "The Evolution of the Monrovia Strategy and the Lagos Plan of Action: A Regional Approach to Economic Decolonization" (UN, 1983), passim.

4. ECA, Secretariat, "Long-Term Trends in the Economic Development of the Regions of the World;" Preliminary Assessment of Long-term Development Trends and Prospects in Developing Africa (Document E/5937/Add.3), 29 March 1977, annex III.

5. Adebayo Adedeji, Africa, the Crisis of Development and the Challenge of a New Economic Order (Addis Ababa: ECA, 1977), p. 16.

6. Ibid., p. 20.

7. Adedeji, "The Evolution of the Monrovia Strategy and the Lagos Plan of Action," p. 1.

8. Ali Mazrui, Africa's International Relations: The Diplomacy of Dependency and Change (Boulder: Westview, 1977), pp. 17-28.

9. Adebayo Adedeji, The Third World and the Search for a New Economic Order, 1976 Turkeyen Third World Lectures (Georgetown, Guyana, 1976), p. 18.

10. ECA Document No. E/CN.14/ECO/90/Rev. 3 of 25 June 1976. The first version of this document was published in November 1975.

11. Adedeji, "The Evolution of the Monrovia Strategy and the Lagos Plan of Action."

12. Statement by the Executive Secretary of the ECA at the formal opening of the Eighteenth Session of the commission on 6 April 1981 at Freetown, Sierra Leone. (Mimeographed), p. 7.

13. Adebayo Adedeji, "Draft Plan of Action for the Implementation of the Strategy for African Development for the 1980s," Statement at the formal opening of the Fifteenth Session of the ECA, Addis Ababa, April 1980, p. 4.

14. Adedeji, The Third World and the Search for a New Economic Order, p. 48.

15. ECA Conference of Ministers, The Declaration of Tripoli on the World Bank Report entitled "Accelerated Development in Sub-Saharan Africa: an agenda for action," Seventeenth Session of the commission, Tripoli, April 1982.

16. See, for example, the Addis Ababa Declaration on the Occasion of the Silver Jubilee Anniversary Celebration of the United Nations Economic Commission for Africa, April 1983.

17. OAU, The Lagos Plan of Action, p. 7.

18. ECA, Revised Framework, pp. 53-54.

19. ECA Resolution 332(XIV), "Development Strategy for the Third Development Decade," requested the "Executive Secretary of the Commission to transmit to heads of state and government through the OAU secretary-general both the recommended strategy as well as a draft Declaration on Guidelines and Measures for the National and Collective

...f-Reliance in Social and Economic Development for the Establishment of a New International Economic Order." The OAU in its Resolution CM/Res.722(XXXIII) endorsed in its first substantive paragraph "the development strategy for Africa...as prepared by the Fifth Meeting of the Conference of Ministers of the Economic Commission for Africa held in Rabat." In the eleventh substantive paragraph of the same resolution, OAU declared, "the strategy for the development of Africa be called Monrovia Strategy for the Development of Africa and the Declaration of Commitment be called the Monrovia Declaration of Commitment."

20. ECA document No. E/CM.14/781/Add.1 of April 1980.

21. Robert R. Browne and Robert Cummings, The Lagos Plan of Action vs. the Berg Report: Contemporary Issues in African Economic Development (Washington: Howard University African Studies Program, 1984), p. 24.

22. Ibid., p. 24.

23. A. Benachenhou, "South-South Cooperation, the Lagos Plan of Action and Africa's Independence," Africa Development 8 (4), (1983): 9.

24. Ibid., p. 12.

25. ECA, Revised Framework, p. 17.

26. Adedeji, "Draft Plan of Action for the Implementation of the Strategy for African Development for the 1980s."

27. Browne and Cummings, The Lagos Plan of Action vs. the Berg Report, p. 33.

28. Ibid., p. 33.

29. Chester A. Crocker, "Expanding the Development Dialogue," Topic 147, (1981): 5-6.

30. ECA, The Declaration of Tripoli.

31. World Bank, Toward Sustained Development in Sub-Saharan Africa: A Joint Program of Action (Washington: World Bank, 1984) 1:3.

32. ECA and Africa's Development 1983-2008: A Preliminary Perspective Study (Addis Ababa: ECA, 1983).

33. ECA document No. E/CN.14/CONF/81/01 of 2 January 1981.

34. Adebayo Adedeji, The African Economic Crisis: An Agenda for Action by Africa and the International Community (Addis Ababa: ECA, 1984), p. 14.

35. Lagos Plan of Action, p. 12.

36. World Bank, Toward Sustained Development in Sub-Saharan Africa, p. 6.

37. A. Bogdanovics-Bindet, "Sub-Saharan Africa: an agenda for action," Journal of World Trade Law, 16 (4), (July-August, 1982): 286.

38. Adebayo Adedeji, Africa in the Year of the ECA Golden Jubilee, (Addis Ababa: ECA, 1983), p. 9.

39. World Bank, Toward Sustained Development in Sub-Saharan Africa, p. 2.

40. ECA document No. ECA/CM.10/37/Rev.2, p. 32.

G. E. A. Lardner

2 Beyond the Neocolonial Nexus: Inheritance, Implementation, and Implications of the *Lagos Plan of Action*

My review of the Lagos Plan and the Final Act of Lagos must begin, in view of the critical role of these two documents as complementary sets of declarations of belief and commitments to action, with some consideration of their background. The most striking feature of this background was the retention by most of the African states of neocolonial socio-economic policies long after independence had been achieved. The principal features of these policies were:

1. retaining monoproduct export dependence;
2. retaining the commodity composition of export dependence;
3. relying on external initiatives for altering this pattern; and intensifying monoproduct export production in order to secure foreign exchange with which to finance imports of factor inputs (entrepreneurship; management; manpower for procurement, production, and marketing; equipment and spare parts; technologies; raw materials, including energy; services, especially institutionalized services and physical infrastructure; and other goods and services).

The maintenance by African states of the neocolonial economy rested on a number of crucial misconceptions and unreasonable expectations. These included:

1. the notion that in Africa economic growth depended on capital investment, which was another name for savings-in-action and that savings meant paper money accumulated in savings accounts in banks. By a simple semantic error, savings (in an environment where money served with reasonable adequacy as a surrogate for created and available factor inputs) was interpreted as having the same substantive and functional meaning in Africa (where factor inputs for developed economic growth hardly existed and where their creation in quantity and relevance was not a major object of socio-economic policy) as in developed economies. For example, few African governments paid much attention to the need for uncovering the natural resource base or for developing national capabilities for extracting natural resources and converting them into raw materials. Yet the range of complementarity of raw materials is a major determinant of the range of feasible production. Since no country is likely to possess all the raw materials needed for structural change and diversification of production, it must be obvious that expanding complementarity requires not only a widening range of production of raw materials but also their transportation and (intra-African) trade;

2. the curious belief that economic growth also meant any increases in the physical output of goods and services, so that producing candies, cigarettes, or cheap gin acquired the same importance as producing energy, engineering spare parts, or pharmaceuticals. Moreover, the lack of discrimination over what was to be produced --since this was determined by (nonexistent) market forces--effectively concealed the problem of market structure, market expansion, and money income distribution, and deprived fiscal and monetary policies of any contemporary meaning;

3. the total failure to recognize the limits of the North-South connection in providing the whole of the Third World plus China, plus the Council for Mutual Economic Assistance (CMEA) states, plus Mediterranean Europe with the factor inputs they required for accelerated development and economic growth, as well as failure to recognize the corresponding limits (economic, social, and political) of the capability and willingness of developed countries to accept, in effect, increasing quantities of primary products, semi-manufactures, and manufactures in repayment for exports to the rest of the world;

4. the failure to recognize that developed economies were really developed <u>domestic market</u> economies and that virtually every aspect of theoretical and applied economics (other than those dealing specifically with international trade) were about domestic economies and markets. Data organization and analysis, policy-making, planning, programming, instrumentation, factor input supply, distribution, competition, etc., were all primarily about the domestic economy and market. African economists, planners, and policy-makers, their advisers abroad and donor agencies have all worked hard during the past 20 years to make theories and practices that basically relate to economies dependent on internal

(e.g., national) stimuli, and factor inputs serve the purposes of economies primarily dependent on external stimuli;

5. the conviction that the processing of one or two primary products for export constituted industrialization or conversely that assembling consumer durables for the high income domestic market was a useful beginning to mastering manufacturing know-how (not to say "know-why");

6. the unrealism of expecting 25 developed countries to supply increasing quantities of relevant factor inputs to the rest of the world at more or less constant real prices and the unreasonable belief that the rest of the world could pay for these imports by competitively exporting to these 25 countries more and more cocoa, coffee, tea, sugar, peanuts, oil palm, fibers, iron ore, bauxite, copper, uranium, petroleum and natural gas, manufactures, etc.,at relatively constant real prices; and the indifference of policy-makers and planners to intra-African trade in particular and South-South trade in general, so that very little effort was consciously made to exploit market opportunities (for food products, beverages, sugar, meat, etc.) in the fast-growing markets of western Asia. The latter is quite remarkable in light of recognition that intra-African trade could simply not rest on the availability of surplus international currencies and that no matter how painful it may be, some alternative bases would have to be found.

Unreasonable expectations were obviously numerous. For example, policy-makers and planners held firmly to the view that the transformation of national economies was possible through the exploitation of only one or two primary export products.

Another staple belief seemed (and seems) to be that foreign exchange was sufficient not only for obtaining the bulk of factor inputs Africa needed for accelerated development, economic growth, structural changes, etc., but also that overample supplies of foreign exchange had wholly failed to further development in the region in general, and in several African (and non-African) countries in particular, seemed to have successfully escaped the attention of most African policy-makers, planners, and their advisors.

Yet another unreasonable expectation was the idea that technologies, if made available reasonably freely by developed countries, would work wonders in promoting development and economic growth in Africa, even though little thought was given to the availability of other complementary factor inputs.

Indeed, the debate on technology for development had for 20 years concentrated attention not on demand but on supply. Governments and spokesmen for Africa regularly insisted on easy access for their countries to mass production technologies designed for mass markets that not only did not exist in Africa but that were rarely the object of African socio-economic policy. It is essential to bear in mind that mass markets require considerable density of population; a high density of national transport and communications systems; the widespread and habitual use of money; standardization of many products and services; extensive distribution networks; the widespread availability of electric power; etc.

So great were the perception confusions that member states, experts, and publicists all continued to bewail the desparate situation of landlocked countries that, all the while, were surrounded by other countries with whom they could trade and share complementary raw materials, exploit larger markets, and create joint facilities for the development of local factor inputs. Meanwhile, the plight of island countries (surrounded by the sea) as well as coastal countries did not seem to have troubled those who formulated the solution to the problems of landlocked countries.

Finally, I come to perhaps the most grievous of all confusions: that planned economic growth (however defined) could be achieved by short-term national development plans that frequently had no real core or motor because they had no genuine long-term goals and targets that reflected self-image of the future state of development at which policy, plan and, programs were aimed. The notion of planning without such a visualized perspective is difficult to comprehend. Equally striking has been the neglect of studies of the world environment where far-reaching changes have taken place. Since the beginning of the century these would include the changing great power system; the emergence of Japan; the rise of the Pacific Rim; the impact of the Newly Industrializing Countries (NICs) on the geo-political as well as the geo-economic system; the trade implications of the international (especially the Third World) debt problem; and the emerging international financial crisis.

Clearly a large program of systematic self-reeducation, sustained over several years, was a necessary precondition and accompaniment of any serious attempts to translate the Lagos Plan of Action into substantive policies, plans, and programs at national and multinational levels. It is not unreasonable to believe that surprising catalytic effects would have been achieved if, for example, the Conference of African Planners, working groups of teachers of economics, management, and technologies, the African Association for Public Administration and Management, the Multinational Programming and Operational Centers (MULPOCs) had been induced to participate in such a program. The participation of some of the staff of the Organization of African Unity, and the African Development Bank, as well as, of course, the Economic Commission for Africa, would have enhanced the catalytic effect beyond anything we can imagine. There were, however, other problems.

There were massive failures in implementation because of organizational deficiencies. The civil services remained predominantly colonial in structure, philosophy, range of competencies, procedures, ambitions, and criteria of performance. They were administrative rather than inventive and innovative and were strongly affected by the anti-intellectualism characteristic of the postwar colonial bureaucracies.

Public enterprises--many of which began as detached segments of civil services--displayed similar characteristics. In addition, they suffered from the inability of governments to make up their minds regarding the roles of public enterprise. This inability rested, first, on the fact that public enterprise in Africa was modelled on public enterprise in Western Europe where there is, for example, no shortage of private entrepreneurship; second, it derived from the extraordinary and basically confused belief that the performance of public enterprise in Africa should be judged by money profits that reflected nonexistent market criteria. As I have noted, the accumulation of "profits" or "savings" in local currency could not be used to buy local factor inputs. The significant profits of public enterprise in developing economies should be the contributions the enterprise makes towards generating relevant factor inputs (in excess of its own needs) for the expansion of the economy; providing critical linkages and multipliers; encouraging and developing small and medium scale enterprises within the sector or subsector in which it operates; and so on.

Policy-makers and planners also were not in the habit of asking and answering questions about entrepreneurial responsibility for critical areas of national development plans. Indeed, they often disdained consulting the experiences of indigenous entrepreneurs or evaluating national entreprenurial capability for plan implementation. It follows therefore that support services for both private and public entrepreneurship were haphazard in relevance, scope, and geographical location. The role of support services carefully designed to enable indigenous entrepreneurs to perform roles allocated (directly or indirectly) to them in the national development plan is thus at least the second if not the first step towards plan implementation.

This leads me to the service sector in Africa, which tends to grow any which way but mostly through rural/urban migration (into petty trade, personal services, low-level clerical jobs, unskilled input into building and construction, etc.). In the meantime, the region pays in large and increasing foreign exchange transfers for business consultancy (especially feasibility studies and project design and planning); management; R&D; industrial and commercial property rights; shipping; civil aviation; telecommunications; foreign banking and financial services; marketing; etc.

Secretariat-type institutions (for organizing meetings, recording minutes, circulating papers, etc.) have dominated economic cooperation. Multinational instruments for procurement, production, and marketing were and are still markedly absent, in spite of the enormous multinational institution-building carried out by the ECA.

MAIN FEATURES OF THE LAGOS PLAN AND THE FINAL ACT

The Lagos Plan of Action rested on two basic objectives. The first was a substantial shift from external to internal demand stimuli, i.e., policies, plans, targets reflecting internal demand (whether the outcome of autonomous markets dominated by oligopolistic producers or a market controlled along socialist lines) rather than the demand of developed economies. The second objective was a shift to reliance primarily on domestic rather than imported factor inputs.

Reliance on internal demand stimuli would involve some of the features characteristic of mass markets in developed countries: a fair degree of density of population; the widespread and habitual use of money; a high density of transport and communications networks; extensive distribution systems; the widespread availability of electric power; standardization of many products and services, and so on. It would involve the deliberate use of fiscal and monetary policies; restraint on the market fragmentation effects of trademarks, advertising and extreme product differentiation, etc.

As I have mentioned earlier, in very few African countries was the domestic market the recognized base of economic growth policies. In some cases the withdrawal of foreign firms from the trade sector actually led to unplanned and unnoticed contractions of the already inadequate distribution system, and market fragmentation was, for personal reasons, actually encouraged. Inflation occurred in a few cities and towns (while money, in fact, continued to play a peripheral role in most economic activity in the large rural sector). The International Monetary Fund (IMF) therefore could describe the whole economy as suffering from double or triple digit inflation and could demand all sorts of mostly irrelevant reforms.

With regard to factor inputs, it is now possible in hindsight to conclude that if someone had calculated, however crudely (piecing together data from NICs with similar population sizes and natural resource endowments), the hundreds of thousands of industrial entrepreneurs (from state enterprises and relatively large private enterprises down to small-scale firms producing batches of screws, nuts, belts, etc.); the tens of thousands of trained managers; the million or two trained men and women needed for procurement, production and marketing, for R&D, including technological search and negotiation, and for key services such as hauling, insurance, consultancy, information, quality control, standardization etc.; the quantities of machines, spare parts, implements, tools, and instruments; the quantities of key raw materials and of electric energy; the amount of buildings, roads, ports, and airports, railways, etc., required for the implementation of the Lagos Plan for the 20-year period following 1981, then policy-makers and planners in Africa would have understood the unlikelihood of such a vast draw of factor inputs from developed countries to Africa. Perhaps an even better idea of physical magnitudes would have been gained if such physical quantities had been broken down and related to some key areas of production, such as natural resources, mining, and other industrial raw materials; electric power and fuels; building materials and building and construction (which usually absorb 30 to 40 percent of plan expenditures in Africa); transport and communications; food production, processing, storage and distribution; etc. African policy-makers and planners would very likely have had to calculate the volume of out-payments in foreign exchange that the region would have to make. They failed to recognize the importance of preparing local expertise, setting up national and multinational enterprises, site selection and planning, and site development and plant construction. Altogether policy-makers and planners could have been prodded into considering what factor inputs would have to come from within the region (and by what measures) in light of what could reasonably be expected to come from outside. It would certainly have been difficult to avoid the question of how to provide education and training facilities in machine-building in African polytechnic schools and universities.

THE PARTING OF THE WAYS

A new and insufficiently recognized element in the African situation now deserves mention. Policy-makers, academics, businesspersons, publicists, etc., in economically developed countries are now of the view that their socio-economic systems are vulnerable to attack by an increasing number of developing countries. The only way to protect these national systems is to transfer their economies to a new, very advanced technological base that developing countries cannot reach for a good while. The matter is not going to be left to chance or to market forces. Active steps at high levels are being taken to create new, relevant factor inputs; to encourage business collaboration; to channel factor inputs into the development of the new technologies and associated industries, etc. In addition, steps are being taken to expand the scope of application of copyright and of industrial property rights, while African countries have acceded to model conventions on industrial property rights. At the same time measures are being considered or taken for effective regulation of bank lending to and private investment in the Third World.

The effects of these developments towards a new international division of labour would include:

1. the diversion of factor inputs to the internal reorganization and development of the economies of developed countries, which would, of course, mean a considerable diminution of real factor inputs available for investment in Africa and the rest of the Third World; consequently, the prices of factor inputs imported from the North to Africa and the rest of the Third World are likely to undergo even steeper rises than in the past and this, together with anticipated economies by developed countries in the use of raw materials imported from the South, may be expected to intensify the decline in the real terms of trade for developing countries;

2. the transfer of much of the conventional technologies of today to Eastern Europe and the NICs. It is to these countries that the African region (which is making too little effort to create the infrastructure, environment, and capabilities for the acquisition and use of these technologies) will have to turn for its supply of technology, capital goods and services and, ultimately, investment and aid;

3. the fairly rapid reduction, within the next few years, of opportunities for teaching African industrial technologies and skills in Organization for Economic Cooperation and Development (OECD) countries as automation (including robotization) takes over. Indeed, this would considerably affect jobs in such areas as medical and health care, secretarial services, teaching, personal services; retail sales; textiles; ticket reservation and issue; telecommunications and postal services; food processing; banking; laboratory technicianship, etc. While the Peoples' Republic of China is busy buying up factories closed down in Western Europe and while resources are transferred elsewhere for use for production and R&D and for use for teaching industrial skills, the African region blandly takes no notice.

4. the power of excitement promoted in African countries related to the belief that, though they are yet far from mastering "sunset" technologies and putting them to effective use, they should immediately begin to make large, indiscriminate claims on the new "sunrise" technologies, which will solve at least half of Africa's development and economic growth problems at once.

In the face of all this, there now seems to be developing a strong effort to persuade African policy-makers and planners, first, of the dominant role of foreign exchange (more foreign private investment and fewer loans) in the search for accelerated development and economic growth and, second, of the validity of North-South "neointerdependence" (to temper the growing inclination to accept self-reliance and autocentric development and economic growth as more than lip service).

In so far as the foreign exchange supply is concerned, we must bear in mind that, at the regional level, vast sums in foreign exchange flowed, as it were, into and out of the African region in the 1970s and left it facing the present debt crisis without contributing much either to structural change or to an ability to repay foreign debts or service foreign investments. This is also true at the national level within and outside the region. It is now time for a reexamination of the genuine role (in the real environment of today) of foreign exchange in, and its effective contributions to, self-sustaining accelerated development and economic growth. The time for fetish claims is over. (It would be an extremely interesting and valuable exercise to review the extent to which aid and loans extended to the African region by the World Bank (IBRD), the International Finance Corporation, the IMF, and the United Nations Development Program (UNDP) have contributed to the expansion in quality, improvement in quality, and relevance of factor inputs for economic growth, and to widening domestic markets and promoting combinations of national markets.)

In so far as interdependence is concerned, this surely was the basis of the colonial and neocolonial economic systems, and it is difficult to see --in the light of the cold realities of on-going trends--what interdependence is expected to yield.

THE LAGOS PLAN AND THE FINAL ACT IN PROCESS

It is sometimes claimed--directly or indirectly--that the Lagos Plan and Final Act have failed. Apart from evidence to the contrary which will be brought up shortly, such judgments are plain nonsense. As I argued earlier, the Lagos Plan and the Act require a massive clarification and orientation of concepts, perceptions, and interpretations to facilitate concrete decisions on the equally massive development of factor inputs, instruments of action, measures for widening domestic markets, as well as for combining them through economic cooperation agreements and mechanisms that reflect the realities of national and multinational procurement, production, and trade. Such a traumatic process would require a minimum of five years and, in some cases, as much as seven to ten years of unrelenting effort.

The proper question to ask, surely, is whether the tangible and obvious forms of the African crisis have taught Africa how to achieve relatively autonomous development and economic growth and whether, therefore, this knowledge will be matched by substantial gains: in know-why as well as in know-how; in self-awareness and a sense of direction; in genuine acceptance of responsibility for shaping the future; in recognition of the limits of North-South relations in fostering desirable socio-economic changes; in the potentialities of South-South relations; in information on meaningful resources and potentialities; in the design of appropriate instrumentation; in the ability to distinguish between money and real factor inputs and other phenomena; in appreciation of the proper role of intra-African economic cooperation; in a realistic grasp of the nature and forces changing the geo-social and geo-political system; and so on.

Of course it would not do to assume that the delinking process on which developed countries have embarked means that African policy-makers and planners and other leading actors would be left to decide for themselves what self-images of the future should inspire them and guide their countries individually and collectively.

Representatives of member states arrive at international negotiating meetings loudly proclaiming their poverty, weakness, and have-not state. Thoughtlessly they accept that all the wealth is on one side and all the needs on the other; that all the strength is on one side and all the weakness on the other; etc. If this were true, negotiations would be virtually unnecessary.

There is also the claim that the real culprit is population growth, an argument that the World Bank, for one, is no longer able to sustain professionally, but is unwilling to abandon. The real issue is not population growth but the rate at which the population of working age acquire the know-why, know-how, and other means for exploiting the astounding natural resource endowments of the region to meet intra-regional needs; and this clearly cannot be simply a matter of importation of factor inputs. The real constraint, I must repeat, on economic growth in the long-run is not so much foreign exchange as the failure to develop domestic factor inputs. The real long-term significance of imported factor inputs is their use in developing, improving, and increasing the quantity of relevant domestic factor inputs. From this point of view, the so-called world financial crisis is a crisis of the availability and movement of real factor inputs to satisfy the needs of developed and developing countries, as well as the rest of the world, and the price and debt consequences of country and regional deficits in real factor input supply, relative to planned production and demand.

I now turn to some results of implementation of the Lagos Plan by describing how its programs have responded to the crisis environment, the pattern of factor input supply, and market development. For lack of space, I will confine my attention to the efforts of the ECA and the OAU.

The secretariat of the ECA first began in 1976 to challenge the basic assumptions of socio-economic policy and practice in Africa and to propose major departures from accepted theory and practice. It has virtually without a break continued to do so until now. The Lagos Plan, sponsored by the secretariats of both the ECA and the OAU, is a major landmark in the process of engineering changes in concepts, perceptions, policies, plans, and programs.

In so far as the first factor input--entrepreneurship--is concerned, the ECA developed a program of field research, consultations, and meetings of African entrepreneurs in both the public and the private sector to help identify bottlenecks and other adverse factors in entrepreneurial development. It also, up to this date, is pressing forward with issues of development of public enterprise. The African Association for Public Administration and Management receives strong support based on the belief that civil services in Africa must play a more significant entrepreneurial and managerial role than hitherto.

In the field of management, the secretariat promoted the establishment of subregional centers of high level modern management (in West, North, and East Africa). It laid emphasis on the need for, inter alia, high level formal and informal courses on international business organization and finance designed to strengthen the capabilities of governments for negotiating with, among others, developed countries and transnational corporations. It virtually salvaged and has consistently supported the growth and expansion of the East and Central African Management Institute in Arusha, Tanzania.

With regard to human resource development, the secretariat of the ECA established, in cooperation with the OAU, UNESCO, ILO, and other agencies, the Conference of Ministers Responsible for Human Resources Development, and it is a strong supporter of the Conference of Vice-Chancellors, Rectors, and Presidents of Institutions of Higher Learning in Africa. The program on the Integration of Women in Development is well known (see chapter 12). It sponsored the establishment of an institute for Higher Technical Training and Research in Kenya. The Institute was expected not only to encourage education and training in subjects of unusual character and importance (for which inadequate facilities existed) in Africa: it was also intended to undertake experiments in curricula design, in the organization of teaching/learning processes, and in educational technology.

Most major programs (e.g., population, statistics, planning, transport and communications, economic cooperation, environment, human settlements, international trade and development finance, natural resources, etc.) either include training courses, seminars, and workshops or envisage the establishment of permanent regional or subregional education and training institutions.

In the field of natural resources/industrial raw materials, attention has centered on programs relating to mineral resource development (including marine sciences and sea-bed mining), to energy, to forest resources, and to water.

Multinational centers on mineral resource development, on cartography, and on remote sensing have been established. The USSR has provided, at the request of ECA, uniquely valuable maps of African geology, minerals, and petroleum.

In so far as equipment and spare parts are concerned, ECA established an African Regional Center for Engineering Design and Manufacturing in Nigeria, in addition to its programs for encouraging the development of the metal, engineering, chemical, and petrochemical industries and for widening national capabilities in building and construction. ECA also, jointly with the OAU, promoted the establishment of an African Industrial Development Fund, managed by the African Development Bank. All these projects and many more are being brought within the program for an Industrial Development Decade for Africa, developed and jointly promoted by UNIDO, ECA, and the OAU.

As regards science and technology, in addition to the African Regional Center for Technology (see chapter 14) and the Engineering Design and Management Center in Nigeria, the ECA also established an Intergovernmental Committee of Experts on Science and Technology Development to guide its programs.

Where physical infrastructure is concerned, in addition to programs in human settlements, building materials, technology, and the building and construction industry, there is a huge transport decade program. The Pan-African Telecommunications Network Project is about to be supplemented by a regional telecommunications satellite. No adequate comment can be made on the ECA's truly astounding institution-building program for economic cooperation. All these have a close bearing on the implementation of the Lagos Plan of Action. It must not be supposed that the brief recapitulation above gives more than a glimpse into the work of this institution and framework.

However, the fact that doubts exist about the Lagos Plan makes it clear that there is first and foremost an insufficient comprehension of some of its basic features. As suggested earlier, a considerable program of education about the plan's assumptions and implications as well as of the changing world environment must be developed for the principal actors. Some aspects of the changes in the world environment ought properly to be handled by the OAU. In addition, a good deal of demonstration (by way of study tours, visits, attachments, films, and video-cassettes, etc.) are necessary to convince governments that some of the steps and projects proposed are not pure invention but have been tested in action elsewhere. This visual aspect of the self-education program will have to be considerably developed.

In addition, the new pattern of policies and activities required must be repeated again and again until it becomes familiar to ministers, senior civil servants, business associations, university teachers and students, and newspapermen. There is a considerable risk of leading actors being seduced into returning to old diagnoses and prescriptions, which can only lead Africa into a new colonial age.

CRITERIA FOR EVALUATING PROGRESS IN IMPLEMENTATION OF THE LAGOS PLAN OF ACTION

Before going to the heart of the matter, we need to consider briefly the use of national accounts in general and their summation in the GDP and GNP as measures of economic growth. My first doubt concerns the adequacy of national accounts for dealing with anything not totally measurable in money in predominantly nonmarket economies, taking into account the misconceptions and illusions referred to above, as well as the sleight of hand by which currencies of developing countries are converted into international currencies and vice versa.

Similarly my doubts concern the suitability of national accounts for evaluating qualitative and relevant changes in factor inputs (which is one of the chief considerations for attacking the *Lagos Plan of Action*) and for reflecting linkages, etc. In effect it is perhaps necessary to reconsider the role of national accounts in evaluation of the progress of the *Lagos Plan*.

Closely associated with these doubts is reliance on published data of the GDP (total as per capita) as measuring anything worthwhile. In any case, since one of the critical variables is the relationship between the GDP and the GNP (indicating the degree of reliance on imported factor inputs), and since the GNP and the net national income indicate the productivity of factor inputs, overtime, and the incremental capital/output ratio, the overemphasis on GDP (explicable in the case of developed countries) is perplexing.

The purpose of these comments is to shift attention from these traditional measures -- partly because excessive reliance on them may easily lead to misleading diagnoses and prognoses and thus to ineffective or even dangerous prescriptions -- and to suggest that, as always, Africa will have to devise different, multiple indices for evaluating the progress of the *Lagos Plan*.

Taking the first of the two principal objectives of the plan as the shift of reliance from external to internal demand stimuli for development and economic growth, indices will obviously have to deal with rates of change in domestic market widening (whether within capitalist or socialist systems) and with degrees of success in market enlargement through economic cooperation.

The next set of criteria would concern the second principal objective of the Lagos Plan, i.e., shifting primary reliance from external to domestic factor inputs. The temptation, ordinarily, would be to assume that the expansion of domestic factor input supplies would be reflected in diminishing inputs from abroad. This is rarely the case, as the tendency is for both imported and domestic factor input supplies to swell rapidly, depending on how fast the economy is expanding. A much more useful index would be to measure changes in the composition of imported factor inputs. A simple way of looking at this would be to inspect the composition of technical assistance supplied to NICs. Experts supplied to these countries tend (as would be expected) to be more highly sophisticated specialists in more complex areas of operation than those supplied to Africa.

However, as pointed out earlier, future circumstances are not going to be ordinary. Within a decade and a half, planned shifts in the technology base of the economies of developed countries are likely to dry up the supply of factor inputs that these countries traditionally supplied to Africa and the rest of the world. This means that the present African complacency about building up their own capital goods industries and their own industrial training facilities is likely to cost the region dearly. With regard to industrial enterprises specially acquired for education and training in industrial skills, it must not be forgotten that for many years transnational corporations have arranged for different stages in a manufacturing operation to be located in different developing countries, which had two purposes: the first was to reduce the risks of nationalization; the second was to isolate segments of know-how so that no one country would gain access to and master the process as a whole. This was not all. Such processes required strict adherence to precise formulae, specifications and operational procedures. There was no room left for experimentation. All this means that close thought should be given to the acquisition of manufacturing plants and in particular those that are to be used mainly for purposes of manpower development.

However, the long-range objective of self-sustainment requires additional activity and involves primarily planned intrasectoral as well as intersectoral linkages, multipliers, spread and backwash effects, which are all, to some degree, physical and institutional infrastructures.

Finally, there are impact indices associated with concepts of poverty and of the quality of life. These indices could include food, water, medical and health care, electricity, and jobs for those discharged from the farm sector as agricultural productivity goes up.

The preceding paragraphs are intended as indicative rather than prescriptive and much more detailed work needs to be done to turn things around. The Lagos Plan encourages and facilitates such a transition.

3 Kwame Nkrumah and the *Lagos Plan of Action*

Twenty-two years after the establishment of the ECA[1] and eighteen years after the OAU was founded, African leaders produced in their extraordinary summit of 1980 a document known as the Lagos Plan of Action (LPA) and its concomitant Final Act of Lagos (FAL) to guide their continent's development up to the year 2000. To be sure, the LPA is the outcome of a rather long series of summit declarations and resolutions by African heads of states and governments in Algiers (September 1968), Addis Ababa (August 1970 and May 1973), Libreville (July 1977), and Monrovia (July 1979).

The Lagos Plan is also a by-product of the acute economic straits experienced by the developing world and especially by the African continent, which in turn is a function of the economic crisis experienced particularly by the capitalist world and its periphery since the early 1970s. To the extent that the economic umbilical cord between the capitalist world and virtually all African countries has not been cut, it is to be expected that the latter would bear the brunt of crises in the former. The Lagos Plan also reflects a new focus of interest and interaction among African states that are making the transition from being preoccupied with decolonization issues to focusing on the imperatives of state-building and development. The issuance of the LPA is, therefore, conditioned by the objective realities of our times.

These objective realities have been adumbrated, explicated, and amplified time and again in the past two decades through lectures, symposia, declarations, resolutions and articles, so that they do not need repeating here.[2] There may still be some debate on the causes of underdevelopment in Africa. There is yet no categorical agreement on the cures, but there certainly is no disagreement about the realities of the worsening state of the continent. So, in this chapter I will spare readers another litany of clichés and figures on the African condition.

The problem at hand is determining the modalities of Africa's extrication from the old capitalist-dominated economic order and the launching of its own development by the year 2000 and beyond. More specifically, the issue is to consider the manner in which the LPA can be made operational and its lofty and worthy goals attained.

The task before us is to examine the political-structural dimensions surrounding the implementation of the Lagos Plan. Technocrats and experts at the ECA and the OAU worked out the wording of the LPA, and African leaders breathed the spirit of life into it; and, with the Final Act, it was launched into the world of action. It is now five years since the adoption of the plan, and this is indeed an appropriate moment for all concerned to pause and take stock of what has transpired in the continent and the world at large since 1980 and to determine what the feasibility may be for the implementation of the LPA. What follows, then, is a brief appraisal, or prolegomenon, of the political implications of the Lagos Plan.

THE LPA FIVE YEARS LATER

By way of recapitulating the serious and solemn resolve of the African heads of state when they issued the LPA in 1980, let me cite a portion of the LPA preamble. Section 3 (iii), (iv) and (v) state:

> We commit ourselves, individually and collectively, on behalf of our governments and peoples, to establish national, sub-regional and regional institutions which will facilitate the attainment of objectives of self-reliance and self-sustainment.
>
> More specifically, we commit ourselves, individually and collectively on behalf of our governments and peoples, to:
>
> (a) give an important place to the field of resource development by starting to eliminate illiteracy;
>
> (b) put science and technology in the service of development by reinforcing the autonomous capacity of our countries in this field;
>
> (c) achieve self-sufficiency in food production and supply;
>
> (d) implement completely the programmes for the United Nations Transport and Communications Decade for Africa;
>
> (e) realize the sub-regional and regional internally located industrial development;
>
> (f) co-operate in the field of natural resource control, exploration, extraction and use for the development of our economies for the benefit of our peoples and to set up the appropriate institutions to achieve these purposes;

(g) develop indigenous entrepreneurship, technical manpower and technological abilities to enable our peoples to assume greater responsibility for the achievement of our individual and collective development goals;

(h) co-operate in the preservation, protection, and improvement of the natural environment;

(i) ensure that our development policies reflect adequately our socio-cultural values in order to reinforce our cultural identity; and

(j) take into account the dimension of the future in the elaboration of our development plans, including studies and measures, aimed at achieving a rapid socio-economic transformation of our states.

We hold firmly to the view that these commitments will lead to the creation, at the national, sub-regional and regional levels, of a dynamic and interdependent African economy and will thereby pave the way for the eventual establishment of an African Common Market, leading to an African Economic Community.

These lofty and worthy commitments were then organized for specific treatment in the plan into some 14 headings, namely, food and agriculture; industry; natural resources; human resource development; science and technology; transport and communication; trade and finance; institution-building; environment and development; least developed African countries; energy; women and development; development planning and population.

As we discuss the _LPA_ now, we have the benefit of consulting, inter alia, the ECA's _Annual Report for 1984_ (E/1984/21-E/ECA/CM.10/38) for the UN Economic and Social Council; the _Joint Progress Report of the Secretary-General of the OAU and the Executive Secretary of the ECA on the Implementation of the Lagos Plan of Action and the Final Act of Lagos_ (CCM/1203 XXXIX), prepared for the Thirty-ninth Ordinary Session of the OAU Council of Ministers; _Report of the Secretary-General, a.i. on the Activities of the Organization Covering the Period from June 1983 to February 1984_ (CM/1233 CXL) Parts I and II; _Special Memorandum by the ECA Conference of Ministers on Africa's Economic and Social Crisis_ (E/ECA/Cm.10/37/Rev.2); Professor Adebayo Adedeji, _The African Economic and Social Crisis: An Agenda for Action by Africa and the International Community_, including his addresses given to the Special Debate on the Critical Economic Situation in Africa at the Second Regular Session of the UN Economic and Social Council in Geneva in July 1984; _ECA and Africa's Development 1983-2008_ (April 1983); the joint ECA, OAU, and UNIDO work, _A Programme for the Industrial Development Decade for Africa_ (1982); the _Resolutions of the Fortieth OAU Ordinary Session of the Council of Ministers_, 27 February-5 March, 1984 (CM/Res.926-958 XL); and the OAU's _Democratization of National Development in Africa_ (Dakar Symposium, March 1982).

Whether one takes the 14 subjects of the _Lagos Plan_ individually or views the overall economic picture generally, the same conclusion is reached. _LPA_ or no _LPA_, the deterioration of the African economic condition is staggering in its scope and appears to be intractable. The secretary general of the UN has established an advisory group and has named the ECA's Professor Adedeji as his special representative to monitor the escalating economic and social crisis in Africa. This must surely be the UN version of declaring the continent a disaster area. Perhaps Adebayo Adedeji's words, five years after the issuance of the LPA, describe the situation unambiguously. In The African Economic and Social Crisis he said:

> I cannot remember any year, particularly since 1980, that I have not, in my statement to your august body, spoken of either the worsening or the deepening economic and social crisis in Africa. Unfortunately, each succeeding year has been worse than the preceding one. In general, the economic crisis in Africa is characterized by a persistent drop in the rate of growth of overall output of goods and services over the years. The rate of growth of output has been decreasing steadily since 1980. It fell from 1.3 per cent in 1980 to zero in 1982 and -0.1 percent in 1983. [Emphasis added.]

Perhaps, things have to get worse before they get better, but it seems that for Africa, even five years after the LPA, what lies ahead is not the expectation of when conditions will get better but the anxiety of how much worse they are likely to become. Dr. Peter Onu, Administrative Secretary-General, a.i., of the OAU, concurs with the bleak picture of the current economic conditions in the continent. In an address to the nineteenth session of the ECA and the tenth meeting of the Conference of Ministers,[3] he referred to the problem of implementing the LPA and offered the following explanation:

> Africa's capacity to implement the Plan and the Act has unfortunately been greatly jeopardized by the drastic fall in foreign exchange earnings and consequent shortages in imported raw materials and spare parts, by the rising cost of energy imports, by the severe liquidity squeeze and by mounting debt burdens. To those adverse factors have been added devastation by natural calamities such as floods, cyclones and, above all, a prolonged drought that had caused acute food shortages. The unprecedented combination of natural and man-made factors, coupled with the rapid growth in population, had created a crisis that called for urgent attention.

According to the Special Memorandum[4] the following 34 countries are declared to be drought-affected and food-aid dependent:

1. Drought-affected and food-aid dependent countries

Angola	Ethiopia
Benin	Gambia
Botswana	Ghana
Cape Verde	Guinea
Chad	Guinea-Bissau
CAR	Lesotho

Mali	Swaziland
Mauritania	Togo
Mozambique	Tanzania
Sao Tome and Principe	Upper Volta
Senegal	Zambia
Somalia	Zimbabwe

2. Drought-affected countries

Cameroon	Niger
Camoros	Nigeria
Djibouti	Sudan
Ivory Coast	Tunisia
Morocco	Zaire

The estimated combined population of the above 34 states is about 300 million or nearly two-thirds of the total African population.

Despite LPA's exhortation that "over the period 1980 to 1985 the objective should be to bring about the immediate improvement in the food situation and to lay the foundations for the achievement of self-sufficiency in cereals and in livestock and fish products [emphasis added]," the FAO/WFP Special Task Force has estimated "the food deficit for 1983-84 for the 24 food aid-dependent countries at about 5.4 million tons of which 3 million tons are required as food aid."[5] It is also observed that food imports in the 34 drought-affected countries listed above soared from 4 million tons in 1970 to over 23 million in 1983.

It may appear as though I am focusing on the Achilles heel of Africa's numerous problems to illustrate the point. But then, I am hard put to find a way to assess the developments on the continent more positively. Any progress towards an establishment of a common market, and through that an African Economic Community, is very much dependent not only on the continent's capacity to withstand the current economic crisis but on the positive outcome of a number of decade-tagged development projects, such as the UN Transport and Communications Decade for Africa, the Industrial Development Decade for Africa,[6] and the Women's Decade. The task of strengthening existing institutions of cooperation and creating new ones envisaged also in the LPA still looms ahead. As the OAU secretary-general, a.i., noted in his Report on the Activities of the Organization Covering the Period June 1983 to February 1984, some progress has been made by Economic Community of West African States (ECOWAS), Preferential Trade Area for Eastern and Southern Africa (PTA) (where 12 of the 18 potential members have signed the protocol), and the newly established 11-state Economic Community of Central African States (CEEAS).[7]

To date some seminars have been held or planned regarding the establishment of an African Economic Community, and some consultants have been contracted to explore the matter. Although none of the 25 resolutions of the Fortieth Ordinary Session of the Council of Ministers meeting in Addis Ababa in 1984 dealt directly with progress in the implementation of the Lagos Plan of Action, there was reference to it in the "Resolution on the Current Critical Economic Situation in Africa."[8] In it the council "urges all member states to intensify their national collective effort to implement the Lagos Plan of Action through, inter alia, a readjustment of their national plans and programs in order to lay a solid foundation for self-reliance and self-sustainment." As far as the question of progress towards evolving programs or structures at the national, subregional, and regional levels is concerned, there is hardly anything that has emerged as a direct outcome of LPA and the FAL.

KWAME NKRUMAH AND THE LAGOS PLAN OF ACTION

In his work, Africa Must Unite, published in 1963 on the eve of the summit conference in Addis Ababa that yielded the OAU, Kwame Nkrumah said, "Just as I was convinced that political freedom was the essential forerunner of our economic growth and that it must come, so I am equally convinced that African Union will come and provide that united, integrated base upon which our fullest development can be secured."[9]

Nkrumah, whose slogan in his struggle for the independence of Ghana was "Seek ye first the political kingdom and all other things shall be added unto you," remained consistent to the theme of unity with respect to the future development of the continent. It is little wonder that Nkrumah has been described as the "Lenin of Africa."[10] He worked hard and untiringly not only to explicate and elaborate on the philosophy of African unity, but he even tried to forge nuclei of union governments or federations in West Africa in the early 1960s, such as his attempts to set up the Ghana-Guinea-Mali Federation or the Ghana-Guinea-Liberian Declaration. As in most other subsequent attempts elsewhere in Africa, these early efforts did not succeed, but right down through his fall from power in 1965, Nkrumah adhered to his proposition that political union precedes meaningful economic interaction, a proposition worthy of reconsideration today in the context of the Lagos Plan.

Nkrumah amplified his ideas succinctly during the Addis Ababa summit of May 1963. A number of the nations now found in the LPA were adumbrated by Nkrumah in his address to his peers on 24 May 1963.[11] He called at that time for common continental planning for industrial development. He recommended the establishment of a Union of African States and for a foreign ministers' committee to work out a machinery for the Union Government of Africa. More specifically he proposed the following:

1. a commission to form a constitution for a Union Government of African States;
2. a commission to work on a continent-wide plan for a unified or common economic and industrial program for Africa; this plan should include proposals for setting up (a) a common market for Africa, (b) an African currency, (c) an African monetary zone, (d) an African Central Bank, and (e) a continental communications system;
3. a commission to draw up details for a common foreign policy and diplomacy;
4. a commission to produce plans for a common system of defense; and
5. a commission to make proposals for a common African citizenship.

Most of the above items are what the LPA now seeks to accomplish, and the OAU is groping to help realize them 20 years later.

To Nkrumah's credit in this regard, he demonstrated exemplary far-sightedness, correct consciousness, and true African orientation. Nkrumah had foreseen and outlined the socio-economic needs of the continent and identified the functional-structural dimensions of socio-economic development within the rubric of a Union Government for Africa. In the past 20 years, Africa has inched its way ever so slowly and hesitantly to attain the very goals identified by Nkrumah two decades ago without even giving the credit that is due to him. The LPA is but a more generalized, a more systematic, and a more contemporary expression of Nkrumah's plans. This, therefore, should be an occasion to salute the memory of that true son of Africa, Osageyfo Kwame Nkrumah.

Though he was a political animal par excellence, his approach was systemic and wholesome. He related economic matters with internal, political conditions and related international, theoretical notions with concrete reality. Thus, he did not perceive his campaigns for African unity in purely political terms. He had enough economic sense and enough grasp of concrete conditions in Africa and the world to blend economics with politics. Through facts and figures he showed the economic advantages of political unity. In other words, Nkrumah did not call for political unity as an end in itself but as a means to economic (in today's jargon--development) ends. These qualities are much in demand in African leaders today. Although few and far between, there have been leaders and intellectuals in Africa who have either emulated or approximated Nkrumah's total dedication to Pan-Africanism, his farsightedness, and his wholesome approach to problems.

In 1963, it may be said that the time was not ripe for Nkrumah's Pan-African ideas. Those same ideas have now resurfaced in different forms in 1983. What separated Nkrumah from virtually all his contemporaries then and what makes reference to him relevant in discussions of the LPA now was his sense of not getting the horse before the cart. Nkrumah did not subscribe to piecemeal or gradual, functionalist integration for the continent. His categorical position, sharply put to his colleagues at the 1963 Addis Ababa summit, was: "The social and economic development of Africa will come only within the political kingdom, not the other way around." That is to say the horse that draws the cart of economic development is a political union of African states.

The mechanics of African unity as envisaged by Nkrumah, or the feasibility of African unity in his time, ideologically or otherwise, may be in question, but the importance of the objective of African unity as articulated by him is not in question. The framework for African unity forged at Addis Ababa in 1963 was very far from the one proposed by Nkrumah, and the result has been mixed. There is no question that, given the spirit of and the desire for African unity, especially in the context of the Lagos Plan of Action, the OAU Charter needs to be drastically revised. A number of concerned Africans and Africanists have analyzed Africa's choices with regard to achieving African unity. Thus, to George Padmore, the choice facing Africa was between Pan-Africanism or Communism. For Reginald Green and Ann Seidman it was Unity or Poverty and for Elenga M'buyinga it was Pan-Africanism or Neo-Colonialism.[12]

Twenty years of experience with the functionalist approach to African unity and economic orientations to continental socio-economic development must necessitate a reconsideration of ideas such as those of Kwame Nkrumah. The experience of the last five years and the problems connected with the implementation of the LPA through existing organizations, namely the OAU and the ECA, dictates a need to reflect on alternative approaches, including those by-passed or misunderstood by others. Nkrumah cited the United States, the Soviet Union, and Switzerland as examples of a federation, a union, and a confederation respectively. African states need to consider which type of overall government would be best for them. Is it feasible to attempt to implement the Lagos Plan outside such a political framework of operation?

POLITICAL IMPLICATIONS OF THE LAGOS PLAN OF ACTION

Doubtless, the issuance of the Lagos Plan represented the most significant political undertaking in the continent since the adoption of the OAU Charter in 1963. It is an ambitious document, and its realization assumes or anticipates drastic political changes. In fact, the success of the LPA depends upon political rather than economic or development adjustments. Yet, paradoxically, it appears that the political implications of the LPA have not been sufficiently studied either before or after its promulgation.[13]

The purpose of this chapter is not so much to fill this gap as to raise some relevant questions and proffer a few suggestions for further investigation. What follows then, is a series of questions and problems for consideration.

In as much as the commitments entered into willingly by Africa's leaders in Lagos are very crucial and very serious, I wonder to what extent and in what manner those leaders related the issues connected with the LPA to their respective peoples at home before arriving in Lagos. Even if, as President Nyerere remarked recently, there may be a tendency to treat the OAU "as a trade union of the leadership,"[14] and even though the urgency of the economic situation dictates quick action, it is nevertheless important to prime the people, to involve the masses in orienting them to the tremendous challenge, and to raise their Pan-African consciousness. Since the OAU was established, it has not permeated to the grass roots and, by and large, it still remains a superstructure far removed from the reach of the average man or woman of Africa. Surely, this cannot also be the fate of the Lagos Plan?

Likewise, I am also bound to ask to what extent the LPA has been popularized, disseminated, promoted, and campaigned for after its issuance? It does not matter who does the promoting; individual government agencies, the ECA and the OAU; but somebody has to do it. How much does the average African know about the LPA, and how much does he or she feel it to be important not only to his or her development but to posterity as well? How many examples do we have today, five years after the LPA, of its provisions being reflected in the national plans of signatory states or in the curricula of their school systems, in the motifs of their novelists, or as topics of seminars and discussions of academics? In other words, what conscious effort is visible to make the actualization of the LPA the responsibility of not only the leaders but also of the people for whose benefit it was issued in the first place? After all, governments come and go, but the people endure, and what is important to them has a better chance of enduring as well.

Insofar as not only its title but its contents denote that the LPA is a plan, it requires an authority structure for its implementation. Enormous decision-making responsibilities are outlined in the Lagos Plan, and it is by now very clear that existing continental structures (the ECA and the OAU) in their present forms cannot carry out these responsibilities effectively without dangerously treading on the sensitive nerves of sovereignty. Quite obviously, there are no other authority structures to coordinate, to monitor, to evaluate, to mobilize, to institutionalize, to generate resources, or to negotiate, as Africa's situation warrants. The issues raised here can perhaps be highlighted if we examine a couple of points in relation to what Professor Adedeji has called "the marching orders" of the LPA.[15] Accordingly, the Final Act proposed that:

> To implement the Plan of Action at the various stages we direct the Secretary-General of the OAU in cooperation with the Executive-Secretary of the United Nations Economic Commission for Africa, to take all appropriate measures, in accordance with Part II, paragraph 7, of the Monrovia Strategy and to submit a progress report to the 1982 Session of our Assembly.

In their Joint Report (E/ECA/CM.9/1) of 1982 these two secretaries-general reviewed what had transpired between 1980 and 1982 and concluded that their work was hampered by "lack of feed-back" by member states with regard to the implementation of the LPA at national levels. More to the point, in an Introductory Note to his 1984 Report (CM/1233 CXL, Part I), the OAU secretary-general, a.i., noted that quite apart from some US$34 million that was already in arrears in the OAU budget, as far as the 1983-84 financial year was concerned only 5 member states had paid their full shares of contributions, while 10 members had paid up partially, and 35 states had paid nothing.[16] Under such circumstances how is the OAU secretariat to fulfill the obligations devolved to it by the FAL? Similarly, the executive-secretary of ECA has observed that of the more than US$32 million in budget allocation for 1982-83 made by the UN General Assembly:

> What is particularly striking and disappointing was the low allocation to natural resources and energy (US$1,794,500) and the very low allocation to science and technology, the two backbones of industrial development, which had been expected to serve as the mainstays for the effective implementation of the Lagos Plan of Action and the Final Act of Lagos.[17]

In light of the concrete realities of the state system in Africa today, what reasonable measure of interstate, regional, and subregional cooperation can anyone expect? Has the LPA, for example, envisaged the manner in which Ethiopia and Somalia, given their present state of tension, can implement the plan's provisions at a subregional level? To the extent that the problems between these countries or between Libya and Sudan, for instance, are contingent and not structural, or given that communication problems among francophone Africa, anglophone Africa, Maghreb Africa, etc., are considered as transient, they will not act as unsurmountable obstacles to LPA implementation. However, even in the short run, strategies have to be worked out to handle such immediate issues. In so far as certain resources such as water are shared by a number of countries, the full development of some resources by one country could adversely affect the resources of other countries. The colonially induced borders that divide united peoples and unite divided peoples in Africa are like time bombs that can detonate at will. How are these tensions to be eased, and how is militarization to be halted in Africa?

Then there is the whole issue of Africa's relations with the external, particularly the Western capitalist, world and the issues related to delinking. Will the LPA be enacted in a business-as-usual manner so that the continent's economic, political, diplomatic, cultural and ideological links will remain fundamentally unaltered or are they to be transformed? Would the development of economic self-reliance entail some form of forgiveness and disengagement or is Africa to deal with the unconscionable US$150 billion debt while pursuing the LPA?[18] To put the question another way, is Africa to pursue primarily self-reliant or primarily outward-directed development? Samir Amin has recently articulated the difference by considering four sectors of production: (1) production of the means for production; (2) production of goods for mass consumption; (3) production and consumption of luxury goods; and (4) production of exports. By my definition, a self-reliant model is determined principally by the interplay of (1) and (2) and an outward-directed model by the interplay of (3) and (4).[19] The question that looms large is whether the economic and political implications of implementing the Lagos Plan as a form of self-reliance are fully appreciated.

Closely linked to the above is the question of models, methods, attitudes, and approaches to development. Africa has agonized through the past two decades or so by regurgitating the old, tired concepts with regard to development, and these have not proven productive. Now the question is do we discard or only change institutions and formal relations? Do we also discard those hackneyed concepts as well and the frame of mind that goes with them? In introducing the recent ECA publication ECA and Africa's Development 1983-2008, Adebayo Adedeji noted that "present development concepts and approaches cannot bring about any improvement in the quality of life of the African people."

The Lagos Plan has invigorated and politicized the ECA, and it has given the OAU a new lease on life. Between these two secretariats, on whose shoulders rest the heavy responsibilities for following through with the implementation of the Lagos Plan, there are a high number of experts and technocrats whose "development concepts and approaches" are critical to the success of the undertaking. Given the fact that the OAU Charter in its present form does not equip the secretariat to discharge properly and adequately its responsibilities connected with the LPA, the secretariat may wish to call for and help draft a revision in the Charter to be more in tune with the LPA. Another small measure of change in attitudes and orientations would be to promote a more activist ECA, much like its counterpart ECLA in another hemisphere, through the espousal of a more integrated political economy approach to problems and plans.

Finally, it behooves all concerned to remember Adedeji's adage that "the nature of development is too complex to conform to clear-cut mathematical or even economic laws."[20]

NOTES

1. It is to be noted that when the ECA was established in Addis Ababa in 1958 there were only 9 independent states; namely, Ethiopia, Ghana, Guinea, Liberia, Libya, Morocco, Sudan, Tunisia and UAR. By the time the OAU was established in 1963 there were 32 independent states, and 30 signed the Charter at the Addis Ababa summit.

2. See, for instance, Professor Adebayo Adedeji's year-end reports and his addresses and lectures in different parts of the world, and at UN forums. His recent paper, "The African Economic and Social Crisis" delivered to the ECOSOC, Geneva, July, 1984, is a case in point. See also OAU, What Kind of Africa by the Year 2000?, (Addis Ababa, 1979) and the periodic reports by ECA, FAO, UNDP, ILO, UNDRO, and other relevant agencies. Reginald Green and Ann Seidman's Unity or Poverty: The Economics of Pan-Africanism, (Hammondsworth: Penguin, 1968) is an important contribution in this regard.

3. See (E/1984/21 E/ECA/Cm.10/38) p. 41 and also the Special Memorandum (E/ECA/CM.10/37/Rev.2) pp. 5 and ff.

4. See (E/ECA/Cm.10/37/Rev.2) annex II.

5. See Adedeji, "The African Economic and Social Crisis," p. 16. It is of comparative interest to note that African countries are said to have imported in 1978 the level that was estimated to be imported in 1990. See A Program for the Industrial Development Decade for Africa (New York: United Nations, 1982), p. 25. See also, "Monthly Early Warning System on Food and Agriculture" in FAO's Food Crops and Shortages. (Rome: 14 September, 1984), pp. 11-21.

6. For details on this subject see the OAU-EGA-UNIDO A Program for the Industrial Development Decade for Africa, (New York: UN, 1983), and the related guidelines for priority actions during the preparatory phase.

7. See (CM/ 1233 XL) Part II. Paragraphs 210 and ff.

8. See (CM/Res/928 XL).

9. Kwame Nkrumah, Africa Must Unite (London: Panaf, 1983), p. 170. Nkrumah went on (p. 221) to say that, "proof is therefore positive that the continental union of Africa is an inescapable desideratum if we are determined to move forward to a realization of our hopes and plans for creating a modern society which will give our peoples the opportunity to enjoy a full and satisfying life."

10. Colin Legum is attributed to have given Nkrumah this nickname. See V. Bakpetu Thompson, Africa and Unity (London: Longman, 1969), p. 27.

11. Proceedings of the Summit Conference of Independent African States, Vol. I. (CIAS/Gen/Inf/36).

12. This last work by a Camerounian activist is in part a critique of the OAU and calls for a Revolutionary Pan-African Organization.

13. While the ECA goes on looking into the economic dimensions of the LPA, the OAU has commissioned studies on the social implications of the LPA. See "The Social Implications of the Lagos Plan of Action for the Economic Development of Africa" (AMSA/III WP.8, 1980) prepared by Dr. Seyoum G. Sellasie for the OAU. See also OAU/ILLS Symposium on Democratization of National Development in Africa (Geneva, 1983). To date, however, there is no substantial study on the political parameters, dimensions and implications of LPA and FAL.

14. See the Special Interview in Africa Now (December 1983), p. 118.

15. See ECA, Biennial Report of the Executive Secretary for 1979-80 (Addis Ababa, 1981), p. x.

16. As an amusing aside, it would be interesting to read the proceedings of the Lagos 1980 meeting and relate them to this record of paying.

17. See Biennial Report of the Executive Secretary 1982-83 (E/ECA/CM.10/11), p. 137.

18. See The Addis Ababa Declaration on Africa's External Indebtedness (CE/ECA/Cm.10/37. Rev. 2. Annex XI). (June 1984).

19. See "Is a Self-Reliant Development Strategy Possible in Africa?" in Democratization of National Development in Africa, p. 108. See also in this regard Bade Onimode, Imperialism and Underdevelopment in Nigeria (London: Zed, 1982) for a micro view of the case for disengagement from the international capitalist system. See also the useful studies in Adebayo Adedeji, ed., Indigenization of African Economics (London: Hutchinson, 1981).

20. ECA, ECA and Africa's Development, 1983-2008: A Preliminary Perspective Study (Addis Ababa: ECA, 1983), p. 1.

Adebayo Adedeji

4 Inter-African Economic Cooperation in Light of the Final Act of Lagos

The Final Act of Lagos (FAL) is both part and parcel of the Lagos Plan of Action (LPA) and at the same time separate from it. Maybe this is the reason why it is not as well known as the LPA itself. Yet, it is not only an integral part of the effort to bring about an increasing measure of self-reliance and self-sustainment in Africa, but it is also one of the foundations on which the economic decolonization of Africa has to be built. Given the balkanization of Africa during the colonial era, with the consequential large number of miniscule states that, with the best will in the world and the most favorable domestic and external economic environments, cannot but have an uphill task in achieving socio-economic transformation, intra-African economic penetration, cooperation, and integration must perforce become an integral part of national economic policy in all African countries.

To its eternal credit, the Economic Commission for Africa (ECA) appreciated this crucial point as far back as 1958 when it came into existence. The ECA further realized that intra-African economic penetration, cooperation, and integration should be promoted from the subregional level rather than to attempt a continental approach all at once. Accordingly, it divided Africa into four subregions--West Africa, Central Africa, Eastern and Southern Africa, and North Africa--and embarked tirelessly to promote a network of economic cooperation among the countries in each subregion.

It is now not generally remembered that the first work program of the ECA secretariat adopted by the commission at its inaugural meeting included, inter alia:

1. a study on how West African countries could derive mutual benefits by increasing their economic contacts with each other;

2. a study on various aspects of economic cooperation among the Maghreb countries of North Africa; and
3. studies on the establishment of an African development financing institution and of an institution for the training of African economists and statisticians.

This program marked the beginning of the 5-nation West African Economic Community (CEAO) and the 16-nation Economic Community of West African States (ECOWAS). For North Africa, this decision led in 1964 to the setting up of the Maghreb Permanent Consultative Committee (CPCM), consisting of Algeria, Libya, Morocco, and Tunisia. It was also the initiative that led to the establishment of the African Institute for Economic Development Planning (IDEP) for the training of African economic planners and to the setting up of Africa's only regional development bank--the African Development Bank (ADB).

Thus, right from the beginning and at a time when only a few African countries were politically independent, the ECA gave intra-African economic integration priority attention. It also adopted a pragmatic strategy of subregional and functional cooperation, which, in spite of all the setbacks of the past 26 years, is still accepted as valid by all the governments concerned. For in spite of the checkered history of intra-African integration and "in spite of the difficulties which have been and are being encountered in different parts of Africa and by different economic co-operation arrangements, there is no viable alternative to intra-African co-operation. Indeed, it is a mistaken belief to regard economic co-operation among African states not as a *conditio sine qua non* for the achievement of determined national socio-economic goals but as an 'extra' to be given thought to after the process of development is well advanced."[1] The African leaders not only endorsed this point of view, but also for the first time in the history of postindependence, Africa formalized the ECA pragmatic approach to economic cooperation by adopting the Final Act of Lagos.

THE FINAL ACT OF LAGOS (FAL), *THE LAGOS PLAN OF ACTION (LPA)* AND THE MONROVIA STRATEGY

However, it must be stated at once that the FAL has gone beyond merely giving a stamp of approval to ECA methodology for achieving intra-African trade and economic penetration, cooperation, and integration. The FAL is, like the *LPA*, the culmination of the series of efforts to reexamine and reappraise the whole strategy pursued by African governments since independence; this effort was initiated by the ECA in 1975 and led to the publication of the now historic and momentous document, *Revised Framework of Principles for the Implementation of the New International Economic Order in Africa, 1976-1981-1982*.[2] This document was the precursor of the Monrovia Strategy, the *LPA* and the FAL. Indeed, it constitutes the intellectual and theoretical foundation of the development strategy propounded in these subsequent documents.[3]

The *Revised Framework* was itself prompted, inter alia, by the ECA preliminary assessment of long-term development trends and prospects in developing Africa; its main finding was that only nine countries--Algeria, Congo, Gabon, Ivory Coast, Libya, Nigeria, Sao Tome and Principe, Tunisia, and Zambia--had managed to achieve during the period 1960-75 growth rates that led to significant increases in per capita incomes. The four major oil-exporting countries in this group--Algeria, Gabon, Libya, and Nigeria--achieved an average GDP growth rate, in real terms, of 6.9 percent per annum, while the corresponding rate for the remaining five countries was 5.8 percent. The study also showed that 22 countries--Botswana, Cameroon, Cape Verde, Central Africa Republic, Egypt, Equatorial Guinea, Gambia, Ghana, Guinea-Bissau, Kenya, Liberia, Madagascar, Mauritania, Mauritius, Morocco, Mozambique, Senegal, Sierra Leone, the Sudan, Swaziland, Togo, and Uganda--just managed to achieve an average GDP growth rate of 4.1 percent per annum, an increase of only 1.4 percent per capita per annum. The GDP growth rates of the remaining 14 countries on which data were available--Benin, Burkina Faso, Burundi, Chad, Ethiopia, Guinea, Lesotho, Malawi, Mali, Niger, Rwanda, Somalia, Tanzania, and Zaire--averaged only 2.6 percent between 1960 and 1975, a growth rate that fell below the rate of growth in population. Thus, throughout the first decade and a half of postindependence Africa, 14 countries experienced a persistent decline in their peoples' standard of living; 22 countries were stagnating; and only 9 countries managed to achieve any significant increase in their per capita income on a consistent basis.[4]

On intra-African economic cooperation, the ECA's preliminary assessment of performance between 1960 and 1975 shows that, although a number of economic groupings have been formed, "progress towards economic co-operation and integration in the African region has not been satisfactory. Some groupings have made progress towards free trade, but multinational industries and other integration activities are still lacking. Lack of political will, together with difficulty in identifying the real benefits from integration have frequently been the main reason for poor performance."[5] Thus, in spite of the increase in number of economic cooperation arrangements, intra-African trade showed a declining trend during the 15-year period. The statistics for four of the then-existing major economic groupings for the period of 1970-74 are shown in table 4.1. Intra-African trade decreased from 9.1 to 4.3 percent, from 16.9 to 13.9 percent, and from 2.2 to 1.8 percent among the countries of the West African Economic Community, the former East African Community, and the Permanent Consultative Committee of the Maghreb, respectively. Among Central African Customs and Economic Union (UDEAC) countries, trade at best stagnated. It unfortunately looked as if there had developed an inverse relation between the number of intergovernmental organizations (IGOs) established and progress in achieving effective intra-African trade, removing trade barriers, and in promoting joint multinational projects.

The proliferation of IGOs has been most marked in West Africa. There are now in existence as many as 32 IGOs in that subregion alone. And if account is taken of bilateral cooperation arrangements, the number will be even greater. Some individual countries belong to as many as a dozen or more. In fact, Niger, which tops the list, belongs to 25 IGOs, followed closely by Burkina Faso, Senegal, Ivory Coast, and Benin, which belong to 22, 20, 19, and 18 IGOs, respectively. Mali and Togo each belong to 17, while Mauritania is a member of 12 IGOs. The Gambia and Nigeria have each joined 10. At the other extreme are Guinea-Bissau and Cape Verde, which joined three and two IGOs respectively. And in between are the remaining four West African countries--Guinea, Sierra Leone, Ghana and Liberia--which have joined seven, six, five and four IGOs respectively.[6] It is not surprising that there is not only overlapping of memberships and

The distribution of MULPOCs in Africa

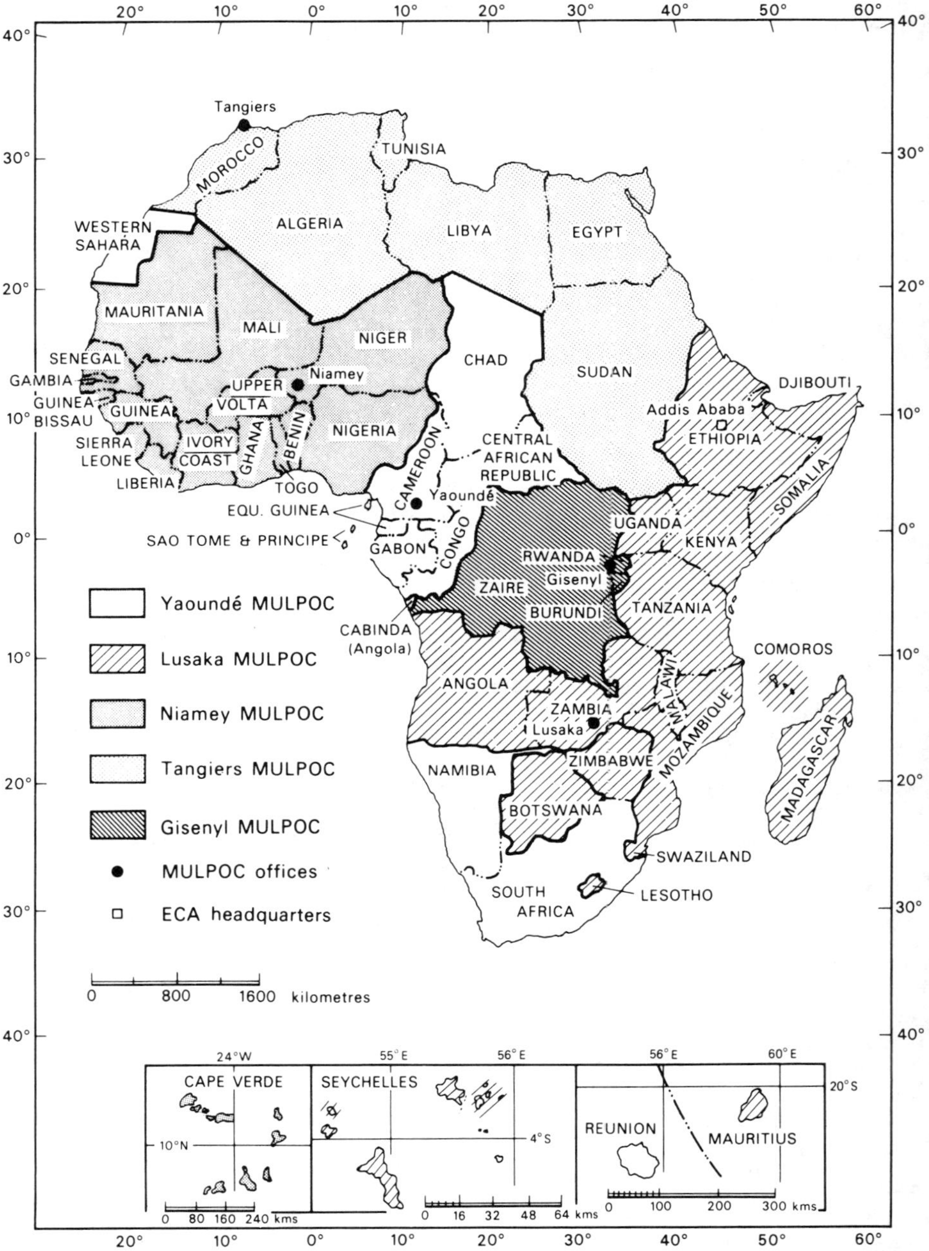

Source: Isebill V. Gruhn, "The Economic Commission for Africa" in African Regional Organization, Domenico Mazzeo, ed. (Cambridge: Cambridge University Press, 1984), p. 42.

Table 4.1

Exports of African countries by economic groupings, 1970-74

	Total exports (1)		Exports among countries in the subregion (2)		(2) as percentage of (1)	
	1970	1974	1970	1974	1970	1974
Central African Customs and Economic Union	437	835	33	62	7.5	7.4
West African Economic Community	803	2,081	73	90	9.1	4.3
East African Community	846	1,350	143	188	16.9	13.9
Permanent Consultative Committee of the Maghreb	1,680	6,947	37	126	2.2	1.8

Source: U.N., Economic Co-operation and Integration among Developing Countries (TD/B/609), Vol. II, p. 63

objectives but also no overall policy or mechanism for ensuring that the activities of these IGOs are harmonious and coordinated and reinforce one another. The result is that they have failed to advance the process of development and subregional economic integration in West Africa. Of these 32 West Africa IGOs, the membership of 17 of them is made up exclusively of French-speaking countries. While this situation is partly the result of geographical contiguity among francophone countries and partly a reflection of the greater unity among these countries during the colonial rule and their desire to maintain many of their previous ties, there is no doubt that "the existence of so many West African IGOs which draw their membership from only one linguistic group cannot but be a hindrance to economic integration at the sub-regional level."[7]

Because of the poor record of economic cooperation in Africa, the ECA's preliminary assessment concluded that not only must cooperation be strengthened but also that steps must continue to be taken to ensure pragmatism and flexibility. It further adds that "for economic co-operation arrangements to be effective, there must be agents of production and distribution able and willing to exploit the opportunities provided by such arrangements. There must be more emphasis on indigenous, rather than external, agents. The difficulties caused by disputes and resistance to the distribution of industries within groups of countries should be removable, provided that the basic framework is effective and that there is a real political will to co-operate."[8]

We then pursued, on an in-depth basis, an exploration of the obstacles standing in the way of effective economic cooperation in the Revised Framework and ended up in providing a package of essential requirements for effective intra-African economic penetration and the achievement of an increasing measure of collective self-reliance. Seven of these basic requirements will be mentioned here. There is, first and foremost, the requirement of political commitment, which itself requires people and their governments to believe that horizontal intra-African penetration is a sine qua non for national development. Second, there is a need for the establishment of mechanisms that will facilitate and foster cooperation. These mechanisms, among other things, must make available on a regular basis a wide range of general and special information supplied by the cooperating countries; must establish marketing and distribution agencies; must set up clearing-house arrangements and commodity exchange markets; and must establish links between different national chambers of commerce and industry. Third, there is an imperative need to establish consultative machinery for the harmonization and coordination of economic policies. Fourth, long-term agreements must be entered into concerning product specialization and product-sharing on the basis of complementarities, including special treatment of less developed countries. Fifth, every effort must be made to ensure that the gains from cooperation are not too long-term or too indeterminate when compared to the other pressing economic objectives of the participating states. Sixth, for economic cooperation arrangements to be effective, there must be agents of production and distribution who are able and willing to exploit the opportunities that cooperation arrangements provide. And finally, a variety of special national measures designed to facilitate cooperation must be taken by each government. Such measures include "the laying of or the improvement of the legislative formation or the formation and operation of companies; the adoption of legislation, machinery and policy relating to the registration of patents and trade marks; the harmonization of policies towards foreign private enterprises and monopolistic business groupings (including financial institutions such as banks and insurance companies); the working out of technical quality and design standards; the orientation of research policy, institutions and priorities; and the regulation of transport, to name only a few."[9]

This package of requirements was put together on the basis of the experience of past years of experimenting with regional and subregional cooperation in Africa. For example, the experience of the East African Community (EAC) has taught us the importance of avoiding promotion of institutional developments that render African economies more vulnerable to penetration by transnationals and other forms of foreign corporate organization than would otherwise be the case. The package of basic requirements was also put together to drive home the point that economic cooperation is not merely a treaty-making exercise. Treaties, important as they are, are means not ends. For cooperation to take root and grow, a thousand and one actions have to be taken, individually, nationally, and collectively by the cooperative states. The pooling of sovereignty in order to advance commonly perceived interests and the loosening of the ties with former metropolitan powers are also essential prerequisites for effective intra-African economic penetration.

The Monrovia Strategy and Declaration of Commitment put to rest whatever doubts might have existed in some quarters about the adherence of African leaders to the principle of intra-African economic cooperation. The governments committed themselves unequivocally to the following goals:

1. to promote social and economic development and integration with a view to achieving an increasing measure of collective self-reliance and self-sustainment;
2. to establish national, subregional, and regional institutions that will facilitate the attainment of the objectives of self-reliance and self-sustainment;
3. to promote the physical integration of Africa in order to facilitate social and economic intercourse;
4. to foster subregional and regional, internally located industrial development;
5. to cooperate in the field of natural resources exploration, extraction, and use; and
6. to cooperate in the preservation, protection, and improvement of the natural environment.

The declaration then ended with these words: "We hold firmly to the view that these commitments will lead to the creation at the national, subregional and regional levels of a dynamic inter-dependent African economy and will thereby pave the way for the eventual establishment of an African Common Market leading to an African Economic Community."[10]

In light of this firm commitment, it was inevitable that the Final Act of Lagos (FAL) would be considered an integral part of the *Lagos Plan of Action*. Indeed, the FAL can be correctly regarded as constituting a major cornerstone of the *LPA*. The preamble to the *Lagos Plan* reiterated the governments' determination "to adopt a far-reaching regional approach based primarily on collective self-reliance."[11] Not surprisingly, the heads of state and governments likened this to the struggle for political independence by asserting "that this same determination that has virtually rid our continent of political domination is required for our economic liberation. Our success in exploiting our political unity should encourage us to exploit the strength inherent in our economic unity."[12]

Accordingly, in all the major sectors dealt with in the *LPA*, action programs and projects that must be undertaken are spelled out at three levels--national, subregional and regional--and sometimes also at the international level. The concern with concerted subregional and regional activities is particularly evident in such sectors as industry, natural resources, trade and finance, human resources development, transport and communications, science and technology, and, environment. For example, in the transport and communications sector, first priority was accorded to regional projects, subregional projects, and national projects with a regional and subregional impact.

It is therefore crystal clear that, although there is the FAL, intra-African economic penetration, cooperation, and integration went beyond those concerns contained in the FAL and was an all-pervasive issue as far as the *LPA* is concerned. But this having been said, the FAL itself complemented and supplemented the *LPA* in at least three ways. First, it provided a time frame for the establishment of an African Economic Community--the year 2000. Secondly, it identified succinctly the various stages of the implementation of this object. Thus, it calls, during the 1980s, for the strengthening of the existing regional economic communities and for establishing new ones so as to cover the continent as a whole; for the strengthening of sectoral integration at the continental level; and for promoting coordination and harmonization among existing and future economic groupings. And during the decade of the 1990s, it calls for sectoral integration. And, finally the FAL realizes that this stage-by-stage approach depends on the political commitment of all African governments without exception. Therefore each stage needs to be carefully monitored with periodic progress reports being submitted jointly by the ECA and the OAU to the heads of state and government.

PROGRESS AND PROBLEMS SINCE 1980

In undertaking any evaluation of the progress that has been achieved in promoting intra-African economic cooperation, (see chapter 5), we must bear in mind two very crucial points. First, many of the initiatives that have come to fruition since 1980 had begun long before the LPA and the FAL. Indeed, rather than being their direct products, the fact that they were in the pipeline played an important role in determining the thrust, orientation, and contents of both the LPA and the FAL. And second, with regard to the initiatives that have been taken as a direct result of the LPA and the FAL in this area, five years may be too short a period to achieve a major breakthrough. What is therefore important at this stage is whether or not there has been a movement in the right direction. And my review and evaluation will perforce be in two parts: (1) progress in each of the major sectors and (2) progress in strengthening the existing and in establishing new economic groupings.

It should be clear from what I have said so far that economic integration is viewed in the LPA and the FAL both as a means and as an instrument for promoting economic liberation. Most significantly, it has never been seen as an end in itself. Second, both the various measures of the LPA and the FAL are mutually reinforcing. For example, the cooperative measures prescribed in the trade field, such as those relating to the reduction and elimination of trade barriers, are aimed primarily at goods given priority attention in the agriculture and industry sectors. And finally, it should also be clear from a careful reading of these documents that there is meant to be a close relation between, on the one hand, the promotion of cooperation at the sectoral level as provided for in the LPA and, on the other, the strengthening of existing subregional economic communities and the setting up of new ones where necessary as provided for in the FAL. There is similarly a relation between the latter goal and the founding of an African Common Market and Economic Community.

These points having been made, it remains for me to review the extent to which all the relevant provisions of the LPA and the FAL have been implemented. Obviously, it will not be possible to do this in a detailed manner in a short chapter such as this. It will be enough to give a picture of the trend and direction, particularly as I have already indicated that many of these provisions are meant to be implemented over a longer time span than has elapsed since 1980.

On the basis of the information currently available to the ECA it seems, regrettably, that not much progress has been made regarding promotion of cooperation at the sectoral level, although there have been a couple of outstanding achievements. But the areas where actions have been lacking since 1980 are so many and so critical to effective intra-African economic penetration that further delay in redeeming the situation will prejudice perhaps irreparably the achievement of the overall objective.

Let me cite some of these crucial areas. First, no effort has so far been initiated in establishing subregional food security arrangements or an African Food Relief Support Scheme, which are intended to assist member countries in times of food emergency. Second, very little has been accomplished in giving fillips to intercountry cooperative agronomic research programs as required by the LPA. Third, effective regional cooperation in tackling environmental problems with transboundary effects is yet to be commenced. In spite of the widespread and severe drought of the past two to three years, which now affects 36 out of the continent's 50 independent countries, and in spite of growing desertification, there has been no breakthrough in effective cooperation to deal with these urgent environmental problems.

In the industrial sector, of the 16 specific action areas that are identified for subregional and regional cooperation, it is only in three areas that action has been initiated. Thanks to the efforts of the ECA and its network of subregional Multinational Programming and Operational Centers (MULPOCs) something is now being done regarding:

1. the preparation of subregional and regional plans for the creation of industrial complexes;
2. the establishment at subregional levels of multinational industries in basic areas such as metallurgy, foundry, chemicals, etc.; and
3. the strengthening of existing ECA-sponsored regional institutions, such as the African Regional Center for Technology and the African Regional Center for Engineering Design and Manufacturing.

Fortunately, all obstacles in the way of operationalizing the African Industrial Development Fund (AIDF) virtually have been removed, and ECA and the African Development Bank (ADB) should be meeting shortly to sort out the remaining problems. In the field of the promotion of trade in manufactures, encouraging steps have been taken by ECOWAS in West Africa and PTA in Eastern and Southern Africa.

Unfortunately, in all the other areas listed in the LPA, no implementation action appears as yet to have been initiated. For example, no multinational regional and subregional institutions have yet been created to make an inventory of and explore shared national resources. Not even the African Regional Center for Consultancy and Industrial Management Services -- on which the ECA secretariat has already undertaken considerable preparatory work -- has yet been organized, thanks to the decision of the ECA Conference of Ministers. The ministers, during the commission's Silver Jubilee session in 1983, decided to set up an ad hoc committee on the evaluation, harmonization, and perhaps merger of the ECA- and OAU-sponsored multinational institutions and also requested that, until the committee had completed its work and the Conference of Ministers had acted thereon, no new institutions should be established by the commission.[13] Unfortunately, the ad hoc committee is yet to complete its assignment, and the freeze on the establishment of new institutions has been extended by a mandate of the committee for another year.[14]

In the area of natural resources, while a few multinational projects and enterprises for the exploitation, production, and processing of useable natural resources have been established and are being established by a growing number of countries, the pace needs to be considerably accelerated. But neither the establishment of joint facilities for applied research, specialized services, and training nor the harmonization of national development programs for the use of mineral, energy, and water resources advocated in the LPA has taken place or has even been initiated. I must add, however, that in June 1983 the ECA successfully set up a mineral resources development center for the Central African subregion in Brazzaville, Congo. This center, which is the second of its kind--the first being the Dodoma-based center--should become operational in 1985.

It is generally accepted that intra-African economic penetration will remain a will-o'-the-wisp unless intra-African trade expands steadily, and indeed faster than total African foreign trade. Hence intra-African trade expansion has constituted a mainstay of the LPA, and different actions that must be undertaken and the time frame within which they should be undertaken have been spelled out in the Lagos Plan under three broad areas:

1. the reduction or elimination of trade barriers;
2. the setting up of mechanisms and measures for the facilitation and development of trade such as commodity exchanges and associations of state trading organizations at subregional and regional levels; and
3. the establishment of African multinational production corporations and joint ventures.

Unfortunately, as in the other sectors, very little progress has been accomplished. The only outstanding exception is the establishment of preferential trade areas in Eastern and Southern Africa and in Central Africa (I will discuss these later) and the founding of the African Federation of Chambers of Commerce (AFCC).

In so far as the AFCC is concerned, it is indeed gratifying to report that, as a result of a series of meetings convened by the ECA secretariat in Addis Ababa and Harare, an ad hoc committee of the presidents and secretaries-general of the National Associations of Chambers of Commerce was able to draft a constitution, rules of procedure of the organs of the federation, and the budget and organizational structures of the secretariat of the federation. These documents were finalized and approved at a meeting of presidents and secretaries-general of African Chambers of Commerce held in Cairo, Egypt, in October and November of 1983. In September 1984, the ECA was able to convene a meeting of plenipotentiaries at which the constitution of the AFCC was signed by no less than 24 national chambers; Cairo was chosen as the headquarters; and the officials who are to lead the organization during its first three years were elected. Thus, in effect, the AFCC came into being more than a year before the 1985 deadline set by the LPA.

In the field of finance, while considerable progress has been made by the ECA in establishing subregional multilateral clearing and payment arrangements (in West Africa several years ago, in Eastern and Southern Africa, and in Central Africa quite recently), a beginning is yet to be made on the setting up of the African Payments Union and development finance institutions. However, the ECA in collaboration with the ADB, the ECA-sponsored African Center for Monetary Studies, and the OAU, has been working hard on the establishment of the African Monetary Fund, although, it must be admitted, progress has been much slower than was initially envisaged by the secretariat. In October 1982, a meeting of experts from ministries of finance and central banks took place at ECA Headquarters and approved the terms of reference and guidelines for the feasibility study for the establishment of the fund. The feasibility study is expected to be completed shortly, and thereafter it is hoped that the process of setting up the fund can be accelerated so that a meeting of plenipotentiaries can take place sometime in 1985.

It should be evident that a lot still remains to be done in pushing ahead with intra-African economic penetration at the sectoral, grass-roots level. There is no doubt that the economic crisis that has engulfed the continent since 1980 is partly responsible for the slow progress, but there is also no gainsaying the need for effective actions at the national level because the types of cooperation being sought by the LPA presuppose the existence of clear, facilitative, and consistent policies at the national level. Unfortunately, this has not always been the case. Also, while intra-African economic cooperation and integration is expected to be given due priority over cooperation with third parties and in particular over cooperation with developed countries, unfortunately this has so far remained a heroic assumption and an unrealized expectation.

But in spite of this slow start, there is no doubt about the intention of the governments to push ahead; as long as we constantly bear in mind that modern Africa is relatively new to the game of international cooperation, we shall understand the rationale behind the hesitation and slow progress. After all, intra-African technical and economic relations were virtually nonexistent some 20-25 years ago unless inherited from the colonial era.

This having been said, no one will dispute that, as far as the second type of cooperative activities are concerned, namely, those having to do with the implementation of the Final Act, major breakthroughs have been achieved. First and foremost, efforts have continued to be made to strengthen and streamline existing economic groupings, namely ECOWAS, CEAO, UDEAC, and CEPGL. And second, new ones, specifically the Preferential Trade Area for Eastern and Southern African States (PTA) and the Economic Community of Central African States (ECCAS), have been established since the adoption of the FAL.

In so far as strengthening and streamlining existing groupings is concerned, the most significant developments to date relate to the strengthening of ECA MULPOCs and efforts are being made to rationalize and streamline the institutional framework for intra-African economic cooperation and integration. As regards the MULPOCs, it will be noted--although no explicit mention is made of them in the FAL--that their main role as intergovernmental policy-making bodies is, with the assistance of the ECA secretariat, to help member states promote cooperation within the five subregions where they are located (namely the Lusaka, Yaounde, Gisenyi, Niamey, and Tangiers MULPOCs for the Eastern and Southern Africa, Central Africa I, Central Africa II, West Africa, and North Africa subregions). As such, they can be regarded as sui generis instrumentalities for multinational cooperation along with the more traditional types of economic groupings that were explicitly mentioned in the FAL.

In addition to strengthening its MULPOCs, for the last two years ECA, at the urging of the ECA Conference of Ministers--which is rightly concerned with the proliferation of the ECA- and OAU-sponsored institutions and the duplication of activities between them--has found itself increasingly involved in helping to rationalize these institutions.

Our first efforts in this direction were made in the form of a comprehensive report entitled Proposals for Strengthening Economic Integration in West Africa, which was produced at the request of the Sixth ECOWAS Summit to help member countries streamline and rationalize the various activities of the large number of IGOs existing in West Africa. The report strongly recommended that ECOWAS, after appropriate restructuring, should be the focal point for economic cooperation in West Africa. The report, after being considered at a number of export and ministerial meetings, as well as at meetings of the IGOs, is now scheduled to be submitted formally to ECOWAS leaders at their next summit.

With regard to developments concerning new economic groupings, one of the most notable achievements since the adoption of the FAL--although the preparatory work and most of the arduous technical negotiations that played such an important part in the creation of the PTA took place before this adoption--was the actual launching of the PTA at the beginning of 1982. Throughout 1982, the ECA secretariat played the role of interim secretariat and, even after the PTA secretary-general and his core staff were appointed, ECA continued to assist the young PTA in every possible way, particularly through technical studies and temporary secondment of staff.

As for ECCAS, unlike the PTA, it is a direct offshoot of the FAL, to the extent that the FAL clearly provided the inspiration for it. In 1981, the UDEAC authorities requested the ECA secretariat to undertake an evaluation study of UDEAC and its institutions with a view to its restructuring and improvement. Following the evaluation report, which recommended the enlargement of economic cooperation in Central Africa for greater efficiency, the secretariat was requested to carry out a series of studies, including one on the implications of the integration process for the economies of the potential member states of the proposed ECCAS, and another to propose a draft treaty and various draft protocols on the basis of which actual negotiations started at the technical level. These were serviced jointly by the ECA and the OAU secretariats and eventually led to the signing of the treaty in October 1983, at Libreville, by 10 heads of state and government of the subregion.

Since then, the ECA and OAU secretariats have been acting as a joint interim secretariat for the ECCAS pending the establishment of its own permanent secretariat, following ratification of the treaty by the required number of countries. In this role, the joint OAU/ECA secretariat prepared, inter alia, an organizational chart for the ECCAS secretariat, a draft budget, job descriptions for the secretariat's professional staff, a draft agreement with the host government, draft staff and financial regulations, and rules of procedure for the policy organs. It is interesting to note that, in the preparation of these various papers as well as in the actual servicing of the negotiations, the ECA secretariat was able to make good use of the experience gained in the course of the PTA exercise, while making the adaptations required for the particular circumstances of the subregion.

EXTERNALLY INDUCED CONSTRAINTS AND IMPEDIMENTS TO INTRA-AFRICAN ECONOMIC COOPERATION

I have already referred in extenso to the constraints and impediments that have continued to vitiate the achievement of an increasing measure of intra-African economic penetration and the realization of collective self-reliance. All the impediments that I have so far identified arise from nationalistic domestic policies and the lack of appropriate facilitative policies. But this analysis would be incomplete if it failed to take into account the externally induced factors that have militated and continue to militate against intra-African economic cooperation.

The relations that prevailed between the major colonial powers (Britain and France, in particular) and their respective African dependencies in the preindependence period are well documented and need not be repeated here. Suffice it to say that apart from their total incorporation into the economies of the metropolitan powers as mere appendages, the African dependencies were, particularly after World War II, beneficiaries of imperial trade and economic and aid preferences. The French African colonies, more than their British counterparts, benefited from substantial assistance and from protected markets in France for their principal exports. They were also recipients of budgetary deficits. Whereas British African colonies exported their products at world market prices and were not protected against price fluctuations for agricultural commodity exports by a price fluctuation fund, their French counterparts enjoyed guaranteed markets and inflated prices for their exports in the protected French market, where the _Fonds national de regularisation des cours des produits d'outre-mer_ guaranteed a _surprix_ substantially above world price levels.[15]

Naturally, the colonial powers were anxious to maintain these preindependence special relationships. And needless to add, many newly independent African countries were themselves not averse to this. In the case of former French colonies, the decision seemed foreordained because France and another former colonial power, Belgium, were the original signatories to the Treaty of Rome, which established the European Economic Community (EEC) and under which there was a provision for the gradual elimination of custom duties between the member states, a provision that necessitated a review of the relations between the colonial member powers and their dependencies. Because the French-speaking African countries had not become independent by the time of the Treaty of Rome in 1957, France successfully obtained from her EEC partners "associated status" for her colonies.

Associated status provided that the exports from the countries concerned be exempt from the provisions of the common external tariff of the EEC. In return for this concession, all the EEC states would extend to member states, albeit progressively, any preferential tariffs that existed within the markets of the associated countries concerned or that might be created for exports by any one EEC member. According to an annex to the treaty, which contains a list of countries with associated status, all French African colonies, including the UN Trust Territories of French Cameroon, Italian Somaliland, Rwanda-Urundi and Togo, and the Belgian Congo were granted associated status. However, Algeria was excluded from the list on the grounds that it was an integral part of France. The treaty also provided for the creation of a Fund for Development to finance development and social projects in the associated countries. Finally, in order to minimize the impact of this additional exposure to international competition on the fragile economies of these countries, the treaty allowed the colonies to establish or retain protective tariffs for their "infant" industries.

Not surprisingly but nevertheless disappointingly, these countries on achieving political independence asked for the continuance of their associated status without considering the repercussions on relations between Africa and the EEC, on intra-African economic and trade cooperation, and on the economies of the nonassociated African states. Rather, they were interested in a renegotiation so that they could "preserve, consolidate, perpetuate, and expand their privileges within the French market and the European Common Market."[16]

Thus, right from the start of independence, Africa was divided--divided into associated and nonassociated countries--and needless to add, this became a constant source of conflict. This conflict came to a head and into the open at the 1962 session of the ECA held in March of that year in Addis Ababa when the francophone countries joined together to defeat an Ethiopian resolution attacking association with the EEC because it was detrimental to the formation of an African Common Market. On their part, the anglophone African countries resisted the pressure from Great Britain to seek associated status if and when she joined the EEC. These countries were unanimous in their rejection of any such link on the grounds that it would (1) perpetuate neocolonialism; (2) constitute a fundamental obstacle to the achievement of African political and economic unity; (3) perpetuate the position of Africa as supplier of primary commodities to Europe; and (4) lead to a loss of freedom to trade freely with non-EEC member states, as well as jeopardize the chances of obtaining capital from the most convenient sources. But in spite of all these objections, the francophone countries entered into a five-year agreement with the EEC from January 1964. This was the so-called Yaounde I, which was replaced by Yaounde II five years later. Thus, during the first decade after independence, independent Africa was "newly divided, in its trade relations with Western Europe, by new barriers to increasing intra-African trade and by the external political, economic and cultural affinities of its independent states."[17]

This division was to have a negative long-term effect on the fostering of intra-African cooperation. It made the realization of effective intra-African economic cooperation, which cuts across linguistic barriers, nearly impossible during the first decade and a half after independence. Thus, until 1975, all the cooperative institutions were set up purely on a linguistic basis. As we have already noted, of the 32 West African IGOs, 17 are made up exclusively of French-speaking countries. Such IGOs tend to reinforce the linguistic division in the region. It was not until the formation of ECOWAS in 1975 that this barrier was at last weakened, if not entirely broken.

It must also be added that all African countries south of the Sahara and including the Sudan have since 1975 become associated states under the EEC-ACP Lomé Convention of that year. Thus, while the distinction between associated and nonassociated states no longer exists, there can be no doubt that the external orientation of economic cooperation in Africa had had and continues to have deleterious consequences for intra-African integration. No one can, or nowadays even bothers to, deny that, contrary to the earlier claims of complementarity and interdependence that used to be made on behalf of EurAfrican cooperation, the benefits arising from cooperation between Africa and Western Europe have been heavily skewed in favor of the latter. This is so for the simple reasons that such cooperation is based on unequal exchange and that the so-called complementarity is artificially induced and the interdependence is asymmetrical.

It is now 10 years since the first Lomé Convention was signed; since then there have been Lomé II (1980) and Lomé III (December 1984). This is not the place for an evaluation of EEC-ACP relations in so far as Africa is concerned. My interest here is to point out the implications of Lomé for intra-African trade and economic penetration. But that having been said, it is also worth mentioning that recent studies by a growing number of independent scholars[18] have confirmed that the gains made by African countries from this relationship have been quite marginal and could definitely not have compensated for the losses that have been suffered as a result of failure to achieve a breakthrough in intra-African trade penetration.

For example, evidence abounds to show that the ACP share of the total EEC imports has continued to fall, whereas other Third World countries that are not part of the Lomé regime have managed to maintain their share of the market. However, this drop in the ACP share of the EEC market has been accompanied by a steady rise in the EEC share of the ACP market. For example, between 1980 and 1981, EEC exports to ACP states rose by about 15.0 percent in value. This negative development has naturally been a source of disappointment to those who had expected that the duty-free access enjoyed by ACP states to EEC markets could play a potentially decisive role in their economic development. As Joanna Moss and John Ravenhill have concluded, for the EEC such disappointing results "must be somewhat embarrassing....Yet it is questionable whether the Community will be particularly upset by the pattern of its trade relations with the ACP. For if ACP aspirations are to be realized, this would obviously impose substantial domestic costs on the Community in the form, for instance, of structural adjustment. To date, the Community has not shown itself willing to bear such costs....It has been less costly--both in economic and political terms--for the community to emphasize financial aid as its principal contribution to ACP development needs."[19]

While intra-African cooperation arrangements such as I have been discussing have imposed considerable strains and stresses on the establishment of a regime of an effective intra-African cooperation, no one is suggesting that Africa should delink itself from the rest of the international economic community. The choice is not either intra-African penetration or EurAfrican cooperation. Rather, the choice is one of priorities and must be made based on the realization that one impinges and affects the other. But that having been said, there is no doubt that as long as socio-economic policy in Africa is still powerfully oriented to the outside world and as long as African countries are still conditioned by strong attachments to preindependence political, economic, social, and cultural relations, then the promotion of intra-African cooperation will continue to prove ineffective.

Regrettably, the African search for regionalism and collective self-reliance has unfortunately received no encouragement from most multilateral international institutions. For example, regional and subregional development and infrastructural projects are accorded very low priority not only by bilateral donors but also by multilateral financing and technical assistance institutions. Not surprisingly, none of the ECA-initiated projects of trans-African highway networks has materialized, due to the unsympathetic attitude of bilaterals and to the lukewarm and ambivalent attitude of multilaterals. No support has been forthcoming on the setting up of clearing and payments arrangements in the various subregions, or on the establishment of the African Monetary Fund, the setting up of preferential trade areas, or the establishment of subregional economic communities. Of course, there are a number of exceptions here and there and the most notable among these is the United Nations Development Program (UNDP), which has supported, within the limits of its resources, multinational projects that aim to bring about intra-African economic cooperation.

The typical approach of most multilaterals is to regard regional cooperation as a long-term issue, as a kind of impracticable African dream that, while it cannot be openly opposed, must remain untouched and unsupported. It therefore surprised no one that the World Bank in its controversial report entitled Accelerated Development in Sub-Saharan Africa: An Agenda for Action relegated regionalism to the category of long-term issues, even though the report explicitly recognized the importance of regional economic cooperation for small states that have limited development alternatives and for the landlocked states that have special problems. While the World Bank (IBRD) report favored the intensification of efforts in joint planning and use of transport and communications links and in the exploitation of energy resources and the use of training institutions, it failed to advocate similar cooperation in the directly productive sectors, particularly in the industrial sector. For the report to suggest that "member states should turn to regional economic co-operation only after they had established effective administrative machinery, developed a more productive monetized agriculture, created physical and social infrastructure, spread suitable education and accomplished similar tasks at the national level" is to ignore the fact that lack of economic cooperation activities particularly in the field of industry may delay and in some cases render impossible the attainment of such objectives at the national level.[20] In contrast to this approach, the LPA sees the solution to the problems of ineffective intra-African economic cooperation as calling for short-, medium-, and long-term actions.

ACHIEVING A BREAKTHROUGH IN INTRA-AFRICAN ECONOMIC PENETRATION

In light of the very limited progress made in implementing the various cooperation projects contained in the LPA and the FAL and in light of lack of encouragement in favor of regional cooperation from the external economic environment as discussed above, what are the prospects for the future? What is the perspective that should be adopted when considering Africa's future? This question is easier posed than answered.

The perspective I support is based on my often-repeated proposition that economic cooperation among African countries, in spite of all the difficulties and obstacles, both internal and external, is imperative for the achievement of any meaningful measure of national self-reliance. Excessive openness and external dependence of African economies are inimical to the achievement not only of national but also of collective self-reliance so that progressive intra-African economic penetration is a sine qua non for the achievement of national and collective self-reliance.

There is no doubt that the developments of the past few years have heralded the emergence of a sound foundation for achieving this objective. ECOWAS, PTA and ECCAS constitute the main instrumentalities for achieving this goal (see chapter 5). Among them these three institutions cover the entire area of Sub-Saharan Africa. Therefore we need urgently to put them into the position of helping direct African development policy.

ECOWAS has been rather slow in making an impact and in advancing the process of integration in West Africa. The proliferation of IGOs in that subregion, the building, until recently, of IGOs along linguistic lines, the lack of a clear vision as to what is intended to be achieved through these IGOs, the lack of effective and efficient supporting structures for ECOWAS to ensure cooperation and implementation at the national level are some of the issues that have to be addressed by West African governments most urgently. These and many other issues have been discussed in the ECA report entitled Proposals for Strengthening Economic Integration in West Africa.

The fact that such a study was commissioned and that its terms of reference included an examination of (1) the effectiveness of the IGOs in the promotion of subregional economic cooperation; (2) the costs and benefits of economic cooperation to the countries of the subregion; and (3) measures that would accelerate the process of economic integration in the subregion, shows an increasing awareness at the highest levels of government that something is seriously wrong and that necessary corrective actions must be taken. The ECA report is already the subject of extensive discussions at the national level in West Africa and in all the West African IGOs. It has also been the subject of two meetings by ministers responsible for economic development and cooperation; and their proposals on actions to be taken are now before the ECOWAS leadership. If the governments could implement vigorously the report's recommendations, this would go a long way in contributing to the achievement of an increasing measure of collective self-reliance in West Africa. Also, the establishment of a development-cum-commercial bank--the ECO Bank--by the West African Association of Chambers of Commerce should help in giving fillip to the spirit of intra-African trade, as this initiative has come entirely from the private sector.

In Eastern and Southern Africa, the newly established PTA is already beginning to make its mark after the usual "teething" problems. Its payments and clearing arrangements have already begun to operate; the gradual reduction in tariffs began on schedule, and an aggressive promotion of intra-African trade has been launched by the secretariat through the organization of a series of national workshops and seminars in cooperation with national Chambers of Commerce. The establishment of joint productive enterprises in the industrial sector is now being vigorously pursued by the organization.

However, there are some problem areas that, unless they are tackled early and successfully, will either adversely affect the progress that is being made or will slow it down significantly. These include the establishment of the Trade and Development Bank for Eastern and Southern Africa; the removal of nontariff restrictions on trade and on the movement of goods and persons; and the joining of the PTA by the six countries that, although they participated in all the negotiations that led to its establishment, have not yet acceded to its treaty. The six countries are: Angola, Botswana, Madagascar, Mozambique, Seychelles, and Tanzania. It is imperative that all the countries of the subregion should participate fully in PTA, otherwise a new and regrettable division will be created. The PTA will also have to work out a modus vivendi with SADCC, which has eight Southern African countries and Tanzania from East Africa as members. Indeed, the ECA MULPOC for Eastern and Southern Africa has already taken an initiative in this regard by forming an intergovernmental ad hoc committee to submit proposals on ways and means of maximizing cooperation between PTA, SADCC, and itself.

The youngest of these new cooperation arrangements, the Economic Community of Central African States (ECCAS), is yet to become operational. Its treaty, which was signed in October 1983, is still being ratified by member states. Nevertheless, the first meeting of the heads of state and government of ECCAS did take place in December 1984 when its program budget was approved, the permanent secretariat established, and the process of launching the community begun. One of the problems that this new organization will encounter is establishing a modus vivendi with UDEAC and CEPGL, each of which caters to some of the countries within the subregion. But since these two organizations worked closely with the ECA and the OAU in the preparation of the treaty, I do not anticipate any difficulty.

The prospects for strengthening and streamlining these three major economic communities appear to be promising. But as is evident from my discussion, there is a great deal that needs to be done and done very quickly. However, it is at the sectoral level that the greatest challenge lies because, as I have already mentioned, not much progress has been achieved. No breakthrough in intra-African economic penetration will be achieved until Africa has set up some major sectoral and functional cooperation institutions. The most important of these institutions are the African Monetary Fund, the Payments Union, the Industrial Development Fund, African Multinational Production Corporations and Joint Ventures, and the Energy Commission. In addition, there is need to take urgent measures to build up and strengthen existing regional and subregional technical cooperation institutions such as the African Regional Center for Technology (see chapter 14), the African Regional Center for Engineering Design and Manufacturing, the Regional Centers for Aerial Surveys and Mapping, and the two Minerals Resources Centers, to mention only a few.

All these ECA-sponsored institutions are suffering from a lack of financial support, which in turn severely limits their effectiveness. I must also not forget to mention that with regard to the transport sector, the focus has centered on four areas: (1) the promotion and development of an integrated infrastructure; (2) the formulation and implementation of harmonized transport and communications rules and regulations on a subregional and regional basis; (3) minimization and facilitation of procedures to permit easier access to landlocked countries and other isolated regions and the faster movement of persons and goods; and (4) promotion of the development of basic communications and transport industries in Africa.[21]

If African countries can devote their considerable energies to all of these areas during what remains of the 1980s, then the groundwork will have been laid for the establishment of an African Economic Community in the 1990s. There is however the question of what special preparatory work needs to be undertaken on this between now and the end of the decade. Should a draft treaty establishing the continental community be prepared now? Is the time opportune?

It is true that the FAL does call for the preparation of such a draft. Indeed it requested that the draft be submitted for consideration to the assembly of heads of state and government in 1981--barely a year after the adoption of the LPA and FAL. In retrospect, and given the fact that no such draft was submitted in 1981 and none has been up till now, we were rather unrealistic in making this provision. Is it really necessary to rush into preparing such a draft treaty when it is abundantly clear that a large number of the prerequisites for ensuring that an African Economic Community, when established, will succeed immediately are not yet present? Treaty-making processes are, after all, not an end but a means. When they cease to be that, they become an exercise in futility.

CONCLUSION

There is no doubt that in spite of all the difficulties and all the constraints, there has been some remarkable progress in laying the foundation for meaningful economic cooperation in Africa. Although there has been no breakthrough yet, there is cause for hope, if not for optimism. The LPA and the FAL eloquently testify to Africa's determination to push ahead with intra-African economic and trade penetration. There is a growing realization that if the "willed future" being advocated by the ECA is ever to be realized, domestic policies must be augmented by appropriate subregional and regional measures. A radical and purposeful pursuit of intra-African cooperation is not only desirable but imperative.

The balkanization of Africa is one of the major constraints to the economic transformation of the continent. Since it now appears too late to change the political map of Africa, the only option available for redressing this hindrance is through effective cooperation. This in turn, difficult as it may be, will require the full and faithful implementation of the LPA and FAL. The progress so far made should be a spur to the further pursuit of this goal. However, to be able to achieve economic cooperation two additional conditions are necessary. First, there must be peace and good neighborly relations among African countries as political tension among countries has often had disruptive effects on economic trade and technical cooperation. There can be no real breakthrough in a situation where political tension exists. Political tension only results in serious economic and social distortion. Thus, it is imperative that African countries should strengthen their solidarity in all fields and stress the factors that unite rather than those that divide them.

Finally, the international community can play a role in facilitating intra-African cooperation not only by supporting regional and subregional projects and the various economic communities but also by encouraging Africa in this endeavor. If it is accepted that it is in the interests of the international community to do all in its power to assist in putting Africa on the path of growth, development, stability, and peace and if Africa cannot be so put unless regional cooperation is seen as part and parcel of national efforts, then the international community must be more positive towards Africa's endeavors to achieve a breakthrough in this area. For their part, African governments must ensure that their extra-African economic and trade relations do not compromise their desire to achieve meaningful intra-African economic penetration.

NOTES

1. Adebayo Adedeji, Africa, the Crisis of Development and the Challenge of a New Economic Order (Addis Ababa: ECA, 1977), p. 16.
2. Document No. E/CN.14/ECO/90/Rev.3 of 25 June 1976.
3. Adebayo Adedeji, "The Monrovia Strategy and the Lagos Plan of Action: Five Years After" (chapter 1 in this volume), p. 10.
4. ECOSOC, Long-Term Trends in the Economic Development of the regions of the world. Report by the Secretary-General Annex III -- Preliminary Assessment of long-term development trends and prospects in developing Africa prepared by ECA (Doc.No.E/5937/Add.3 of 29 March 1977).
5. Ibid., pp. 23-24, para. 88.
6. ECA, Proposals for Strengthening Economic Integration in West Africa (Addis Ababa: ECA, n.d.), pp. 22-3.
7. Ibid., p. 23.
8. ECOSOC, Long-Term Trends, p. 3.
9. Revised Framework, p. 17.
10. "Monrovia Declaration of Commitment of the Heads of State and Government of the Organisation for African Unity on Guidelines and Measures for National and Collective Self-reliance in Social and Economic Development for the Establishment of a New International Economic Order" Resolution AHG/ST.3 (XVI) Rev. 1.
11. OAU, Lagos Plan of Action for the Economic Development of Africa 1980-2000 (Geneva: International Institute for Labor Studies, 1981), p. 2.
12. Ibid., p. 8.
13. ECA Conference of Ministers Resolution 477 (XVIII) of 30 April 1983.
14. ECA Conference of Ministers Resolution 519 (XIX) of 29 May 1984.
15. Aaron Segal, "Africa Newly Divided," Journal of Modern African Studies 2(1) (1964): 74.
16. Ibid., p. 77.
17. Ibid., p. 90.
18. See for example, Joanna Moss and John Ravenhill, "Trade Developments during the First Lomé Convention, World Development 10 (10) (1982) and Nantang Jua, "Towards Renegotiating the Lomé Regime: Some (non) Policy Options Considered," African Development 8 (4) (1983), passim.
19. Moss and Ravenhill, "Trade Development during the First Lomé Convention," pp. 853-4.
20. "Accelerated Development in Sub-Saharan Africa: an assessment by the OAU, ECA and ADB secretariats" (ECA Edited Version), Africa Development (3) (1982), p. 124.
21. ECA, ECA and Africa's Development 1983-2008: A Preliminary Perspective Study (Addis Ababa: ECA, 1983), pp. 41-42.

S. K. B. Asante

5 Development and Regional Integration Since 1980

Economic co-operation among African states is a *sine qua non* for the achievement of national socio-economic goals, and not an "extra" to be given thought to after the process of development is well advanced. African states have also to learn very soon how to insulate economic cooperation institutions and arrangements from the vagaries of political differences.

Adebayo Adedeji, Africa: The Crisis of Development and the Challenge of the New International Economic Order [1]

Economic co-operation and integration, like the political will or the will to develop, is a qualitative attribute of immense significance which cuts across all the development scenarios under discussion. It can, therefore, be said that its absence or ineffectiveness is an inherent part of the development problem that Africa faces today.

ECA, *ECA and Africa's Development, 1983-2008*[2]

> We resolved to adopt a far-reaching regional approach based primarily on collective self-reliance....This is not to say that the continent should totally cut itself off from outside contributions. However, these outside contributions should only supplement our own effort: they should not be the mainstay of our development.
>
> OAU, Lagos Plan of Action for the Economic Development of Africa, 1980-2000[3]

The promotion of regional economic integration among developing countries is now a well-accepted part of international development policy. Many issues in international economic relations are currently subordinated to the quest for regional economic associations among more or less geographically contiguous areas. Linking the concept of regionalism with development has become so important that some scholars like John Sloan would prefer to substitute the term "developmental regionalism"[4] for that of regional economic integration, because the latter, they contend, is imprecise, static, and irrelevant to the development issue. In most recent economic literature, the terms "integration" or "common market" have tended to become nearly synonymous with "rapid economic growth," "acceleration of economic development," or "big push." Regardless of the terminology used, there can be no doubt that the process of regional integration is now inextricably linked to that of economic development.

Significantly, the concept of development is now closely associated with the process of regional integration because the integration process has been redefined; it is no longer regarded as merely a supportive measure. Regional integration efforts are no longer inspired mainly by considerations of pure efficiency, as exemplified by the East African Common Services Organization; neither are they structured to be only adaptations of the doctrine of import-substitution as part of a policy for "industrialization by invitation" on a regional scale, as in the case of the Latin American Free Trade Association.[5] Regional integration is now designed primarily as a tool to combat and reduce external economic dependence, as in the case of the Andean Common Market, and it is being vigorously advocated as a grand strategy for solving the problem of underdevelopment. It is in this sense that Edward Milenky has referred to regional integration as "developmental nationalism," that is, a "strategy and rallying point for the rejection of all forms of external dependence on the advanced countries."[6]

Regionalism of this kind, therefore, follows the approach to development that emphasizes collective self-reliance and incorporation into the international economic system. Such regional integration is now an essential component of "alternative" strategies for the elimination of external dependence and exploitation that have been responsible for the distortion of the development process throughout much of Africa and the rest of the Third World. Hence, Johan Galtung refers to the concept of collective self-reliance as an effort to "undo five centuries of dependency on the West, to turn the tide started when Columbus travelled west and Vasco da Gama east...and to work for a world where each part is a center."[7] In the last decade, UN development agencies have put more emphasis on collective self-reliance as a means of economic independence for developing countries. In the case of Africa, this strategy has been examined in various studies conducted by ECA.

Regionalism in Africa has been given a new lease on life with the adoption of the Lagos Plan of Action (LPA), a historic document that constitutes the first comprehensive continentwide formulation and articulation of preferred long-term development objectives. The Lagos Plan is a response to the elusiveness of postcolonial development in Africa, to the shattering of "the African dream," and to the dismal development prospects for Africa in the 1980s. Its main theme is Africa's reduction of dependence on external exchange and strategy. By adopting the Lagos Plan and the Final Act of Lagos, African leaders have demonstrated, inter alia, their desire for a far-reaching, indigenously determined regional strategy, primarily based on collective self-reliance. With the advent of the LPA, Africa therefore has effectively shifted its focus away from the New International Economic Order (NIEO) demands for higher prices and guaranteed markets for developing countries' exports and called for the retention, processing, and use of more of these raw materials at home. Regionalism, which is discussed in virtually every chapter of the plan, constitutes an integral condition for its implementation. Without regional integration, comment Robert Browne and Robert Cummings, the LPA "collapses as a concept" and a strategy.[8]

To be sure, even before the adoption of the Lagos Plan, the Executive-Secretary of the ECA, Dr. Adebayo Adedeji, who had done more than any one person to draw attention to Africa's "continental crisis," had advocated the restructuring of national and regional economies as an alternative strategy for reversing the deterioration in Africa's economic performance:

> It will now have become clear that, if we are to reverse the past and present trends of low development and accelerate the rates of socio-economic advancement, we will need to install... a new economic order.
>
> It is therefore imperative that African states should reformulate their policies and economic strategies and instruments with a view to promoting national and collective self-reliance.[9]

What is new is that, for the first time, collective self-reliance, self-sustaining development, and economic integration have been formulated by the supreme organs of both the ECA and OAU as strategies designed to create new economic structures and to change fundamentally the existing pattern of economic relationships.

It is within this framework of regionalism, related to the strategy of collective self-reliance, that I intend to review the progress and prospects of African regional integration since the adoption of the Lagos Plan in 1980 (see also chapter 4). In considering Africa's incorporation into the world system, such a review addresses the problem that has given rise to two contending approaches to the evaluation of regionalism in Africa.[10] The first is the orthodox approach, which is vigorously espoused in the writings of scholars like I. William Zartman.[11] Based on the premise of decolonization and dealing primarily with continental and national institutions, the orthodox perspective "assumes that political decolonization has already been won" and that "regional integration and autonomy are already possible if functional and federal strategies are successful." Disregarding the importance and impact of external linkages and interests in African economies, the orthodox approach assumes that countries in Africa "have sufficient sovereignty to determine their own individual and collective foreign policies."[12]

By contrast, the radical approach, which is the approach I shall take, is based on the premise of external dependence. This approach lays special emphasis on the effects of historical processes, international dependency, and class analysis. It sees Africa's historical incorporation into the world system as constituting a fundamental constraint on the viability of regionalism on the continent.[13] From the radical perspective, there exists a "fundamental incompatibility between regionalism and the world system." Regional integration is advocated as an "alternative to global incorporation."[14] The effects of dependency are evident given that one cannot isolate the process of change in any given African country from that occurring in the world economy as a whole. This is especially true in view of external economic and social penetration, which has characterized the recent history of most African countries. Hence the contention of Philippe Schmitter that no matter what regional negotiations may intend to accomplish, it should "prove difficult to isolate regional deliberations from their context of global economic and political dependence."[15] The radical perspective also brings into focus the interrelationships of external and internal factors that affect regional integration, which enables us to understand the extent to which the dynamics of the international politico-economic system affect the viability of African regional integration. Significantly, the radical rather than the orthodox perspective is reflected in recent publications of the ECA.[16] Repudiating the orthodox approach, Dr. Adedeji recently stressed that:

> We challenged the orthodox view which indeed many well-meaning donor countries and highly reputable international institutions still hold dear....
>
> We have also put to question the external orientation of the African economy and its virtually total external dependence....Instead we have argued with all the forces at our command that self-reliance, either national or collective, cannot be achieved while African governments run externally-oriented, excessively-open and externally-dependent economies.[17]

It is from this radical approach, reinforced by the *dependencia* perspective of the *LPA*, that this chapter attempts to investigate the extent to which regional integration in Africa is being implemented in line with the goals and objectives of the *Lagos Plan*. Thus the problems, potential, and prospects of recently created regional schemes merit special attention.

THE NEW REGIONAL SCHEMES

By 1980--when the *LPA* was adopted--almost all the economic cooperation schemes optimistically launched in the 1960s--the halcyon years of African integration--had become largely moribund. The fundamental causes of their decline, which included regional inequalities and intractable problems of politicization leading to institutional tensions and decay, have already received adequate attention elsewhere.[18] Suffice it to say that one of the organizations that barely survived the disintegration and decay of the 1960s is the Customs and Economic Union of Central Africa (UDEAC).

Two other organizations established in 1973 in West Africa remain operational: the Mano River Union (MRU) and the West African Economic Community (CEAO).

Since the mid-1970s, however, the world recession and its severe impact on Africa's economic performance have strengthened interest in the establishment of new regional groups and the geographical extension of existing ones. Hence, the past several years have witnessed the reemergence of a rash of regional integration schemes in Africa, as more or less explicit challenges to the external domination of the continent inherited from the colonial era. Among the most ambitious and dynamic is the Economic Community of West African States (ECOWAS), which brings together 16 countries covering an area of six million square kilometers and extending from Mauritania in the northwest to Nigeria in the southeast. The area has a total population of about 150 million. Established in Lagos in May 1975, ECOWAS is the first serious attempt at economic cooperation and integration in the West African subregion cutting across divisions of language, history, and existing affiliations and institutions (see chapter 4).

Besides ECOWAS, the two major organizational offspring of the Lagos Plan and the Final Act are in Southern Africa. The first group is the Southern African Development Coordination Conference (SADDC), which was formally inaugurated in April 1980 by the signing of the Lusaka Declaration on Economic Liberation by the five Front Line States (FLS)--Angola, Botswana, Mozambique, Tanzania, and Zambia--joined by Lesotho, Malawi, Swaziland and Zimbabwe. Originally conceived as the economic counterpart to the FLS, which, since 1974, have been most closely involved in assisting and, to some extent, directing--militarily, politically, and diplomatically--the liberation struggle in Rhodesia, Namibia, and South Africa, the nine SADCC countries cover an area of five million square kilometers, with a total population of some 60 million. The second regional group to be initiated is the Preferential Trade Area for Eastern and Southern Africa (PTA), which was ratified in Lusaka in December 1981 by nine out of the potential 18 states. PTA was finally launched in Harare in July 1984. Despite its name, the PTA does not confine itself to trade alone; the treaty is much more than an elaborate definition of trading relationships. It addresses itself to virtually every sector relating to the promotion of regional economic integration.[19] Like ECOWAS, the PTA is the brainchild of Adebayo Adedeji. But, whereas the PTA is an example of painstaking development, SADCC, like ECOWAS, is much more an act of deliberate political will, carrying the personal imprimatur of its members' presidents and prime ministers. Just as the six French-speaking CEAO members are signatories to the ECOWAS Treaty, so all SADCC members are potential members of PTA. And like ECOWAS and CEAO, although the purposes and programs of SADCC and PTA are substantially similar and steadily converging, differences are apparent in the origins of the two organizations, their institutional structures, financial patrons, ideologies, and strategies.

Another manifestation of the concern with regional cooperation in Africa was the creation in December 1981 of the Senegambian Confederation, which propels Gambia and Senegal towards an economic and monetary union. This confederation is the culmination of many years of efforts to create closer economic cooperation between these two countries. The latest initiative made in response to the goals of the Lagos Plan and the

Act is the treaty signed in Libreville, Gabon, in October 1983 to establish the Economic Community of Central African States (ECCAS), comprising the present members of UDEAC and those of the Economic Community of the Great Lakes. This community is intended to be the Central African equivalent of the ECOWAS.

The basic objectives of these new regional integration schemes is substantially the same: apart from deriving the more orthodox benefits such as expanded trade and investment, they intend to reduce dependence and help improve the bargaining position of Africa. ECOWAS, for example, has as its central objective the promotion of cooperation and development in virtually all fields of economic activity for the purpose of "reducing gradually the Community's economic dependence on the outside world." The lessening of a high degree of external dependence is seen as a precondition for achieving basic structural development goals. Similarly, SADCC came about as the result of a common desire among its nine members to gradually reduce and eventually eliminate economic dependence upon South Africa. The emphasis in SADCC on reducing dependence is focused especially, but not exclusively, on Pretoria. As President Machel of Mozambique stressed in his opening address at SADCC 2 in Maputo in 1980: "The effects of colonial domination are still present in our countries...the mentality of dependence, the fatalist spirit."[20] On the other hand, PTA, with its broader membership, makes no direct attempt to address the issue of reducing dependence on South Africa. Instead it advocates a positive approach to the problem, contending that, to the extent that it succeeds in promoting intraregional trade and development, dependence on South Africa will decrease. Viewed within the context of the elusiveness of any NIEO, all these regional initiatives must also be regarded as indicative of the desire of the poor nations of Africa to eliminate, or at least reduce, the inequalities inherent in the present international economic system.

But what have the new regional schemes achieved so far, in only a few years of existence, particularly in the area of dependency reduction? Because of the recent emphasis on the concept of collective self-reliance among developing countries, it is too often assumed that any form of economic integration or cooperation will have a positive impact on development. Yet schemes such as ECOWAS, PTA, SADCC, or UDEAC will not automatically lead to accelerated development. Indeed, without a well-considered and intensive effort to restructure the economy and without adequate planning, these regional schemes could lead to the perpetuation of neocolonialism, underdevelopment, and inequality and to increased rather than decreased external dependence. For, as Osvaldo Sunkel rightly remarked in the case of Latin America, "integration, in fact, can be either a basic instrument of national realization in Latin America, or it can be the instrument of accelerated dependence (sucursalizacion) of the region."[21] In the case of Africa, Shaw and Grieve have similarly warned that regional integration "is not always an escape from Africa's inheritance of subordination," and that it may not "advance disintegration from the global economy." It may even lead to "regional inequalities and continued dependence," particularly when "some of its major advocates are foreign actors or collaborationist groups."[22]

Viewed from the radical perspective, to what extent are the present regional schemes in Africa effectively equipped to confront the disturbing problems posed by dependency and the neocolonial "mesh"? And since, as noted above, regional self-reliance is incompatible with global and trans-

Figure 5.1 Regional Organizations in Africa

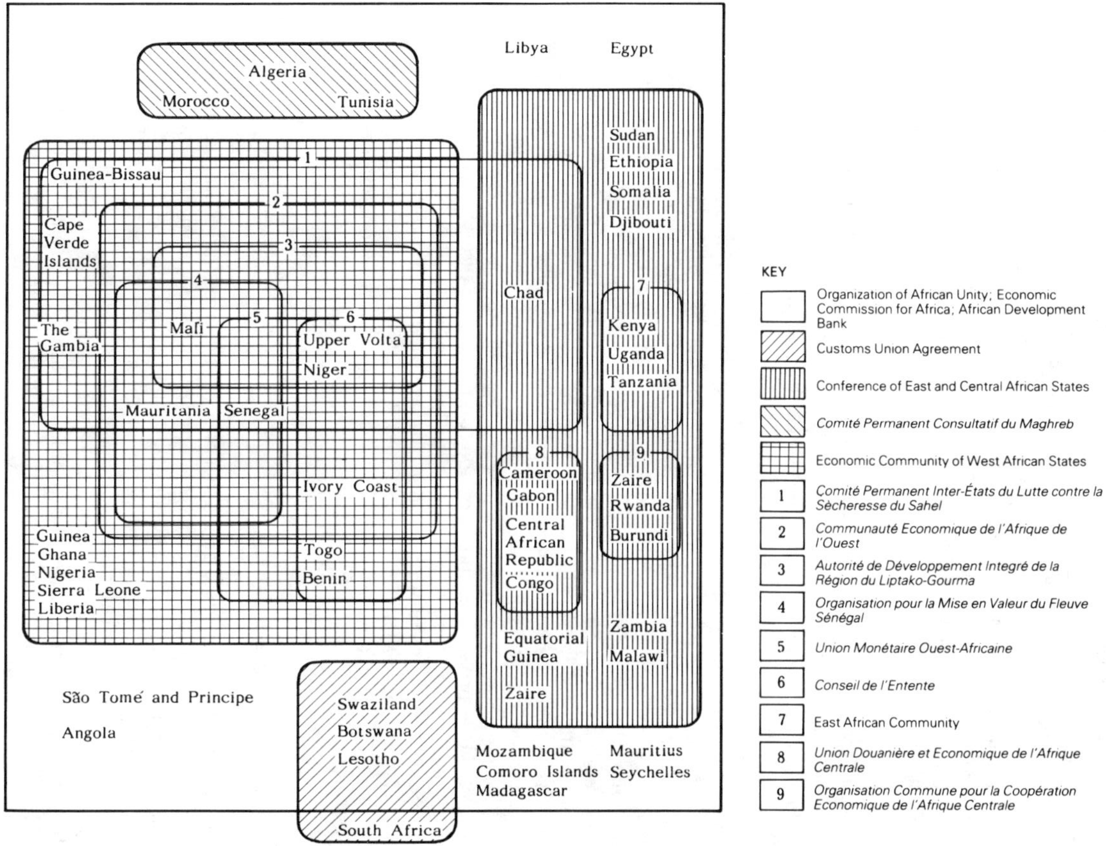

Source: Oliver, Roland, and Michael Crowder, The Cambridge Encyclopedia of Africa (Cambridge: Cambridge University Press, 1981), p. 359.

national integration, just how far have the new regional initiatives attempted to restructure both national and regional political economies as the prerequisite for integration and development? Or to what extent have they, for example, initiated efforts towards intraregional trade or horizontal exchange in order to overcome the inherited vertical integration with former metropols and thereby achieve greater self-reliance at both national and collective levels? Put differently, how far have they effectively challenged the established pattern of trade and division of labor? Finally, are African regional groupings in a position to create conditions that will make self-sustained, autonomous development possible? In the African setting, such development can only come about through the transformation of productive structures. Can ECOWAS, PTA, or SADCC really contribute to this type of change?

REGIONALISM, COLLECTIVE SELF-RELIANCE, AND DEVELOPMENT

The goal of reducing dependence lies behind the concept of collective self-reliance espoused in the LPA. Given the pervasiveness of neocolonial structures in Africa and the nature of external and internal linkages between the elites of the continent and their international and domestic constituencies, it is easy to envisage the kind of problems likely to confront African regional groupings in the area of dependency reduction. There is, for example, the problem of initiating effective measures to combat attempts by extraregional powers to take advantage of the newly created regional opportunities and thus derive more benefit from integration than would the intraregional participants. There is also the problem of extricating the member countries of ECOWAS, SADCC, or PTA from existing dependency relationships and of using national and regional institutions to bring about greater local control over resources. Given the complexity of these problems, the question that arises is, How adequate are the provisions of current regional treaties to confront the issues posed by dependency? What institutions under the treaties have been specifically charged with what Schmitter has termed "policy externalization"?[23] And what efforts have been made to give substance to the concept of collective self-reliance?

The Issue of Disengagement

Evidence suggests that to date none of the regional schemes has adequate provisions for attacking the all-embracing issue of dependency reduction; nor have efforts made towards this objective had any significant impact. Although ECOWAS, for example, promotes collective self-reliance in West Africa, in several crucial areas it does not go as far as might be desirable. A case in point is the ECOWAS protocol on the rules of origin, which, although it anticipates the problems posed by external linkages, does not effectively confront the issues of foreign control, ownership, and participation. The ownership level requirements approved at the May 1983 ECOWAS meeting still fall short of expectation. These requirements alone do not necessarily ensure effective local control, especially when greater reliance is to be placed on foreign technology and know-how. Majority equity ownership, as a recent ECA report has concluded, "will neither reduce the technological dependence of the host country nor ensure a genuine transfer and diffusion of the imported technology."[24] The main problem is how to exercise or acquire effective control over the activities of extra-regional actors and their local affiliates. For unless the control that foreign actors exercise over the ECOWAS market is carefully circumscribed and progressively minimized, they may remain a dominant force within the community.

Of significance, also, is the fact that, although Article 32 of the ECOWAS Treaty specifically calls upon the community's Council of Ministers to take effective steps towards gradual dependency reduction, there is no institution or machinery in ECOWAS that is empowered to enter into negotiations with external actors on behalf of the community.[25] Neither does the ECOWAS Treaty include any provisions for a common regime on foreign investment and divestment; nor has any institution been established to control the importation of technology, as has been done in the Andean Common Market. Therefore, the redefinition of the ECOWAS economic relationship with the outside world, which is crucial for reduction of dependence, is largely ignored. Yet, for economic integration to be meaningful and lead to collective self-reliance, a very advanced form of integration, such as control of new technology transfer and industrial location, is required. In addition, ECOWAS can only play a meaningful role in the economies of integrating countries if these countries change their production and ownership structures. Without such measures, the degree of success of West African economic integration will be sharply limited. Thus, although ECOWAS can undoubtedly contribute to the achievement of self-reliance in West Africa, it will not, by itself, lead to such collective self-reliance.[26] I thus agree with Langdom and Mytelka that, in order to transform integration into an instrument for autonomous development, "regional policies that regulate external linkages in the interest of domestic development must be enacted."[27]

While neither UDEAC nor CEAO has formulated a policy regarding disengagement, SADCC and PTA have each attempted to initiate policies in this direction. Of these two southern African organizations, the latter would seem to have more potential for combating dependence on both South Africa and the West. PTA is generally perceived as a powerful vehicle for radically restructuring the economies of eastern and southern African states to achieve collective self-reliance and self-generating growth. Toward this end, it has established a technical committee of experts to advise on "ensuring economic restructuring of the BLS (Botswana, Lesotho, and Swaziland) states and reduction of their dependence on South Africa."[28]

On the other hand, although the SADCC countries have identified transport and communications as the first sector targeted for a reduction of dependence on South Africa and have consequently established the Southern African Transport and Communications Commission (SATCC) for this purpose, this strategy is fraught with the danger of creating new dependencies. First, SADCC's concentration on the rehabilitation of transport systems inherited from colonialism may perpetuate and reinforce neo-colonial patterns of trade and production and hinder intra-SADCC trade. Specifically, most of the 112 projects (as of 1983) on SATCC's list involve rehabilitation of already existing traffic routes designed principally by the colonial powers "to facilitate exportation of primary commodities...from the mining and agricultural centers of the interior to the ports for shipment to the metropoles."[29] Whether SADCC will, at some future stage, succeed in redirecting the transportation network to promote intraregional interaction and collective self-reliance remains to be seen.

Second, the reduction of dependence on South Africa may be replaced with new forms of dependence, probably on the West. For despite the Lusaka Declaration that SADCC must aim at reducing economic dependence "on any single external state or group of states," SADCC's efforts have almost exclusively been directed towards the objective of reducing dependence on South Africa. Consequently, dependency relations with extraregional powers have been a secondary concern so far. Thus, anxious as SADCC members are to escape from the South African "frying pan," they run the risk of landing in the "fire" of Western economies.

And third, even though SADCC is dedicated to self-reliance, much of its efforts have gone into cultivating beneficial relations with sympathetic international organizations, resulting in very heavy dependence on external financial support--75 percent to 80 percent in some estimates.[30] This tendency is not in line with the LPA. It also threatens SADCC's ability to set priorities for its member states. For SADCC has had to recognize that its priorities are not necessarily the same as those of the parties from whom it seeks assistance. As a result, SADCC has, in the past, advanced projects on the basis of their appeal to prospective donors, rather than because they were considered most beneficial for its region. Donors are free to choose items from SADCC's "shopping list" on the basis of their own preferences.

On the whole, then, there is considerable uncertainty concerning the degree to which SADCC members are committed to the goal of disengagement from South Africa. It is not even certain whether South Africa's immediate neighbors are anxious to reduce their imports from the south. Douglas Anglin has recently observed that Botswana and Swaziland "are even planning new rail links with South Africa."[31]

Intraregional Trade Expansion

Closely related to the issue of disengagement is commitment to the promotion of intraregional trade expansion with the consequent reductions in inherited North-South links. For, as Adedeji points out:

> The North-bound vertical orientation of the African economy has also made effective intra-African economic cooperation difficult. Many African countries are still conditioned by a strong attachment to preindependence colonial economic ties, whatever the rhetoric giving the contrary impression may be. This attachment to preindependence ties even twenty years after independence has inevitably militated against the development of policies and instruments essential for bringing about effective intra-African economic cooperation on regional and subregional levels.[32]

Thus promotion of intra-African trade, as opposed to continuous dependence on trade with outside economic blocs, is one of the major challenges to African regional integration schemes.[33]

Yet, whereas ECOWAS and PTA are attempting to respond to this challenge, SADCC has mainly concentrated on production rather than exchange, despite the sharp contrast between intraregional SADCC trade flow and trade flow with South Africa and individual Southern African states.[34] Trade expansion, as such, has been seen as a means to validate production rather than as an end in itself. As a result, there has been no trade sector priority and no meeting held primarily to discuss trade and payments questions.

By contrast, PTA, like ECOWAS, aims at reducing customs tariffs and other trade barriers between countries as diverse as Marxist Ethiopia in the north and pro-Western Lesotho, landlocked within South Africa. PTA members have also undertaken to eliminate gradually customs duties they charge each other for imports of selected commodities produced within the PTA region; tariff and other trade barriers are to be eliminated on 132 commodities.[35]

But while PTA has not yet advanced much beyond ratification of its treaty, ECOWAS, CEAO, and UDEAC have each adopted a trade liberalization scheme aimed at promoting intraregional expansion.[36] However, despite the LPA's emphasis on intraregional expansion which, to quote the Lagos Plan, is "meant to constitute the mainstay for the present strategy"[37] of collective self-reliance, none of these schemes has made substantial progress in this sector of the economy.[38] Preindependence North-South economic ties have been the major cause of this unhappy situation. For example, a recent ECA report on UDEAC has shown, inter alia, how intraregional trade flows respond not so much to conditions in the UDEAC countries as to the global and regional strategies adopted by the transnational firms that benefit from intraregional trade.[39] Similarly, Wilfred Indongko in a recent study has demonstrated how UDEAC is more concerned with its links with Europe, particularly France, than with partner states.[40] Politico-economic commercial arrangements, such as the three Lomé agreements, reinforce these links and effectively tie Africa to Europe, thereby further discouraging intra-African relationships. EurAfricanism, exemplified by the Lomé "regime," not only symbolizes the "continuity of an unequal division of labor between the two sets of parties," as Shaw has shown;[41] it is also essentially incompatible with the self-reliance and self-sustainment objectives of the LPA.

Food and Agriculture

Given Africa's colonial heritage and recent reinforcement of African incorporation into the world system, it is not surprising that regionalism in Africa to date has not made much progress in responding adequately to the number one LPA priority: self-sufficiency in food production and supply. For instance, the UDEAC states, which are collectively harnessed to the French system, have made agricultural development a secondary consideration.[42] And, although both ECOWAS and SADCC have adopted comprehensive agricultural programs as a means of (1) fighting the serious food problem of their respective regions and, especially, (2) reducing the high degree of external dependence on food imports,[43] they have not yet transformed LPA concepts regarding the food and agriculture sector from political slogans into policy frameworks. ECOWAS member states are still without an explicit food policy. By contrast, SADCC would seem to have made some substantial progress towards the implementation of projects for "enhancing the productivity of the land on a permanent basis, and towards national and regional food policies."[44] High priority has been given to food security, and nine projects, including an early warning system for regional food security, have been listed for implementation.

Thus far, I have attempted to focus attention on the top priorities of current regional schemes in Africa. Obviously, a comprehensive evaluation of these schemes at this time would be premature, as most are so new. Moreover, integration, particularly in the developing world, is a process likely to take a long time, with its effects on development taking even longer. It has become evident, however, that regional integration has not yet made any appreciable impact on the objective of dependency reduction in response to the LPA's central philosophy of collective self-reliance. Achievement of collective self-reliance and self-sustaining development will require substantial changes in external and internal relationships. Fundamental questions regarding Africa's inheritance of incorporation within the world system and the transnational linkages of its bourgeoisie with external classes and corporations must be confronted. These issues are a major impediment to progress. Since, in the final analysis, there is no realistic alternative to economic integration for most African countries, let us focus attention on the current problems, possibilities, and prospects.

PROBLEMS OF INCORPORATION

A crucial policy issue that confronts regional groupings in Africa is the issue of equity in the distribution of benefits. Most of these schemes are characterized by substantial economic disparities among members. To compensate less industrially developed partners, ECOWAS and PTA, in particular, have adopted measures designed to produce an equitable interstate distribution of the benefits of integration. But, in view of the dominant presence of external actors in integrative systems, such compensatory mechanisms have proven in the past to be ineffective, resulting in heightened conflicts over cost-benefit issues within integrative systems. The conflicts within and ultimate collapse of the East African Community (EAC), the West African Customs Union (UDAO), and the Customs Union of West African States (UDEAO) over cost-benefit issues bear out this point. By making use of the transnational linkages established between foreign capital and the local political and economic elite, external actors tend to weaken the effectiveness of mechanisms designed to correct the inequitable distribution of integration costs and benefits. Thus the contemporary crisis of regional integration in Africa, as Langdon and Mytelka have emphasized,

> is not a purely nationalist affair in which states are pitted against each other in conflicts over the interstate distribution of the gains from integration. Rather, this interstate conflict is a reflection of more fundamental problems that are associated with the distribution of gains between national and international capital as the MNC seeks to structure not only national but also regional markets around its own needs and interests.[45]

The analyses by Langdon and Mytelka of UDEAC[46] and by Peter Robson of CEAO[47] provide excellent case studies of the way in which transnational corporations (TNC) and other external interests derive benefits from African regional integration to the disadvantage of partner states.[48] There is thus a major problem in Africa today, because economic integration, which is the backbone of collective self-reliance, cannot be effectively implemented as an instrument for regional development so long as the participating countries have no effective control over resources flowing into joint projects or sovereignty over the key sectors of their economies.

Another significant aspect of this incorporation is the symbiotic relationship that has been established between the African ruling classes and external actors. The former, as "junior partners" of the external system, as Shaw and Grieve have argued, are "able to rule only through collaboration with external interests; to disengage meant isolation, intimidation, and obscurity, a situation that most first-generation national leaders strenuously sought to avoid."[49] Given the nature of the postcolonial state, collaborationist groups in Africa are likely to resist any efforts by the current regional groupings towards higher levels of integration that might involve reduction of dependence.

This largely explains the inability of the SADCC countries to disengage from South Africa, despite rhetoric to the contrary. Because of the existence of class alliances between member governments of SADCC and Pretoria, recent observers have expressed serious doubts about whether "there is either the wish or the will to accept the economic sacrifices that may initially be necessary" in the process of disengagement.[50] No one would argue that certain class elements in respective SADCC countries "have vested interests in maintaining close links" with South Africa. The actions of such elements, as Torstensen has observed, vary "from overt sabotage" and "overt active opposition," to passive disobedience or indifference by "retarding implementation of decisions."[51]

More worrisome, as we might expect, SADCC leaders themselves have on occasion made conflicting statements about disengagement from South Africa. Some leaders have insisted that SADCC is not an anti-South African initiative or even a reaction to Pretoria's own project for a Constellation of Southern African States; at SADCC's inauguration in April 1980, for example, Seretse Khama of Botswana assured South Africa that it was not the objective of the SADCC governments "to plot against anybody or any country." Samora Machel of Mozambique was even more explicit: "We are not declaring a war against South Africa."[52] Yet on another occasion, Kaunda of Zambia, among others, linked PTA and SADCC to "our effort to contain and finally defeat the theory of a Constellation of Southern African States."[53] But in spite of this, Zimbabwe has retained an important trade agreement with South Africa, which gives its manufactures privileged access to the large South African market. And there are those who still hold that it is in Zimbabwe's best interest to increase trade with South Africa.[54]

Given interests held in common by Africa's ruling classes and extra-regional actors, I must conclude that, in the short term, the prospects for a significant restructuring of Africa's economy involving substantial disengagement remain limited. But does it follow, then, that African countries must resign themselves to dependence and limited development? Are there no other measures that can be adopted to reduce somewhat their vulnerability to outside forces?

POSSIBILITIES AND POLICY OPTIONS

Since autarky or even very greatly diminished reliance on economic relationships with the rest of the world--trade, borrowing of capital, skills, and technology, etc.--is currently out of the question for small, poor African states, the potential for overcoming dependence lies in their opting to be part of the system, while simultaneously seeking ways to exercise greater control over the industrialized world. I thus accept the premise of Gerald Helleiner that "'turning inward' or 'reducing dependence' need not mean diminishing external relationships so much as consciously employing them as one of several instruments for the pursuit of a truly independent strategy."[55]

In this regard, mobilization of external assistance for implementation of regional projects--and, by extension, implementation of the LPA and the Final Act--can be viewed as means to an "inner-directed" development effort. As indicated above, the Lagos Plan recognizes the important contribution that external assistance can make towards Africa's socio-economic development. However, both the plan and the ECA stress the importance of the use of external resources only as a supplement to domestic resources for financing development "in the spirit of national and collective self-reliance."[56] And, moreover, external assistance should not be beyond the control of the African beneficiaries--as is the case in SADCC--as it can be effective only if it is based on priorities set by recipients.

Briefly stated, external assistance can no doubt significantly affect the current integration process in Africa by increasing total resources available to integrative systems, thereby lowering the costs of integration and making possible a more equitable distribution of benefits. It can also be used to assist in underwriting regional clearinghouses, thus facilitating trade expansion within the integrative system. It should, however, be emphasized that, in the long run, external aid can only be of marginal assistance to the regional effort, even when it is being used by members collectively to resolve problems of distribution and development. As Webster Mutharika once stressed, "aid should never be taken as...a substitute for domestic resources."[57]

External assistance therefore is a mixed blessing for regional integration schemes, as the experiences of the defunct EAC[58] and UDEAC[59] have demonstrated. In both organizations, the capacity of donors to affect the integration process in both ways deemed desirable for development remained very much circumscribed. Rather, external resources tended to reinforce dependence, exacerbate problems of nationalism, and maintain economic disparities.[60]

For external assistance to play a positive role in the integration process in Africa, it is imperative that recipient regional schemes coordinate their aid policies. Drawing on the experience of the UDEAC, Mytelka has suggested that, for foreign aid to be beneficial to regional integration, it should be multilaterally coordinated by recipients in order to "enhance the learning of integrative behavior through joint negotiations with aid donors; reduce the political leverage of donor states and international institutions; eliminate the drive towards national competition in seeking aid; and ensure the prior coordination of policies thus avoiding duplication of projects."[61] Multilateral aid, especially from the UN and its specialized agencies, is almost always potentially beneficial.[62] Nevertheless, it is necessary for regional integration schemes in Africa to diversify their financial base.

Indeed, when support for integration comes from a mix of southern and northern countries and agencies, it can only benefit the integration process.

Closely related to the coordination of aid is the need for current regional integration schemes to diversify their external economic relations--trading partners and sources of technology and capital--to include not only Western Europe, the United States, Canada, Australia, or Japan, but also the industrialized countries of the socialist community, such as members of the Council for Mutual Economic Assistance (CMEA). And to achieve rapid industrialization, each regional grouping should seek to establish, on the strength of its regional policies, collaboration with particular donor countries to achieve specific objectives. For example, through CARICOM and the Caribbean Common Market, the countries of the Caribbean have negotiated long-term industrialization arrangements with Canada, the United States, and other industrialized countries. A case in point is the Trade and Economic Cooperation Agreement between Canada and the CARICOM members signed in 1979.[63] This kind of arrangement makes it possible for industrialized countries to lend their support through special financing, incentives to private investment, transfer of technology, and the protection of markets on both sides.

Diversification, not elimination, of dependencies in the initial stages of regional integration would seem almost a sine qua non for regionalism in Africa today. A more diversified structure of dependencies would improve the maneuverability of SADCC, ECOWAS, and PTA, which, in the long term, bodes well for a collective self-reliance and genuine reduction of dependence. Diversification also has the potential of strengthening the bargaining position of regional governments by enabling them to "play off" one developed economy against another. As Ali Mazrui stressed in his recent BBC Reith Lectures:

> There are occasions when freedom begins with the multiplication of one's masters. If one is owned and controlled by only one power, freedom is often particularly restrictive. But if an African society cultivates the skills to have more than one hegemonic power competing for it, this has possibilities for liberation. To be dependent on two giants, especially when the giants have rivalries between them, is sometimes an opportunity to play one against the other--and maximize one's own options.[64]

Another option available to African regional groups for transcending dependency is to develop preferential economic links, first among themselves, and second, with integration schemes in developing countries in Asia (e.g., ASEAN) and Latin America (e.g., the Andean Pact). This type of "horizontal integration" promotes economic cooperation among developing countries--"the new imperative of the 1980s," to quote Elvin Laszlo. Vast opportunities for cooperation exist in the fields of South-South economic and technical cooperation.[65] By taking full advantage of opportunities of mutual interdependence and complementarity of their economies, the countries of the South, concludes Adedeji, "will sooner or later put themselves in a position to seize the initiative and assume the leadership for bringing about the establishment of the new international economic order."[66]

By diversifying its relationships beyond exclusive reliance on Western Europe, Africa would blunt the impact of its continuing dependence on the industrialized nations. Such contacts would furthermore enhance Africa's "collective bargaining strength" and allow it to exercise its "countervailing power, thereby creating the compulsions" that would, for example, make Europe willy-nilly negotiate changes in Lomé.[67]

Then, too, African countries and leaders should be willing to introduce fundamental policy and institutional changes. These should include a redefinition of the development objectives at national and regional levels to recognize fully regional integration as an effective approach to the issue of dependency and underdevelopment. But a regional development strategy cannot be fully realized unless countries develop a common policy towards the problem of foreign investment and technology dependence through regional regulation and planning. This should be backed by an agreement to build a joint industrial research and development institute, which would also investigate foreign technology and arrange for its purchase, acquisition, or adaptation for joint development projects.[68]

To this may be added one other issue that has not yet been adequately addressed: the mobilization of public support. The current regional schemes were and are very much an act of will on the part of their political leadership. Yet, in order for them to achieve their fundamental aims, they will have to enlist active popular support. Specifically, the success of any regional strategy for collective self-reliance hinges on a common political will of national governments, which in turn requires the backing of its citizens. What appears to be lacking in African integration movements is group or popular support. Where are the interest groups or pressure groups needed for the mobilization of public opinion in favor of integration? As long as groups in West, Central, Eastern, and Southern Africa remain more or less on the sidelines, there will be little or no dynamic, propelling, and supporting integration. For, though economic integration may be a powerful means for the acceleration of development, in the final analysis "man is both the means and the end. The best study of the strategy of economic integration is man."[69]

Thus, the mobilization of public support should be regarded as crucial for implementing and maintaining African regional cooperation oriented towards collective self-reliance and endogenous, self-sustaining development. What is needed as the internal precondition for integration is the mobilization of human resources: entrepreneurs, parliamentary groups, religious groups, trade unions, journalists, chambers of commerce and industry, and professional associations. These social, political, economic, labor, and business groups can act "as a countervailing force" against uninformed integration obstructionists, in particular, and raise the consciousness of the nation in general as to the meaning and advantages of regional integration. The reality of regionalism in Africa in the future probably rests largely in the hands of these groups.

Finally, whatever strategy is adopted for transcending dependency, priority should be given to internal policy reforms or a "new domestic order," to which Adedeji and the ECA have already drawn attention in recent years.[70] For, to think that the way is open for spontaneous development of the economy once external difficulties are also necessary. This calls for self-discipline and sacrifice. We in Africa must accept the restraint and austerity required for establishing such new domestic orders if we ever hope to transform our relationship with the industrialized nations from one of permanent dependence to one of beneficial interdependence.

CONCLUSION

Viewed from the radical perspective, regional integration in Africa has not made any significant progress since 1980. The problem of dependency poses difficulties for African countries attempting a strategy of regional integration. Dependency serves as an obstacle to development; it not only limits the beneficial effects of integration, but it also foments disintegration in both national and regional economies. None of the regional schemes reviewed in this chapter is sufficiently equipped in terms of resources and power to overcome dependency and to bring into reality a process of autonomous, self-sustaining growth. Africa's incorporation within the world system and subsequent persistent internal-external linkages have been so pervasive and are so entrenched, impinging on so many aspects of African life, that the narrow focus of current regional groupings may be just an exercise in chasing shadows. The forces of incorporation can only be eliminated through a radical restructuring of existing modes of production and subsequent reorientations of political economies: the prerequisites for integration and development.

Since none of the existing regional integration schemes--ECOWAS, SADCC, PTA, UDEAC, or CEAO--is currently adequately equipped to bring about a profound change in both the internal political economy and the external state, the only alternative open to them is to pursue more immediate objectives. In this regard, these regional groups need to mobilize external assistance to supplement domestic resources, diversify economic and financial relations, increase bargaining power through South-South linkages, mobilize mass support to strengthen government initiatives in integrative systems, and demonstrate leadership by having the will to sacrifice self-serving interests and the stature to win popular support. Taken together, these efforts may reduce somewhat the continued vulnerability of these subregions to outside forces.

NOTES

1. Adebayo Adedeji, Africa: The Crisis of Development and the Challenge of a New International Economic Order, (Addis Ababa: ECA, 1977), p. 16.
2. ECA, ECA and Africa's Development, 1983-2008: A Preliminary Perspective Study (Addis Ababa: ECA, 1983), p. 15.
3. OAU, Lagos Plan of Action for the Economic Development of Africa, 1980-2000 (Geneva: International Institute for Labour Studies, 1981), paras. 1 & 14 iii.
4. John W. Sloan, "The Strategy of Developmental Regionalism: Benefits, Distribution, Obstacles and Capabilities," Journal of Common Market Studies 10 (2), (December 1971): 142.
5. W. Andrew Axline, Caribbean Integration: The Politics of Regionalism (London: Frances Pinter, 1979), p. xvi.

6. Edward S. Milenky, "Developmental Nationalism in Practice: The Problems and Progess of the Andean Group," Inter-American Economic Affairs 25 (3), (1971): 49.

7. Johan Galtung, "The Politics of Self-Reliance," in From Dependency to Development: strategies to overcome underdevelopment and inequality, ed. Heraldo Munoz (Boulder: Westview, 1981), p. 173.

8. Robert S. Browne and Robert J. Cummings, The Lagos Plan of Action vs. The Berg Report: Contemporary Issues in African Economic Development (Washington: Howard University African Studies Program, 1984), p. 37.

9. Adedeji, Africa: The Crisis of Development, pp. 16 and 18.

10. For a scholarly and interesting discussion of the two approaches see Timothy M. Shaw, "Africa," in Comparative Regional Systems: West and East Europe, North America, The Middle East, and Developing Countries, eds. Werner J. Feld and Gavin Boyd (New York: Pergamon, 1980), pp. 355-397.

11. See I. William Zartman, "Europe and Africa: Decolonization or Dependency," Foreign Affairs 54 (2), (1976): 325-43.

12. Shaw, "Africa," pp. 385-358.

13. For this view see, for example, Steven Langdon and Lynn K. Mytelka, "Africa in the Changing World Economy," in Africa in the 1980s: A Continent in Crisis, Colin Legum et al. (New York: McGraw-Hill for Council on Foreign Relations 1980s Project, 1979), pp. 177-179; and Kenneth Hall and Byron Blake, "Collective Self-Reliance: The Case of the Caribbean Community (CARICOM)," in From Dependency to Development, Munoz ed., pp. 197-206.

14. Shaw, "Africa," p. 363.

15. Philippe C. Schmitter, Autonomy or Dependence as Regional Integration Outcomes: Central America, Institute of International Studies, Research Series No. 17 (Berkeley: University of California, 1972), p. 8.

16. See for example, Biennial Report of the Executive Secretary of the United Nations Economic Commission for Africa 1977-1978 (E/CN.14/695), (Addis Ababa: UN, February 1979).

17. Adebayo Adedeji, address at the formal opening of the Annual Policy Meeting of the Cooperation for Development in Africa Conference, Washington, D.C., 26 October 1982.

18. See, for example, Timothy M. Shaw, "Regional Cooperation and Conflict in Africa," International Journal 3 (4), (Autumn 1975): 671-688.

19. Adebayo Adedeji, opening address at the inaugural Ministerial Council meeting of PTA, Lusaka, 22 June 1982, pp. 9-10.

20. A. Kgarebe, ed., SADCC 2--Maputo: The Proceedings of the Second Southern African Development Coordination Conference, held in Maputo, Peoples Republic of Mozambique on 17/18 November 1980 (London: SADCC Liaison Committee, 1981), p. 23.

21. Osvaldo Sunkel, "National Development Policy and External Dependence in Latin America," in Contemporary Inter-American Relations, ed., Yale Ferguson (Englewood Cliffs: Prentice-Hall, 1972), p. 478.

22. Timothy M. Shaw and Malcolm J. Grieve, "Dependence as an Approach to Understanding Continuing Inequalities in Africa," Journal of Developing Areas 13 (3), (April 1979): 243.

23. Schmitter refers to "policy externalization" as the process whereby integration units jointly elaborate a common position in negotiations with outsiders. See Schmitter, Autonomy or Dependence, p. 1.

24. See ECA Secretariat, _Transnational Corporations in Africa: Some Major Issues_ (Document E/ECA/UNCTC/21), (Addis Ababa: ECA, January 1983).

25. John P. Renniger, "The Future of Economic Cooperation Schemes in Africa, with Special Reference to ECOWAS," in _Alternative Futures for Africa_, ed. Timothy M. Shaw (Boulder: Westview Press, 1982), p. 170.

26. _Ibid_.

27. Langdon and Mytelka, "_Africa in the Changing World Economy_," p. 189.

28. _PTA Treaty_, annex XII.

29. Arne Tostensen, _Dependence and Collective Self-Reliance in Southern Africa: The Case of the Southern African Development Conference (SADCC)_, Research Report No. 62, The Scandinavian Institute of African Studies, (Uppsala, 1982), p. 132.

30. Reginald H. Green, "SADCC and South Africa in Confrontation," _Africa Contemporary Record_ 15 (1982-83): A81.

31. Douglas G. Anglin, "Economic Liberation and Regional Cooperation in Southern Africa: SADCC and PTA, "_International Organization_ 37 (4), (Autumn 1983): 701.

32. Adebayo Adedeji, "Development and Economic Growth in Africa to the Year 2000: alternative projections and policies," in _Alternative Futures for Africa_, ed. Shaw, p. 281.

33. Jonathan H. Chileshe, _The Challenge of Developing Intra-African Trade_ (Nairobi: East African Literature Bureau, 1977), p. 51.

34. Compared with overall intra-African trade the southern African region is slightly worse off. Intraregional SADCC trade has averaged 2 to 3 percent relative to total foreign trade at the level of overall trade flows. See Amon J. Nsekela, _Southern Africa: toward economic liberation_ (London: Rex Collings, 1981), p. 218.

35. For details see _South_ (September 1984), p. 86.

36. For details about ECOWAS trade liberalization scheme see ECOWAS Document, _Final Communique of ECOWAS Summit_ (ECW/HSG. VI/4/Rev. 1) (Conakry: ECOWAS: May 26-30, 1983).

37. OAU, _Lagos Plan_, para. 250.

38. For details about ECOWAS implementation of trade liberalization scheme, see S.K.B. Asante, "Seven Years of ECOWAS: trade problems and prospects," _West Africa_ (24 May 1982).

39. ECA, _Report of the ECA Mission on the Evaluation of UDEAC_ (Libreville, Gabon: ECA, 1981), p. 80.

40. Wilfred A. Ndongko, "Central Africa Regional Co-operation in the Context of the Lagos Plan of Action: the UDEAC," _Africa Development_ 7 (1 & 2), (1982): 53.

41. Timothy M. Shaw, "From Dependence to Self-reliance: Africa's Prospects for the Next Twenty Years," _International Journal_ 35 (4), (Autumn 1980): 836-7.

42. Ndongko, "Central Africa Regional Co-operation," p. 50.

43. For example, in 1980, the SADCC states food imports amounted to US $340 million. See Kgarebe ed., _SADCC 2--Maputo_, p. 240.

44. See _Overview_, Southern African Development Coordination Conference, Lusaka, February 1984.

45. Langdon and Mytelka, "Africa in the Changing World Economy," pp. 178-9.

46. _Ibid_., pp. 179-80.

47. Peter Robson, *Integration, Development and Equity: Economic Integration in West Africa* (London: George Allen and Unwin, 1983), p. 41.

48. For details see S.K.B. Asante, "Expectations and Reality: Transnational Corporations and Regional Self-reliance Objectives of the *Lagos Plan of Action*," paper presented at the Conference on OAU/EAC *Lagos Plan of Action* and the Future of Africa, University of Ife, Nigeria, March 1984.

49. Shaw and Grieve, "Dependence as an Approach," p. 236.

50. Anglin, "Economic Liberation and Regional Cooperation in Southern Africa," p. 701.

51. Tostensen, *Dependence and Collective Self-Reliance in Southern Africa*, p. 120.

52. *Record of the Southern African Development Coordination Summit*, Lusaka, 1 April 1980, pp. 2 and 30.

53. Opening Address, PTA signing ceremony, Lusaka, 21 December 1982, p. 12.

54. See statement by Richard Hove, Trade Minister of Zimbabwe, *Daily Times* (Malawi), 21 June 1982, p. 2.

55. Gerald K. Helleiner, "Aid and Dependence in Africa: Issues for Recipients," in *The Politics of Africa: Dependence and Development*, eds. Timothy M. Shaw and Kenneth A. Heard (New York: Africana for Dalhousie University Press, 1979), pp. 225-6. (Emphasis in original.)

56. See ECA, *ECA and Africa's Development*, p. 84.

57. B.W.T. Mutharika, *Toward Multinational Economic Cooperation in Africa* (New York: Praeger, 1972), p. 332.

58. Thomas S. Cox, "Northern Actors in a South-South Setting: External Aid and East African Integration," *Journal of Common Market Studies* 21 (3), (March 1983): 283-312.

59. Lynn K. Mytelka, "Foreign Aid and Regional Integration: The UDEAC Case," *Journal of Common Market Studies* 12 (2), (December 1975): 138-158.

60. For details, see S.K.B. Asante, "International Assistance and International Capitalism: Supportive or Counter-Productive" in *African Independence: The First 25 Years*, eds. Gwendolen M. Carter and Patrick O'Meara (Bloomington: University of Indiana Press, 1985).

61. Mytelka, "Foreign Aid and Regional Integration," pp. 157-8.

62. See Susan A. Gitelson, "Can the U.N. Be an Effective Catalyst for Regional Integration? The case of the East African Community," *Journal of Developing Areas* 8, (October 1973): 65-82.

63. For details of the agreement see K. Venkata Raman, "The Achievement of Specific NIEO Objectives by Means of Regional Approaches: Access to Markets, International Trade and Industrialization," in *Regionalism and the New International Economic Order*, ed. Davidson Nicol *et al.* (New York: Pergamon, 1981), p. 273.

64. Ali A. Mazrui, *The African Condition: A Political Diagnosis* (London: Cambridge University Press, 1983), p. 82.

65. For further details see Benno Engels, "The Global Approach to South-South Cooperation," *Development and Cooperation* (Bonn), 1 (January-February 1984): 14-16; and Elvin Laszlo, *RCDC (Regional Cooperation among Developing Countries* (New York: Pergamon Press, 1981).

66. Adebayo Adedeji, "Africa and the South: Forging Truly Interdependent Economic and Technical Links," *Africa Quarterly* 20 (1 & 2): 13.

67. See S.K.B. Asante, "Africa and Europe: Collective Dependence or Interdependence?" in Africa and Europe: From Partition to Interdependence, ed. Amadu Sesay (forthcoming) and "The Lomé Conventions: Towards Perpetuation of Dependence or Promotion of Interdependence?," Third World Quarter 3 (4), (October 1981): 658-672.

68. See Developing Local Technical and Managerial Capabilities for Dealing with Transnational Corporations in Africa (ST/ECA/CTNC/3), July 1981.

69. George C. Abangwu, "Systems Approach to Regional Integration in West Africa," Journal of Common Market Studies 13 (1 & 2), (1975): 133.

70. See for example, ECA, ECA and Africa's Development, pp. 17-18.

Part 2

Ambiguities in Assistance for African Development

Julius Olu Aiyegbusi

6 Collective Self-Reliance and External Assistance

In the first paragraph of the preamble to the Lagos Plan of Action (LPA),[1] the heads of state and government of Africa declared, "The effect of unfulfilled promises of global development strategies has been more sharply felt in Africa than in the other continents of the world. Indeed, rather than result in an improvement in the economic situation of the continent, successive strategies have made it stagnate and become more susceptible than other regions to the economic and social crises suffered by the industrialized countries. Thus, Africa is unable to point to any significant growth rate, or satisfactory index of general well-being, in the past 20 years. Faced with this situation, and determined to undertake measures for the basic restructuring of the economic base of our continent, we resolved to adopt a far-reaching regional approach based primarily on collective self-reliance [emphasis added]." In paragraph 14 of the preamble, Africa's leaders went on to say, inter alia, "Africa must cultivate the virtue of self-reliance. This is not to say that the continent should totally cut itself off from outside contributions. However, these outside contributions should only supplement our own effort: they should not be the mainstay of our development."[2]

At first glance, these two passages from the Lagos Plan may seem to propose contradictory courses of action. But do they? I can offer two reasons why some degree of dependence may be necessary to achieve self-reliance: (1) Africa is part and parcel of the world and cannot, even if it wants to, be an island unto itself; and (2) post-World War II international economic relations are based on the premise that the strong must help the weak to become stronger (even though differences exist between promise and practice). Moreover, this basic philosophy continues to be affirmed by the strong. Therefore, there is no real contradiction between these two important passages from the LPA.

Given that this is true, my purpose is to advocate more resources for collective self-reliance activities in Africa. And in so doing, I will re-examine the rationale for a regional approach based on collective self-reliance; describe and explain the poor response of external assistance to collective self-reliance efforts in Africa; restate the case for collective self-reliance; and propose forms of effective external assistance for collective self-reliance efforts in Africa.

A REGIONAL APPROACH BASED ON COLLECTIVE SELF-RELIANCE

Increasingly, planning and management of economies in developing countries in general, and African economies in particular, are being viewed in the context of national economies. This is particularly the approach of the World Bank.[3] Such management and planning stresses the efficient use of resources, particularly financial and material resources. But, according to the standard economic theory on which resource efficiency is based, economies of scale and the associated division of labor inevitably depend on the size of the market, in terms of income levels and distribution, population, and the geographical area covered. Therefore, in talking about planning and managing African economies, intercountry planning and management cannot be ignored.

The reasons for this regional or multinational approach are fundamental. First, for historical reasons many African countries are so small that managing their economies leads to insurmountable problems. In terms of population levels, the 50 countries that belong to ECA are distributed as follows: 10 countries have populations of fewer than one million each; 13 have between one million and 5 million each; 15 have between 5 million and 10 million each; 4 have between 10 million and 20 million each; 4 have between 20 and 30 million each; and only 4 have populations over 30 million each. Second, there is the problem of uneven distribution of natural resources, which at least for the early stages of development and economic growth, is crucial. It is instructive to note that 15 countries have less than one hundred thousand square kilometers each, 24 between one hundred thousand and one million, and 11 between one and three million. In all cases, the mean is nearer the lower end of the spectrum. Yet, in the region as a whole, there is an abundance of natural resources, as emphasized in the Lagos Plan. And third, there is the problem of low level per capita income. Thus, in 1982, seven African countries had a per capita income of less than US$200, with one country having a per capita income of less than US$100; two had per capita incomes between US$200 and US$400; twenty-two had between US$400 and US$1000; five had between US$1,000 and US$2,000; and only four had per capita incomes over US$2,000.

As a result, African countries find it difficult to achieve development on an individual basis. Therefore, in the face of fundamental handicaps at the national level, the regional or multinational approach is the answer. Through this approach, African countries would be in a position to capture economies of scale by sharing joint institutions and increasing agricultural and industrial production capacities. With appropriate policies, they would be able to take advantage of the growth potential of a larger market area and the gains derivable from competition in a large market.

In the foregoing paragraphs, the case for the regional approach, as propounded by the heads of state and government, has been briefly restated. However, these leaders went further and affirmed that the regional approach is linked to the principle of collective self-reliance. In this context, what is collective self-reliance and its rationale in Africa?

Unfortunately, this concept is not defined in the LPA document. But this does not mean that the leaders did not have concrete ideas about what they meant when they affirmed the principle of collective self-reliance. Indeed, the various expert meetings and working documents that formulated the plan produced precise ideas about collective self-reliance and the associated concept of national self-reliance.

Thus, as far back as 1976, when the ECA adopted The Revised Framework of Principles for the Implementation of the New International Economic Order in Africa,[4] which provided the main intellectual and theoretical foundation for the preparation of the Monrovia Strategy and the Lagos Plan of Action, the central elements of the concept had been defined. Put briefly, self-reliance was conceived in terms of (1) the internalization of the forces of demand and patterns of output, and the increasing substitution of factor inputs derived from within the region for those derived from outside; and (2) the increasing participation of the mass of the people in the production and consumption of the socially produced product. In addition, the concept of self-sustainment was related to that of self-reliance and defined as the deliberate installation of patterns and processes of development and economic growth in which different components mutually support and reinforce each other, so that, when related to the internalization of the forces determining demand and supply, the whole system develops its own internal dynamics.[5] This process has to start at the national level and culminate at the regional level.

In effect, my approach to the concept of self-reliance is very similar to that of Roy Preiswerk and Johan Galtung[6] in the book edited by them with Peter O'Brien, Self-reliance--A Strategy for Development. Indeed, the very concept that underlies the Lagos Plan is to make "it possible for local, national or regional (African) communities to use more resources for themselves, to assert their own value systems, to have confidence in their own ingenuity--in other words, to be less dependent on international organizations, foreign governments or giant corporations when trying to attain a better life."[7] Yet, "such efforts at the local, national and regional levels, still require some co-operation with the outside world,"[8] although the ultimate aim is to decrease heavy dependence on external sources in the fields of trade, technology, and finance. Therefore, such self-reliance cannot be at the expense of the self-reliance of others; it only implies autonomy to set and realize goals as far as possible through our efforts, using our own forces, including economic factors.

In a way, this concept captures some of the elements identified by Samuel Parmar in his interesting article, "Self-reliant Development in an Interdependent World."[9] Thus, it emphasizes the need to formulate concepts and policies of development based on African socio-economic realities rather than on ideas inherited from other regions of the world. It rejects imitative approaches, and emphasizes structural issues, including social and institutional change and the assurance of social justice in the process of development and economic growth.

Unfortunately, when this principle was openly announced by African leaders, it received hostile reaction from some quarters.[10] Yet, as Preiswerk has correctly put it, although "the concept of self-reliance is receiving serious attention and being properly defined only today, as a form of social behavior it has probably existed at all times of human development and in almost every part of the world."[11] Moreover, "it is first and foremost a constructive idea."[12]

But how do we expect to achieve the objectives of national and collective self-reliance in Africa? The answer to this crucial question lies in the basic characteristics of the Lagos Plan, four of which I give here for purposes of illustration.

First, the need for a thorough understanding of the natural resource base--that is, a complete knowledge of all the available land, mineral, and other resources--is considered vital if national and regional planning is to be executed in a rational, coordinated, and effective manner. The planning process must focus on the exploitation of the natural resource base to produce goods and services for the improvement of the general well-being of the peoples of Africa. The expectation also is that the implementation of the Lagos Plan will lead to the complete participation of all the peoples of Africa in the ongoing planning and implementation process. Hence, emphasis is placed on human resource development as the sine qua non for the realization of planning objectives. This inevitably calls for an adequate knowledge of the population, including its gender composition and other characteristics. The link between natural and human resources is basic; once the natural resources are known, the products to be produced from them can be determined, and these will in turn affect the technologies and the skills required.

Second, the Lagos Plan stresses the importance of technology and institutions. Hence, it emphasizes the need to have a thorough knowledge of existing institutions and technologies and to build on what already exists.

Third, the initiation and sustainment of economic interdependence among sovereign African states envisaged in the plan requires a complete restructuring and transformation of present economies. The Lagos Plan places special emphasis on the importance of national, subregional, and regional markets and calls for their reexamination and restructuring so as to streamline distributive structures and maximize their contribution to socio-economic development. The role that these markets would have to play in the internalization of factor inputs (skills, raw materials, machinery, technology, etc.) is also considered important. Along with the restructuring of national, subregional, and regional markets must come the restructuring of the transport and communications sector. Its importance derives from its provision of critical services (carrying of goods and materials) for all the social and economic sectors, its use of products of the engineering subsector, and its carrying of people and messages from one place to another. Consequently, the transport and communications sector takes on critical importance because of its role in promoting growth in other sectors; in addition, it serves the socio-economic integration of Africa. The objectives of any transport and communications sector restructuring are, therefore, to open up land-locked countries and isolated regions; to integrate the transport and communications infrastructure with a view to promoting intra-African trade; to coordinate the various transportation systems (multinational, intermodal transport networks) and regulations; and to use local engineering products.

The objectives of self-sufficiency in food production--cereals, livestock, and fish products to meet the basic needs of the population--and establishment of growth and linkage-promoting activities for industry call for a considerable restructuring of those sectors. It is believed that for agriculture, the "fundamental requisite is a strong political will to channel a greatly increased volume of resources to agriculture and reorientation and transformation of the social systems...equitable distribution of the means of production and the proceeds of such production"[13] with the objective of attaining higher levels of productivity. Industry, on the other hand, "demands for creation, in each member state, of an industrial base designed to meet the interest of that country and strengthened by the complementary activities at subregional and regional levels."[14] In addition to stressing the importance of subregional and regional interdependency for industrial development, the Lagos Plan expects the industrial sector to play a leading role. Basic industries that enhance inter- and intrasectoral linkages at the national and multinational levels are proposed for study and establishment. These basic industries include food and agro-industries, building, metallurgical, mechanical, electrical and electronic, chemical, and energy industries.

Finally, development planning as conceived in the Lagos Plan is based on a scenario for the future that has been developed, discussed, and collectively adopted as more desirable than and preferable to the present. This scenario can become operational in three stages: first, by determining what ought to be done; second, by setting time-specific or plan-specific goals; and third, by implementing decisions formulated at high levels. Putting into sharp focus the problems, issues, and priorities for attaining a willed future creates the commitment and unity of purpose necessary for the achievement of national and collective self-reliance and self-reliant and self-sustaining economic growth and development. Planning as conceived in the Lagos Plan of Action is devoid of ideological consideration. Consequently, the plan insists on individual and collective self-reliance and calls for the articulation of a "national institutional and economic development infrastructure"[15] to "provide a framework for the involvement of the entire population."[16]

It is clear therefore that emphasis in the Lagos Plan is placed on self-reliance at the national level. And collective self-reliance is clearly defined in the Final Act of Lagos annexed to the Lagos Plan. Thus, the heads of state and government laid down the stages for implementing the plan by commiting themselves to:

1. strengthening the existing regional economic communities and establishing others;
2. strengthening, effectively, integration in the fields of agriculture, food, transport and communications, industry and energy; promoting co-ordination and harmonization among existing and future economic groupings with a view to creating an African Common Market as a precursor of an African Economic Community.[17]

As it is, integration can only be achieved by creation of joint institutions, implementation of joint projects, and harmonization of strategies and financial and monetary policies. Thus, although significant progress has been made towards the creation of economic groupings and efforts are being made to promote cooperation among them (as ably reflected in chapters 4 and 5),[18] the success of economic groupings will ultimately depend on the benefits that can be derived through joint projects, including the use of the services of multinational institutions. In "joining the club," the gains are quite salient[19] for economic cooperation. Such gains are particularly important in the critical areas of agriculture and industry. And if we apply Professor Harry Johnson's[20] concept of "industrialization"--namely, the organization of production in business enterprises, characterized by specialization and division of labor, and the application of technology and of mechanical and electrical power to supplement and replace human effort, and motivated by the objectives of minimizing costs per unit and maximizing returns to the enterprise--the emphasis on collective self-reliance in the Lagos Plan of Action can be defined as a "paradigm for industrialization."[21] In this context, as the chapters by Kimani[22] and Pallangyo and Odero-Ogwell[23] clearly show, big programs for "industrialization" already exist for implementing the Lagos Plan.

EXTERNAL ASSISTANCE RESPONSE TO COLLECTIVE SELF-RELIANCE EFFORTS

In the foregoing two sections I have attempted to justify the collective self-reliance approach to development and economic growth in Africa and to highlight measures for achieving such reliance, all with a view to laying the basis for a review of the response of external assistance to collective self-reliant efforts.

Since I am interested in external assistance for collective self-reliance efforts, in my review I will apply Lynn Mytelka's[24] four models of donor-recipient interaction. I will concentrate primarily on the two-way multilateral and bilateral-multilateral recipient components.

In discussing the two-way multilateral component, I am inevitably interested in UN institutions like the European Economic Community (EEC), the Organization for Economic Cooperation and Development (OECD), OPEC, the different Arab funds, COMECON, and the African Development Bank, to name only a few. With respect to the bilateral-multilateral recipient category, I will examine a few individual governments and their development institutions.

Criteria for Evaluating Contributions to Collective Self-reliance Activities

In discussing the impact of aid agencies on collective self-reliance, I am concerned about such donors' philosophies and attitudes to collective self-reliance, since these are likely to determine the amount of resources allocated. Similarly, since their philosophies are also likely to determine areas of concentration, there is also a need to review sectors and activities, such as institution support, training and research, studies and surveys, and investment projects, particularly in the critical areas of agriculture (including food) and industry.

Indeed, as J.P. Renniger has correctly stated about the clinker plant project sponsored by Ghana, Ivory Coast, and Togo and financed by the IBRD, "it is relatively easy to determine the integrative impact of projects such as this. It is much more difficult to develop criteria which can be used to evaluate the integrative impact of technical assistance activities. In the United Nations, intercountry projects and programs refer to those which involve more than one country. But this alone does not ensure that the projects promote the integration process. It appears reasonable that a genuine integration project is something more than a project which simply involves two or more countries. Technical assistance projects which promote integration would, first of all, be those that are directly related to the establishment, strengthening, or maintenance of subregional organizations which promote integration. Other projects that might qualify would be those that result in new types of integrative behavior through, for example, the creation of new knowledge. Such creation could conceivably come about through training and research activities."[25] There is a need to increase joint investment projects, such as the clinker plant.

The United Nations System

United Nations Development Program (UNDP). In this context, what has been the role of the UNDP in helping to implement collective self-reliance, as defined in the *Lagos Plan*? In general, it can be said, that whenever the *Lagos Plan* is mentioned, the role of UNDP cannot be ignored. In fact, most of the expert group meetings, at which the basic ideas of the *Lagos Plan* were discussed, were financed by the UNDP. Similarly, since the adoption of the plan, UNDP assistance to institutions created for the promotion of economic and social integration in Africa has been impressive. However, recent trends, which reflect the increasing financial difficulties of the UNDP, give cause for concern. There is no doubt about the commitment of UNDP to self-reliance efforts in Africa.

However, despite this commitment to collective self-reliance efforts in Africa, there is a problem with the size of the UNDP resource allocation. Thus, while the regional allocation for the period 1977-81 was about 13 percent, it is only about 17 percent for the period 1982-86 (figures are purely illustrative). In effect, since 1977 and even earlier, the regional allocation has never reached the maximum 18 percent recommended. This figure is definitely too low as far as Africa is concerned.

However, the story does not end there. While there were 300 approved and ongoing projects during the 1977-81 cycle, there are only 183 during the 1982-86 cycle. Moreover, there is no assurance that all of these are going to be financed, given increasingly poor responses to annual pledging for UNDP and other development funds.

Moreover, although these projects come under the title "Regional Program for Africa," only about 25 percent were really projects involving all the countries of the region or a group of them together. Further, in terms of instruments for collective self-reliance -- in the sense of projects whose main purposes are to either act as catalysts for integration activities or enable the group of countries to develop joint capacities and produce commodities or services jointly for the use of their members or for export -- only a few of them can be so regarded. And, most of these projects are oriented to individual national needs. The result is that, as far as joint investment projects in the agricultural, industrial, and energy areas using the enormous resources of the region, there are big gaps. Hence, these are the areas where joint activities for collective self-reliance have to be vigorously pursued. But that is not the total picture. These figures are allocations based on the UNDP's view as to the likely level of resources available during the cycle. If there are shortfalls, allocations are scaled down accordingly. Indeed, as a result of such difficulties, UNDP has had to cut down or withdraw assistance to some ongoing instruments for the promotion of development cooperation.

In highlighting the commitment of UNDP to the promotion of integration in Africa, Renninger has indicated that "this commitment is, however, accompanied by the firm conviction that such assistance must be a step in the direction of making the organizations self-sufficient,"[26] and he has quoted a UNDP policy statement which said that "care should, however, be taken to ensure that the institutions become truly local endeavors as soon as possible and do not become isolated enclaves transplanted from abroad."[27] This point is well taken. However, before established support to an ongoing institution or project is terminated, it is necessary to ensure that such termination will not lead to the loss of the benefits so far generated.

Other United Nations Organizations. I have highlighted the role of the UNDP because it is not only the leader of the UN systems development activities, but also because its resources overshadow those of the other units; in fact, it finances a lot of their operational activities. While UN organizations like UNCTAD, the Department of Technical Cooperation for Development (DTCD), and the Department of International Economic and Social Affairs (DIESA) have been mandated to play a significant role in the promotion of regional cooperation among developing countries and UNCTAD has done a lot to strengthen the capacities of some economic groupings in the region, in general, the activities of these bodies are oriented toward the national level. The activities of such organs as the Center for Science and Technology for Development, the United Nations Industrial Development Organization (UNIDO), and the United Nations Center for Human Settlements (Habitat) are also nationally oriented. However, because of the recognition of the transnational character of some environmental problems such as desertification, the United Nations Environment Program (UNEP) is allocating increasing shares of its resources to collective self-reliance.

Among these diverse bodies, it is the regional economic commissions that mandate more economic cooperation and hence assistance to collective self-reliance efforts. In this connection, refer to the preceding chapters by Adebayo Adedeji and S.K.B. Asante for the activities of the ECA in promoting economic and technical cooperation in Africa in the context of the Lagos Plan. In terms of investment projects, a lot has been and is being done in identifying and promoting projects for collective self-reliance at the subregional and other intercountry levels, as the chapter by George Kimani demonstrates. In general, about 70 percent of ECA regular and extrabudgetary resources was devoted to promoting collective reliance activities in the biennium 1982-83; the same percentage is likely to be allocated in the 1984-85 biennium.

Unfortunately, as indicated in the 1982-83 Biennial Report of the Executive Secretary, while the ECA and its secretariat have, over the years, accumulated experience in dealing with African economic growth and development problems, particularly in the context of collective self-reliance, "that position is unfortunately likely to be weakened by shrinking resources, both human and financial."[28] "Such weakening is particularly serious in the context of the Lagos Plan of Action and the Final Act of Lagos. In such crucial areas as industrial development, science and technology, and education, training, labor, management and employment, which do not appear to be particularly favored by the regular budget or extrabudgetary resources, this is especially true. Industrial development and science and technology in particular, are not generally favored by bilateral donors. The same applies to economic co-operation and integration, whose good showing in the biennium 1982-1983 was due to an increased allocation from the regular budget."[29]

Specialized Agencies of the UN System. While, in general, UNDP funds a lot of activities executed by the specialized agencies of the UN and quite a number of these are projects for the promotion of collective self-reliance, it is still true to say that the bulk of the assessed and voluntary resources of the specialized agencies are devoted to national activities. Indeed, the principle of concentration on national activities is clearly followed by the specialized agencies. Although this orientation may not be too bad as far as support to institutions and to research and training are concerned, since benefits from these areas can spill over into collective self-reliance projects, it is detrimental to investment projects in agriculture (including food), industry, and transport and communications sectors, which are crucial for integrative and collective self-reliance efforts.

It is in the context of investment projects that one should view the activities of the World Bank and its affiliates--the International Development Association (IDA) and the International Finance Corporation (IFC). Although reference has already been made to the financing by the World Bank of the clinker plant owned by Togo, Ivory Coast, and Benin in 1977, a search for the World Bank's support for similar projects in subsequent years has so far proved abortive. Similarly, enlistment of the World Bank's support for the regional approach has also yielded no positive results.[30] In fact, in the World Bank's first report[31] after the adoption of the Lagos Plan of Action, regionalism was treated as one of the long-term issues, despite the fact that economic cooperation and integration activities have had a long, though checkered, history on the continent. One paragraph in the report on the roles of donors in economic integration and functional cooperation is not enough to defeat the clear opposition demonstrated in the preceding six paragraphs. Inevitably such an attitude can only lead to lack of support for such activities. Of course, the World Bank has shifted its position on this issue, as is evidenced in its latest document[32] on the Lagos Plan of Action. But in view of the importance of the World Bank and its affiliates in the field of development, not only in terms of financial resources but also of technical competence, I would like to see a more definitive statement by them on the rationale of the regional approach, backed up by an increase in activities in this area.

That the activities of the specialized agencies of the UN are predominantly state-centered is particularly clear in a recent report[33] by the secretary-general on special measures for the social and economic development of Africa in the 1980s. In very few cases are UN organizations promoting joint projects between two or more African countries.

Non-UN Multinational Agencies and National Donors

Of all the non-UN organizations in a position to support collective self-reliance activities in Africa, OECD and EEC top the list. As far as OECD is concerned, all available information,[34] particularly on Development Assistance Committee (DAC) member activities, indicates only bilateral activities with individual African countries.

With regard to EEC, records of assistance within the EEC-ACP framework show strong emphasis on assistance to national activities, although here and there the European Development Fund and the European Investment Bank support infrastructure projects, including research activities, that benefit groups of countries. But in terms of joint projects in such critical areas as agriculture and industry, there are serious gaps. Realization of this situation is probably responsible for specific reference to the need to support regional projects and economic cooperation and integration among the developing countries in EEC's new development policy, which laid the basis for the negotiation of a new convention between the community and the ACP countries.

In the new development policy the EEC has indicated that one of its objectives is to "help countries to apply development policies based on self-reliance."[35] Moreover, the community now acknowledges that "often, development operations cannot be fully effective unless they are undertaken over several countries concurrently, in the areas of trade relations and industrial co-operation. In its co-operation ties with the various groups of developing countries, the community will continue to press for the necessary regional aspect of development work to be taken into account; it will adjust its co-operation instruments to give greater weight than in the past to this important factor, with the aim of building up complementarity and contributing to the economic balances of regional groupings."[36]

This is a welcome change particularly for Africa, where the EEC has prided itself on being most active and where, at the same time, the impact of two decades of aid has been disappointing. What is now needed is following up the policy with action.

As far as individual EEC states and their aid agencies are concerned, their assistance to collective self-reliance projects is rare, although the new development policy of the community may be a reflection of a change of policy at the individual state level. That being so, one may anticipate a reorientation of the activities of the members of the Interact Group.[37] Indeed, a review of the objectives and operations of the members of Interact confirms that the problem is not a lack of resources and institutions to support collective self-reliance activities in Africa. Rather, the problem may be the lack of will based on rigid ideology.

In terms of size and power, the CMEA constitutes another possible source of aid and technical assistance to collective self-reliance in Africa. However, just as in the case of the OECD and the EEC, the cooperation arrangements of the members of CMEA are usually oriented towards individual African states.

OPEC and Arab Development Funds are relatively new in the aid and technical assistance field. But again, just as in the cases of the other groups of donors, multilateral-bilateral and bilateral-bilateral arrangements still constitute the order of the day.

The African Development Bank (ADB)

Although the African Development Bank was established by the ECA, its activities over the first 20 years of its existence were predominantly devoted to national projects. However, the new program for the period 1982-86 not only recognizes the importance of the _Lagos Plan_ but also emphasizes the need to allocate more resources to collective self-reliance activities in Africa. Allocation to multinational projects only started in 1982.

Overall, it is clear from this review that collective self-reliance activities and projects have not received the support which the OAU heads of state and government envisaged in their Lagos Plan of Action. Why has this been so? One important reason is undoubtedly the diehard belief that the twentieth century is predominantly a nation-state century. As a result, all development activities are expected to be centered at the national level. This belief is the basis for the preference of donors for bilateral assistance. There is of course the question of the difficulty of dealing with multinational institutions for cooperation or the governments interested in joint projects. But is economic development mainly a national phenomenon? Of course, there are certain activities that must be organized and implemented at the national level. However, in situations where nations are economically small, and yet rapid growth is envisaged, collective self-reliance seems imperative. In fact, there are certain circumstances where national development can be meaningful only within the framework of collective self-reliance. The majority of African countries would benefit most from development derived from collective self-reliance.

If the view that development is mainly a national phenomenon is the reason for a lack of effective external support for collective self-reliance in Africa, then a major problem exists: namely, donors have refused to accept the basic philosophy underlying the Lagos Plan, the regional approach based on collective self-reliance. This being so, the next question is: Of what use are the repeated pronouncements of donors, particularly bilateral donors, that they support the efforts of the developing countries to promote more cooperation among themselves? Another question is: To what extent are independent development programs and projects developed by African countries used as bases for making aid and technical assistance? In view of the need for donors to provide assistance based on priorities established by the developing countries themselves, it seems imperative that donors should review and change their attitudes towards collective self-reliance efforts, particularly in the context of the Lagos Plan.

THE CASE FOR COLLECTIVE SELF-RELIANCE

At the beginning of this chapter, I argued the case for the regional approach based on collective self-reliance, particularly on the basis of the small economic size of the majority of African states and the problem of uneven distribution of natural resources, including human resources. In view of the reluctance of donors to respond positively and effectively to this approach, it seems necessary for me to restate the case in order to make practical suggestions for meaningful support for collective self-reliance activities.

While political problems have so far retarded the progress of collective self-reliance activities in the African region, there is no doubt that the economic arguments for such an approach are quite sound. First, there is the basic economic argument that fast economic growth and the associated diversification of goods and services depend, at least in the early stages of development, on natural resources. Similarly, the required demand is definitely a function of per capita income and population size, particularly in the context of a development strategy geared to the satisfaction of the basic needs of the population. As is widely known, Africa possesses enormous amounts of natural resources. Unfortunately, their distribution among countries is abnormal. And the same problem exists with population distribution. Yet, if basic needs are to be met, there is need for efficient allocation of resources and their optimal utilization. Hence, the need for economies of scale. And as Adam Smith has said, the division of labor, hence economy of scale and improved productivity, is determined by the extent of the market. As far as Africa is concerned, there is no gainsaying the fact that the collective self-reliance approach is imperative.

With the adoption of this approach, it would be possible for African countries to achieve the 13 components of self-reliance as outlined by Galtung,[38] namely, change in priorities towards production for the basic needs of those most in need; mass participation; better utilization of local factors; stimulation of creativity; more compatibility with local conditions; more diversity of development; less alienation; attainment of ecological balance; internalization of important positive externalities; solidarity with others at the same level on a more solid basis; increase in the ability to withstand manipulation because of trade dependency; increase in the defense capability of each country and hence of the group of the countries involved; and establishment of the present relationship between center and periphery on a more equal footing. These could be achieved without the five negative effects that Galtung also identifies: the possibility of inequalities remaining while inequities may decrease; the possibility that local exploitation may solidify as long as the base remains unchanged; the likelihood of organic ties between units being reduced; the possibility of reduction of mobility between units; and the possibility of a new vertical distinction being created between self-reliant and non-self-reliant units.

All these have implications for Africa's future international economic relations. Indeed, as Galtung says, using trade as an example of the general pattern of interaction that may develop as a result of effective collective self-reliance in Africa, "the most important dynamic tendency will be in the direction of decreased centre-periphery inter-sector trade (in other words across genuine gaps in the level of processing) as an expression of increased periphery tendency to process their own raw materials and use their own tertiary sector, their own services. As a result, and equally much as an expression of self-reliance, one may hypothesize increased intra-sector trade (raw materials against raw materials, (semi)manufactures against (semi)manufactures, services against services) both in the center and in the periphery. Consequently, the periphery will not only preserve more of the positive externalities and distribute them more evenly among themselves; they will also be better protected against terms of trade fluctuations since there will be more focus on intra-sector trade. What will happen in the other three cells in the table is hard to postulate, but the general hypothesis is that increased self-reliance involves redirection and recomposition of trade and, consequently, will have an impact on the total world trade picture. Whether total world trade volume will increase, diminish or remain about the same under a system of self-reliance is another matter, however--there is hardly any base for predicting."[39]

Such a situation should be welcome since a series of "centers of development and economic growth" all over the world operating under their own inner strength would lead to meaningful interdependence and create a situation preferable to the present asymmetric one that exists between North and South. It is in the interest of all aid donors to support strongly such a move since viable regional groups are likely to relieve traditional donors of some burdens. Moreover, such a situation is more in tune with the views of some leading politicians[40] in Europe, who advocate collective self-reliance in Western Europe so as to reduce the dependence of that part of the world on the United States. It is also in agreement with the views of one of the leading development economists of our time--the late Professor Dudley Seers.[41] Indeed, if Mr. Giscard d'Estaing and Professor Dudley Seers could argue for collective self-reliance for Western Europe, given its present economic and military power, a call for collective self-reliance for the poorest region in the world should be praised and supported.

Finally, there is the fact, as already stated, that "the idea of self-reliance in the sense of the small community relying on its own forces is as old as humanity itself: this was the normal form of human existence."[42] The progress of history and the consequent enlargement of human contact have extended the idea to the subregional and regional levels. Therefore, if the expression of solidarity with developing countries in general and African states in particular is to have meaning, the desire to become self-reliant individually and collectively should receive greater support than at present from those who claim also to believe in such solidarity.

EFFECTIVE EXTERNAL ASSISTANCE FOR COLLECTIVE SELF-RELIANCE

It is important to recall that there are already many arrangements for collective self-reliance efforts on the continent. Thus, there are different economic groupings such as ECOWAS, PTA, ECCAS, SADCC, UDEAC, etc. There are also such institutions as the mineral resources development centers, one for Eastern and Southern Africa based in Dodoma, Tanzania, and one for Central Africa based in Brazzaville, Congo. Other institutions include the African Regional Center for Technology based in Dakar, Senegal, the African Regional Center for Engineering Design and Manufacturing based in Ibadan, Nigeria, and the African Regional Center for Technology, to name only a few. There are also training and research institutions such as United Nations African Institute for Economic Development and Planning (IDEP), the African Center for Advanced Research and Training in Social Development (ACARYSOD), the ECA Multinational Programing and Operational Centers (MULPOCs), the ECA itself, and the specialized agencies of the OAU, to name only a few.

But more importantly, as already mentioned, collective self-reliance is a paradigm for industrialization in the widest sense of that word. Moreover, the necessary industrial, agricultural, and infrastructural projects for the implementation of such industrialization programs are already being analyzed in the framework of economic cooperations arrangements such as ECOWAS, ECCAS, PTA, the MULPOCs, etc. For these institutions to become effective to the point that they can be supported by their member states, they need continuous and substantial external assistance in the form of money, equipment, and experts, including training specialists. As far as the agricultural, industrial, and infrastructural projects are concerned, investment capital, particularly in concessional terms, is needed. With respect to the channels through which these resources could be provided, I have already mentioned the UN system, OECD, EEC, OPEC, the Arab funds, COMECON, etc. There is also, of course, the ECA.

Unfortunately, contributions to multilateral technical assistance institutions are declining fast, although donors have indicated their willingness to continue to support such institutions. With the case for collective self-reliance in Africa now well established, I can only appeal strongly to aid donors to take the case of "additionality" very seriously. It is only by increasing contributions substantially that collective self-reliance activities can be promoted, since the level of bilateral assistance should not be reduced. With increases in contributions to multilateral aid and technical assistance agencies with emphasis on collective self-reliance, the idea that development and economic growth are only national phenomena will be modified. Accordingly, allocations to intercountry projects and other collective self-reliance activities in the African region will be increased, and collaboration with institutions created for promoting collective self-reliance will be strengthened.

With respect to investment activities in multinational agricultural, industrial, and infrastructure projects, the World Bank and its affiliates will have to increase their contributions. The World Bank must make a change in philosophy to benefit collective self-reliance programs and projects.

With regard to bilateral assistance to multinational collective self-reliance activities, bilateral donors will have to take into consideration the participation of member states in collective self-reliance projects. It has often been said that member states do not show an interest in multinational projects when discussing aid and technical assistance with donors. While this may be true, there is no doubt that bilateral donors can use their influence and technical capability to encourage member states to consider the implications of projects for collective self-reliance. They can even point out such implications in their own review of existing and future projects. It is hoped that bilateral and multilateral aid donors will henceforth use the Lagos Plan of Action as the primary basis for determining aid allocations and will constantly remind members of the relevance of collective self-reliance.

In general, I would suggest the increasing use of roundtables and consultative meetings for raising support for collective self-reliance activities in Africa. The role of the ECA, the ADB and other regional or subregional multinational development institutions in this area cannot be overstressed. Of course, these institutions can profit from the experience of the World Bank and the UNDP in organizing consultative meetings and roundtables.

SUMMARY

The main purpose of this chapter has been to argue for increased aid and technical assistance to collective self-reliance activities in Africa in accordance with the Lagos Plan. In pursuing that objective, I have reexamined the case for the regional approach based on collective self-reliance and concluded that it is well founded, not only because of the small economic size of many African countries and the uneven distribution of natural and human resources but also because of the need for solidarity among African countries and the fact that the idea of collective self-reliance is natural and universal. I have also emphasized that African collective self-reliance should not be at the expense of other regions' collective self-reliance. While such self-reliance will inevitably involve some decoupling, which is also practised by the developed countries, it should not and cannot mean autarky. Hence, developed and other countries should support economic cooperation among developing countries and provide assistance to collective self-reliance activities in Africa.

It has often been said that the United Nations, other international organizations, or even bilateral donors cannot force governments to cooperate if they are unwilling to do so. This may not be entirely true, at least in the case of international institutions, such as the World Bank, and as far as bilateral donors are concerned. In any case, there have been cases when donors refused assistance to recipients who were not prepared to accept their conditions. Similarly, the assistance being proposed in the framework for the Joint Program of Action of the World Bank is being made on condition that members are prepared to take the recommended measures. Is it not possible to make a condition for aid the readiness of groups of countries to initiate and implement jointly institutions, investment projects, etc.?

It has also been argued that the lack of genuine integration projects is a reflection of the fact that many governments are simply not interested in cooperative approaches. In addition, intercountry projects in general, and integration projects in particular, are more difficult to formulate and implement than national projects for a variety of reasons; and the number of factors that must be considered is larger, thus making agreements more difficult since decision-making is more complex.[43] While there is no doubt that some governments show no interest in integration projects, such reluctance may not be blamed solely on these governments but also on donors who discourage such cooperative efforts. There are a lot of donor practices, such as insistence on financing only national projects, providing assistance only for training in donor countries, and encouragement to continue to patronize institutions that tie recipients and donors--even when the interests of the recipients dictate a different approach--that discourage attempts to initiate and sustain local collective self-reliance efforts. It is hoped that the expressions of support for collective self-reliance activities among the developing countries that are now being made by donors will lead to the stoppage of such practices and result in concrete action for collective self-reliance in the Third World and in Africa.

NOTES

1. OAU, Lagos Plan of Action for the Economic Development of Africa, 1980-2000 (Geneva: International Institute of Labor Studies, 1981), p. 5.
2. Ibid., p. 8.
3. See World Bank, World Development Report, 1983 (Washington, 1983).

4. ECA, The Revised Framework of Principles for the Implementation of the New International Economic Order in Africa, (E/CN.14/ECO/90/Rev.3) mimeographed. As indicated, this document provided the main intellectual and theoretical foundation for the "Monrovia Strategy for the Economic Development of Africa." For a summary of the process that led to the formulation of the Lagos Plan of Action and the ideas contained in the Revised Framework, see Adebayo Adedeji, "The Evolution of the Monrovia Strategy and the Lagos Plan of Action: A Regional Approach to Economic Decolonization," (Addis Ababa: ECA, 1983).

5. Adedeji, "The Evolution of the Monrovia Strategy," p. 10.

6. Self-Reliance-- a strategy for development, Johan Galtung, Peter O'Brien and Roy Preiswerk, eds., (London: Bogle - l'Overture, 1980), introduction and chapter 1.

7. Ibid., p. 11.

8. Ibid., inside cover page.

9. Samuel L. Parmar, "Self-reliant Development in an "Interdependent World," in Beyond Dependency -- the developing world speaks out, Guy F. Erb and Valeriana Kallab, eds., (Washington: Overseas Development Council, 1975).

10. See especially OECD, "1980 Review-Development Co-operation" (Paris, November 1980), Chapter II - "Focus on Africa."

11. Galtung, O'Brien and Preiswerk, eds., Self-Reliance, p. 11.

12. Ibid., p. 15.

13. Lagos Plan of Action, p. 11.

14. Ibid., p. 20.

15. Ibid., p. 121.

16. See "The Lagos Plan of Action--Progress, Problems and Prospects of Implementation by OAU and ECA Secretariats," mimeographed, International Economic Association Regional Conference on Structural Change, Economic Interdependence and African Development (Addis Ababa, July 1983), pp. 5-6.

17. Lagos Plan of Action, annex 1, p. 128.

18. See chapters 4 and 5 by Adebayo Adedeji and S.K.B. Asante in this volume.

19. See Lynn Mytelka, "The Salience of Gains in Third World Integrative Systems," World Politics 25 (January 1973).

20. See Harry G. Johnson, Economic Policies Toward Less Developed Countries (Washington: The Brookings Institution, 1967), pp. 45-46.

21. Mytelka, "The Salience of Gains in Third-World Integrative Systems."

22. See George M. Kimani, "Industry in Africa: Continental Co-operation and the Industrial Development Decade," chapter 13.

23. See E.P. Pallangyo and L.A. Odero-Ogwel, "The Persistence of the Food and Agricultural Crisis in Africa," chapter 10 in this volume.

24. See Lynn Krieger Mytelka, "Foreign Aid and Regional Integration. The UDEAC Case," in Journal of Common Market Studies 12 (2), December 1973, figure 1: 141.

25. See J.P. Renningar, Multinational Cooperation for Development in West Africa (New York: Pergamon, 1978), p. 84.

26. Ibid., p. 86.

27. Ibid.

28. ECA, Biennial Report of the Executive Secretary, 1982-1983 (E/ECA/CM.10/11) (Addis Ababa, 1984), p. 157.

29. Ibid.

30. See World Bank, _Annual Report, 1983_ (Washington, 1984).

31. See World Bank, _Accelerated Development in Sub-Saharan Africa: An Agenda for Action_ (Washington, 1981), pp. 118-120.

32. See World Bank, _Toward Sustained Development in Sub-Saharan Africa: A Joint Program of Action_ (Washington: World Bank, 1984).

33. See United Nations General Assembly and Economic and Social Council, "Special Measures for the Social and Economic Development of Africa in the 1980s. Report of the Secretary General" (A/39/289; E/1984/107), 1984.

34. See any issue of OECD's _Review-Development Co-operation_ (Paris: OECD).

35. See "Memorandum on the Community's Development Policy," _The Courier_ 76 (November-December 1982): 56.

36. _Ibid._, p. 57.

37. See J. Leech, "Towards More Effective Investments in Development," _The Courier_ 82 (November-December 1983): 31-35.

38. Galtung, O'Brien and Preiswerk, eds., _Self-Reliance_.

39. _Ibid._

40. See Valery Giscard d'Estaing, "New Opportunities and New Challenges," _Foreign Affairs_ 62 (1), Fall 1983: 185-192. Note particularly the section on "Current Problems in International Relations."

41. See Dudley Seers, "Time for a Second Look at the Third World," _Development Policy Review_, 1 (1) (May 1983).

42. Galtung, O'Brien and Preiswerk, eds., _Self-Reliance_, p. 19.

43. See Renninger, _Multinational Cooperation for Development in West Africa_, p. 85 et seq. for these views.

Amir Jamal

7 Self-Reliance, International Assistance, and Managing the African Economy

Through the adoption and promulgation of the Lagos Plan, the OAU has achieved something quite significant. It has set into motion continent-wide African thinking on economic and social issues very specifically aimed at "promoting the economic and social development and integration of the economies of African countries with a view to achieving an increasing measure of self-sufficiency and self-sustainment," at "facilitating and reinforcing social and economic intercourse," and thereby establishing "national, sub-regional and regional institutions which will facilitate the attainment of objectives of self-reliance and self-sustainment."

Economists belonging to the classical, the neoclassical, and the non-conformist schools will have no difficulty in understanding and appreciating these objectives. All the arguments arising since the adoption of the Lagos Plan of Action have quite predictably centered around the implications for policy-makers in bringing the plan's objectives to fruition.

I have to point out at the outset that given the political realities of more than 50 sovereign states, the task facing policy-makers is extremely difficult. It is fair--though not necessarily pleasant--to observe that the odds very much favor a series of agonizingly frustrating experiences before any agreement regarding a political union of African states is signed by sovereign members with the same solemn commitment as they have given the Lagos Plan. Yet, this political framework is essential for implementation of the Lagos Plan. If the actual efforts of national governments to carry out their commitments under the Final Act of Lagos precipitate a commitment for a political union to be achieved within, say, two generations, then the Lagos Plan will have performed a historic task of monumental significance.

This is not to say that the Final Act of Lagos is not itself a political commitment. The Plan of Action speaks of Africa's immense resources, Africa's overwhelming reliance on exports of raw materials, Africa's own internal market, and Africa's need for self-reliance. The challenging task of national policy-makers is to devise national policies that, taken together with those of other African states, will reinforce all common endeavors rather than cancel out one another's efforts. The political framework within which the Lagos Plan is expected to be implemented is the OAU, which is necessarily founded on the principle of sovereignty.

The subject of my chapter is planning and managing the African economy: the balance of international assistance and self-reliance within the framework of the Lagos Plan and the Final Act. To begin, I will assume that an "African economy" is an economy that is within the scope of policy-makers. For the large part, this means a national economy, since all African states at present retain ultimate sovereignty within their respective borders. Regional groupings will take on increasing significance, to the extent that both the actual, contractual commitment, and the commensurate national management of the political economy make this possible on a sustained basis. As is recognized by the signatories of the Lagos Plan, ability to manage the political economy at the national level is very highly constrained and circumscribed by an inherited weakness of the physical and social infrastructure, as well as by overdependence on the industrialized countries. It is perhaps a truism to say that the degree to which managers of national economies successfully reduce external dependence, while at the same time increasing African interdependence, will determine the pace of progress toward achieving the African Economic Community, as envisaged in the Lagos Plan.

THE PROBLEMATIQUE OF PLANNING

No examination of economic management in each of the major sectors of the economy covered by the Lagos Plan will be meaningful without beginning with a consideration of three of the plan's injunctions: first, that there ought to be national development plans based on a commitment to national and collective self-reliance and self-sustaining development; second, that such plans should have short-, medium- and long-term goals that should be "integrated at the sub-regional, regional, and continental levels"; and third, that there should be institutional arrangements in place "for the implementation, continuous evaluation and monitoring of the (national) plan, both at macro as well as sectoral levels, to ensure proper co-ordination and to avoid undue duplication of efforts and resources." The Lagos Plan, in this regard, lays emphasis on "manpower, technology and financial planning" and on "comprehensive statistical data and information on population and natural resources as a basis for effective policy-making and planning."

Finally, the Lagos Plan informs the African countries that "institutional arrangements for the implementation, continuous evaluation and monitoring of the Plan at both macro as well as sectoral levels should be clearly specified and developed and existing ones strengthened, to ensure proper co-ordination," etc. Obviously this applies both to the national plans and the subregional, regional, and continental commitments that evolve from the process of integration.

It is fair to say that most African countries do not possess the adequate capability to plan and to monitor the performance of a national plan, much less possess the institutional framework for the monitoring of the performance of regional integration. The task of ensuring consistency among sectoral, macro, and micro planning is an extremely exacting assignment. A theoretical exercise can be most harmful because it almost inevitably leads to much greater distortion in the use of resources than would be the case under the operations of the real market, within certain broadly planned parameters.

Without developing adequate capability for data collection and evaluation -- on which the Lagos Plan lays particular emphasis -- planning an economy can be dangerously ambitious. It has often been said that "to plan is to choose." The obvious choice -- that of planning the capability to plan as *the* priority -- has been rarely made. It is true that it was first necessary to develop sectoral priorities. However, depending on a rigid framework, based on a theoretical exercise of reconciling macroeconomic targets (including overall GNP growth) with sectoral targets, in the absence of data on available manpower, infrastructure, productivity, weather conditions, world market prices, external resources, and entrepreneurial and managerial capacity, has often led to inflexibility in responding to rapidly changing, exogenous factors. Also, too many unforeseen consequences related to the interaction of internal factors have arisen from wholly inadequate data and its evaluation. In the end, this has meant a waste of scarce resources.

To monitor the performance of a plan based on so many variables and imponderables becomes even more intractable if properly coordinated, self-assessing mechanisms are not built into the decision-making structure at the outset. To mention this need is to underline the magnitude and complexity of managing the economy in many African countries, since a major problem is the inability to take appropriate, corrective action in time, in order to remain on course. To describe, thus, the immensity of the difficulties of planning in an underdeveloped economy is not to decry the importance of planning. It is to suggest that governments need to be extremely realistic and, in the early stages, to remain content with first identifying and then securing the elements that together constitute a critical capacity to plan and monitor performance, while concentrating on certain broad macroeconomic targets, as well as defining the basic socioeconomic principles that will guide the efforts of all sections of the community.

Conditions differ from country to country in so vast and diverse a continent as Africa. Even so, certain basic principles have been accepted by almost all African countries. Self-reliance has been accepted as a fundamental tenet. What has not been done adequately is to interpret this principle in the context of actual conditions prevailing at a particular time. In order to develop the social awareness of the people, it is necessary to equip *local communities* with the capacity for data collection and evaluation, based on the resource potential existing within their own environments. The training of district statisticians, capable of collecting and evaluating data relevant to the sustained development of the population in a given locality (e.g., soil and weather conditions, particular food and agricultural crop suitability, minor irrigation and local energy potentials, etc.), needs to be made a high priority in manpower development. An inventory of locally available manpower including tradesmen and craftsmen, educational and health institutions, economic enterprises in actual operation, known natural resources, etc., would be an essential part of such data. The next stage would be its evaluation with a view to enabling the local community to judge for itself what it could do with its own efforts, and what it was ready to do with the assistance of the national government.

It is the equipping of local authorities with such capacity that will assist in establishing a national data collection and evaluation network. This data will provide reliable information to planners involved in increasingly more comprehensive national planning, based on the fundamental premise of self-reliance. In the absence of such a capacity, it is not surprising that so many projects and programs become influenced disproportionately, either by donor preferences or by urban-based officials, including planners, who can only conceive what they are capable of conceiving given their own personal preferences and prejudices.

The absence of this local capacity shows in the long-term trend of increasing dependence on external factors, leading countries away from taking greater control over their own national potential. It is this situation which, having been unavoidable perhaps for a certain period after achieving political independence, has nevertheless now become manifestly endemic, and it needs to be reversed with resolution and insight.

Without governments being able to set the management of their respective national economies on a path of decreasing external dependence and without their development of the countervailing power to negotiate with external partners on more equal terms, subregional, regional, and continental integration will be an uphill task. It is not suggested that the national process should take priority, in allocation of time, over the regional process. What is essential is to develop regionally integratable priorities based on achievable national capacities. If Africa is to have an economically and politically viable common market, it is essential that national governments give priority to the development of the capacity of their respective local communities first, to collect and evaluate data of immediate relevance to them, and then, to apply the knowledge so as to realize their own potential for sustained economic and social development.

In the next 25 years, management of African economies will increasingly lose ground to internal upheavals and external influences if priority is not given to education and population growth. A national policy which gives the opportunity of an education to every child of six years of age -- and which is aimed at giving an education that realistically prepares the youth to become productive in a predominantly peasant, agricultural environment -- will provide a rich reservoir from which to draw manpower for more specialized and complex management and supervision. As long as the political leadership clearly understands the importance of this issue, it should be possible to avoid the risk of producing too many highly trained citizens, who either cannot be absorbed in the economy or who will form pressure groups demanding the disproportionate allocation of capital and consumer goods, thus contributing to internal imbalance. The long-term consequences of such a situation are all too predictable.

At the same time, African countries can no longer ignore the question of population growth. A 3.5 percent rate of annual growth in population with a 4.5 percent growth in GDP is much less manageable than a 1.5 to 2 percent population growth with a 3.5 to 4 percent rate of economic growth. And of course a 2 percent rate of economic growth with a 2.5 percent rate of growth in population speaks for itself. If sustained over a period of time, the medium- and long-term consequences are quite predictably unwholesome. Other things being equal, a reasonable rate of growth in population of, say, 1.5 percent every year would generate a high rate of economic growth over the long term, because more savings would be available to be reinvested in the economy. Whether one looks at it from the point of view of achieving a higher standard of living, or improving the health of every mother and child, an active population policy is an indispensable socio-economic instrument.

Looking at the subregional, regional, and continental prospects, it must be said that if inflexibility has inflicted a high cost on national economies, then inflexibility at the regional and continental levels will also extract high costs. While it is understandable that the UN system needs to identify groupings of neighboring countries for there to be effective programming from the ECA, it would be a very costly error to assume that these are necessarily natural groupings for the purposes of promoting regional integration. There are geographical, political, and historical realities that need to be accommodated in such a continent-wide endeavor. An artificial regional framework will only contribute to frustrations and costly delays. In the final event, the process has to be a politically motivated, organic affair, with the participants, by definition, propelling themselves towards a point of convergence.

Considering Africa's current progress toward continental economic integration, I am reminded that Africa consists of sovereign states, each of which is a member of the IMF, the World Bank, the GATT, and a number of other international arrangements and institutions spelling out the rights and obligations of their respective constituent members. All of these states are dependent on external technology and capital. In their respective macroeconomic and sectoral planning exercises, they incorporate such commitments as they have with these international institutions, as well as the bilateral commitments they have with donors, lenders, and investors. The assumptions behind such contractual obligations are not necessarily aimed at reducing overdependence on external elements, nor are they based on compliance with the disciplines involved in coherent and consistent macroeconomic and sectoral planning. The Bretton Woods institutions are predicated on the operation of a market economy and "the rules" to be applied for its "proper" functioning. These institutions, as well as most of the donors, lenders, and investors, do not have any abiding faith in a comprehensively planned economy. For the most part, they promote their national or commercial interests by selecting particular projects. In addition, countries with planned economies that have relations with African countries are not impressed by the capacity and capability of most African countries to devise coherent macroeconomic and sectoral planning and continuously to evaluate actual performance.

As we move from the comprehensive objectives of the Lagos Plan to the task of the actual identification, mobilization, and allocation of available resources within the confines of national economies -- in a manner which reconciles both national and regional claims on those resources -- the extremely limited range of options available to the managers of the respective national economies becomes all too clear. To refer to the African economy in general, as though the various African states had comparable political, social, and economic frameworks, managerial capability, resource endowment, geopolitical entanglement, historical legacy, access to sea, etc., is not very helpful. All this is not a plea for perfection. It is necessary to view realistically the environment in which policy advisers are expected to assist policy-makers in devising actual programs capable of implementation within the overall context of the Lagos Plan. The fact that subregional, regional, and continental institutional frameworks, as they exist, are more mechanistic than organically rooted makes the task ahead a most challenging one.

As I examine the implications of subregional and regional cooperation and integration for sound economic management, the significance of this issue will perhaps become clear.

REGIONALISM RECONSIDERED

The Lagos Plan rightly places food and agriculture on the top of its list of priorities. The technical recommendations relating to food and agriculture, including conservation and storage, soil husbandry, livestock, fisheries, incomes and prices policy, forest development, and the crucial role of research and extension services, are all absolutely relevant. Ministries of food, agriculture, livestock, and forestry development in all member states will not be worthy of their names if they do not incorporate the technical recommendations of the Lagos Plan. Indeed, these recommendations found their place in the plan because they were agreed upon collectively by the member states.

However, when it comes to incorporating these recommendations into any subregional or regional arrangement, the severe limitation of human and material resources becomes of paramount importance. In this context, the significance of the transport sector has been accepted by most governments. And yet, within national plans the priorities accorded to this crucial sector are, for the most part, at the cost of subregional or regional needs. The development of extremely costly transport infrastructures in response to national programs of food and agriculture leaves little surplus capacity to accommodate regional schemes.

For the development of food and agriculture, the Lagos Plan has calculated that, for the period 1980-85, some US$21.4 billion would be needed as a total investment, which would mean an annual investment of US$560 million. It is not clear whether investments in the transport sector, together with recurrent maintenance and amortization costs, have also been taken into account. It would be instructive to know how much of the US$10 billion from external resources as envisaged by the Lagos Plan has actually flowed into African economies. Even more instructive would be the disaggregation of the inflow, in terms of each national economy, as well as how much was actually mobilized from domestic resources. It is also relevant to inquire, when assessing financial requirements of this order, whether manpower was assumed to be in place or whether the amount included training the needed manpower. In the first place, it would be difficult to mobilize external resources without the necessary manpower being available; and second, if finances were made available and allocated to this sector without ensuring the necessary technical, enterpreneurial, and managerial manpower, it would be a waste of a scarce resource.

In any case, we are dealing with peasant societies that are captive to the handhoe and the axe. It is the challenge of making the hoe and the axe as productive as possible, while at the same time transforming these elementary implements into oxen and ploughs and eventually the tractor, that should determine the kind of enterpreneurial and managerial skills as well as field technicians needed. It must also be the challenge of imaginative and creative research scientists and economists, who are committed to carrying out the transformation, even as the hoe and the axe continue to provide both goods for immediate consumption and the surplus for continuous investment.

How does the economic infrastructure, bank credit in particular, harmonize with the program of reaching these target areas? How do the macroeconomic policies and related sector priorities (such as transport) synchronize with programs that aim both at using existing technology and transforming it at the same time? Almost all African countries are involved in various forms of donor-recipient relationships, from downright food aid, year after year, to the provision of rather sophisticated inputs, which tend to marginalize the men and women with the hoe.

Correct foreign exchange cost accounting, with respect to each major user-earner of foreign exchange, would reveal an extremely serious dilemma facing the managers of African economies. Departments of state -- such as those of defense, foreign affairs, internal security, education, health and welfare, judiciary, parliamentary and local government affairs -- all these are users of foreign exchange, which is earned by others, mostly by the efforts of the peasants with the handhoe and the axe. Road building and maintenance consume foreign exchange and so do activities such as water supply, power production and distribution, and mail and telecommunications. While these services are all necessary for the production of goods and services, a disproportionately large, direct consumption of these amenities takes place for purely personal convenience or for maintaining overgrown administrations. Further, the goods produced by the users of these services and inputs (e.g., textiles, sugar, cement-building materials, etc.) are in large part consumed internally, leaving relatively small amounts for export. In such a situation, a marked imbalance of trade is sustained, even when a country can potentially produce enough to meet the basic needs of its whole population. Even after deciding what should be produced, the cost of producing the basic-needs items remains uncompetitively high. The result is that only a small proportion of the minimum needs of the peasant community is actually met out of this production.

The task of devising macroeconomic and sectoral policies requires not only professional competence but political commitment and political leadership in support of such professional management. Regional cooperation and integration requires a widening of the mental horizon of the population involved. Horizons will not widen, indeed they may contract, if regional linkages do not yield tangible benefits because of deficient macroeconomic and sectoral management, which, in turn, receives little help from political leadership.

Obviously, in dealing with food and agriculture, it has not been possible to remain confined to that crucial sector alone. The sectors of transport and industry have had to be considered at the same time. Indeed, in theory, the whole industrial strategy proposed by the Lagos Plan is fully consistent with the input factors implied and explicit in a correct policy for developing food and agriculture, which at the same time safeguards the essential elements of a basic-needs strategy. But again, policymakers need to address themselves to the all-important question of setting a priority within priorities. The point does not need to be labored that sustained social transformation in Africa, as elsewhere, will only be possible through industrialization. All the areas of concern covered by the Lagos Plan -- that is to say, natural resources, human resource development and utilization, science and technology, transport and communications, trade and finance, environment, and the strengthening of institutional frameworks for effective regional cooperation -- have to be given due attention with a view to successfully developing food and agriculture and industry.

A major lesson learned in the past 20 years of managing African economies is that, more often than not, governments have failed to take into account the recurrent costs arising from a particular project or program commitment. This is especially true when it comes to assessing, at the point of decision-making, the recurrent foreign exchange cost of a particular project or program upon completion. The rapid, indeed dramatic, inflation in the 1970s has of course not helped African governments at all. But the fact remains that there has not been built into government practice the discipline of calculating the actual recurrent burden that is being undertaken when a particular project or program is approved for implementation. This applies not only to tangible programs and projects, such as roads, schools, hospitals, and specialized institutes, but also to decisions to expand existing government departments or to add new ones. The cost of this failure has been incalculable, not only in terms of money, but even more, in terms of making the journey towards the goal of a sustained, self-reliant economy infinitely longer and more difficult.

No management of a typical, underdeveloped African economy can bring about transformation without producing investable surplus from within the economy, augmented by capital resources from outside. The external resources need to be utilized on two distinct planes: (1) for altogether concessional investments to develop physical and social infrastructure, especially transport and communications, schools and training institutions, as well as the rural health and water supply, and (2) for investments aimed at expanding and improving food and agricultural production, exploitation of natural resources, and industrialization, starting from simple and expanding to more complex technology. However, the key element is the internal balance between production and consumption. While external resources may assist in bridging short-term gaps, they will not be available to meet long-term deficits in consumption needs. If planning is deficient or too ambitious to be implemented and monitored, if goals are disproportionately weighted in terms of consumption rather than production, if consumption is inequitably distributed, and if there is a refusal to make evaluations within a reasonable period of time, it will not be possible to lay a dependable foundation for regional cooperation and integration.

As we have seen, the question of whether the US$10 billion investment for the food and agriculture sector from external resources was actually secured is as important as whether the money was directed toward priorities determined by the reality of a predominantly peasant economy. Indeed, the former has to be a function of the latter, and not the other way around. The domestic component of the five-year investment program -- equal to another US$10 billion -- can only be provided by way of surplus, from the use of the handhoe and the axe for the most part. This is the dilemma and the challenge.

The next question that needs to be asked is whether the Lagos Plan target of Africa achieving 1.4 percent of world industrial output by the year 1990 is based on an appropriate development strategy for food and agriculture and the attendant technological environment. Does it incorporate a progressive organic transformation along the path indicated? If not, are we not straying from the path that leads toward a self-sustained, self-reliant economy and going in the direction of still greater dependence?

Whatever applies to industry applies also to transport and communication, to energy development, to science and technology, and to human resource development. In each of these crucial areas, the same questions need to be asked. Do the programs and projects strengthen self-reliant efforts in the field of food and agriculture, and are they consistent with an industrial strategy that is oriented towards technology within the reach of the majority of peasants and workers? While a certain type of technology may be bypassed by developing countries, for the most part it is imperative that African countries adapt the technology already tried and found productive elsewhere at a time in history (be it 30, 50, or 70 years ago) when it made sense to the society that used it. In other words, any attempt to take a shortcut is bound to make the journey even longer. Only when sufficient momentum is generated through a process of organic growth will it be possible for African industry to pick and choose technology from available options. But again, this crucial choice can only be exercised optimally by those in Africa whose credentials in the field of science and technology will have evolved from their own intimate association and identification with Africa. Such a choice cannot be exercised by armchair scientists.

Particular mention needs to be made of energy. There is still an inadequate realization of the serious implications for national economies of failure on the part of policy-makers to look carefully at this sector. While a considerable amount of time is spent on debating the issue at various regional and subregional forums, the fact remains that there is as yet little sign of an active national policy that applies to all users and potential users of energy. There is no way that costly, capital-intensive hydrocarbons can replace wood fuel resources, which are being increasingly depleted. In fact, technology and consumption patterns based on hydrocarbons need to undergo major adjustment, so as to reduce dependence on them. Unless government policies force every user and potential user to begin to depend on clearly identified forms of energy other than hydrocarbons, and to take the necessary measures to conserve and develop such alternatives, economic growth will be seriously retarded. Again, for the most part, a correct policy will mean involving a large section of the population through specially devised programs of education and training, so as to meet clearly identified targets of a national energy program.

CONCLUSION: SECTORS, SCIENTISTS, AND SAVINGS

To conclude, then, the managers of African economies would do well to take a very serious look at the Lagos Plan of Action. All the values and areas of emphasis contained in this historical document are most relevant. They are indeed fundamental. However, the political component of the management of African unity is of decisive significance. Unless the professional and scientific community of Africa is able to rely on a firm, enlightened political leadership -- committed to the strategy of providing basic needs for the majority by equipping them with the capacity to be productive and to earn surpluses to be invested in furtherance of a basic needs strategy -- managing the African economy will not only be devoid of social purpose, it also could lead to social tensions.

And members of the professional and scientific community too must realize that no political leadership will be able to ignore the needs of the majority for an indefinite period of time. Priority must be given to education, vocational training, and training on the job for tasks to be performed in the service of local communities, as well as for larger interests. These tasks include food self-sufficiency, the development of agriculture as a springboard for industrial development, and the maintenance of a steady momentum towards regional and continental integration. The professional and scientific community needs to show its full understanding of these socio-economic and political objectives and make its maximum contribution, as a privileged minority possessing immense potential for promoting swift development.

With the best intentions, achieving these goals will be an arduous task, in a world environment that is weighted heavily in favor of those who possess the capital, technology, and capacity to influence markets to serve their own interests. The balance will remain tilted against the underdeveloped countries for a considerable period of time. The all-too-familiar problems of managing any economy combined with external factors will tend to erode whatever little surplus is accumulated by African countries. This being so, international assistance from progressive societies will become even more valuable in the future than it is now.

The cost to Africa of investing in the Lagos Plan for the next 20 years can be calculated in a number of ways, depending on the strategy of development chosen by African countries. Capital needed could be as low as US$200 billion if reliance is placed fully--as it should be--on domestic resources to meet the recurrent costs of operations and maintenance and to produce some surplus for reinvestment. The amount could be as much as US$400 billion, not taking into account how recurrent costs would be met. Such a projection, in all likelihood, will have a stultifying effect and thus effectively prolong the journey towards a self-reliant, self-sustaining economy and a continental economic community.

The implications of one external orientation are more than just quantitative; they are qualitative. Assistance from friendly, progressive, and farsighted societies is much more likely to be forthcoming if planning and managing the economy is aimed, in quite specific terms, at developing a self-reliant society, and if those responsible for managing the economy command the confidence of the people. It is the people who are, after all, the true partners in the process of self-development. In the final analysis, it is in retaining their confidence and in sustaining their spirit of self-reliance -- to work for a better future in the direction of a common destiny --that the price of managing the African economy lies.

Ibrahim H. El-Issawy

8 The Aid Relationship and Self-Reliant Development in Africa

The purpose of this chapter is twofold: (1) to discuss the implications of current trends in foreign aid flows and policies for the goal of self-reliant development in Africa; and (2) to explore the conditions that must be satisfied by foreign aid and the national and international environments that determine the aid relationship if foreign aid is to contribute positively to the attainment of self-reliant and self-sustained development.

I begin with a brief discussion of Africa's development crisis and the credibility of the Lagos Plan of Action (LPA) in view of the systematically poor performance of the continent in the four or five years since the plan's formal adoption. In spite of major differences of opinion as to the primary causes and the best way out of the crisis, there appears to be a fair measure of agreement on the need for substantial outside assistance in order to help Africa reverse current tendencies towards stagnation and deterioration. Given the well-established association between foreign aid and dependency-promoting policies and practices, it appears legitimate to enquire whether there is a place for foreign aid in self-reliance-based development, and if so, to specify the nature of its role in a self-reliant framework. It also seems worthwhile to examine current trends in the volume and composition of aid, as well as in the aid relationship. In conclusion, I present a number of ideas for maximizing the supportive role of foreign aid in self-reliant development and minimizing its negative influence on the continent's independence and sovereignty.

AFRICA'S DEVELOPMENT CRISIS, THE LAGOS PLAN OF ACTION, AND FOREIGN AID

The year 1980 witnessed an event of great historical significance: the adoption by the OAU of the LPA. African leaders were able, perhaps for the first time, to elaborate and commit themselves, in unambiguous terms, to a unified strategy reflecting their own understanding of the causes of their problems and their own prescription for the collective salvation of their continent. The same year witnessed the onset of a global recession which turned out to be the "deepest recession of the post-war period."[1] The past four or five years have been a time of tremendous strains and stresses for the Third World; its growth in 1983 was "slower than in any year since World War II."[2] African countries in general, and those of Sub-Saharan Africa in particular, were especially hard hit. Since 1980, Africa has been "going from one economic and social crisis to another, which in the last year (1983) has become so grave as to threaten the very survival of the continent."[3]

Some Facts

Africa's rate of growth of output per capital went down from -1.7 percent in 1980 to -3.0 percent in 1982 and -3.1 percent in 1983. Food output per capita registered negative rates of growth in both 1981 and 1983 (-2.0 percent and -2.9 percent respectively; the rate for 1982 was a mere +0.6 percent). The rate of growth of manufacturing output per capita was very small and disappointing in comparison with the Lima target of +9 percent (+0.6 percent in 1981, +0.7 percent in 1982 and -2.6 percent in 1983). Exports declined in real terms at the rate of 2.4 percent in 1982--though a positive rate of growth was expected for 1983 (2.9 percent)--and the terms of trade have declined by about 30 percent since 1970. Africa's external debt is currently estimated at US$150 billion, which is about 20 percent of the external debt of all developing countries, compared to less than 12 percent in 1973. It represents 223.5 percent of Africa's exports, compared to 70 percent in 1973 and 78 percent in 1980. The debt service ratio has also risen from 8.8 percent in 1973 to 25 percent at present.[4] Distressing as these statistics may be, it must be emphasized that they are but very imperfect and inadequate measures of Africa's escalating economic and social crisis, which is having a devastating impact on the continent's fragile economies and on the African peoples' very modest standards of living.[5]

Causes of Crisis

By all accounts, the continental crisis did not arise suddenly. Economic development has been sluggish in most African countries during the past two decades, and the signs of an escalating crisis became apparent as of the mid-1970s. Indeed, increasing awareness of long-term stagnation was the major reason for initiating the activities that led to the formulation and adoption of the LPA.

The list of possible causes of the crisis is well known. It includes three major sets of causes, namely (1) adverse ecological conditions, including not only the prolonged drought and rapidly spreading desertification, but also other natural disasters such as earthquakes and volcanic eruptions; (2) deteriorating international economic conditions and the prolonged recession in the North; and (3) inappropriate domestic policies in most African countries. The fact that this list may be accepted by most students of Africa's development crisis does not mean, however, that there is general agreement on the diagnosis. As a matter of fact, views differ substantially regarding the interpretation of each of the causes just listed and the weight attached to each. Moreover, these differences can be traced back to diametrically opposed views on the origins of the malfunctioning of the world capitalist system and the growing disarray in the international trade, monetary, and financial systems, as well as on the primary causes of Africa's underdevelopment. Clearly, conflicting views on these issues lead to divergent views concerning the ways and means of surmounting Africa's development crisis, as can be easily ascertained from a comparative study of, for example, the OAU's LPA and the World Bank's Agenda for Action.[6]

This is not the place for a detailed review and evaluation of strategies for the development of Africa; the lines of debate are clear and have already been thoroughly reviewed.[7] But it may be appropriate to make a number of points regarding this issue to establish the general intellectual framework for considering the question of foreign aid.

General Framework

My point of departure is that the failure of Africa to achieve respectable rates of growth on a sustainable basis is due to the fact that "African countries still remain, by and large, the most 'satellitized' and exploited countries coerced into the periphery of the global economic system."[8] Together with other Third World countries, African countries are economically and technologically "locked into the economies of the North and into the maze of international economic relations which are controlled by the North."[9] African countries are the dependent and powerless victims of an international economy based not on genuine interdependence, but on unequal exchange and major structural inequities in North-South economic relations.

Under these circumstances, the obvious task for African countries is to make a clear break from their "colonial dependent economic inheritance with a production structure heavily dominated by export-oriented agriculture and with a small industrial base, fractured and only minimally linked with the region's natural resource base, with mining output being predominantly for export, and with the most open and exposed economy in the world."[10]

An agriculture-based and export-crop-oriented strategy, including devaluation, reduction of import controls and greater reliance on the market mechanism and private enterprise, would only exacerbate Africa's problems, since it would perpetuate its disadvantaged, dependent position in the world economic order and tighten the grip of transnational conglomerates on the continent's destiny. To help African countries swallow this medicine by calling for a doubling, in real terms, of foreign aid (by the end of the 1980s) can only confirm the widespread belief that foreign aid is being used as an instrument for "system maintenance."

Africa's development crisis cannot be treated as if it were a problem of economic management based on well-ordered national systems and a proper international economic environment. In fact, this seems to be the assumption underlying most foreign aid programs. As one scholar put it:

"Both bilateral and multilateral aid programmes were premised on one fundamental assumption: that external assistance can play a positive and effective role in fostering development in LDCs within their existing political systems and the international economic order."[11] Of course, no fair observer can deny that there are various aspects of economic mismanagement, corruption, etc., in all African countries. But the contribution of these aspects to Africa's development crisis is relatively marginal, and in any case closely linked with the dependency issue. This is because dependency cannot persist in the absence of internal social structures, power relations, and ruling elites who favor its perpetuation.

It is my belief that the patterns of power distribution prevalent in most African countries provide ample support to the dependency relations of their countries. The industrialized countries and their transnational corporations do their best to exercise all sorts of pressures and temptations (including foreign aid) to keep this balance of power undisturbed. International organizations, such as the World Bank and the IMF, have a crucial role to play in this process. As a study of IMF stabilization programs has shown: "It is no accident that in the widely varying conditions of Peru under progressive military rule, post-fascist Portugal, and People's National Party (PNP)-led Jamaica, the political result of IMF stabilization programs has been the same: the discrediting of processes of social and economic restructuring aimed at improving the lot of the deprived majorities and the strengthening of the position of the conservative opposition to the governments and to the personalities who have attempted to implement these processes."[12]

The unfavorable world economic environment, therefore, cannot be narrowly interpreted to mean the recent recession. It includes a wide range of aid, and economic, financial, technological, and military policies and instruments used by the industrial capitalist countries to maintain and preserve the world capitalist order, to ensure that Third World countries will continue to play a marginal and dependent role in the international division of labor, and to shift a good part of the burden of global crises onto the shoulders of the Third World. It is important to note that the recent recession is but an integral part of a global structural crisis of the world capitalist system which was triggered in the late 1960s, and became manifest throughout the 1970s.[13]

Likewise, inappropriate domestic policies in Africa, cannot be narrowly interpreted to mean economic mismanagement. They should be broadly understood as inappropriate orientation of development strategies enforced by socio-economic groups and ruling minorities who are "tied up" with dependency relations. No program for accelerated development can succeed in Africa unless it strikes at the heart of the prevailing system of subjugation and exploitation, both nationally and globally. The struggle for a New International Economic Order (NIEO) must go hand in hand with the struggle for politically and economically equitable systems at home.

As the LPA pointed out, Africa "cannot wait for the New International Economic Order to arrive. It must help create it."[14] But how can Africa help create a NIEO except through the national and collective efforts of the African countries to restructure their political and economic systems and to reorient their regional and international political and economic relations? Such restructuring and reorientation must be attempted in a way that enables African countries: (1) to smash dependency relationships and achieve political and economic liberation; (2) to gain control over their natural resources; (3) to bring their production structures in line with the basic human needs of the African peoples; (4) to internalize the sources of growth and hence ensure its sustainability; (5) to eradicate poverty and ensure an equitable distribution of the benefits of growth; and (5) to participate on an equitable basis in international decision-making processes. Such are the objectives and goals of the LPA!

The recent economic and social crisis in Africa has not shaken the confidence of African leaders in the LPA. On the contrary, at every opportunity they have reaffirmed their confidence in and commitment to both the philosophy and objectives of the LPA.[15] The trouble, however, is not with the willingness of African governments to declare their commitment to the LPA, but with the political will to follow such declarations with the sort of policies necessary for the implementation of the objectives of the LPA. In this regard, the record is disappointing. As a recent ECA report has noted: "In general, there are hardly any encouraging signs that the necessary policy reorientation in individual member states is being vigorously undertaken."[16]

More Aid

It is interesting to note that in spite of conflicting views on the fundamental causes of the crisis and ways of dealing with it, there is a wide measure of agreement over the inadequacy of current aid levels to Africa and the need for considerable increases in them if the continent is to overcome not only its current crisis but also generate the necessary momentum for self-sustaining growth.

The LPA clearly states that to implement the plan, "the region shall need aid, investment and technical assistance from all parts of the world." Moreover, the achievement of the objectives of the LPA--"requires having recourse to massive external resources which represent an essential contribution."[17] An ECA perspective study also found that, although the implementation of the LPA would lead to "a substantial reduction of the trade gap as a proportion of GDP,...domestic efforts will undoubtedly need to be supplemented by external assistance and aid."[18] Finally, African ministers responsible for economic development and planning have recently stressed Africa's need for "increased and sustained international support, not only on an emergency basis but also on medium- and long-term bases."[19]

On the other hand, the World Bank maintains that a "profound commitment is necessary from the international community--a commitment to increase aid and to provide assistance in ways more suitable to Africa's needs than in the past...." More specifically, the World Bank has called upon the international community to double net disbursements of ODA to Africa in real terms by the end of the 1980s, since "policy reform without substantially increased aid...does not provide a satisfactory solution."[20]

Finally, with regard to food aid, a recent study has shown that current levels of such aid fall considerably short of the desirable targets, and has urged the international community to increase food aid immediately "to help low-income developing countries, particularly in Africa, to meet acute food import needs and help relieve balance-of-payments crises."[21]

This agreement on the need for more aid by the LPA and its official supporters as well as by the World Bank (which, incidentally, claims that its Agenda for Action took as its point of departure the "long-term objectives of African development as expressed in the Lagos Plan of Action")[22] is rather curious. It raises important questions about the need for and place of external assistance in self-reliant development strategies.

THE PLACE OF FOREIGN AID IN A SELF-RELIANT STRATEGY FOR AFRICAN DEVELOPMENT

Foreign aid, particularly bilateral aid, was not originally designed to help Third World countries achieve economic and political independence and establish conditions conducive to self-reliant development. Historical evidence suggests that, in general, benevolence has not been a major motive in the aid process and that foreign aid has not been politically neutral. Rather, aid has frequently been used by donors as a means of exerting political leverage over recipients, for creating or strengthening economic, political, and military relations beneficial to the donors, and for supporting conservative socio-economic groups and unpopular ruling elites who are willing to furnish domestic conditions favoring the preservation of those relations.

In view of the foregoing, it seems appropriate to ask: Is it legitimate to seek foreign aid while raising the banner of self-reliance? Is foreign aid compatible with the pursuance of self-reliant development, and, if so, under what conditions? What kind of role can foreign aid play in a self-reliant development strategy?

The Question of Legitimacy

First of all, let us be quite clear about the question of legitimacy. When African countries ask for aid from the North, they are neither begging nor requesting something that they are not entitled to obtain. African countries, like all other Third World countries, have a historical right to a transfer of resources from the North, even in the form of outright grants. Moreover, this historical right to assistance remains valid irrespective of the manner in which such aid may be utilized by the recipients and independent of the domestic and external policies that the latter may pursue.

The *LPA* was quite right when it asserted that external assistance "should come to a large extent and above all from the developed countries, which owe some of their present wealth in large measure to the exploitation of the African continent. In this connection, the massive transfer of resources to the African continent must take the form either of grants or of soft loans."[23] The industrialized capitalist countries should not overlook the fact that they are responsible for the appalling conditions that Africa experiences today, on account of both their colonial policies in the past and their neocolonial practices at present. As a recent African document noted with regard to the problem of indebtedness: "The industrialized countries share the responsibility for the Third World indebtedness, which results in part from historical circumstances and in part from the developed countries shifting to the developing countries of an excessive share of adjusting to the world economic crisis."[24]

In addition to Africa's historical right to aid, other arguments can be advanced to justify Africa's need for substantially augmented flows. Suffice it to note here what the World Bank has had to say on this point. The Bank gave five reasons for the required increase in foreign aid to Africa:

(1) "the continent contains many of the poorest and most vulnerable people in the world"; (2) "Africa's medium term prospects for growth are worse than those of any region"; (2)" Africa is even less well situated to take advantage of the growth of world trade"; (4) "Africa remains highly dependent on concessional capital (aid) because of limited creditworthiness"; and (5) "increased aid together with policy reform holds the promise of a highly fruitful investment which will be able to accelerate growth during the 1980s."[25]

Aid and the Aid Relationship

In addition to the obvious need for aid in meeting emergency situations, aid could serve a number of useful functions, particularly during the difficult phases of policy reorientation. As the World Bank put it: "Outside help is necessary to lubricate the process of change and of policy adjustment, to finance new departures, and to help African governments soften the effects of change on groups that fear losses of income [namely, in the event the World Bank implements its policy package] such as urban consumers."[26] Aid could increase the size of the development effort beyond what would otherwise be possible without running into severe problems of inflation and unmanageable balance of payments deficits.

Note, however, that none of these benefits is guaranteed; they may be completely negated or reversed by a host of frequently debated negative aspects of foreign aid. For instance, aid may diminish the attention that is urgently required to increase domestic savings. It could support inappropriate consumption habits and encourage the adoption of inappropriate technologies. Certain types of aid, specifically food aid, may have a distinctive effect on domestic agriculture and food production. Above all else, aid may lead to the entrenchment of those socio-economic groups that oppose structural reform, redistribution policies, and dependency-reducing measures.

Again, this is not the place for a detailed commentary on the pros and cons of foreign aid; there is no shortage of such commentaries.[27] What is important to emphasize is that the trouble with foreign aid does not lie in aid as such, but in the set of relationships that arise from granting and accepting aid, i.e., the aid relationship. Depending on the donor's position in the international division of labor and its global economic, strategic, and political interests, and also depending on the recipient's socio-economic orientation, the extent to which its economy is exposed to external influences, and the degree of its reliance on external assistance, aid may give rise to a set of donor-recipient relationships that either support self-reliant growth or intensify dependency relationships.

If the donor is committed to the preservation and expansion of a particular social system, aid will naturally be used as an instrument for system maintenance and for expanding the sphere of influence of that system. If commercial and business interests of the donor press for the opening up of external markets and for outside opportunities for investment, the donor will obviously use aid to protect those interests (e.g., through aid tying) and furnish a more hospitable environment for them in the recipient country. Furthermore, if the recipient is heavily dependent on foreign aid and is not willing to pursue vigorous policies to increase domestic savings and restrict nonessential imports and the consumption of the affluent minorities, there will be little room for maneuverability in dealing with donor conditions. If the social framework into which aid funds flow is characterized by structural inequities that favor the rich, the benefits from aid-supported projects and programs will not reach the poor.[28] Finally, the recipient is less likely to negotiate the terms of aid and more likely to be subject to externally imposed policies when it faces the donor individually, with little bargaining power and without the collective strength that could emerge from cooperation with other Third World countries.

Self-Reliance Aid Support

It is grafitying to note that African leaders have defined the role of foreign aid in a way that is compatible with the goal of self-reliance. As stated in the LPA:

1. Outside contributions are "supplements to our efforts and cannot be substitutes."[29] Thus while asking for increased and improved aid, African governments have frequently emphasized that "the burden of developing our economies...rests with our governments and our people."[30]

2. Outside contributions "must be supplements genuinely relevant and substantially meaningful in terms of the purposes and programs the member states have collectively resolved to pursue."[31]

3. There should be no trade-off between foreign aid on the one hand, and national sovereignty and freedom of decision-making on the other hand. "It is [therefore] not the region's intent to make the approval of the outside world a condition of what it does or how it does it for the African peoples, African countries, and the African region."[32]

However, the real challenge for African countries is to bring their policies and actions in line with these principles. African countries must abandon the traditional attitude towards foreign aid, namely, "any aid is better than none," no matter what strings are attached. They have to demonstrate to the rest of the world that the era of excessive reliance on aid is being terminated and that their plans will no longer stand or fall depending on the flow of foreign aid. Africa must show, through drastic reorientation of national and external policies, as well as through the collective efforts of its governments and peoples, that it will no longer accept the role of the dependent, exploited, and powerless victim in the international economic order, no matter what the amount of foreign aid may be. In short, African countries have got to turn the philosophy and objectives of the LPA into tangible actions at the national and regional levels; otherwise, aid will not support, and may in fact subvert, all attempts at development based on the principles of national and collective self-reliance.

The Promise of Aid

We must never forget that the promise of increased foreign aid to Africa is conditional upon the acceptance by African countries of a particular policy package that is considered appropriate by major donors and the international organizations subject to their control. This is clearly expressed in the World Bank Agenda for Action: "The increased aid and related technical assistance recommended in this Report can only be mobilized if they support deliberate and well-formulated programs to reverse the downward trend of development in Africa."[33] Such programs are obviously those that reflect the policies recommended by the World Bank (and the IMF); they would exacerbate rather than alleviate the African crisis by their failure to strike at the heart of Africa's predicament, namely its dependent and peripheral situation in the world economic order.

In addition to the technical arguments against these policies, experience has shown that such policies have often been unpopular and, as the World Bank puts it, "politically thorny."[34] Because these policies normally shift a disproportionate share of the burden of adjustment onto the shoulders of the poor and yet leave their needs unmet, they are not easy to introduce through normal democratic procedures. They have, therefore, been enforced in the countries that adopted them at the expense of civil liberties and human rights.[35]

Foreign aid plays a cardinal role in enforcing the policies favored by donors in at least two ways. First, to ensure that reform programs are formulated in line with recommended policies, donors are called upon (by the World Bank) to assist African recipients in undertaking the required policy analyses. In so doing, they "can help governments, both directly and indirectly, formulate macro and sectoral action programs."[36] This type of aid is traditionally favored by donors because it is "amenable to continuous review and assessment of precise costs and benefits," and leads to "concrete and tangible results." More importantly, "it facilitates a special link between donor and recipient in a particular sector, enabling the provision of goods and services for the project by the donor country."[38] In contrast, recipients have often found project lending rather restrictive, inflexible, and costly (because it affords great scope for aid tying). Moreover, it provides donors with ample opportunities to create an influential presence in the recipient country and to make specific interventions in its economic affairs, including choice of projects. Clearly, the promise of augmented aid is fraught with a significant reduction in the "number of degrees of freedom" available to aid recipients.

To conclude, African countries committed to implementing a development strategy based on the principle of national and collective self-reliance should recognize that traditional aid relationships are likely to encroach upon their sovereign rights of decision-making and may therefore hamper their efforts to carry out such a strategy. They must be well-prepared, therefore, for the alternatives, including not only aid taps being turned off by traditional donors, but also of other forms of retaliation, including economic embargoes and military action. True, other donors may be willing to fill the aid gap, namely the socialist countries. But it must be emphasized that the three principles expressed by the LPA regarding self-reliance-aid support should be equally applicable to both capitalist and socialist donors. Strict adherence to these principles, while pursuing equitable growth nationally and joint plans and policies regionally, is the only guarantee for minimizing the possible conflict between the aid relationship and the pursuance of self-reliant development.

CURRENT TRENDS IN FOREIGN AID AND THEIR IMPLICATIONS FOR SELF-RELIANT DEVELOPMENT

Volume and Sources of Aid

According to the 1983-84 edition of World Bank World Debt Tables, disbursements from bilateral and multilateral sources to the countries of Sub-Saharan Africa (SSA) declined from US$9.18 billion in 1980 to US$8.12 and US$8.10 billion in 1981 and 1982, respectively. Since debt service payments have been absorbing an increasing proportion of disbursements, net transfers declined much faster than disbursements. The deterioration in disbursements and net transfers was much worse for the low-income countries of Africa (LIA), as the figures in table 8.1 clearly demonstrate. Many small countries in SSA had to reschedule their external debt to official creditors through the Paris Club, and some had to conclude debt-relief agreements with creditor commercial banks at the expense of an increase in service charges and reduced creditworthiness. These developments must be seen against a general background in which "almost as many developing countries have had to reschedule loans in the last two years as in the previous twenty-five years."[39]

As for official development assistance (ODA) to developing countries as a whole, a decline of about 5 percent in real terms was registered between 1980 and 1981. Although ODA increased by 70 percent during the 1970s, most of the increase occurred during the first half of the decade, owing to the sharp increase in OPEC contributions (from a mere 5 percent in 1970 to 30 percent in 1975). ODA grew at a slower rate in the second half of the 1970s and did in fact decline in some years, i.e., 1975-77. OPEC's share declined to 25 percent in 1980 and 22 percent in 1981. Overall, ODA's share in total net resource flows to developing countries has been fluctuating around one-third during the 1978-81 period (1978, 33 percent; 1979, 36 percent; 1980, 38 percent; 1981, 34 percent).[40]

Only four countries had been able to surpass the 0.7 percent ODA-GNP target by 1982, namely, Denmark (0.77 percent), Norway (1.01 percent), Sweden (1.02 percent), and the Netherlands (1.08 percent). However, the total share of these countries in total ODA was no more than 9.2 percent in 1982. Altogether, DAC countries contributed 0.39 percent of their GNP in 1982, and their share in total ODA amounted to 72 percent in 1981. In contrast, OPEC countries contributed 1.46 percent of their GNP, and their share in ODA was 22 percent in 1981. Impressive ODA-GNP ratios were attained by some OPEC countries in that year, e.g., Kuwait (1.98 percent), UAE (2.88 percent), and Saudi Arabia (4.77 percent). Finally, the socialist CMEA countries contributed around 6 percent of total ODA, and their ODA-GNP ratio was 0.14 percent in 1981.

Net disbursements of ODA to Africa have been declining throughout the 1979-83 period as is shown below (in billion U.S. dollars):[41]

1979	1980	1981	1983
5.9	4.9	3.5	3.3

Although the ratio of concessional loans to disbursed debts rose between 1980 and 1982 (from 38 percent to 39 percent for SSA and from 51.4 percent to 54.7 percent for LIA), it appears to have experienced

Table 8.1

Resource transfers to African countries, 1973-82

	Sub-Saharan Africa				Low Income Africa			
	1973	1980	1981	1982	1973	1980	1981	1982
Disbursements (billion US dollars)	2.165	9.178	8.120	8.099	0.985	3.762	3.117	2.496
Rate of change in disbursements			-12%	- 1%			-18%	-20%
Debt service payments as percentage of disbursements	53.8%	43.3%	50.3%	64.6%	35.6%	28.0%	30.4%	43.5%
Net transfers (billion US dollars)	0.999	5.200	4.032	2.865	0.635	2.708	2.171	1.410
Rate of change in net transfers			-23%	-29%			-20%	-35%

Source: World Bank, World Debt Tables, External Debt of Developing Countries (Washington, D.C., 1984), 6-9 and 26-29.

Notes: Net transfers = disbursements-debt service payments (including both interest and principal repayments).

Dollars = U.S. dollars.

The number of countries included in SSA is 41, of which 24 were classified as low-income countries because their GNP per capita was less than 410 dollars in 1981. *Ibid.*, pp. xxvii-xxxii.

a sharp decline when compared with its 1973 level (SSA, 47.2 percent; LIA, 58.3 percent). These developments reflect the increasing "privatization" of financial flows to Africa during the last decade, i.e., the significantly increased reliance of African countries on the international financial market for nonofficial, nonconcessionary flows. This phenomenon can be further illustrated by the rising share in SSA's disbursed debt of loans that carry variable interest rates (i.e., interest rates that float with movements in key financial markets) from 8.8 percent in 1973 to 19.2 percent in 1980, and 21.4 percent in 1982. As for LIA, this share has been declining from 7.4 percent in 1973 to 5.4 percent in 1982, owing to substantial reductions in creditworthiness.[42]

The region's capacity to develop was dealt a severe blow by these unfavorable developments in external resource transfers. Their effects were compounded by the fact that they occurred at a time when many African countries were suffering not only from drastic declines in their export earnings and sharp increases in the burdens of debt servicing, but also from a severe and protracted drought as well as a number of other natural disasters with social and economic consequences that have been extremely tragic. Emergency situations developed in many countries, which had to be dealt with promptly at the expense of upsetting medium-term plans and relegating long-term plans, whether the plans were made for self-reliant or traditional development. Apart from the increased cost of external resources resulting from the increasing reliance on international financial markets, the increasing privatization of financial flows to Africa meant further integration into a world economic order that consistently discriminates against African countries. Instead of progressively delinking from this dependency-promoting system, many African countries have found their links considerably tightened in recent years. This is obviously a condition which renders future attempts at national and collective self-reliance more difficult.

Composition of ODA

The multilateral component of donor ODA has been persistently declining in relative terms in recent years (see chapter 7). Donor contributions to multilateral institutions have declined from 32 percent to 23 percent of donor ODA between 1978 and 1981.[43] This situation has been causing serious difficulties for these institutions both in negotiating their replenishment programs and in reconciling growing demands for multilateral aid with their tight budgets. The trend towards reduced multilaterism (which means increased bilateralism) is fraught with dangers for self-reliant development. Although multilateral institutions are not completely free agents in the aid field--they are, in fact, controlled to varying degrees particularly by major donors--multilateralism does ensure some degree of detachment of aid relationships from commercial, security, and political relationships. This is very important for countries with self-reliant-development plans because it broadens the range of economic and technical options available to these countries. Given current practices in bilateral aid (e.g., aid tying, emphasis on project aid, etc.), increased bilateralization of ODA is bound to narrow the already limited range of choices for using foreign aid to support self-reliant development. This danger is quite serious in view of the fact that a substantial portion of ODA is controlled by a handful of major donors.[44]

An important characteristic of ODA is its large portion designated as food and technical aid, and this portion appears to have been rising in recent years. This trend serves the interests of donors rather than recipients, as donors may determine the composition of ODA, as will be explained below.

The share for food in total ODA rose from 8.9 percent in 1973 to 11.4 percent in 1981, although it was as high as 21 percent in 1960-62. In contrast to the downward trend in the percentage of total ODA channelled through multilateral institutions, the percentage of multilateral contribution to total food aid rose from 16.2 percent in 1973 to 21.4 percent in 1981, although it was 33 percent in 1960-62. The fact remains, however, that the bulk of food aid is disbursed on a bilateral basis. Note also that the proportion of grants in total food aid declined from 68.2 percent in 1978 to 66 percent in 1981.[45]

Food aid is a convenient form of aid from the viewpoint of many donors. It serves as a useful avenue for the disposal of surplus food output, and its actual cost is usually far below what is recorded in aid agreements. Food aid is not bad in itself. Its usefulness from the viewpoint of self-reliant development is predicated, however, on a number of conditions similar to those discussed in the previous section regarding foreign aid in general. It is believed that most of these conditions are absent in most African food aid relationships. Given serious food deficits, African countries tend to be passive recipients of food aid, with little or no say in the determination of its contents and terms.[46] Given also the predominantly bilateral nature of food aid, it is easily employed in these circumstances to mobilize support for donor foreign policies, to impose certain economic policies that help strengthen certain types of socio-economic relationships in line with the requirements of global system maintenance, and to foster donor-recipient dependency. This argument should not detract, however, from the importance of food aid in meeting present emergency situations in many African countries.

Like food aid, technical assistance is also a form of aid much favored by the industrialized countries. It accounted for some 25 percent of DAC's bilateral aid in 1980.[47] Technical assistance draws upon resources that are relatively abundant in the industrialized countries. Its cost is often overrated by donors. More importantly, technical aid serves as an effective mechanism for the marketing of technologies and all sorts of goods and services that may not be appropriate from the recipient viewpoint.

Given the specific circumstances surrounding the disbursement of technical assistance (mostly bilateral, mostly tied to the donor's country, and not infrequently regarded as a component of capital projects with goods and services procured from the donor country), it is believed, in general, that this form of aid militates against self-reliant development in many ways. Technical assistance increases cultural dependence and weakens self-confidence--a factor of crucial significance for the initiation and continuation of self-reliant-development efforts. Technical assistance helps to propagate development concepts and to popularize economic theories that are favorable to the expansion of the transnationals and the preservation of the existing world economic order. It is a vehicle for the universalization of Western culture and life-styles, whereas self-reliant development presupposes cultural diversity and respects and adapts to traditional values and modes of life. In fact, it could be argued that a certain measure of calculated insulation from external cultural influences is necessary, at least in the early stage of self-reliant development. Again this general conclusion should not detract from the usefulness of carefully selected types of well-designed technical aid programs for the formation of skills and the improvement of scientific and technological capabilities of recipients, even in present circumstances.

Terms and Conditions

Table 8.2 shows changes in the average terms of Africa's official external debt (i.e., debts owed to official creditors including governments and international organizations) over the past decade. All indicators clearly point to the hardening of terms of borrowing for both SSA and LIA. Compared to 1973, in 1983 there was a marked increase in interest rates on the one hand, and a reduction in average maturity, grace period, and grant element on the other hand. Some improvement is observed, however, between 1980 and 1982 in all indicators except the interest rate.

Table 8.2

Average terms of borrowing from official sources, 1973-1982

Region	Interest (%)	Maturity (years)	Grace period (years)	Grant element (%)
SSA				
1973	2.8	29.1	8.0	55.3
1980	3.7	25.3	6.6	45.7
1982	4.4	28.7	6.9	43.8
LIA				
1973	1.5	33.3	8.5	66.7
1980	2.6	27.6	6.9	53.5
1982	2.8	31.8	7.6	56.5

Source: World Bank, World Debt Tables, External Debt of Developing Countries, 1983-84 edition, (Washington, D.C., 1984), 6 and 26.

Note: The average terms of borrowing for a given year relate to all new loans contracted during that year. The grant element is the grant equivalent of a loan as a percentage of its commitment value. The grant equivalent of a loan is the difference between its commitment value and the (discounted) present value of its contractual debt service. As a measure of the concessionality of a loan, it is believed that the grant element tends to be overestimated by the choice of the discount rate and also because of the inflated cost of borrowing that results from the tying of aid.

As previously noted, aid tying and project aid continue to be distinct features of ODA. It is reported that over 50 percent of ODA is still tied to procurement from the donor countries and that at least 55 percent takes the form of project aid.[48] Reference has already been made to the World Bank's recommendation that project aid should continue to be "the major channel of donor financial assistance to Africa." These two factors may obviously lead to economic and technological choices that are not consistent with the philosophy of self-reliance. Indeed, they may reinforce the same economic and technological biases that characterize outward-oriented dependent development.

More alarming, however, is the increasing insistence on the part of donors that particular economic reforms be implemented in recipient African countries. As noted earlier, the World Bank has made it quite clear that increased aid to African countries is predicated on the acceptance of its recommendations for policy reform. Moreover, donors are blamed for Africa's poor development record and for the persistence of "inappropriate policies" and "unsuitable project concepts," precisely because they have not insisted to a sufficient extent on the domestic policy changes deemed necessary for the success of aid-supported projects and programs.[49] Finally, more coordination among donors with respect not only to "aid procedures" but also to "project selection and aid allocations" is considered to be desirable by the World Bank, notwithstanding its awareness that the latter type of coordination arouses suspicions of donors "ganging up" and fears of "loss of maneuverability" on the part of recipients.[50] Such suspicions and fears, however, are not groundless, particularly regarding coordination of aid policy among bilateral donors, which could very well lead to excessive donor pressures on recipients to adopt projects and policies that are not compatible with self-reliance.

Donor Motivations

It seems appropriate to conclude this section with a few remarks concerning recent trends in donor motivations. Donors appear to be attaching increasing importance to aid serving to promote their commercial and business interests. This is reflected in their growing insistence on aid tying and project aid, the diminishing of donor contributions to multilateral institutions, and the rising share of food and technical aid in total ODA. It is also reflected in the growing expectations of a slow-down or a partial reversal of the movement toward giving greater ODA allocations to the low-income developing countries and especially to the least developed among them.[51]

This movement to help low-income countries, however, has been grossly exaggerated for two reasons. First, the higher share in ODA going to the low-income countries was relative to a stagnant ODA total, so that the real increase involved may not have been as great as widely publicized. And second, the shift in favor of low-income countries occurred at a time when donor contributions to multilateral institutions declined--a change that has been disadvantageous to the low-income countries.[52] Note also that the slight shift in aid allocations in favor of the low-income countries applies on the average to donor countries. It does not necessarily apply to all donors or even to the major donors. In this connection, it is of interest to note that the claim of a shift in favor of the low-income countries in U.S. bilateral aid allocation has been seriously challenged.[53]

Whatever gains may have resulted from this shift in aid distribution are at present in danger of being wiped out, as donors redirect ODA to middle-income developing countries, in search of greater benefits for donor business and commercial communities.

The implications of these donor motivations to self-reliant development are precisely those already discussed in relation to the consequences of changes in aid policies and practices; namely, resurgence of bilateralism, emphasis on aid tying, project aid, etc.

TOWARD AID RELATIONSHIPS IN SUPPORT OF SELF-RELIANT DEVELOPMENT

As shown in the previous section, aid policies governing the bulk of ODA (over 90 percent), which originate in the advanced capitalist countries and in the OPEC countries and which pursue by and large liberal market economy policies, are primarily designed to serve donor national and global interests. Foreign aid is used, as a rule, to maintain the status quo of a global economic order, which is impeding progress in Third World countries, and to support the ruling classes, who keep their economies open to the transnationals and resist redistribution of power in favor of the supporters of self-reliance. Recent developments in aid policies clearly indicate that these deplorable features are being reinforced, notwithstanding donor claims to the contrary.

As noted earlier, the promise of increased aid to Africa is an integral part of an elaborate program of economic reform that donors may cease to support, leading to further economic and social deterioration. Even so, from the recipient and self-reliant perspectives, implementation of such a reform could only exacerbate Africa's problems and perpetuate its peripheral position in the world economy. If current trends in aid relations continue, along with an unfavorable international division of labor and submissive Third World attitudes, there is a real danger that attempts at self-reliant development will either fail or turn into isolationistic autarky.

Proposals for Aid Reform

There is no shortage of proposals for increasing aid flows and improving aid quality. L. de Silva was able to compile no less than 27 sets of recommendations aiming at improving ODA alone.[54] They include proposals for subsidizing interest rates on loans to developing countries, international taxation and other suggestions for achieving ODA autonomy, utilization of IMF gold holdings, establishment of an SDR-development financing link, inclusion of an ODA element in primary exports stabilization schemes, debt relief as ODA, restriction of ODA disbursements to countries pursuing poverty-alleviating policies, etc. A variety of aid-related recommendations can also be found in a recent Special Memorandum by the ECA Conference of Ministers, as well as in the Addis Ababa Declaration on Africa's external debt.[55] Further discussion may also generate many suggestions for the amendment of available reform proposals and for the addition of new ones. But, given the abundance of unimplemented proposals for aid reform, it seems more appropriate to discuss the conditions under which existing proposals can be translated into aid policies and practices.

As would be expected, the implementation of many of the current proposals for aid reform presupposes a change of climate on a worldwide scale. Acceptance of these proposals requires the emergence of an international spirit, particularly in the donor countries, favoring the establishment of a more equitable international economic order. However, in view of the failure of North-South dialogue and given African countries' decision (expressed in LPA) not to wait for a NIEO to arrive, there seems to be no choice but to start at home, i.e., at Africa's national, subregional, regional, and continental levels. In any case, it should be clear that no amount of improved foreign aid can by itself eradicate poverty, hunger, and unemployment. Nor can it transform a country's development orientation from outward and dependent to internalized and self-reliant. The initiative and impetus for such a transformation can only originate from within the developing country concerned.

African countries have no choice but to reorient their national development policies and plans along the lines of national and collective self-reliance expounded in the LPA. The failure of Africa's economic performance to match the expectations raised by the LPA and by the repeated declarations of commitment to this plan by African governments should give no cause for despair. After all, the lesson to be drawn from Africa's experience since the adoption of the LPA is quite clear and must not be overlooked: the political stage has not been prepared for the drastic changes in development thinking expressed by the LPA. The obvious task for the peoples of Africa is to remove the political hurdles that block the road to self-reliant development. This involves a political struggle aimed at the redistribution of political and economic power currently held by the socio-economic elite, who are tied into dependency relationships, to those who suffer from the perpetuation of these relationships, i.e., the majority of the people.

Given such a redistribution of power, African countries can then begin to reshape their development policies and their development effort to be consistent with the philosophy and objectives of the LPA. While continuing to insist on their historical right to a massive transfer of resources from the developed capitalist countries, African countries should:

1. demonstrate to the outside world, both capitalist and socialist, that foreign aid is only supplementary to domestic efforts, and that their planning will no longer be at the mercy of aid donors;
2. be quite vigilant as to the content and terms of foreign aid and extremely selective in keeping with the philosophy, methods, and objectives of self-reliance; and
3. plan on a much reduced volume of foreign aid, and prepare contingency plans to handle situations where foreign aid is sharply reduced or completely suspended.

To hedge against such contingencies, there is no viable alternative to foreign aid but African self-help, cooperation, and collective self-reliance. Coordination and integration of development efforts among African countries is an absolutely necessary condition in a continent with a large number of small countries that "do not have the critical mass nor the economy of scale to survive by themselves."[56] African cooperation, undertaken in the wider framework of South-South cooperation, is in fact an essential prerequisite for a change in the global economic status quo in favor of the marginalized and exploited South. Through a series of cooperative activities undertaken by African countries, Africa can gradually build up its missing countervailing power vis-à-vis the North, which would be highly instrumental in reorienting aid policies in support of self-reliant development. For how "can the North take the South seriously unless the South gives some tangible proofs of its commitment to a minimum of cohesion, coherence and solidarity"?[57]

African cooperation, however, ought to be perceived and designed not merely as a defensive or offensive mechanism vis-à-vis the North, but also as a permanent feature of the strategy for economic liberation of the continent and as a necessary activity towards the full realization of its potential. African cooperation is desirable, no matter what the external environment is like. It is, as President Nyerere put it, "through self-reliance and organized cooperation on a South-South basis (that) we can--even in the existing adverse economic circumstances--promote our own declared national objectives."[58]

As for the developed countries, they ought to recognize their responsibility for the plight of more African countries by virtue of past colonial policies and current neocolonial practices. They must acknowledge the validity and genuineness of African and other Third World countries' historical right to aid, before the debt problem of these countries turns into an unmanageable problem with unpredictable consequences for world peace and stability. They must work towards a historical settlement of world debts, i.e., a settlement that recognizes the forced debts that the developed countries owe to the developing countries. Perhaps more important, developed countries ought to admit that African countries are mature enough to decide for themselves what economic policies seem best for getting their economies on the path of self-sustained growth.

But how can such changes in concepts and attitudes take place in the donor countries except when (1) the South demonstrates, through systematic collective action, that it has to be taken seriously by the North, and (2) public opinion in the North presses hard for a shift in donor-recipient relationships away from their one-sided traditional path? This brings me to the responsibility of intellectuals, developmentalists, and sympathizers with the Third World in the North. As the experience of the "successful donor countries" has shown, "an articulate and vocal domestic constituency in favour of ODA is an extremely important factor in ensuring a dynamic program. General public opinion in most rich countries does not attach great significance to the issue (ODA), partly because it is not presented with the facts."[59]

It is the responsibility of intellectuals in the North to see to it that their general public is not misled by groundless and empty slogans that have nothing to do with actual aid policies. Public opinion in the North ought to get the following facts right:

1. that every nation has an indisputable right to choose, without outside pressure, its own path to development, and that such a path need not be similar to the path chosen by the developed countries under completely different historical circumstances;
2. that the North owes the South a considerable debt, and that a substantial part of the North's wealth and affluence has been obtained at the expense of exploitation and marginalization of

the South;
3. that the countries of the South have a historical right to aid, no matter what development policies they may pursue;
4. that foreign aid is not "a purely one-way flow of resources, providing 'benefits' to 'recipients' through 'sacrifices' on the part of 'donors'";[60] foreign aid must be demystified and ODA balance sheets must be correctly presented to the public;
5. that the current tendency on the part of donors to overemphasize short-term trade and commercial benefits of ODA policies is in the long-run counterproductive and detrimental to the establishment of healthy North-South relationships and world peace; and
6. that large sums of foreign aid are used by their governments to reinforce the obstacles that impede progress of Third World countries towards self-reliant and self-sustained development, e.g., military assistance to entrench elite-dominated and repressive regimes, donor-aided corporate interventions in Third World countries, which reinforce opposition to redistribution of power and control over the use of resources in favor of the masses, etc.

What Africa needs from public opinion in the North, much more urgently than improved ODA, is sympathetic understanding of its problems, greater appreciation of the specificity of its conditions, and increased awareness that in the long run both North and South will benefit from a change in the world economic order, which initially compensates African and other Third World countries for the historical loss of a substantial part of their economic surplus.

To conclude, it is only when all parties in the aid process recognize their responsibilities in the manner expounded above, and act accordingly, that the world can begin to experience aid relationships that effectively support self-reliant development in Africa and the rest of the Third World.

NOTES

1. See the statement of IMF Managing Director J. de Larosiere in IMF Survey, 4 June 1984, pp. 172-3.

2. World Bank, World Debt Tables, External Debt of Developing Countries, 1983-84 edition (Washington, D.C., 1984), p. vii. According to the World Bank Annual Report, 1983, the rate of growth of GDP per capita was -0.1 percent in both 1981 and 1982, compared to 2.7 percent in 1973-80 and 3.5 percent in 1960-73, for all developing countries, p. 27.

3. See the statement delivered by ECA Executive Secretary at the UN ECOSOC Conference, Geneva, July 1984, Adebayo Adedeji, The African Economic and Social Crisis: an agenda for action by Africa and the international community (Addis Ababa: ECA, Sept. 1984), p. 2.

4. The statistics in this paragraph are quoted or derived from: Ibid., pp. 3-4; ECA, Special Memorandum by the ECA Conference of Ministers on Africa's Economic and Social Crisis, (E/ECA/CM. 10/37/Rev.2) 1984, p. 40; World Bank, World Debt Tables; and World Bank Annual Report, 1983 (Washington: World Bank, 1983), p. 29.

5. Note also that the multiplier effect on African economies of the recession in the industrialized countries is considerable and much bigger than is commonly believed. See H.W. Singer, "North-South Multipliers," World Development, 11 (5) (May 1983): 451-454.

6. World Bank, Accelerated Development in Sub-Saharan Africa: an agenda for action (Washington: World Bank, 1981).

7. For a comparison of the LPA and Agenda for Action, see North-South Institute, "Africa's Economic Crisis, Briefing" (Ottawa, Feb.-May 1983); and the Arab Bank for Economic Development in Africa, Africa's Development Strategies between Lagos Plan of Action and the World Bank's Agenda for Action (Jan.-May 1983).

8. See Adebayo Adedeji, "Introduction" to ECA, 25 Years of Service to African Development and Integration (Addis Ababa: ECA, 1983), p. 5.

9. Julius K. Nyerere, "South-South Option, The 1982 Third World Lecture," IFDA Dossier 31 (September-October 1982): 65-66.

10. Adedeji, "Introduction," p. 15.

11. Ozay Mehmet, Economic Planning and Social Justice in Developing Countries (London: Croom Helm, 1978), p.260.

12. Norman Girvan, "Swallowing the IMF Medicine in the Seventies," Development Dialogue, 2 (1980): 73.

13. See "Strategies for the Future Africa: an Outline of a Research Programme Directed by Samir Amin," IFDA Dossier, 20 (November-December 1980): 2.

14. All references to LPA in this paper are based on ECA, Plan of Action for the Implementation of the Monrovia Strategy for the Economic Development of Africa, (E/CN. 14/781/Add. 1), p. 14.

15. See ECA, "Special Memorandum by the ECA Conference of Ministers," p. 29.

16. ECA, Biennial Report of the Executive Secretary, 1982-1983, (E/ECA/CM. 10/11) (February 1984), p. x. The report notes, however, that "significant progress was made in the biennium in implementation of the requirements of the Final Act." See p. x. As President Nyerere observed in 1982, "our different countries have still not faced up to the need to change the emphasis of our development planning," "South-South Option," p. 70. See also "Strategies for the Future of Africa," pp. 74-75, where it was observed that "no preparations have been made" for the implementation of self-reliant endogenous development.

17. ECA, Plan of Action for the Implementation of the Monrovia Strategy, p. 4 and p. 5 respectively.

18. ECA, ECA and Africa's Development, 1983-2008; a preliminary perspective study (Addis Ababa: ECA, 1983), p. 84.

19. ECA, Special Memorandum on the ECA Conference, p. 8. See also pp. 15, 21, and 29. (Emphasis by author.)

20. World Bank, Accelerated Development in Sub-Saharan Africa, pp. 121-123.

21. Hans Singer (with S.J. Maxwell), "Development through Food: Twenty Years Experience," in Report of the World Food Programme/ Government of the Netherlands Seminar on Food Aid (The Hague, October 1983), p. 39. (Emphasis by author.)

22. World Bank, Accelerated Development in Sub-Saharan Africa, p. v.

23. ECA, Plan of Action for the Implementation of the Monrovia Strategy, pp. 5-6.

24. ECA, Special Memorandum by the ECA Conference of Ministers, p. 46. According to IMF Managing Director J. de Larosiere, "every percentage point on international interest rates adds US$4 billion a year to the cost of servicing their (i.e., the developing countries') external debt." See IMF Survey, May 21, 1984. Needless to say, such a rise in interest rates is an integral part of the industrialized countries' policies to combat domestic inflation.

25. World Bank, Accelerated Development in Sub-Saharan Africa, pp. 121-122.

26. Ibid., p. 123. (Emphasis added by author.)

27. See, for instance, the recent publication by the Third World Forum in cooperation with the UN Non-Governmental Liaison Service Geneva: L. de Silva, Development Aid: A Guide to Facts and Issues (1983), chap. 3.

28. See the two interesting case studies of food aid to Ethiopia and Bangladesh in Report of the World Food Programme, pp. 93-100 and pp. 179-190.

29. ECA, Plan of Action for the Implementation of the Monrovia Strategy, p. 4.

30. ECA, Special Memorandum by the ECA Conference of Ministers, p. 29. See also p. 35. (Emphasis by author.)

31. ECA, Plan of Action for the Implementation of the Monrovia Strategy, p. 4.

32. Ibid., p. 4.

33. World Bank, Accelerated Development in Sub-Saharan Africa, pp. 132-133. See also p. 8. (Emphasis by author.)

34. Ibid., p. 133. On the criticisms levelled against the Bank's Agenda, see North-South Institute, A Balance Sheet, p. 7. On the irrelevance of IMF-supported policies, see I.S. Abdalla, "The Inadequacy and Loss of Legitimacy of the International Monetary Fund," Development Dialogue 2 (1980): 25-47.

35. See Girvan, "Swallowing the IMF Medicine in the Seventies." See also the very interesting quotations on this issue from the Congressional Record in A.G. Frank, "Some Limitations of NIC Export-Led Growth from a World Perspective," IFDA Dossier 33 (January-February 1983): 82-85.

36. World Bank, Accelerated Development in Sub-Saharan Africa, p. 124.

37. Ibid., p. 125.

38. Quotations in this sentence and the previous one are from de Silva, Development Aid, pp. 10-11.

39. World Bank, Annual Report 1983 (Washington: World Bank, 1983), p. 34.

40. Figures in this and the following paragraphs are derived from Ibid., p. 33 and de Silva, Development Aid, pp. 42-43, and p. 66.

41. The 1979 and 1980 figures are taken from the World Bank, Accelerated Development in Sub-Saharan Africa, p. 123. The 1981 and 1983 figures are taken from ECA, Special Memorandum by the ECA Conference of Ministers, p. 10.

42. World Bank, World Debt Tables, p. 7 and p. 27. On the privatization issue, see de Silva, Development Aid, p. 39 and ECA, Special Memorandum by the ECA Conference of Ministers, p. 10. Note also that the share of private creditors in the outstanding debt (including undisbursed debts) of SSA has risen from 31.3 percent in 1973 to 39.4 percent in 1982.

Within this debt category, the share of financial markets has risen from 48.7 percent in 1973 to 86.7 percent in 1982 for SSA, and from 47.9 percent to 71.3 percent for LIA, according to the World Debt Tables, p. 6 and p. 26.

43. de Silva, Development Aid, p. 45.

44. In 1981, five industrialized countries (namely the U.S.A., West Germany, U.K., France, and Japan) accounted for about 50 percent of ODA.

45. The statistics quoted in this paragraph are from Report of the World Food Programme, p. 33 and p. 43.

46. de Silva, Development Aid, p. 17.

47. As the North-South Institute put it, "all studies of donor behavior in food aid have documented the predominance of 'surplus disposal' over 'need' in the determination of the types, levels and conditions of food distribution programmes." Moreover, an inverse relationship was found between global need (as reflected in rising food prices) and food aid supplied by all donors, including Canada. See North-South Institute, "A Balance Sheet of Third World-Canada Relations," IFDA Dossier 10 (August 1979): 1-14.

48. de Silva, Development Aid, p. 50. The proportion of ODA in the form of project aid goes up to 70 percent if the 15 percent sectoral aid is treated as project aid.

49. See World Bank, Accelerated Development in Sub-Saharan Africa, p. 121. See L. Kleemeier, "Domestic Policies Versus Poverty-Oriented Foreign Assistance in Tanzania," Journal of Development Studies 20 (2) (January 1984), where it is argued that poverty-alleviating foreign assistance in the form of rural development projects has failed because Tanzania did not pursue the domestic policies deemed necessary for the success of those projects.

50. World Bank, Accelerated Development in Sub-Saharan Africa, p. 130. See also, de Silva, Development Aid, pp. 55-56, on the case for and the case against donor coordination.

51. Such expectations apply even to some donors with reasonably good reputations such as Canada, as is shown in the North-South Institute study: "A Balance Sheet of Third World-Canada Relations," pp. 12-13.

52. See de Silva, Development Aid, p. 46 and p. 50. According to this source, 22 percent of DAC's ODA was targeted towards the least developed countries in 1980 , as compared with 16 percent in 1974. Yet, DAC's allocations of ODA to the least developed countries falls short of the UN target of 0.15 percent of donor GNP (the DAC percentage is 0.08 percent).

53. This challenge is based on an analysis of U.S. aid in 1980, which showed that "U.S. bilateral assistance is highly concentrated on a few countries, with 10 countries receiving well over half of the total. Israel and Egypt receive a full 40 percent. Of the top 10 recipients, only 4 are considered low income. Among the top 10 are the governments of Indonesia, the Philippines and Bangladesh. In each of these countries vast increases in foreign assistance in the last decade have gone hand in hand with the increasing impoverishment and repression of the majority of the people." See F.M. Lappe, J. Collins and D. Kinley, "Aid that Doesn't," IFDA Dossier 20 (November-December 1980): 117.

54. de Silva, Development Aid, chap. 7.

55. ECA, Special Memorandum by the ECA Conference of Ministers, pp. 21-28.

56. Mahdi Elmandjra, "South-South Cooperation: A Peaceful Decolonization of the Future," IFDA Dossier 38 (November-December 1983): 52.

57. Ibid., p. 52.

58. Nyerere, "South-South Options," (Emphasis added by author), p. 71.

59. de Silva, Development Aid, p. 45.

60. North-South Institute, "A Balance Sheet of Third World-Canada Relations," p. 6.

Robert S. Browne

9 International Resource Mobilization for the *Lagos Plan of Action*: ADB and Self-Finance

Africa's leadership has realized that the weakening of the linkages that nurture Africa's dependence is a sine qua non for their continent achieving the sustained economic growth and the peership with the developed countries that a meaningful "interdependence" genuinely calls for. The Lagos Plan of Action (LPA)[1] sets forth the strategy of self-reliance by which these linkages may be relaxed. This is a collective strategy, which means that the leadership must begin to focus on the continent as well as on the nation-state.

Global interdependence has a parallel at the local level, especially in Africa, where the well-being of most countries is highly affected by what is happening in neighboring countries. For countries to be responsive to this phenomenon, the lesson of Pan-Africanism must be learned and internalized by all Africans--possibly a difficult task for many Africans whose loyalties have traditionally been narrower even than the nation-state. But if the experience of the past decade has illustrated any truth about development, it is that African problems can only be addressed effectively on a supranational basis. The fact that this perspective is gaining acceptance in Africa is especially gratifying to American blacks. Pan-Africanism comes naturally to black Americans. We can never know exactly from what part of Africa our ancestors came. Consequently, our African nationalism, our emotional ties, are to the continent as a whole, not to any particular nation. It is comforting indeed to note that economic reality has pushed Pan-Africanism to the forefront of the African struggle for economic independence.

Paradoxically, the LPA, a program designed to minimize Africa's dependence, calls initially for increased assistance from others as a prerequisite for eliminating such assistance altogether. Self-reliance--the basic objective of the *LPA*--is achievable only after a period of reliance on others. Most industrialized nations have passed through a similar cycle, having been capital importers, or debtor nations, for prolonged periods before they achieved a level of development wherein net external assistance was no longer necessary for them. The *LPA* recognizes that Africa will require a continuation, and indeed the augmentation, of its present flow of resources from abroad for some years into the future. But the *LPA* prescribes a strategy that is specifically designed to eliminate, ultimately, the need for this external flow.

Despite its continental focus, however, the *LPA* must be implemented mainly at the national level. There are, of course, a host of vital regional and multinational entities, programs, and projects that constitute the core of the self-reliance strategy. Their effectiveness will be a major determinant of the success of the *LPA*. But underpinning every multinational effort, there must be solid national support from the member nations involved. Until the African nations begin to perceive their economies as parts of a larger, collective system, the *LPA* cannot be applied as a viable strategy. This observation has particular relevance with regard to the mobilization of internal and external resources. In this chapter I will consider the availability of both domestic, or internal, resources and of foreign resources that might be enlisted in support of the *LPA*, and attempt to draw some conclusions that might help to serve as guides to policy formulation in this area.

MOBILIZING INTERNAL RESOURCES

The *LPA* must be implemented by each and every African country. There is no supranational entity that can implement projects within countries, select cadres, plant crops, market produce, issue currency, or incur debt. Nor are these tasks foreigners should do. They are the responsibilities of national governments and of private citizens functioning within the nationally constituted framework. The choice of tasks to be performed and the method of carrying them out, however, may have significant implications for the *LPA*, and it is therefore important that each African country, in formulating and implementing its own national plans, take full account of how its efforts fit into the larger picture. This, in itself, can constitute a first step toward resource mobilization because it can lead to significant economizing in the use of scarce resources. If complementarity rather than competitiveness with neighboring economies is to be encouraged, if wasteful duplication of facilities is to be avoided, if optimally sized installations are to be constructed, and if other similar economies are to be realized, then the first step must be a coordination and harmonization of national economic activities within regions. The *LPA* offers many suggestions in this regard, including the development of intra-African trade, the substitution of local goods and local foods for imports, replacing of foreign technicians by an indigenous cadre, and the abandoning of European lifestyles in favor of more traditional customs. Such suggestions are, of course, easily made but are implemented only with considerable difficulty.

A demonstration of vigorous support for the *LPA* by African countries is absolutely essential for the successful mobilization of large amounts of external resources for the *LPA*. Although none of the industrialized powers has expressed any opposition to the Lagos Plan, this absence of verbal opposition does not mean that they support it. In Washington, for example, the LPA is not given much attention in official circles. One can attribute this to the urgency of Africa's immediate needs, such as emergency food relief, refugee problems, debt-servicing requirements, and to the current fascination with policy reforms and expanded conditionalities. An equally likely explanation for ignoring the Lagos Plan, however, is the absence of any significant pressure from Africa demanding support for the LPA.

Furthermore, the LPA's objective of reducing Africa's dependency and directing the continent's efforts toward the development of internal rather than external markets is not viewed with equanimity in all quarters of the industrialized world. Consequently, the developed nations might perceive the LPA as threatening to their African supply of raw materials, as well as to their markets in Africa for manufactured goods. The LPA implies a drastic revision in the existing international division of labor, which may not suit the plans of the industrialized nations.

The prospect of Third World countries assuming control over the disposition of their resources has historically provoked consternation. Who can forget the strident calls for Washington to invade the Middle East and take over its oil fields when OPEC first began to flex its muscles? And as recently as last year, the U.S. representative at the UN stated that "We must take careful reckoning of a sinister aspect of the policies of many developing countries--I refer to their efforts to achieve full state control of their natural resources...in complete disregard of our own interests....We might be unable to satisfy in full our requirements of strategic raw materials and of others essential to the prosperity and welfare of our people."[2]

Clearly, the effective implementation of the LPA would create some problems for the industrialized nations, which have anticipated quite a different role for Africa to play in the global economy. Although in the long run a self-reliant Africa can become a valued trading partner for the industrialized nations, both for imports and for exports, the terms of this trade relationship are expected to be more equitable under the LPA scenario, so there will be some costs imposed on those developed countries that are currently extracting disproportionally large benefits from African trade.

Thus, it is not surprising that the developed nations have not rushed to embrace the Lagos Plan; it is therefore mandatory that Africans mount a major initiative to win support for it. Such an initiative must begin at home, where both leadership and popular support must be mobilized under the LPA banner. The amount of support that can be garnered abroad for the LPA will be gained in direct proportion to the amount of support the LPA has at home; so, the first step toward mobilizing external resources is to mobilize internal support. This entails African governments and institutions drumming up popular support and taking concrete actions that are unambiguous steps in the direction of LPA implementation. The mobilization of domestic savings for private investment, of course, would be highly useful in this regard but can probably not be relied upon as a major source of funds in many African countries because extensive savings may not be present. In some countries, however, it may be possible to tease out a substantial volume of investment capital that may currently be in hiding or housed outside the continent.

For undertakings requiring large amounts of resources, however, Africa has no institution better suited to facilitate the task of resource mobilization for the LPA than the African Development Bank (ADB). As a continent-wide organization, controlled by Africans and with a relatively substantial capitalization, it is admirably suited to channel financial resources toward activities that support the LPA and to encourage other donors and lenders to do likewise. The ADB group (which consists of the African Development Bank, the African Development Fund, and the Nigerian Trust Fund) is presently lending at a rate approaching US$1 billion per year, which represents about 7.5 percent of official development assistance (ODA) for Africa. Disbursements are, of course, considerably less, owing to the lengthy delay that generally ensues between the commitment of a loan and the widespread implementation of a project.

The importance of the ADB for the LPA does not rest upon the magnitude of ADB loans, however, nor even upon the considerable additional monies that ADB attracts via cofinancing many of its loans, i.e., bringing in funds from other lenders to supplement those of the ADB. The real promise of the ADB lies in the manner in which it proposes to utilize its resources.

In a highly significant speech delivered at the twentieth anniversary meeting of the ADB governors in Tunis in May 1984, ADB president Wila Mung'Omba set forth the program for the ADB's next two decades.[3] The thrust of this program foreshadows a commitment to the achievement of the goals of the LPA. A seminar on the future role of the ADB provided much of the focus for this anniversary meeting, and an ADB paper set forth in greater detail the program that Mung'Omba was proposing. This paper recommends a lending program that will be supportive of LPA in meaningful ways.

In his address, President Mung'Omba spoke of the next two to three years as a period of transition at the African Development Bank, during which time priority would be given to food security and to project rehabilitation. After this transitional period, the bank's program will stress: (1) alternatives to project lending; (2) multinational projects; (3) support to the private sector; (4) population issues; (5) policy dialogue with member countries; (6) trade promotion; and (7) support to the industrial sector. Indeed, the paper goes on to state that "in adopting these priorities, reference should be made to setting the objectives and developing activities in the context of the Lagos Plan of Action for economic development...."[4]

Three of these ADB priority areas--multinational projects, trade promotion, and industry--can address a major thrust of the LPA in a particularly synergistic fashion: the production and distribution of manufactured goods for a multicountry region. With the ADB taking the leadership in providing financing for such programs, other donor and lender agencies may be persuaded to follow suit; so, the role of the ADB becomes a crucial one in terms of attracting external resources for the Lagos Plan.

MOBILIZING EXTERNAL RESOURCES

The effective implementation of the Lagos Plan will require vast sums of external resources. These resource needs are in addition to those that are necessary just to keep the continent lurching along in its present unsatisfactory condition. Preliminary ECA estimates for 1983 indicate that

Africa experienced a US$13.6 billion deficit on current account, down from US$24.7 billion in 1982. Official net transfers remained steady at US$3.3 billion for both years; net capital transfers fell from US$14.2 billion to US$7.8 billion and the drawdown in reserves declined from US$7.1 billion to US$2.4 billion.[5] These figures must be read with caution, however, because the US$11 billion decline in the current account deficit was achieved by cutting imports by a comparable amount--imports which were, for the most part, essential to Africa's economic growth and development.

The resources necessary for achieving the goals of the LPA probably exceed by far the resources likely to become available under the best of circumstances. I am in no position to estimate either Africa's total resource needs or the sums that it may be able to obtain. It may be useful, however, to examine current trends in development assistance with a view toward identifying resources that might be sought via an effective resource mobilization campaign. (See also previous chapters, i.e., 7 and 8.) The bulk of external resources flowing to Africa will be (1) multilateral, (2) bilateral, or (3) private, including both debt- and equity-type capital. A modest amount will come from voluntary organizations.

When considering multilateral assistance, one almost inevitably thinks of the World Bank and its sister institution, the International Development Association (IDA). These are by far the largest single institutional sources of aid monies for African development (although funds from EEC countries, collectively, are larger). In 1984, they committed in excess of US$3.4 billion in loans to African governments, almost exclusively for the funding of specific projects, which presumably had been requested by the recipient country (although it is possible that the requests had, in some cases, actually been prompted by the donor). IDA, which makes its loans on highly concessional terms and affords priority to the poorer countries, was responsible for US$1.2 billion of this total.[6]

There appears to be a general disposition to allocate about one-third of IDA's resources to Africa in the future,[7] so the actual size of the total IDA resource base becomes the major determinant of the amount available for Africa. The U.S., as the largest contributor to IDA, plays a major role in shaping IDA policy, and in recent years it has drastically reduced its support for IDA, a decision that slashes IDA resources by a multiple of about four, in terms of what other donors would have given if only the U.S. were willing to be more generous. For the period 1985-87, an IDA replenishment of only US$9 billion was agreed to, a 25 percent decrease from the 1981-83 figure of US$12 billion. If the allocation of one-third of IDA resources of Africa is in fact adopted, then the IDA allocation for Africa will presumably run in the neighborhood of US$1 billion annually for the next three years, roughly comparable to the ADB's current level of commitment. Loans from the World Bank totaled US$2.2 billion for Africa in 1984, and while this sum could conceivably be substantially escalated without a new cash levy being required of its members (by a change in the gearing ratio, for example), the World Bank's loans are not particularly attractive to many African nations because their cost is too high.

In 1981, the World Bank released a special study focusing on Africa's development problems. This highly controversial Agenda for Action (popularly known as the Berg Report) placed the principal blame for Africa's desultory economic performance on improper policies being pursued by most African countries. It prescribed a number of policy reforms that African governments needed to institute to rectify the situation and called upon donor nations to increase substantially the resource flow to Africa as a means of helping to persuade African governments to make reforms. To facilitate borrower compliance with policy reforms, a shift away from project lending in favor of "structural adjustment lending" was recommended, with the policy reforms mandated as preconditions for receiving the loans.[8]

In effect, what was being urged was a shift in the World Bank's entire lending program, rendering it more akin to the International Monetary Fund (IMF), which lends to meet balance of payments financing needs, tying its loans to strong "conditionality" requirements that effectively place national economic policy in its hands. IMF lending in Sub-Saharan Africa, which tends to be short-term in nature (generally less than three years) and highly subject to cancellation for noncompliance with IMF-determined policy targets, has increased rapidly in recent years, going from US$161.2 million in 1973 to US$3,987.9 million in 1983 (excluding the Reserve Tranche and the Trust Fund).[9]

As a supplier of resources for implementation of the LPA, the IMF is not likely to be a significant agent. Its role in influencing capital flows, however, can hardly be overstated. Because of its current disposition toward extracting policy reforms from African borrowers as a precondition for obtaining development aid--a movement that may have been sparked by the World Bank's report and that shows signs of being adopted for bilateral as well as multilateral assistance--the "good conduct" cachet of the IMF is becoming a requirement for obtaining significant external assistance from any source, including commercial bank loans and private investment capital.

None of this bodes well for the prospects of obtaining the large sums of resources needed for effective implementation of the Lagos Plan. The IMF's policies in Africa are already under severe criticism because they are often inappropriately tailored to the African situation. The LPA, with its emphasis on self-reliant development, is out of step with the export-oriented World Bank report and is probably viewed with skepticism if not hostility in the major industrialized capitals that set the policies for the IMF and the World Bank. Thus the probability of a sympathetic response to calls for resources to implement the Lagos Plan is not likely to be great, unless considerable effort is made to convince the major powers that support for the LPA is actually in their own self-interest. To make that case will require considerable wizardry, given the fact that the whole purpose of the LPA is to wean Africa from the economic clutches of these same industrialized powers. Can it realistically be in their interests to assist Africa to break free of them?

There would appear to be two types of arguments that Africa might use in this regard: (1) an effectively implemented Lagos Plan offers the best, perhaps the only, prospect for assuring stability in Africa, and (2) an effectively implemented Lagos Plan will produce an economically prosperous Africa, which can offer expanded markets for imports, attractive prospects for foreign investment, and plentiful supplies of raw materials. The first argument, based on political considerations, presumably presents no problems to the African states, who are as eager for continental stability as anyone else. But it is an argument that can be persuasive to donors only insofar as the African states remain united around a common objective. If this unity proves to be easily shattered by a few states succumbing to the blandishments of the great powers and allowing themselves to be split off from the others in return for momentary gain, then the LPA will be stillborn and unable to attract resources. Whether African leadership has matured to the point where such unity is achievable remains to be seen.

The second, or economic, argument is less persuasive than the first. A highly prosperous Africa is clearly in everyone's interest, but a coincidence of interests between a self-reliant Africa and today's great powers cannot be automatically assumed. Indeed, a commitment to satisfy the interests of the capital-surplus nations could effectively nullify the very purpose of the LPA and make the entire exercise futile. Yet within certain limitations and with adequate safeguards, there may be some basis for negotiation of resource transfers within the framework of the second argument.

What is quite clear is that the obtaining of external resources for implementing the LPA will not be easy, and a realistic assessment of these prospects suggests that the most effective strategy may be for Africa to seek multilateral and bilateral assistance primarily for the financing of national programs that make a complementary contribution to the LPA. LPA objectives would be achieved through the intimate coordination of the national development activities of countries within regions, with African resources being utilized to fund appropriate collective and integrative activities.

There are, of course, multinational projects that are capable of attracting external financing, as has been demonstrated by foreign support for some of the projects of the Southern African Development Coordination Conference (SADCC), although even here much of the non-African support has been for projects that are as much national as regional in nature. For the next few years, the competition for the limited pot of money available for Africa is likely to be so intense that there will be few possibilities for convincing donors to fund new initiatives that are not of their own design.

The current trend in foreign economic assistance is strongly toward structural adjustment and sectoral lending, linked to policy reforms. This is true not only at the level of the World Bank, but it is also being considered as a model for future bilateral assistance. The U.S. is a prime example of this trend. Washington has proposed a new program entitled the Economic Policy Initiative, which would set aside US$500 million over five years, to be allocated among a very limited number of African countries who agree to accept Washington's direction in setting policy for the sector in which funds are to be used.[10] Principal emphasis would be on private sector initiatives in agriculture. Although the program was denied funding by the U.S. Congress on its first hearing, it is still being pushed vigorously by the Administration and may well be funded during Reagan's second term.

Meanwhile, Washington appears to be leading an effort to bring about greater coordination and cooperation among all donors to Africa, with policy "conditionalities" standardized to prevent one donor from being played off against another. It will be particularly interesting to note the extent to which this trend is reflected in the Lomé III regime and in future bilateral assistance of EEC countries.

The recent annual meeting of the World Bank (September 1984) recognized the severity of Africa's economic plight and gave its informal endorsement to the idea of a special meeting to be held in the spring of 1985 to explore more intensely how the international community might be of assistance. Meanwhile, a sequel to the World Bank's 1981 report on Africa was released at this annual meeting.[11] This document took a second look at Africa's economic situation, focusing particularly on what had transpired since the 1981 report. Although its conclusions were in large measure reaffirmations of what had been said in the earlier report--namely, that African policies were faulty and needed to be changed and that there was too much public and not enough private sector involvement in African economies--there was also a greater recognition that Africa's problems were not entirely of its own making and that a pure export-led development strategy would not suffice to put Africa on a satisfactory growth path. Particular stress was placed on the urgency of the need for expanded capital flows to Africa and on the gloominess of the outlook if such flows were not forthcoming.

Just before the formal opening of the meeting, the World Bank's policymaking development committee called for the creation of a supplemental fund of US$2 billion for Africa. According to news reports, only Germany and the U.S. were opposed to this proposal, which was clearly an effort to help counteract the disastrous underfunding of IDA-7 and the U.S. shortfall in IDA-6. The U.S. will be pressured to ante up some additional resources, but in turn, the U.S. will battle to see that these resources are made available with strong restrictions on their use. Increased private sector involvement and other policy reforms will be mandated, and the LPA philosophy will almost certainly be ignored unless a major campaign is organized to make the African voice heard.

CONCLUSION

A realistic assessment of the prospects for mobilizing substantial resources for the LPA at the present time must necessarily be pessimistic. The minimum resources needed just for Africa's survival are barely forthcoming and are increasingly made subject to harsher conditionalities, some of which may not be in Africa's best interest and some of which are predicated on the assumption that an export-led development strategy is the only appropriate path for Africa to pursue. The economic philosophies of donor countries, as well as their perceptions of their own self-interest, lead them to favor continuation of the present export-led development strategies for Africa and to be unreceptive to the LPA program of collective self-reliance. Indeed, the very concept of a "collective" Africa, rather than of 50 separate states, may frighten some donor countries. The concept of a collective Africa, however, may be attractive to U.S. private investors, who have heretofore not found Africa to be a particularly attractive arena.

Private foreign investment is a mixed blessing, as we all know, and the LPA is ambiguous in terms of the role that it envisions for such investment. Assuming that Africa does desire to have an inflow of this sort of capital, it can be attracted. However, the terms whereby its availability is acceptable to both parties are likely to require considerable negotiation and may in fact vary from one agreement to another. Regardless of whether such decisions are made on a national or a Pan-African basis, it is virtually mandatory that these terms be worked out and made public if an enlarged flow of such capital is to be forthcoming. The International Finance Corporation (IFC) is beginning to display some interest in Africa and is a capital source worth exploring.

So the search for funds to implement the LPA will require a variety of skills. Unless Africa is perceived as being solidly united behind the Lagos Plan, donor nations will have neither an incentive nor an obligation to take the plan seriously, and they will proceed to undermine it with impunity through the simple act of buying client states with bilateral aid monies. At the same time, as a capital-short area, Africa cannot afford to frighten off potential capital flows, so it must exhibit unity in a non-threatening manner, seeking assistance but accepting it only when its utilization is in harmony with the LPA. The difficulty of attracting external resources highlights the importance of Africa striving to mobilize its domestic resources to the maximum extent possible, although such resources can never entirely take the place of outside help. The China experience demonstrates how difficult it is to develop without external assistance, but it also proves that a great deal can in fact be accomplished if the level of discipline and of sacrifice is sufficiently high. Africa enjoys neither the homogeneity nor the unity of China, so there are obvious limits to applying the Chinese experience of domestic resource mobilization to Africa.

Africa would be well advised to use its internal resources as leverage for gaining external resources. As the only Pan-African institution with significant funding capabilities, the ADB must inevitably bear much of the burden and will have a dual role to play in this regard. It should not only fashion its lending program in ways that are strongly supportive of the LPA, as it has indicated it intends to do, but it must recognize how admirably suited it is to fill the void and serve as an African economic voice in influential foreign and international circles. This void is especially noticeable in Washington, where so many of the decisions that have strong economic impacts on Africa are made. Rarely, if ever, is there an authoritative spokesperson for the continent available to present a continental perspective at the endless forums that provide the underpinnings for many U.S. foreign policy decisions. Occasionally an African from a particular embassy or from an international organization, or an African expatriate resident in America, may participate in such forums, but even such chance participation is likely to bring a narrow, rather than a continental, perspective to the discussion. A few of Africa's American friends attempt to fill this void, but inasmuch as we are merely private citizens, with no official authority to speak for Africa, our views carry little weight.

If the LPA is to acquire credibility among donors, it must achieve some degree of acceptance in the U.S. But if the acceptance of the donor community is to be achieved, it will require an ongoing campaign by a team of persons who are tuned into the relevant structures on both sides of the Atlantic and who are totally dedicated to the cause of African development. U.S. policy largely shapes Western donor policy, and U.S. policy is in turn heavily influenced by a fairly elite group of foreign policy specialists, who may move in and out of government as political fortunes change but who continue to affect policy. The LPA perspective must be strong and persuasively introduced within these circles, and an ADB liaison office, properly staffed and mandated, would appear to be the most promising way to launch this effort.

U.S. policy is also influenced by pressure groups within the American populace. Virtually the only constituency that Africa has within the U.S. is the black American community. This group has become highly influential in recent years, and while it wields considerably less influence during Republican administrations than during Democratic ones, the Democrat-controlled House of Representatives takes the lead on many African issues from the increasingly influential Black Caucus (the black congressmen). The Jesse Jackson presidential campaign substantially expanded the scope of black influence in American politics and publicly established the black community's interest in international affairs. Although the average black American's interest in Africa (other than South Africa) is less intense than one would wish, the black American community, with proper nurturing, can be fashioned into a highly influential lobby on behalf of such issues as U.S. policy toward Africa, U.S. aid levels for Africa, and other Africa-related topics. Here again, however, an African agency is essential. Sympathetic black Americans can help, and indeed are already doing much in this regard, but what is missing is some African liaison agency, which, by virtue of its official status, would render such efforts more credible and more authoritative.

In this regard it is interesting to note that Israel received US$2.6 billion in U.S. economic and military assistance for fiscal year 1984, or approximately one thousand dollars per inhabitant. This invites comparison with the US$1.1 billion that the U.S. provided to all of Sub-Saharan Africa for the same year. Even if we add on the U.S. share of multilateral assistance to Africa, total U.S. aid to Africa works out to only five dollars per inhabitant. While Israel's special relationship to the U.S. is well known, a disparity of this magnitude dramatically illustrates how meaningless the U.S. argument is that "it cannot afford" to be more generous with Africa. The disparity highlights just how ineffective we have been in selling Africa to the U.S., and we all share the blame.

The _Lagos Plan_ can have a future if sufficient numbers of Africans wish it. Resources can be mobilized if Africa convincingly demonstrates its support for it. This will not be an easy task, but with sufficient perseverance the necessary resources can be raised. In the spirit of the Civil Rights movement, I feel confident in saying that "we shall overcome."

NOTES

1. OAU, _The Lagos Plan of Action for the Economic Development of Africa 1980-2000_ (Geneva: International Institute for Labor Studies, 1981).
2. Jeane Kirkpatrick, _Congressional Record_, 7 March 1983, 52181-84.
3. Mung'Omba, Wila, "Statement to the Board of Governors," _ADB/ADF Annual Conference_, Tunis, 9 May 1984, p. 5.
4. African Development Bank, "The Future Role of ADB in Promoting Economic Development and Social Progress in Africa," Tunis, May 1984.
5. ECA, _Special Memorandum by the ECA Conference of Ministers on Africa's Economic and Social Crisis_ (Addis Ababa, May 1984), p. 11.
6. World Bank, _Annual Report_ (Washington, 1984), pp. 80-85.
7. _Ibid._, p. 50.
8. World Bank, _Accelerated Development in Sub-Saharan Africa: an agenda for action_ (Washington: World Bank, 1981), p. 127.
9. E.I.M. Mtei, "An Evolving Relationship," _Africa Report_ (September/October 1984), p. 21.
10. U.S. Department of State, "Background on the Economic Policy Initiative for Sub-Saharan Africa," handout distributed at press conference of Secretary of State George P. Schultz, Washington, 30 January 1984, mimeographed.

11. World Bank, *Toward Sustained Development in Sub-Saharan Africa: a Joint Program of Action* (Washington: World Bank, 1984).

Part 3

Sectors, Strategies, and Self-Sufficiency

E. P. Pallangyo and L. A. Odero-Ogwel

10 The Persistence of the Food and Agriculture Crisis in Africa

THE FOOD AND AGRICULTURE SECTOR IN AFRICAN ECONOMIES

The food and agriculture sector is the mainstay of most African economies. This is evidenced in its generation of employment (67 percent in 1981), in its percentage of national output (40 to 60 percent of GDPs), and in its contribution to total export earnings. Agriculture provides income, livelihood, and security for a large majority of Africa's 537 million people. Although the contribution of this sector varies from one country to another,[1] for most, agriculture remains the single most important generator of overall economic growth and sustained further development, including the supply of raw materials and labor for industrialization.

Yet, despite this predominant role, food and agriculture output, in decline since the 1960s, has precipitated a crisis of continental proportions. Chronic food insecurity, mounting food import bills, serious dietary deficiencies, and stagnating agricultural exports plague the continent, while depletion of natural resources and environmental degradation loom large.

The food crisis facing the region is now one of the gravest challenges of our time. According to FAO estimates, acute food shortages and widespread human suffering are to be found in almost half of the African countries, with a population of some 150 million people seriously affected.

The ECA's Executive Secretary has summarized the problem thus:

> Whatever other factors may be responsible for the present plight of the continent, there is no doubt that the fortune and misfortune of the food and agriculture sector have up to now determined the progress or non-progress of the majority of the countries of the region. This is mainly because of the

importance of the sector in terms of employment, food supply, industrial inputs supply, income generation and foreign exchange earnings.[2]

The poor performance of this sector has been the principal factor underlying Africa's current economic dilemma. What was initially a crisis of agriculture has become a severe economic malaise with all sectors of African economies, as well as all areas of national activity, affected. It is therefore not surprising that national output (GDP) has been stagnant or in decline in much of the continent since the late 1960s. African countries have now become acutely aware that the food and agriculture sector, in particular smallholder agriculture, holds the key to the continent's destiny.

This chapter seeks to identify some of the main causes of the present food and agriculture crisis and its resulting cumulative effects. Policy issues, both domestic and external, as well as drought and other geophysical factors are considered. The most important political actions, expressing determination by the African governments to deal with the crisis, are to be found in the Regional Food Plan for Africa (AFPLAN) and the Lagos Plan of Action (LPA). The objectives of the LPA and efforts to realize them are analyzed in the context of the deepening African food and agriculture crisis. The final section of the chapter suggests future directions to be taken, and the role of the international community is discussed.

THE GENESIS OF THE CURRENT FOOD AND AGRICULTURE CRISIS

Africa, so generously endowed with natural resources, is today, paradoxically, in the throes of a crisis for survival. Growing food deficits and hunger have begun to undermine the economic and social systems of many African nations.

The need for a technological breakthrough in African agriculture, whether seen in terms of the expansion of land under cultivation or land-intensification, is overwhelming. An indication of the gap between existing and potential technology is shown by comparing yields in Africa with those in other developing regions and the world (see table 10.1).

A recent FAO study points out that Africa has enough land to feed three times the population it had in 1975, and more than one and a half times the population projected for the year 2000, even with low levels of technology.[3] This is predicated, of course, on easy and massive movements of food and population across borders. African countries therefore have the potential to improve their overall food self-sufficiency ratio (SSR).

$$\text{SSR} = \frac{\text{Domestic Production} \times 100}{\text{Domestic Utilization}}$$

They can also disengage themselves from the present poverty trap, especially if they vigorously pursue appropriate national policies and strategies and strengthen intercountry trade and cooperative development of resources.

The present crisis is spawned by a combination of factors. Hardly any African country achieved independence without inheriting colonial institutions and structures. These have not yet been adapted to national needs and to do so will require far-reaching policy changes. Some of the manifestations of the legacies of the colonial past include urban-biased development, export-

Table 10.1

Percentage increase, 1969-1971 to 1979-1981, in average crop yields in Sub-Saharan Africa in relation to all developing countries

	Sub-Saharan Africa	All developing countries
Maize	4.1	29.8
Wheat	7.1	41.1
Paddy	22.2	20.1
Cassava	-4.1	-1.2
Groundnuts	1.3	3.8
Coffee	-11.2	21.4
Tea	13.5	-6.2
Cocoa	-11.4	2.3
Seed cotton	2.7	17.1
Milk	5.0	8.0

Source: FAO, The State of Food and Agriculture 1983, Rome, p. 76, table 1-26.

oriented strategies, technological dependence, scarcity of trained manpower, and a largely unknown resource base, especially in a neglected smallholder agriculture without domestic and external development resource allocations. These have been the major bottlenecks in Africa's postindependence economic growth.

On the continent, agriculture continues to consist of two separate and sometimes unrelated components: the export-oriented, highly commercialized estate-type agriculture and, side by side, subsistence-oriented and family-based smallholder agriculture. The latter, as a major producer of food and raw materials for industries, makes small use of commercial inputs. Therefore, peasants wallow in their backwardness, unrelieved because of their low levels of technology, among other constraints. Meanwhile, the export-oriented, commercialized agriculture is subject to the pressures of distant and anonymous world market forces.

African countries originally saw industrialization as the symbol of modernity and advancement. Accordingly, the past two decades witnessed a deliberate tilting of policies in favor of industry and of commercial and industrial crops. The industrial sector was expected to create jobs, provide markets for agriculture, and generate surpluses for further investment. But these hopes were smothered due to inefficiency, high costs, excessive operational capacity, minimal links with the resource base, and overdependence on imported inputs. The anticipated structural transformation of the urban-biased policies of the 1960s and 1970s did not come. Agricultural development suffered, and countries are now paying dearly for this oversight.

In the aftermath, declining overall growth rates and plummeting agricultural exports have made increasing reliance upon food imports and food aid inevitable.

Agricultural production (food and nonfood) showed a temporary rise from 1980 to 1982, but this was only the prelude to a sharp downturn in 1983 that continued into 1984. Figures 1.1 and 10.1 and table 10.2 illustrate the depressing annual trend of the last two decades. The most recent estimate for 1980-83 shows a per capita decline of 2.7 percent, with the food sector alone declining at 2.9 percent per capita. The significance of this shortfall becomes apparent when viewed against rising food demand and the widening food gap, which for all of Africa has shown a deterioration of 1.3 percent in the decade 1971-80.

Figure 10.1

Index of food production per capita (% of 1960-65 average)

Per Capita Grain Production in Twenty-four African Countries Affected by Drought, 1970–84

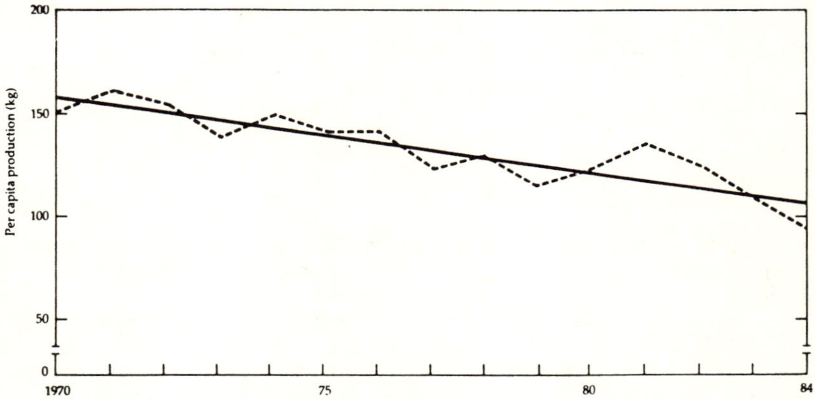

SOURCE: World Bank, Toward Sustained Development in Sub-Saharan Africa: A Joint Program of Action (Washington, D.C.: World Bank, 1984, pp. 14-15)

Table 10.2

Index numbers and rates of change in African agricultural production

Subregion	1980	1981	1982	1983[a]	1971 to 1980	1972 to 1981	1981 to 1982	1982[a] to 1983	1980 to 1983
	Agricultural Production								
	1974-76=100				Percentage of annual change				
North-eastern	92.9	94.6	88.4	90.7	-1.2	1.9	-6.6	2.6	-1.5
North-western	95.4	80.5	87.9	81.4	-1.5	-15.6	9.3	-7.4	-3.1
Western	95.6	95.6	95.2	93.0	-1.0	0.1	-0.4	-2.4	-0.7
Central	92.4	91.6	91.6	89.5	-1.1	0.6	-0.3	-2.3	-0.6
Eastern	92.2	92.5	90.9	89.7	-1.3	0.3	-1.8	-1.3	-0.9
Southern	86.1	93.2	91.4	91.7	-2.8	8.3	-1.9	0.3	1.7
Total[b]	94.0	92.2	92.5	90.0	-1.2	-1.9	0.3	-2.7	-1.0
	Food Production								
North-eastern	93.2	96.7	89.2	91.5	-0.5	3.7	-7.7	2.5	-1.4
North-western	95.5	80.3	87.8	81.2	-1.5	-15.9	9.4	-7.6	3.1
Western	96.0	95.7	95.9	93.8	-0.9	-0.2	0.1	-2.1	-0.5
Central	93.6	93.0	92.6	90.6	-0.8	-0.7	-0.4	-2.1	-0.6
Eastern	92.2	93.2	91.5	89.2	-1.2	1.1	-1.9	-2.5	-1.0
Southern	84.4	91.6	93.1	90.5	-1.1	-2.0	0.6	-2.9	-0.9
Total[b]	94.4	91.6	93.1	90.5	-1.1	-2.0	0.6	-2.9	-0.9
	Nonfood Production								
North-eastern	90.7	81.9	83.2	86.3	-4.7	-9.7	1.6	3.6	-1.9
North-western	90.3	89.1	92.6	92.0	-1.7	-1.3	3.8	-0.6	1.1
Western	84.2	92.4	75.1	67.2	-2.4	9.7	-18.7	-10.6	-6.8
Central	70.5	71.3	73.7	68.1	-7.2	1.1	3.4	-7.6	-0.3
Eastern	92.7	88.1	87.2	93.0	-2.0	-5.0	-1.0	6.6	-0.5
Southern	118.9	112.9	103.5	104.9	3.0	-5.1	-8.4	1.4	0.8
Total[b]	87.4	86.5	82.6	83.3	-2.8	-1.1	-4.5	0.7	-1.8

Source: FAO, ESS, Computer Printouts on Index Numbers (Rome: FAO, February 1984).

[a]Preliminary

[b]Total for Africa excludes north-eastern Africa

African countries have failed to satisfy the higher demand for food from domestic production, thus more food imports have been necessary to maintain the essential dietary energy supply, now put at below necessary levels in some 27 African countries. Information received from the FAO/WFP Special Task Force indicated the following 27 countries as being most seriously affected by food and agricultural emergencies as of October 1984: Angola, Benin, Botswana, Burkina Faso, Burundi, Cape Verde, Central African Republic, Chad, Ethiopia, The Gambia, Ghana, Guinea, Guinea Bissau, Kenya, Lesotho, Mali, Mauritania, Morocco, Mozambique, Rwanda and Sao Tome and Principe, Senegal, Somalia, Tanzania, Togo, Zambia, Zimbabwe. (However, if the current favorable climatic situation continues in some parts of West Africa, Benin, the Central African Republic, Ghana and Togo may soon be off this list).

Yet, apart from food aid, there has been an estimated 9 percent rise a year in commercial food grain imports for two decades. Cereal imports alone have gone up nearly six-fold since 1970. Agricultural imports rose 15 percent between 1980 and 1981 with a value of US$18.99 billion, although they dropped by 8 percent the following year (US$17.54 billion). Food, the bulk of total imports in recent years, went down in value by 9 percent in 1982, compared to the previous year, demonstrating Africa's inability to offset food deficits through commercial imports. Meanwhile, food aid remains stagnant in that actual deliveries are below pledges.

The present structure of the world market, including unfavorable movements in world prices,[4] has not only resulted in a decline in the volume and value of exports by African countries but also in a deterioration of the terms of trade. Exports declined by about 50 percent between 1977 and 1981, thus inhibiting capabilities of countries to import. According to FAO, the 24 African countries critically affected[5] would require about five million tons of cereals in 1983/84, an increase of 0.6 million tons over 1982/83 requirements. The continent's combined export of agricultural, forestry, and fishery products fell from US$13.3 billion in 1980 to about US$11.6 billion and US$11 billion in 1981 and 1982, respectively. In many African countries, food imports claimed 30 percent of total agricultural export earnings, and, in some countries, it accounted for all these earnings, forcing serious cutbacks in development outlays.

An export-led development strategy has therefore failed to bring about progress in Africa because the anticipated gains from trade have not materialized. In fact, there have recently been a number of very serious developments in the world economic scene with far-reaching implications for the food and agriculture sector. These will continue to have a significant impact on the economies of African countries in the foreseeable future. Some of these are of immediate concern: (1) the long-term decline in the African share of primary commodities in total world trade;[6] (2) the rise in developed countries' exports of primary commodities; and (3) the increase of developing countries' imports of primary commodities, in particular food.

Africa therefore faces, for the rest of the 1980s, declining world trade in primary agricultural commodities, which most African countries depend upon, almost exclusively, for their foreign exchange earnings. Africa will, in essence, be paying higher import bills with decreased export earnings, both of which are externally determined.

THE LAGOS PLAN OF ACTION (LPA) AND THE AFRICAN AGRICULTURE CRISIS

The gravity of the food and agriculture crisis, which has been developing for the past 20 years, has been fully recognized by the African governments and the international donor community only recently. Hitherto, African and foreign planners and politicians seriously underestimated both the importance and the complexity of the food and agriculture sector. Biases against this sector were reflected in the very low priority given to domestic food production, as well as in the relatively low prestige attached to the farm sector and to those associated with it, such as farmers and agricultural scientists and administrators. In the current crisis, efforts are being made to rectify this dereliction.

Deeply concerned with the poor overall performance of their economies, the menacing food and agriculture crisis, and deepening rural poverty, African governments have responded by taking positive action, individually and collectively, at all levels on a multisectoral and multidimensional basis. The attempt has been to reorientate Africa's development strategies by defining priorities more rigorously and laying major emphasis on the reconstruction of Africa's economic base. These efforts culminated, among others, in the *Revised Framework of Principles for the Implementation of the New International Economic Order for Africa*, (1976-1981-1986) of 1978 and the *Regional Food Plan for Africa* (AFPLAN) of 1978, which became the basis for the preparation of the *Lagos Plan*. The *LPA* is Africa's strongest expression of political will ever formulated for the social and economic development of the continent.

The *Lagos Plan* outlines a policy-oriented, macroeconomic framework in which the region's resources, both domestic and external, human and physical, are to be developed. It has accorded highest priority to agricultural and rural development through appropriate and courageous policies, strategies, and programs for increasing food availability, reducing the region's growing food import dependency, combating hunger and malnutrition, and alleviating poverty. Without doubt, therefore, there is a growing affirmation among African leaders of the primacy of food and agriculture in fostering balanced development. The general objective of the plan's food and agriculture chapter for the period 1980-85 was to bring about an immediate improvement in the food situation and lay the foundations for the achievement of self-sufficiency in cereals and in livestock and fish products. This objective was to be achieved through efforts aimed at revamping food and agriculture policies in African countries.

Renewed efforts are being made, especially with respect to specific priorities. Progress is anticipated in bringing about viable food security at national and subregional levels through a 50 percent reduction in postharvest food losses, accompanied by measures to set up strategic food reserves of about 10 percent of total food production. Special emphasis is being put on the increased production and quality improvement of such staple foods as maize, millet, sorghum, and roots and tubers, to replace food imports. There is considerable emphasis on improved livestock production and management. A one million ton target in fish production, based on 1 kg. of per capita annual consumption, was set for the period 1980-85. Other major objectives are coherent policies on prices, incentive systems, research, extension, and other essential support services. A 10 percent annual forest resources expansion is also included in the *Lagos Plan*. The estimated cost is US$21,400 million, with an extra US$560 million for agricultural inputs; 50 percent of this cost is expected to come from domestic sources.

The long-term provisions of the Lagos Plan outline programs that will take Africa over the 20-year period to the year 2000, by which time the continent's population will have nearly doubled to 900 million. The agricultural program, however, does not go beyond 1985; and with 1985 rapidly approaching, African food and agriculture problems still loom large.

HAVE ANY IMMEDIATE GOALS BEEN ACHIEVED?

In spite of some efforts made by African governments, there has been no appreciable improvement in overall food production to match population increases, and there has been only limited success in the achievement of targets. Food insecurity has worsened. Although there has been a 4 percent increase in fish production during the 1980s, and a fair performance by the livestock subsector, the production of cereals and pulses has either dropped or remained stagnant. The calls to "channel a greatly increased volume of resources to agriculture," still awaits a response. Stopgap measures have failed to relieve hunger and malnutrition. Inappropriate policies have spawned short-term improvisations, perpetuating the problems.

Compounding this situation are such adverse factors and constraints as difficult climatic and geographical conditions; poor planning and management due to inadequate planning resources (personnel, data, etc.); diverse individual national development strategies and policies; institutional and bureaucratic weaknesses; technological deficiencies, especially input packages for smallholders; and exogenous shocks. Political and social upheavals have merely aggravated an already serious situation.

The influence and unpredictability of exogenous forces on the development of the African food and agriculture sector must also be recognized. The international economic and aid environment has become more unfavorable in recent years, particularly since 1980, unleashing, as it were, a series of negative external factors, including worsening terms of trade and declining development assistance (see previous chapters in this section).

For the African people, the vision of the UN World Food Conference of 1974 remains far from being realized today. That conference came up with 20 substantive recommendations, including what now has turned out to be an ambitious goal: that in a decade no child would go to bed hungry, no family would fear for its next day's bread, and no individual's potential would be stunted by malnutrition.

LPA AND RESOURCE FLOW INTO AGRICULTURE

Official pronouncements declaring agriculture to be the major sector deserving priority attention, however, have not always been backed up by budgetary allocations. Besides, agricultural surpluses have often been siphoned off to other sectors. Although the more readily available data are those on planned rather than actual expenditures, it is nevertheless certain that, for most African countries, public investment (i.e., capital and recurrent outlays of central, regional, and local government, as well as expenditures of public enterprises engaged in agricultural activities) for the development of the sector, which has been minimal in the past two decades, continued to be marginal and on the decline during the post-LPA era. During 1967-73, only 5 to 6 percent of total public recurrent expenditure was allocated to food and agricultural development, while capital expenditure was less than one-third of the sector's contribution to GDP.

The Lagos Plan's annual investment target is some US$4.4 billion, half of which is to come from African governments; only about US$1 billion was raised toward the 1981 domestic target of US$2.2 billion. This gap can only be closed by substantially increasing domestic resources in the remaining years of the plan. As figures indicate in table 10.3, over the period 1979-82 average annual planned public expenditure declined in real terms in all subregions, except in West Africa where there was a slight increase of about 2 percent. The sharpest decline occurred in the Yaounde-based MULPOC[7] group of countries[8] and the Gisenyi-based MULPOC countries of Burundi, Rwanda, and Zaire.

Table 10.3

Average annual growth rates of total public expenditure for all sectors and for the agriculture sector (at constant prices)

	All sectors					Agriculture				
	1979	1980	1981	1982	Average 1979-82	1979	1980	1981	1982	Average 1979-82
North Africa	6.1	4.0	- 6.0	3.6	1.8	- 6.3	2.2	- 0.3	- 5.8	-2.5
West Africa	9.1	-15.7	-18.4	- 1.7	-7.3	-10.4	18.9	- 5.4	8.0	2.1
Central West Africa	20.3	- 3.0	3.1	- 8.8	2.4	68.7	- 7.5	-34.2	-34.5	-9.5
Central Africa						-13.5	-48.6	10.0	39.1	-9.2
Eastern and Southern Africa	14.5	- 3.9	-11.0	-18.7	-5.5	27.0	4.9	- 1.1	-30.7	-2.2

Source: FAO, Public Expenditure on Agriculture Computer Printouts (Rome: 1983, FAO, 13/12/83).

Although total official development assistance for world food and agriculture doubled during the period 1973-78, reaching US$10 billion in 1978,[9] aid almost stagnated until 1981 and declined to an estimated 4 percent in multilateral assistance in 1982. This was due mainly to difficulties in replenishing the funding of IFAD, UNDP, and IDA.

For the Africa region, official commitments of external assistance to agriculture (whether by narrow or broad definitions)[10] had been on the increase during the 1974-81 period. Concessional and nonconcessional, multilateral and bilateral aid all showed upward trends in absolute and in real terms. However, it is perhaps true to say that about one-third of this assistance went into emergency situations rather than for strict investment expenditure in the sector. And as with domestic resources, shortfalls still exist in external funding.

In addition, on the basis of subsectoral allocations, studies reveal a drastic decline in official external resource flows into crop production,[11] implying that the food sector has been denied high priority in donor allocations. River basin and regional development, so essential for extending agricultural land frontiers and tackling the problems of regional imbalances and inequalities in income and wealth, have also received less in official external commitments. It is significant also that in recent decades, apart from earlier investments such as the Aswan Dam in Egypt, the Sudan Gezira Scheme, and the Akosombo project on the Volta Lake, there have not been major investment programs or projects in agriculture and related sectors in Africa. It is wise to remember that India was only able to extricate itself from similar crises through improved and vastly increased investments in the food and agriculture sector, in particular in fertilizer development, river basin and irrigation development, as well as expanded manpower and institutional development. Massive investment is therefore required to achieve modernization in African agriculture.

The relatively long lag between commitment and disbursement of funds is also a significant factor explaining suboptimal resource allocation to African agriculture. Over a period of time, disbursements of funds committed have shown a decline; very often only about 50 percent of these funds were disbursed after a long time (four to five years) following a commitment. For example, of the funds committed in 1974 only 34.6 percent were disbursed in the first three years and only 66.8 percent by the fifth year. Similarly, of the funds committed in 1976, only 51 percent were disbursed in the first five years. Moreover, by reading table 10.4, it can be seen that the rates of disbursements also declined over time, thereby affecting the level of resource allocation to agriculture.

THE ROLE OF DONORS AND INTERNATIONAL AGENCIES

International agencies and donors have been playing an important role in Africa's development for more than two decades. They have been especially influential in shaping the direction of development in African countries. Therefore, like African governments, they must necessarily share responsibility for the imbalances and inadequacies in development.

Problems of External Assistance

Whereas in recent years there have been important improvements in external assistance to African agriculture, the international community has yet to focus on critical issues that are at the heart of Africa's food and agriculture problems. A shortcoming of agency and external assistance is that their approach to development is based narrowly on project criteria, which are followed without adequate attention being paid to the national policies essential for the maximization of economic and social returns. This disaggregated and partial approach focusing on narrow project criteria has tended to limit the benefits that would accrue from a broader approach

Table 10.4

Annual cumulative disbursements of multilateral capital commitments to agriculture in Africa, 1974-81 (in percentages)

	Cumulative disbursements							
Year of commitments	1st year	2nd year	3rd year	4th year	5th year	6th year	7th year	8th year
	(1974)	(1975)	(1976)	(1977)	(1978)	(1979)	(1980)	(1981)
1974 (1st yr.)	0.2	18.2	34.6	52.8	66.8	76.4	84.3	90.2
1975 (2nd yr.)	0.3	8.5	23.3	41.8	59.9	72.8	79.6	
1976 (3rd yr.)	0.9	7.0	21.7	36.3	51.0	63.1		
1977 (4th yr.)	1.9	11.1	30.2	48.7	60.8			
1978 (5th yr.)	2.9	14.5	26.4	38.9				
1979 (6th yr.)	0.4	7.2	18.7					
1980 (7th yr.)	1.7	7.4						
1981 (8th yr.)	0.7							

Source: FAO, Cumulative Disbursements Printouts (Rome: FAO, 8/2/84).

involving policies and programs.

Also, external assistance has tended to focus much more on technical rather than policy analysis. Moreover, because agency and donor missions are generally composed of experts from abroad, without the inclusion of local experts, it is hardly surprising that some of the projects formulated by these missions have not been successful. What is more, donors and agencies have tended to apply very strict conditionalities, accountability, and procedural requirements, which are far beyond the capabilities of most African governments to satisfy.

By and large, welfare issues, such as employment generation, improvement of the nutritional status of the population, and the provision of training to meet exploding manpower requirements, have been ignored in external assistance. Yet such welfare components are essential for establishing viable social and political systems in Africa. Moreover, project design and administration sometimes places a heavy burden on the managerial and technical skills of African governments by stretching their institutional capabilities to the limits, with a resulting loss of efficiency.

The complexity and diversity of donor procedural requirements, as well as the multiplicity of agencies, remain a critical problem. In countries with weak administrations--and this the case with many African countries--the way that many agencies make aid available, when inappropriately coordinated, can have a serious destabilizing effect on governments' abilities to cope with manifold missions.

A serious weakness also exists in the way donors and agencies appraise development returns. To date, project formulation criteria, mainly borrowed from private company financial analysis practices in the developed countries, can hardly address adequately the social and welfare issues that are essentially linked to progress. There is an urgent need for donors and agencies to examine their aid criteria, including those relating to project preparation. Considerations of social justice may demand placing a more positive valuation on such social and economic objectives as assured food supplies, drinking water, minimum health care, nutritional improvement, and reversal of environment degradation. Achievement of these goals cannot be measured by the application of excessively narrow cost-benefit criteria, which have been hitherto applied by aid agencies for addressing African development, sometimes with disastrous consequences.

The issue of the recurrent, as well as counterpart (local), costs of financing is still proving to be an elusive problem for the poorer African countries. Many African governments cannot meet these obligations out of their recurrent and development budgets. Given the current magnitude of indebtedness among African countries, shrinking export earnings, and the inability of African governments to increase domestic savings, meeting local and recurrent costs merits donor consideration.

Donors and agencies should assist African governments in improving and expanding manpower development. This is especially necessary because, while external technical advice is required in the short term, it tends to become less suitable to African sensitivities and needs in the long run. Moreover, such training and manpower development programs are the only way to ensure continuity and sustainability of projects and programs initiated with external assistance.

There is also a tendency for donors and agencies to prefer formulation of new projects rather than improving many existing, poorly maintained, and underutilized projects. There is a need to rethink this approach since greater benefits may accrue through the improvement of existing projects and governments' abilities to maintain them.

In assisting African nations, donors and agencies must realize the overriding importance of the food and agriculture sector as the major generator of economic and social development. Some development agencies have been slow to recognize this. The underlying assumption has been that if general economic advance is promoted then agricultural development, including domestic food production and consumption, will follow. The experience of Africa, with its deteriorating food and agriculture production, does not bear out this assumption. As in the case of India, a healthy agriculture has to be recognized as the basis of and the prime mover for overall development. In the food emergency currently being experienced by the African continent, food aid will continue to be required in the interim period for feeding the hungry masses, while ways are sought to rehabilitate the most seriously affected areas. However, unless food aid is accompanied by increasing indigenous food production in a framework of effective food policies, then food aid dependency can only continue to grow with disastrous consequences on African economies and political systems. (Growing food aid dependency is illustrated by the fact that Africa has now replaced Asia as the world's principal food aid recipient, currently receiving some 50 percent [about four million tons] of all cereal food aid, mostly wheat, as compared with 5 to 6 percent in the 1960s and early 1970s.)

Increased external assistance, aimed at supporting African food and agriculture objectives, must address critical areas such as smallholder agriculture, so as to enable African governments to get out of the poverty trap and the impasse of a growing food import dependency. Only in this way can donors accelerate development and avert major human suffering and political upheaval throughout the continent.

As indicated earlier, external assistance directed to the production of crops, including food crops, in Africa has been declining drastically over the past years. While data is incomplete, a recent study indicates that the U.S. Agency for International Development (USAID) found that only an insignificant proportion of projects undertaken in Africa were related to food crop production. According to this analysis, out of 570 projects in Africa, 218 were expected to have some impact on food production. However only 22--representing about 7 percent of the total projects in monetary terms--were directly concerned with food crop production. Thus, on the whole, it would appear that development projects supported by external assistance are having only a limited impact on changing the steadily worsening food production situation in most of Africa.

Progress by Donors and Agencies

International agencies and donors are becoming increasingly aware of this problem and are beginning to shift emphasis from external crop specialization to more adequate food and agricultural production. It is being recognized that increasing self-sufficiency in food production constitutes the best strategy for creating viable food security and general economic development in Africa. The Swedish International Development Agency (SIDA), for example, noting that food production is declining in the region and causing serious social and political discontent, has been undertaking an assessment of how best to redirect its aid to food production and to general rural development in Africa. Indeed there is a growing consensus among donors that fundamental rethinking is required to bring about solutions to Africa's food and agriculture problems. The EEC countries are already changing the mode of their technical assistance to support crucial areas, notably the food sector. Through a mutual commitment, EEC has entered into agreements with a number of African governments to support their policy adjustments and reforms to increase food production and establish food security.

Multilateral agencies, notably FAO and IFAD, are already allocating the largest shares of their funds and technical assistance to food and agriculture in Africa and are assisting African nations to reverse unfavorable trends in the food and agriculture sector. FAO has responded very effectively in the past to African food and agriculture emergencies. In the case of the current crisis, FAO took steps as early as February 1983 to focus international attention on the most critical aspects of the situation. A series of appeals were made to the international community to mobilize food aid and financial, material, and other resources for the emergency and for agricultural rehabilitation of the most seriously affected countries. To continously monitor progress of the African emergency, FAO set up a FAO/WFP Task Force in the region. Similarly, ECA through the Joint ECA/FAO Agriculture Division has been undertaking investment and other policy studies in support of the African effort to implement the agricultural aspect of the Lagos Plan. Moreover, ECA recently published a special economic memorandum, which has been debated extensively, both in ECOSOC, and in the UN General Assembly. The purpose of this memorandum was to draw international attention to the critical socio-economic crisis in Africa and to galvanize international action to support the African effort to deal with it.

Because of the serious economic difficulties facing the continent, the donor community should increase concessional assistance, especially for the African food and agriculture sector. Recent difficulties in replenishing funds of organizations such as IFAD, IDA, UNDP, and WFP can only exacerbate the problems of the world's poor countries, the majority of which are to be found on the African continent.

It is significant that the present gap between estimated investments required for African agriculture and available domestic and external resources is very large. The critical mass of resources required to develop Africa's food and agriculture is considerably larger than what is currently being made available. LPA estimated about US$22,000 million needed during the period 1980-85, as compared to current commitments of official development assistance to agriculture (ODA) estimated by FAO to be US$9,000 million over the same period. As already indicated, actual disbursements will be less, perhaps about 60 percent of the amount committed, or only about US$5,400 million in external assistance (instead of the US$11,000 million required), leaving a shortfall of US$5,600 million over the period 1980-85.[12]

Clearly, flows of ODA to Africa must at least be doubled if accelerated agricultural development is to be achieved to cope with population growth and increased demand for capital. The World Bank estimates that faster growth in this region can only be achieved by a two-fold increase in real terms of the annual flow of development assistance in the decade 1980-90.[13] If this level of flow were to be achieved and appropriate policy changes brought about among African countries, African per capita incomes would rise from current stagnation about 25 percent in the coming decade. The World Bank also emphasizes that besides the doubling of aid, better quality aid that gives more emphasis to programs and less to project-based technical assistance is required. Moreover, the increased volume of aid should be more flexible, with a greater accent on rehabilitation and other quick-yielding projects and long-term programs, and it should cover more local and recurrent costs. These, therefore, are among the challenges that face the international community in assisting Africa's effort to implement the Lagos Plan.

THE LAGOS PLAN OF ACTION AND FUTURE PRIORITIES

Since the launching of the Lagos Plan, the ECA has continued to monitor the food and agriculture aspect of the plan, and an evaluation is currently being prepared for the period 1980-85 to determine the bottlenecks in the implementation process and to chart priority areas for the next decade. The report will also document new proposals for 1986-90.

Information already available indicates that the past decade has been a difficult one for the continent and the situation could get worse, with an uninterrupted food disaster, if no action is taken now to reverse adverse food and agriculture trends. A recent paper by the Rome-based African Group (members of the Group of 77), endorsed by the second session of the OAU African

Interministerial Committee for Food,[14] outlined critical areas that must be tackled immediately to overcome constraints on food production and agricultural development in Africa. The committee called for a serious reorientation of strategies and policies for the decade ahead. Special emphasis was placed on bringing about structural changes and policy adjustments among African governments. It was pointed out that this must also be accompanied by similar adjustments on the part of developed donor countries and international agencies to bring about realignment of aid policies and practices.

However, given the current emergency situation on the continent, attention must be paid first to the rehabilitation of the food and agriculture sector of the affected countries. In the meantime, emergency actions should concentrate on mobilizing food, financial, and technical assistance to avert further starvation. On the one hand, attention should be paid to the provision of logistics, storage facilities, and transport and distribution systems and, on the other, to the adequate provision of seeds, fertilizers, tools and other production requisites, including pesticides, vaccines, and drugs to combat plant and animal diseases and pests.

The medium- and long-term priorities that urgently require increased resources from the donor community and multilateral agencies include the following areas:

1. Research, Technology, and Delivery Systems: Considering that most African agriculture is still at the minimum stage of technology, and that it will only be entering the intermediate stage by the turn of the century, the development of agricultural research and technology transfer is a major policy issue. But to date agricultural research and delivery systems in Africa are grotesquely understaffed, under-financed, manifestly weak and inadequately focused to the crucial task of raising agricultural productivity.

   Ensured growth can come from improved application of available research findings and technology packages, including a combination of modern inputs. The development and application of agricultural technology must take into account ways to conserve natural resources and protect the environment. Research on farming systems is necessary to modernize small-scale, traditional agriculture. Research should also aim at the development of low cost technology packages and quick-maturing crops necessary for extending agricultural frontiers into semiarid areas. Development of dry farming has also been minimal so far and merits support.

2. Manpower Development: There is an acute shortage of manpower in many development fields in Africa. Manpower is particularly short for agricultural research, managerial planning, and for formulating and developing appropriate policies; but, above all, many countries lack trained personnel for carrying out the critical tasks of repair and maintenance and for operating equipment. This manpower shortage is partly due to inherited colonial education systems, which primarily trained students for white-collar jobs. However, part of the problem is due to the fact that many African governments have not identified national manpower requirements and priorities. Moreover, even when local personnel have been trained,

government policies do not provide adequate incentives to keep trained manpower in Africa and stop the brain drain. There is also an urgent need to train farmers, including women, in practical home economics, nutrition, and child care, as well as to train the youth to be productive members of the national labor force.

Fortunately there is an increasing awareness among African governments and international agencies about this problem. The FAO Regional Conference held in Algiers in 1982 singled out lack of manpower development as one of the most important constraints hampering modernization of the food and agriculture sector in Africa. Other organizations, such as the World Bank and IFAD, have also recognized this fact and, like FAO, are now placing a high priority on the development of African manpower.

3. Development of Smallholder Agriculture: Since smallholder cultivation forms the bulk of African agriculture, it merits greater attention. Because of its share in national output and total employment, this subsector holds the key to agricultural and overall progress. It is increasingly being recognized that the African smallholder is an "economic man" who, given the right incentives and income-generating opportunities, is quite prepared to change and modernize. Therefore external assistance directed to the smallholder will benefit society as a whole.

   Emphasis on smallholder development should focus on staple food crops, which hitherto have been woefully neglected, contributing greatly to the current food crisis. Recognition must also be given to women as major producers in African agriculture, and funds are urgently required to improve their condition.

4. Institutional Development: In some African countries, the institutional issue may be even more important than land reform. The multiplicity of parastatal organizations has resulted in a serious lack of progress. The continent is full of examples of state agencies with statutory, monopolistic powers that have done no more than distort resource use, markets, and pricing policies, in addition to dampening individual initiatives. The resulting inefficiency has been very costly for governments and taxpayers. There is therefore a need to support African efforts to develop proper institutional capacities to handle development tasks. Instead of rushing to establish new institutions, there are distinct gains to be made by improving existing institutions through providing training in management and planning.

5. Infrastructure: A grossly inadequate physical infrastructure, which severely blocks transport and trade in the movement and marketing of products, constitutes a major bottleneck to development in Africa. Great distances and few navigable inland water courses are severe constraints. This is compounded by rugged terrain and deeply incised water courses, as well as seasonally flooded swampy areas. In many parts of Africa, gravel and other road building materials are not readily available and have to be moved long

distances or replaced by inferior surfacing material that can hardly withstand the severe climatic conditions. With the need for greater subregional and intercountry cooperation in trade and development, the lack of infrastructure is an increasingly serious impediment. Even within a country, the transport infrastructure is a prerequisite to input supply, produce movement, and the extention of technology and training to farmers. African governments, though handicapped by lack of funds for investment in an infrastructure, are aware of the problem. The building of Pan-African highways is an example of the determination of African governments to solve it. Thus the development of adequate infrastructure in African countries is another area that commands donor support.[15]

CONCLUSION

The deteriorating African food and agriculture situation constitutes a major challenge to the international community. Worsening trends confirm the inadequacy and unpreparedness of African governments in particular and the international community as a whole. It is, however, African governments and peoples themselves who must be the prime movers and arbiters of their destinies, especially in the drive for increased self-reliance. To this end, they must be supported in a more resolute and concerted manner by donors and international organizations, who must increase investments and make appropriate policy adjustments for reviving and accelerating food and agricultural development.

NOTES

1. For countries like Algeria, Djibouti, Gabon, Libya, Reunion, Seychelles, Zambia and Zimbabwe, the contribution is relatively small (3 to 15 percent) and large (52 to 64 percent) for Burundi, Comoros, Gambia, Guinea Bissau, Niger, Rwanda and Uganda.
2. Professor Adebayo Adedeji's opening statement at the Fifth Meeting of the Technical Preparatory Committee of the Whole, Addis Ababa, May 1984.
3. FAO/UNFPA/IIASA, Potential Population Supporting Capacity of Lands in the Developing World, Report of Project FPA/INT/5/3, Land Resources for Population of the Future (FAO, Rome, 1982).
4. During 1982 for example, these prices declined sharply: cotton, 14 percent; sugar, 49 percent; and tea, 4 percent.
5. Angola, Benin, Botswana, Cape Verde, Central African Republic, Chad, Ethiopia, The Gambia, Ghana, Guinea, Guinea Bissau, Lesotho, Mali, Mauritius, Mozambique, Sao Tome and Principe, Senegal, Somalia, Swaziland, Tanzania, Togo, Upper Volta, Zambia, Zimbabwe.
6. During the 20-year period between 1960 and 1980, the African share in world trade of most of the continent's commodities declined. World trade in these commodities grew in volume by 1.8 percent and by 3.3 percent in value annually, while comparable rates for Africa were zero and 1.8 percent per year.
7. MULPOCs (Multinational Programming and Operational Centers) are decentralized arms of ECA.
8. Cameroon, Central African Republic, Chad, Congo, and Gabon.

9. Development Assistance Committee of the OECD; DAC (83) 14, in constant prices.

10. The narrow definition of agriculture refers to activities relating directly to sector and includes the appraisal of natural resources, development and management of natural resources; research; supply of production inputs; fertilizers; agricultural services; training and extension; crop production, livestock development, fisheries; etc. These are all activities that are directly in support of agriculture. On the other hand, the broad definition includes in addition activities defined as relating "indirectly to sector." These additional activities are forestry; manufacturing of inputs; agro-industries; rural infrastructure and rural development; regional development; and river basin development.

11. ECA, Apparent Discrepancy between Increasing Resource Allocation to Food and Agriculture in Africa and the Declining Performance of the Sector (Document E/ECA/CM.10/21), 1984.

12. FAO, The State of Food and Agriculture (C 83/2), August 1983, p. 41.

13. World Bank, Accelerated Development in Sub-Saharan Africa: an agenda for action (Washington: World Bank, 1981).

14. OAU, The African Food Crisis: Basis for Future Action, Tenth Session of the UN World Food Council, (AIMCF/II), Addis Ababa, June 1984.

15. World Food Council, The African Food Problem and the Role of International Agencies (Document WFC/1982/4 Part I), May 1982.

Cyril Kofie Daddieh

11 Recovering Africa's Self-Sufficiency in Food and Agriculture

If you want to help hungry people, don't give them food, teach them how to fish.

A Chinese Proverb

Before people can do anything they have got to eat. And if you are looking for a way to get people to lean on you and be dependent on you, in terms of their cooperation with you, it seems to me food dependence would be terrific.

Hubert Humphrey

The tragic human drama that has been unfolding in Ethiopia in recent months is merely the latest episode of an enduring development crisis on the African continent. It may be characterized as a gradual but continuing deterioration in the continent's capacity to meet the dietary needs of its burgeoning population. In comparison to a high annual population growth rate of roughly 3 percent, coupled with rising urbanization, food production is estimated to have increased by a mere 1 percent for 1980-81, a modest 3.7 percent for 1981-82, and then to have plummeted to 0.2 percent between 1982 and 1983. Persistent declines in food and agriculture have been recorded in many parts of the continent since the late 1960s, perhaps even earlier. And historical trends reveal that Africa has been lagging far behind Asia and Latin America in per capita food production (see figure

10.1).

The trend toward falling prices for most of Africa's traditional export raw materials has combined with the rather sluggish performance of the agriculture sector to seriously undermine the continent's capacity to successfully compete on the world market for grains intended to shore up domestic food production. The oil price hikes of the early 1970s have had an even more devastating impact on Africa's development prospects and on food and agriculture in particular.[1]

The pressures on both food production and food supplies have been pervasive and persistent rather than confined to a few countries on the continent. However, this development condition is, as the LPA has suggested, paradoxical rather than inevitable, especially given Africa's immense human and natural resources.

> In addition to its reservoir of human and natural resources, our continent has 97 per cent of world reserves of chrome, 85 per cent of world reserves of platinum, 64 per cent of world reserves of manganese, 25 per cent of world reserves of uranium and 13 per cent of world reserves of copper, without mentioning bauxite, nickel and lead; 20 per cent of world hydro-electrical potential, 20 per cent of traded oil in the world (if we exclude the United States and USSR); 70 per cent of world cocoa production; one-third of world coffee production, 50 per cent of palm produce, to mention just a few.[2]

The crisis in agriculture is particularly distressing because of the rural character of African economies and the overwhelming participation of the continent's population in the agriculture sector. Well over 70 percent of the continent's labor force is engaged in some form of agricultural pursuit. Yet the continent is even less self-sufficient in food production now than it was only a decade ago. As a result, a growing proportion of import expenditures is now devoted to food. Food imports have outstripped even fuel as a percentage of total imports.[3]

The composition of food imports raises serious questions about the efficacy of public policy with respect to equity goals subscribed to in official documents and the promise of recovery of national and continental self-sufficiency in food and agriculture, both as means to self-sustaining economic development and as adjuncts to recovering the continent's political salience in international affairs.[4] Such issues are germane to any serious discussion about the future recovery of self-sufficiency in food and agriculture, partly because wheat and sugar, the major components of food imports, have a much higher demand elasticity than either coarse grains (maize, millet, and sorghum) or roots and tubers (cassava, plantain, yam, cocoyam, etc.). Despite a certain degree of homogenization of tastes between town and countryside, as well as between different classes in Africa, the latter set of foods remain the primary staple foods of the majority of the African population. these staple foods have been largely neglected in the past in favor of costly food imports and food handouts, Africans in lower income brackets have lacked the kind of political and economic clout that would have effectively entitled them to imported food items.[5] More lamentably, food imports and foreign food subsidies have had a depressing impact on farm incomes and subsequent productivity. As Shamsher Singh has noted:

> The preference for wheat and rice is being fueled by consumer subsidies, food aid, and indirect subsidies through overvalued exchange rates. Subsidized prices for wheat and rice have not only depressed prices of traditional food crops, but also destabilized them.[6]

If historical trends are allowed to continue and current deprivations become exacerbated, Africa's future is likely to be characterized by greater competition for scarce public resources and associated conflicts over the policy process as it relates to location-allocation issues and the chances for social mobility. Such a future is unlikely to produce significant shifts in resource allocation in favor of the unorganized poor and farm sector in Africa. In this regard, even where particular African countries are able to manage a food import strategy, the benefits are likely to accrue largely to the fortunate few. The need, therefore, to recover national and regional self-sufficiency in indigenous staple crops is not only indispensable, it makes good political sense.

We need to pause, briefly, to reiterate not just how ubiquitous and persistent the crisis in the agriculture sector has become but also the unevenness of its impact on classes, communities, villages, and households. The responses to the crisis, too, have varied at state, community, continental, and international levels. While many rural households, classes, and countries have witnessed a steady decrease in their disposable incomes and have been compelled to withdraw from commodity production and the state nexus, a few have been well served by continued participation and association. Thus, there are bound to be both tensions and discrepancies between those indigenous communities, classes, and international associates that advocate and work toward the implementation of a self-reliant strategy for national and continental self-sufficiency in food and agriculture and those that seek to uphold Africa's seemingly immutable role in the international division of labor.

GENESIS OF THE CURRENT CRISIS

In order to comprehend fully the nature of the current demise of agriculture and associated food problems on the continent as well as the prospects for future recovery, it is useful to view the continent's historical role in the international division of labor. A detailed analysis is beyond the modest scope of this chapter. It will suffice to indicate that by the time African states gained formal political independence in the 1960s, the continent's role in world trade had already been carved out for it. This role involved the production and export of a rather narrow range of commodities and raw materials. A measure of the degree of African involvement in the world economy and the relative success achieved are reflected in the phenomenal growth of such crops as cocoa, coffee, groundnuts, palm oil, cotton, etc., which remain primary sources of state revenues. Success was achieved by the exemplary exertions and economic motivations of indigenous peasant producers.[7]

Although some coercion was applied through poll and hut taxes, labor legislation, and location-allocation decisions in an effort to induce whatever peasant response was desired,[8] the seemingly more benign instruments proved most effective. An important case in point is the penetration of relatively low-cost European goods, much of which, incidentally, were consumed and therefore did not enter directly into the production process. This penetration did, however, strengthen the linkages between the countryside and newly created urban/commercial and politico-administrative centers. More importantly, the presence of various merchant capitalists and their products stimulated a further monetization of rural African economies and generated intense pressure for cash in many areas. The resultant socio-political and economic impacts were far-reaching. They involved both social differentiation and conflict stemming from the sale of communal land for commodity production, growing indebtedness from loans and land rents, increased social stratification, and subsequent social struggles. Most regrettably, the onslaught of European manufactures also undermined indigenous industries and contributed to the deterioration of their technological capacity.[9]

In addition to the introduction of European goods, particular mention must also be made of the important influence of various missionaries, indigenous ruling elites, and colonial institutions. For instance, the Basel Mission played a pioneering role in promoting the Gold Coast cocoa industry. In addition to starting trial plots and distributing seedlings to converted farmers, the mission also opened up schools. It must be recognized that schooling was and remains an important investment outlet for cash accruing to farming households from commodity production. Since the need to invest in education acted as a catalyst for cash, which in turn stimulated increased participation in commodity production, the influence of such missions cannot be underestimated.

The involvement and acquiescence of influential rulers and indigenous elites was another important influence on the peasantry. Elite household heads became important commodity producers in their own right and often acted as conduits between colonial administrations and their communities. As so-called progressive farmers, they benefited from select seeds, marketing stations, and research results (arguably few and of limited value), provided by the Royal Botanic Gardens and Department of Agriculture officials.[10]

The available historical evidence indicates that the responsiveness of African peasants to commodity production was based on rational calculations that were both immediate (the differential rates of return as compared with other economic and social activities) and anticipatory (What are the likely pay offs? Will they be enough to satisfy future wants?). The nature of the involvement in commodity production by individuals, households, and communities depended very much, however, on access to suitable land, and, no less importantly, on the labor available to the production unit.[11]

In the early decades of this century, the trade in export commodities made possible an expansion in the area of cultivation and brought new lands under the hoe and the cutlass. Since African farming systems were frequently characterized by intercropping, the early stages of export commodity production stimulated food production as well. Moreover, there appeared to be an unlimited supply of land, especially in the forest zone, that could be devoted to food production. Hence no real anxieties arose over the penetration of new crops into the interior.

This apparent lack of population pressure on the land encouraged the continuation of technologies and techniques that, while compatible with the often harsh environment, could only support extensive rather than intensive cultivation. Thus shifting cultivation or rotational bush-fallowing or concentric ring farming all came to characterize the African farming technique. This system of allowing farm land to lie dormant for several years in order to recuperate soil nutrients was effective as long as population pressure and demand for land were kept within manageable limits. How intensively a particular piece of land was cultivated and the length of the fallow period also depended on environmental conditions and on changing patterns of household organization. Households that possessed fewer farm hands or smaller acreages were more likely to shorten the fallow period and cultivate more intensively.[12]

Crop selection was important to the success of this system of production. Generally speaking, the crops that were selected were among those that were genetically more resilient and well suited to the prevailing ecological conditions. They were thus less vulnerable to pests and diseases. This partly explains why grains such as sorghum and millet and roots and tubers such as cassava, yam, cocoyam and plantain are such popular staple crops. Of course, their storage capabilities and savings in labor time are additional merits.

Market linkages between towns and countryside provided an outlet for agricultural surpluses and stimulated increased production. Grains and other food items were actively traded both locally and over relatively long distances. Some settlements gained considerable prominence as market towns and grain centers. They witnessed an expansion in the scope of their functions as well as in their populations. Bamako, Salaga, and Kano are illustrative cases in point.[13]

The labor process in this system of agriculture was predicated on a sexual division of labor. With few exceptions, the critical role of producing, processing, and marketing food was assigned to women, while men were free after performing their land clearing and burning duties to pursue other economic interests. Women were also responsible for supplying the staple side of the dietary needs of the household. Quite clearly, this sexual division of labor within the African household was partly responsible for the monopoly by men of the export commodity sector (leaving aside the transfer of European sexist notions to African society.)[14]

Moreover, the heads of households and community elites exercised control over the available labor force. Since they had prior claim to the labor services of young men and women, there was often marginal labor available to women food producers. Under such circumstances, the proximity as well as quality of the land available to women food producers were keys to the self-sufficiency and food surpluses achieved by women. If future recovery of the food and agriculture sector is to become a reality, such sexual divisions of labor and differential access to resources must be recognized and redressed (see chapter 12).

The inducements to produce cash crops for export had a number of profound implications for the system and structure of agriculture as it was practiced. First, the balance of priorities shifted from devotion to food crop production to a concern for cash from export commodities. Either as peasant producers or state functionaries dependent on the revenues from export trade, Africans were so consumed by these cash crops that they neglected their food consumption needs. As a Ghanaian Commissioner for Agriculture put it, the "major cause of food shortage in previous years is that never in our history has there been a purposeful plan for the growing of such crops as cassava, plantain and cocoyam."[15]

Not only did the crop priorities change but, second, local and regional market linkages were left to decay because the locus of demand for the new crops was external rather than internal or contiguous. And third, by their very nature cash crops represent a withdrawal of farm land from the collective pool. The problem was not just the privatization and collection of farm lands by fortunate pioneers, although that in itself is a potentially explosive issue in Africa as elsewhere. These crops undermined the access of food farmers, predominantly women, to farm lands.

Land dispossession is not a general condition of the African peasant food producer. But even where landlessness is not a critical problem, the expanded reproduction of cash crops has pushed available food farms further inland. Thus, fourth, the cash crop revolution has, at the very least, increased the walking distance to food farms. As distances to food farms have increased, the combination of backbreaking activities connected with food farming and fatigue has taken its toll on labor productivity in the food sector.

Cash crops competed with food producers for more than just land; they also competed for increasingly scarce household labor resources. Again, labor resources have been controlled in most communities by male heads of households and villages. Thus, fifth, male involvement in commodity production tended to draw labor resources away from female food producers. It is easy to see how rural outmigration and the improved availability of educational opportunities for rural youth would exacerbate the problems of labor supply to food producers. The underdevelopment of rural transport infrastructure has left the food sector woefully underserviced, resulting in high production and marketing costs and leaving the food farmer particularly vulnerable to the accumulating tendencies of ambitious transport owners. High transportation costs act as barriers to attempts by small-scale producers to bring the food to market. And often what one finds in the market place is the sum of what women producers and suppliers, together with young helpers, have been able to bring in on foot. Is it any wonder, then, that there are food shortages?

These various constraints have led to intensive cultivation and shortened fallow periods, which, without adequate nutrient compensation using fertilizers, have inflicted serious ecological damage. The current ecological crisis is the logical outcome of the introduction and commercialization of crops such as groundnuts and cotton that have different nutrient requirements than those produced by African farmers as staple food crops. The ancient methods of resource utilization in the harsh lands of Africa remain functional but, as Earl P. Scott suggests, "they have been knowingly displaced, substantially altered or uncritically expanded in favor of methods intended solely to produce select crops for export to overseas markets."[16]

Meanwhile, a combination of external and internal forces, some of which I have already alluded to above, have exacerbated the problems of production and supplies in Africa. Externally, the market, as reflected in falling prices for Africa's raw materials and export commodities, has had a serious dampening effect on production. The trend toward falling tropical commodity prices is due to several factors, including excessive competition among producers on the one hand and monopoly buying by a few giant TNCs, the availability of substitute products, and speculation by various brokers. Subsequent declines in state revenues are a measure of the elusiveness of cartelization attempts and stabilization arrangements. The decline in commodity prices has been accompanied by a continuing rise in import prices.

A leading advocate of the export-oriented strategy of development in Africa, President Felix Houphouet-Boigny of the Ivory Coast, was recently compelled to issue a warning that the newly educated generation of Africans will not tolerate for long the same meager compensation their ancestors received for their coffee and cocoa. He questioned the equity of rising consumer prices for coffee, cocoa, and chocolate bars as compared with falling producer prices. The seriousness of the predicament is reflected in a 25 percent drop in revenues from cocoa and coffee for the Ivory Coast from their 1981 levels. This drop has also posed serious problems for balance of payments management. And for the first time since independence, the country's debt has had to be rescheduled, much to the chagrin of the president because of the implications to continued attraction of foreign factor inputs.[17]

The failure of the export market and the deteriorating terms of trade have had domestic repercussions. Faced with the expectations of independence and the mounting demands for schools, roads, hospitals, clinics, housing, clean water, etc., the African state borrowed the one seemingly effective policy instrument bequeathed to it by the colonial state for generating revenues. The state extracted resources from the peasant agriculture sector through the mediation of marketing boards and combined that with the policy of trying to secure food as cheaply as possible for the urban consumer. The latter strategy was intended to placate the urban working class in particular and dissuade it from making too many salary demands.[18] Such a strategy impacts heavily on rural women, who are by far the most important producers and suppliers of staple food crops in Africa.

Not only do African states pay their peasant producers less than the real value of their basic commodities, but they have invested marginal resources for research and development in agriculture. It has been noted that agriculture expenditures lag behind education, defense and general services, partly as a result of the cost structure of these various services and also the class background of occupants of state offices. In the first instance, the agriculture sector in Africa is less dominated by recurrent costs, especially wages, which tend to enjoy priority claims on government expenditures. The lack of cohesion and independent political organization among peasant producers, as compared to teachers and the military, may be an even more crucial consideration. The peasantry's lower class position and the depoliticization as well as departicipation of a majority of the rural population have enabled revenue shortfalls to be made up through reductions in the agriculture budget.[19]

Neglect of rural socio-economic interests and the extraction of surplus from the rural sector have resulted in a gradual deterioration of state-local relationships, leading to the apparent withdrawals by the rural sector from commodity production, the rediscovery of local self-help and self-reliance, an increased incidence of informal cross-border trade, and national economic decay.[20] A good example is the case involving peasants smuggling cocoa across Ghana's borders into neighboring countries where black market exchange rates make the effort particularly lucrative. It has been estimated that in 1977 alone some 40,000 tons of cocoa were smuggled out of Ghana. This represented over 12 percent of that year's total output and is believed to have cost the state US$100 million in foreign exchange earnings.[21]

There is evidence to suggest that where the terms of trade actually improved for farmers, there were positive shifts in favor of food production. In Ghana, where the terms of trade index for cocoa growers dropped steadily from 170 in 1956 down to 47 in 1976, the exit rate from cash cropping has been quite pronounced--in the neighborhood of 125,000 acres per annum. By contrast, the high domestic market prices for coconut oil have bolstered the coconut industry. The entry of new producers into this cash crop industry since the late 1960s has been simply phenomenal.[22]

SOME POLICY IMPLICATIONS

The foregoing overview is filled with several important lessons for future policy formulation. Since there is now evidence to suggest that under favorable conditions African peasants respond to state initiatives for increased production of particular commodities, the task ahead involves providing those requisite conditions. These include access by Africa's peasant producers to land and labor, an adequate cash remuneration for their backbreaking efforts, and the enjoyment of economic support services (transport, markets, institutional credit, etc.) and human services (schools, clinics, housing, etc.). It is important to remember that the provision of some of these services, rudimentary though many were, and the anticipation of improvements in rural standards of living through involvement in commodity production stimulated the successes of the past several decades.

Conversely, the recognition that the anticipated development has bypassed them is partly responsible for peasant producers withdrawing their support for national economic interests. The recovery will not get off the ground until African policymakers are able to convince peasant producers that their interests will be protected under new state-local exchanges and relationships.[23]

Furthermore, since past successes were achieved without the benefit of extension support services from the state (rather, farmers learned from their neighbors and from locally recognized successful farmers), the recovery will require imaginative changes in extension-farmer relationships. African states must recruit locally reputable peasant (as opposed to progressive) farmers and hone their skills for disseminating their knowledge more widely. However, if the need arises for young graduates from the university and agricultural institutions to do agricultural extension work, it would be unwise and ultimately counterproductive to thrust them upon local communities as change agents unless they have experience in local farming and environmental conditions. In short, the current interventionist modus operandi that characterizes agricultural extension work needs to be replaced by a participatory approach.

To illustrate the point, during a visit to northern Nigeria in 1911, E.D. Morel, the European agronomist, was so impressed by the wealth of ecological and farming knowledge possessed by local farmers that he remarked, "in the northern part of Zaria and in Kano 'the science of agriculture' had attained remarkable development....There is little we can teach the Kano farmer. There is a lot we can learn from him."[24] We may, of course, be able to do both. But the essence of the above assessment is corroborated by recent research among rice farmers in Sierra Leone and indicates that this is not an isolated instance. As Paul Richards contends:

> Farmers are knowledgeable about land resource management issues. Often, villagers are the _only_ experts on the specific processes and problems affecting their farm lands....It is unreasonable (and unfair) to expect extension services to try and force through changes, the need for which is not yet apparent to the majority of small-scale farmers and which are incompatible with their existing land management strategies, solely in the interests of a long-term land use policy recommended by agricultural planners on 'text-book' grounds.[25]

Richards goes on to submit in a manner consistent with my earlier arguments that "there would be more merit (and job satisfaction) in a _participatory_ approach to agricultural extension, in which the extension worker is trained to recognize and develop a creative response to land management processes and problems which farmers are already addressing."[26]

The above reflections highlight the need for identifying problems and planning agricultural programs and strategies through the consultative and participatory process. They call for a democratization of the development process, combined with a certain measure of decentralization of planning and budgetary control. These measures are also likely to minimize the pressures on the central budget, since communities are more apt to mobilize their own financial resources for project implementation through self-help. As already indicated, implementation of such measures implies fairness; it is desirable for reasons of equity and increased productivity that more of the benefits resulting from local efforts remain within the community and that some share of national resources be available in rural areas.

The extant historical evidence and recent developments point to the imperative need for reviving and strengthening old market linkages and creating new ones. The focus therefore should turn from serving the extracontinental markets to developing the domestic and regional markets as a way of stimulating production and exchange. A recent survey I conducted of the growth of a locally contrived produce market in a border village has convinced me of the generative influence of a "liberated" and sustained market on production and exchange.[27]

Of particular relevance to the issue of market linkages and increased food production and supplies is the preponderant role of women. The strength of the recovery will depend in part on the degree to which women in Africa are given encouragement and resources to produce and supply nutritional foods to their communities and urban consumers. It is important to remember that the plight of women producers is somewhat analogous to that of small-scale farmers. The problem is partly gender and partly class. And we need to ensure that the small-scale female or male farmer has access to land, institutional credit, labor, and the market. Needless to say, male or female farm producers must receive prices for their products that are reflective of the real value of their labor.

African states need to do more than ensure fair prices for farm products. As I have already suggested, they need to create conditions and opportunities not only for generating incomes in the rural sector but also for spending it. We cannot expect peasant producers to continue to produce if opportunities for spending incomes thus generated are not made available to them. In the past, schooling and housing improvements have provided two important avenues for rural investment. There are indications that these two investment outlets are no longer sufficient to sustain peasant interest in the farm sector in Africa. In order for the recovery to be sustained, it is imperative that investment opportunities in rural areas be improved based on local resources and geography, especially if the trend toward outmigration of rural youth is to be reversed.

The recovery of food self-sufficiency requires more than the enhancement of opportunities for small-scale female and male farmers. Where opportunities have been available to them and producer prices have warranted the investment, women, like their male counterparts, have gone into cash crop production or into alternative economic pursuits. Future strategies can ill afford to ignore the profit margins of cash crops and competing alternatives in the economic arena. Research on food must also be given high priority in budgetary allocations as a way of restoring the balance between commodity production for export and food production and supplies for domestic consumption.

THE CONTINENTAL RESPONSE

The LPA has recognized the centrality of food and agriculture to self-sustaining socio-economic development in Africa. It proposes to transcend the continent's unenviable inheritance in this area by striking a more appropriate balance between the production of commercial or export crops and staple foods for the African diet. It has shown uncanny appreciation for some of the essential needs of the food and agriculture sector as outlined above. While it does not ignore the contingent factors that have been militating against African agriculture in recent years, it focuses greater attention on the long-term structural constraints. It notes with uncharacteristic bluntness that "at the root of the food problem in Africa is the fact that member states have not usually accorded the necessary priority to agriculture, both in the allocation of resources and in giving sufficient attention to policies for the promotion of productivity and improvement of rural life."[28]

> For an improvement in the food situation in Africa, the fundamental requisite is a strong political will to channel a greatly increased volume of resources to agriculture, to carry through essential reorientations of social systems, to apply policies that will induce small farmers and members of agricultural cooperatives to achieve higher levels of productivity, to set up effective machineries for the formulation of relevant programmes and for their execution. The development of agriculture, however, should not be considered in isolation, but integrated within the economic and social development processes. Emphasis should also be put on the latter aspect, particularly on the problem of improving the conditions of rural life.
>
> For an effective agricultural revolution in Africa it is essential to involve the youth and to arrest the rural-to-urban drift. Policies have to emphasize consistently the need not only to improve the living conditions on the farms but also to increase real farm income as a means of making agriculture more attractive and remunerative.[29]

The corrective measures that the LPA has proposed revolve around two main axes: the creation of adequate incentives through the adoption of effective and coherent income and pricing policies, and the provision of essential farm inputs on the one hand and the building of physical infrastructure and institutional mechanisms for facilitating market linkages and intercountry exchange and cooperation on the other. The LPA calls for joint efforts in the application of science and technology to the problems facing the agriculture sector, such as pest control, seed selection, dissemination of information via extension services, etc. The LPA proposes that:

> Within the context of agronomic research, special emphasis should be placed on improvement of selected seeds, fertilisers, pesticides and other chemicals suitable for African conditions.
>
> Agricultural research is crucial to the transformation of agriculture in Africa. National research systems and inter-country co-operative research programmes should be strengthened. Agricultural research work should be geared to supporting the objective of food self-sufficiency, and liaison between research and extension should be made more effective.[30]

THE ROLE OF THE INTERNATIONAL COMMUNITY

The road to the recovery of Africa's self-sufficiency in food and agriculture will be fraught with difficulties and painful reorientations of priorities, resources, and interests. For the foreseeable future, external assistance will be needed to supplement Africa's efforts. This assistance need not have the same negative effects on the continent's development prospects as long as African interests have been clearly identified and strategies for the attainment of continental goals clearly mapped out as the LPA has attempted to do. It is vital in this regard to summon a political will that can only come from the mobilization of popular political support; hence, another plea for democratization of the policy and development processes.

It is important to recognize that just as there may be divergencies in continental responses, so the international community's responses will also vary. I am confident that there are enough progressive as well as relatively benign associations in the international community who will assist African efforts. I will focus briefly on the kinds of contributions that nongovernmental and private voluntary organizations (NGOs and PVOs) can make toward the recovery.

International assistance will be necessary in three main areas: research, action-oriented programs, and lobbying. In the first instance, research and training institutions and funding agencies can assist in data collection and analysis by providing institutional and financial support to researchers whose work is geared toward problem identification and solution or to teachers imparting similar relevant skills to Africans. Universities are well placed to facilitate the dual tasks of training and research. To date, however, university findings have not been adequately disseminated because few institutional mechanisms exist in Africa for tracking down relevant research, let alone for incorporating findings into policy formulation. Proper dissemination of research findings can be usefully combined with collaborative research between Africans and Africanist researchers from abroad. Funding agencies such as the International Development

Research Center (IDRC) and the Canadian International Development Agency (CIDA) can facilitate such tasks.

A number of action-oriented associations have been doing invaluable work in Africa and elsewhere. Some of these groups are so small that their contributions have often gone unnoticed. For an Africa concerned about avoiding the pitfalls of chemical and mechanized agriculture, the emergence of ecologically oriented farming groups and alternative farming options, such as organic farming, augur well for the future. The ECA or the OAU should collect and coordinate information about such groups in order to advise African governments about possible uses for their activities.

The International Small Farm Exchange Association of Prince Edward Island (PEI) in Canada exemplifies the kind of action-oriented programing I have in mind. This group recently entered into an exchange agreement with small farmers in Tanzania and Kenya, and both groups have visited each other's countries to exchange ideas about farming. The PEI group even made the important gesture of bringing Tanzanian and Kenyan coffee to sell outside channels controlled by the coffee barons. Hidden in one corner of the Midwestern U.S., in Iowa, is another group, SELF HELP, which describes itself and its mission as "a non-profit foundation dedicated to alleviating hunger by assisting small farmers worldwide to become self-sufficient in meeting the food needs of their communities. Efforts are focused on teaching the skills necessary to manufacture, operate and maintain appropriate farm equipment." There are other important examples ranging from church groups to the more familiar CUSO, OXFAM, and Match International that can be cited. But the key point is that the activities of such groups need to be properly coordinated and channelled to have a lasting impact in Africa.

Finally, in the international community there are grass-roots organizations that can bring pressure to bear on national policies to make them reflect the new international economic order. Africa's diplomatic missions should actively cultivate the support of progressive groups in the international community. In the U.S., blacks represent a neglected constituency in Africa's political and development strategy. Continental leaders must make a concerted effort to cultivate this "ethnic" link if Africa is to be successful at attracting more resources for development from Washington (see chapter 9).

CONCLUSION

The intention of this chapter was to explore the historical antecedents of the current crisis in African agriculture in order to gain insights into the kinds of reorientations in policy and planning that will be required for fashioning a self-reliant and self-sufficient future in food and agriculture. I have highlighted a number of measures that can enhance the prospects for recovering Africa's self-sufficiency in food, if they are pursued diligently. I have stressed the importance of reviving and strengthening domestic and regional market linkages and enhancing the role of women and small farmers by making available to them a greater share of agricultural resources than has been the case to date. I have also called for decentralized planning and budgetary control, at least as far as agriculture is concerned. The chapter has also noted the need to ensure that there are investment opportunities in rural areas for spending incomes generated from improved agricultural production. At the national and regional level, collaborative research on food crops needs to be intensified and the information disseminated through local extension agents. These reorientations may be particularly painful for some countries, but Africa's recovery lies in sustained pursuit of these goals.

NOTES

1. For more on this conjuncture and its impact on Kenya and Tanzania, see Yash Tandon, "New Food Strategies and Social Transformation in East Africa," Africa Development 6 (2) (1981).

2. OAU, Lagos Plan of Action for the Economic Development of Africa (Geneva: International Institute for Labour Studies, 1981), p. 7.

3. See Shamsher Singh, Sub-Saharan Agriculture: Synthesis and Trade Prospects (Washington: World Bank Staff Working Papers Number 608, 1983).

4. The relationship between food and diplomacy is revealed in our second opening citation and given practical expression in the Reagan administration's linking of military aid to El Salvador with food aid to Africa. On the interrelatedness of food scarcities and African diplomatic weakness, see Okello Oculi, "Food Imperialism and African Diplomacy in the 1980s," Africa Development 6 (3) (July-September 1981), pp. 63-73 and Carl K. Eicher, "Facing Up to Africa's Food Crisis," Foreign Affairs 61 (1) (Fall 1982): 151-174.

5. On the importance of thinking in terms of ownership and effective entitlement instead of aggregate food availability per capita, see Amartya Sen, "The Food Problem: Theory and Policy," Third World Quarterly 4 (3) (July 1982): 447-459.

6. Singh, Sub-Saharan Agriculture, p. 4.

7. See Polly Hill, "The History of the Migration of Ghana Cocoa Farmers," Transactions of the Historical Society of Ghana 4 (1) (1969: 14-28 and her seminal study The Migrant Cocoa-Farmers of Southern Ghana: A Study in Rural Capitalism (Cambridge: Cambridge University Press, 1963).

8. For illustrations, see Nii-K. Plange, "Underdevelopment in Northern Ghana: Natural Causes or Colonial Capitalism?" Review of African Political Economy 15/16 (May-December 1979): 4-14 and Kankuenda M'Baya, "Sous-Developpement de l'Agriculture et Pauvrete d'un Pays Riche: Cas du Zaire," Africa Development 5 (2) (April-June 1980).

9. For an illuminating study of these pressures and their impact, see Kwame Arhin, "The Pressure of Cash and Its Political Consequences in Asante in the Colonial Period," Journal of African Studies 3 (4) (Winter 1976/77): 453-468.

10. See Beverly Grier, "Cocoa Marketing in Colonial Ghana - Capitalist Enterprise and Emergency of a Rural African Bourgeoisie," Ufahamu, 1 and 2 (Fall-Winter 1980-81): 89-113 and her "Underdevelopment, Modes of Production and the State in Colonial Ghana," African Studies Review 24 (1) (March 1981): 21-43.

11. For more on this, see Cyril K. Daddieh, "The Political Economy of Food and Agriculture and Social Change in Nzimaland, Southwestern Ghana" (Ph.D. dissertation, Dalhousie University, 1984); John Tosh, "Lango Agriculture during the Early Colonial Period: Land and Labour in a Cash Crop Economy," Journal of African History 19 (3) (1978): 415-438 and

Jane I. Guyer, "Household and Community in African Studies," African Studies Review 24 (2/3) (June/September 1981): 87-137.

12. Ibid. and John Levi and Michael Havinden, Economics of African Agriculture (London: Longman, 1982).

13. See Plange, "Underdevelopment in Northern Ghana" and Richard Roberts, "The Emergence of a Grain Market in Bamako, 1883-1908," Canadian Journal of African Studies 14 (1) (1980): 55-81.

14. See Ester Boserup, Woman's Role in Economic Development (London: Allen & Unwin, 1970).

15. Quoted in Emmanuel Hansen, "Public Policy and the Food Question in Ghana," Africa Development 6 (3) (1982): 99.

16. Earl P. Scott, "Land Use Change in the Harsh Lands of West Africa," African Studies Reivew 22 (1) (April 1979): 3.

17. See "Ivory Coast--Houphouet's Gloomy Forecast," West Africa 3443 (8 August 1983): 1850 and Lyse Doucet, "Ivory Coast -- Rescheduling Progress," West Africa 3469 (13 February 1984): 341.

18. Robert Bates, Markets and States in Tropical Africa (Berkeley: University of California Press, 1981).

19. For a useful overview of state policies, see Albert D.K. Agbonyitor, "Central Government Expenditure Allocation for Agriculture in the Sub-Saharan African Economies," African Studies Association (Boston, December 1983).

20. Field research notes in Ghana. See also Merrick Posnansky, "How Ghana's Crisis Affects a Village," West Africa 3306 (1 December 1981): 2418-2420.

21. See Assefa Bequele, "Stagnation and Inequality in Ghana," in Agrarian Policies and Rural Poverty in Africa, eds. Ghai and Radwan (Geneva: International Labor Office, 1983), pp. 234-235.

22. This is fully reported in Daddieh, "The Political Economy of Food and Agriculture and Social Change."

23. Recent proposals for local governments in Ghana, Kenya, and Upper Volta, for instance, are promising first steps in this direction.

24. Quoted in Scott, "Land Use Change," p. 5.

25. Paul Richards, "The Ecological Knowledge of Sierra Leone Rice Farmers--Its Relevance to Extension," Workshop on The Role of Extension on Environmental Management and Agriculture (Freetown, May-June 1983).

26. Ibid.

27. Field notes partly reported in Daddieh, "The Political Economy of Food and Agriculture and Social Change." See also Jane I Guyer, "Female Farming and the Evolution of Food Production Patterns Amongst the Beti of South-Central Cameroon," Africa 50 (4) (1980): 341-356.

28. OAU, Lagos Plan of Action, p. 11.

29. Ibid.

30. Ibid., p. 16.

Agnes Akosua Aidoo

12 Women and Development in Africa: Alternative Strategies for the Future

The concern and action of many African women and some of their governments regarding women's role and participation in national and regional development predate the proclamation of the United Nations Decade for Women (1975) and the adoption of the Lagos Plan of Action (1980). But the advent of these two landmark strategies has provided a framework for review and appraisal of the issue in a broad context.

The Decade for Women is ending in 1985, at a time when Africa is impelled by worsening economic and social conditions to review and adjust its development efforts in order to attain the supreme goals of the Lagos Plan: self-reliance and self-sustaining development. In a sense the multi-faceted crisis may be regarded as Africa's crucial opportunity to reconsider the condition of its primary resource: its people. And women constitute the majority of the continent's population. Certainly the lessons learned from the past 10 years in the struggle for the advancement of women can be used to facilitate the implementation of a revitalized Lagos Plan for Africa's total development.

This chapter briefly outlines the situation of women and African development before the adoption of the Lagos Plan of Action. It then reviews the plan itself with respect to its limited emphasis on women and the steps taken so far at national, subregional, and regional levels to advance the cause of women in the plan's implementation. However, in view of the identified limitations, an attempt is made in this chapter to suggest alternative strategies for women and the LPA from now until the year 2000. The proposals are based mainly on strategies adopted at the Regional Conference on Women and Development held in Arusha, Tanzania, in October 1984. Finally, the urgent need for international assistance and cooperation for the implementation of these strategies is underlined.

WOMEN AND AFRICAN DEVELOPMENT BEFORE THE *LAGOS PLAN OF ACTION*

African women have had a strong historic role in the economic development of the continent, particularly in the agricultural and so-called informal sectors. Out of 50 million African women described as "economically active" in 1975 by the UN International Labor Organization (ILO), 34 million were engaged in agriculture, the highest female participation rate in this sector in the world.[1] Their strong economic role combined with their fundamental moral and cultural position in society should make African women a formidable force indeed. In many respects this force is only potential; it has yet to translate into power that would ensure the coresponsibility of women and men for Africa's development and the equitable sharing of the rewards from such development.

The factors that prevent such an equitable relationship are complex, but many aspects are well known. They include: (1) social attitudes of both women and men that define the proper roles and functions of women in subordinate terms with respect to men; (2) perceptions of the value of women's work in social (i.e., service) rather than economic (i.e., reward) terms; (3) conflicts in customary and statutory definitions of women as individual personalities and actors, especially in the area of property rights; (4) structural imbalances in African economies that favor the modern and urban sectors to the detriment of the majority of women found in the traditional, rural, and informal sectors; (5) the stress on economic growth in development planning with no corresponding emphasis on social equity; and (6) the unequal access of women to education, training facilities, and scientific knowledge at a time when an education provides access to employment, wealth, and power.

It is now generally recognized that women are an integral part of the production process in developing countries. In Africa their unrealized potential has a direct bearing on the quality and quantum of development. President Mwalimu Julius Nyerere underscored this point when he opened the Regional Intergovernmental Preparatory Meeting for the World Conference of the United Nations Decade for Women and the Third Regional Conference for the Integration of Women in Development held in Arusha, Tanzania, in October 1984. He said:

> The problem of women's development in Africa is inextricably bound up with the problem of African poverty. And it cannot be solved outside the attack on that poverty....Yet just as women's development in Africa is dependent upon national economic development, so national development is dependent upon the women of Africa and cannot easily take place without them. A person does not walk very far or very fast on one leg; how can we expect half the people to be able to develop a nation?...The attack on poverty needs to be waged in a manner which is liberating to the whole population. But that will only happen if women are involved in both the decision-making about development, and the implementation of those decisions.[2]

In general, development plans of African countries, like those in many parts of the world, have tended to incorporate quantitative targets for the entire economy rather than for different social groups. Overall development programs are supposed to cater to all, and there are no basic policy elements or specific programs calculated to improve the economic status of women. Women's consumption of certain social services such as health, social welfare, and community development are taken for granted as arising out of their natural condition and ascriptive roles.

The limiting of women's role in development to the social sector, where they are viewed mainly as beneficiaries rather than agents of change, has persisted in most African countries. It has characterized much of the effort to integrate women into the development process in the last two decades. Yet, besides their important productive roles already noted, some women in Africa took initiatives in political activities long before the United Nations Decade for Women was proclaimed. Their active participation in independence and national liberation movements and mass political parties in the 1950s and 1960s helped to raise African women's awareness and strengththen their organizational skills.

Women's organizational skills were also developed through social, cultural, and marketing associations, for example in Ghana, Nigeria and Sierra Leone. Thus the period before and immediately after independence saw women leaders from such associations--educated and noneducated--committing themselves voluntarily to programs for vocational training for young girls and for leadership, domestic science, and child care training for adult women in many countries.

The ECA played an important role at this early stage in promoting awareness and influencing policy at a broader level. It sponsored a series of regional meetings for the exchange of views and technical cooperation for the advancement of women. Such meetings included the Seminar on the Participation of Women in Public Life (Addis Ababa, 1960); Seminar on the Status of Women in Family Law (Lomé, 1964); Seminar on the Civic and Political Education of Women (Accra, 1968); Regional Conference on Education, Vocational Training, and Work Opportunities for Girls and Women in African Countries (Rabat, 1971); and the Regional Conference on the Integration of Women in Development, with Special Reference to Population Factors (Addis Ababa, 1974). This last Conference formulated the Plan of Action for the Integration of Women in Development in Africa, which called for (1) a series of measures to improve opportunities and services for women in practical fields and to change attitudes, (2) administrative and legal actions to improve the position of women in decision-making, and (3) the creation of the African Training and Research Center for Women (ATRCW). The center was established in March 1975 in pursuance of Resolution 269 (XII) adopted by the ECA Conference of Ministers of Economic Development and Planning. The African Plan of Action became the model for and was incorporated in the World Plan of Action, adopted at Mexico City in 1975 by the Conference on the International Women's Year (IWY) and later endorsed by the United Nations General Assembly.

The ferment on women's issues in Africa as elsewhere in the world received a great boost with the proclamation of the Decade for Women (1976-85). National programs and projects were initiated in many sectors, and several countries established commissions, councils, departments, and bureaus as focal points for women's issues. The ECA, through the ATRCW, gave considerable assistance to the strengthening of these national machineries and to the development of subregional and regional cooperation activities before the Lagos Plan was formulated. The Commission's efforts were strengthened by the generous support of bilateral and multilateral donors, NGOs, and UN agencies.

Between 1975 and 1980 the ATRCW made significant impact in the continent in a number of fields, such as:

1. technical consultancy services and catalytic support to women's groups, national machineries, and governments in the development of suitable approaches to women's issues: national machineries for the advancement of women have been established or strengthened in almost all African countries with the ATRCW's assistance;

2. action-oriented research in such fields as agriculture, nutrition, childcare, appropriate technology for farm and home, economic enterprises of women, cooperatives, law, etc., as well as research on topics such as the impact of economic changes on women, women under apartheid, refugee and displaced women, and research on methodology;

3. information networking and dissemination of research findings, workshops, and seminar reports: to date over 40 research publications,[7] annotated bibliographies, and numerous other reports and publications have been issued by the Center in English, French, Arabic, and Portuguese. These are disseminated to women's groups, focal areas, and to governments free of charge;

4. regional technical cooperation (TCDC) activities under the African Women's Development Task Force, which has enabled hundreds of African women and men to serve as experts and agents of change for the advancement of less fortunate women. This activity, which began in 1978, has been innovative in concretizing regional collective self-reliance in the area of expert service, particularly of women who assist relatively disadvantaged rural and peri-urban women in various economic enterprises to either travel to other African countries to broaden their horizons and expand their knowledge or to learn from African trainers and role models, who help them to develop confidence in their ability to succeed. The Task Force has also extended its assistance to some of the most disadvantaged women in Africa, such as refugee and displaced women, women in the national liberation movements, and women from the newly liberated Portuguese-speaking countries; and

5. training and technical assistance through workshops, seminars, and study tours to enhance women's skills and capabilities in agricultural and nonagricultural production, management of small-scale enterprises, development and project planning. Women in nearly all African countries have received some training assistance from the ATRCW.

Africa has led the rest of the regions of the world in developing institutions for subregional and regional cooperation on women's issues. In 1977 a Regional Conference on Women and Development was established; it meets every three years to review progress on the advancement of women. The third meeting was held in Arusha in October 1984. Between 1978 and 1981 five subregional committees (SRCs) on the Integration of Women in Development were established within ECA's regional cooperation network of MULPOCs based at Gisenyi (Rwanda), Lusaka (Zambia), Niamey (Niger), Tangier (Morocco), and Yaounde (Cameroon). The SRCs are comprised of representatives from the national machineries. With financial support from the United Nations Development Program (UNDP), ECA was able to place women coordinators in the five MULPOCs to serve as secretariats to the SRCs and develop and monitor subregional women's activities. In 1979 the Africa Regional Coordinating Committee for Women in Development (ARCC) was inaugurated at Rabat on the twenty-first anniversary of the ECA, with 15 member states agreeing to advise, coordinate, and monitor ECA's entire women's program.

The above machineries and institutions should not be seen by African governments as mere structural glorifications. They clearly anticipated the *Lagos Plan* strategy of technical and economic regional cooperation. In the face of common problems, the limited size of many countries and, even more serious, limited resources for development, collective solutions and mutual sharing are an inescapable necessity in Africa. Thus the various committees help to mobilize resources, coordinate development programs especially as they relate to women, and advise the respective policy organs at the national level, the MULPOCs, and the ECA on the needs of women. It is significant, for example, that the annual meetings of the ARCC are held at the same place and immediately before the annual meetings of the ECA Conference of Ministers. ARCC's reports go directly to the ministers, whose resolutions every year since 1979 have included policy and action directives regarding women.

WOMEN: THE NEGLECTED MAJORITY IN THE *LAGOS PLAN OF ACTION*

A cursory glance at the table of contents of the *LPA*--which addresses women and development in chapter 12--can lead one to sigh at the apparent low priority given to women in Africa's master plan of development. More serious still is the fact that a close reading of the sectoral and policy analyses reveals that the *LPA* is largely gender-blind until one arrives at chapter 12, which, in the words of an eminent African woman scholar, Marie Angélique Savané, seems to reinforce the "ghetto" status of women's issues:

> It is clear that this chapter does not have its place in a document like this one. The economic problems of women are in food and agriculture, industry, science and technology, environment, energy, etc....in fact in all the other chapters. The specific chapter on women only reinforces the "ghetto" status usually attributed to women's problems. A conceptual effort should be made to introduce specific problems of women within the analysis of the economic situation of Africa. It is only in this way we will effectively deal with the cause of women.[3]

In the above statement, Savané, who is the president of the Association of African Women Researchers for Development (AAWORD) based in Dakar,

Senegal, underscores the problem that I would call the dilemma of method in development planning. There is a persistent tendency for planners and strategists to conduct their work with a conscious or unconscious disregard of classes, social groups, and gender in society. They adopt an amalgamated approach towards the agents and beneficiaries of development, which appears satisfactory on the surface but in effect can be unrealistic and damaging when it conceals gross inequalities among segments of the populations.

The class and gender blindness of development planning has forced many disadvantaged groups in society to adopt the dual strategies of group self-preservation through renewal and remedial action and struggle for entry, integration, or incorporation in ongoing mainstream processes. This remedial approach has characterized women's programs not only in Africa but in the rest of the developing world. Indeed it was the approach with respect to women advocated by the International Development Strategy for the Second UN Development Decade in the 1970s. That global strategy influenced African and world plans of action for women.

Thus most of the efforts made before 1980 by African women, governments, and the ECA to provide opportunities for women to develop socially relevant skills, to gain experience, and to influence policies on development reveal certain limitations. These were due to: (1) the macrolevel planning methodologies that emphasize global (and often impersonal) targets for entire economies and populations; (2) the philosophy that viewed women's issues as primarily social, if not social welfare, problems; and (3) prescriptions of special remedial measures for disadvantaged social groups--in this case, women--who must struggle to integrate themselves in the ongoing mainstream development. These approaches not only assume the marginality or peripheral position of women in development but quite often perpetuate that concept.

The Lagos Plan unfortunately bears some of these characteristics and limitations. Most of the sectoral analyses and strategies in the plan require much greater refinement and specification to identify who, by class, social group, or gender, is meant by the "population," "manpower," "personnel," "human resources," "bulk of the rural population," etc., and how they are to be developed, assisted, or utilized in the development process.

The first and preeminent chapter in the LPA discusses food and agriculture and quite rightly so. The African economy is based primarily on agriculture and the current tragedy of the growing numbers of food-aid-dependent countries[4] compels the continent to take bold measures to alleviate the food crisis. But in this war against hunger, women have a fundamental role. They account for more than 60 percent of the subsistence agricultural labor, and they are responsible for the bulk of the processing, storage, and preservation. Yet chapter 1 of the LPA mentions women only in one place, where it calls on extension workers to focus their attention on "youth and women."[5] There is no recognition of FAO's estimate that only 3.4 percent of African agricultural extension staff are female, or the well known fact that farming and rural women grossly lack access to land, technical training, credit, and other inputs.

The relevant chapters on industry, natural (including water) resources, transport and communications, trade and finance, environment and energy make no specific mention of women or any particular social groups. The dawn-to-dusk work of women--reaching 16 hours a day in most countries--in tedious agriculture work, food processing, water and firewood collection, and trading in food and consumer goods is nowhere specified in these sectoral analyses. Therefore it is not clear that the sectoral strategies will alleviate the particular problems of women.

Only chapter 5 on science and technology makes clear and direct proposals for the provision of scientific and technological knowledge for women and for the utilization of women so equipped. Thus program element 2.4 calls for the development of programs to train and encourage more women to enter science and technology; program element 2.5 on the mobilization of the creative and adaptative technology potential in the informal sector proposes the training and orientation of the rural population, in general, and women in particular, to deal with technical problems; program element 2.6 on mass popularization of science and technology advocates campaigns using national languages, where possible, "with the primary object of getting rural women to participate more effectively in agricultural and rural technology programs and projects (e.g., food production, preservation, storage and use, and nutrition, etc.)"; program element 6.1 proposes the provision of an institutional infrastructure for training the required manpower, especially women, in identified priority areas of need; program element 8.3 calls for the development of subregional and regional exchange programs for women for the improvement of specialized skills; and finally, program element 9.1 urges financial and technical assistance at the international level for the programs of concern to women within the whole science and technology field.[6]

Perhaps the issue of women as the neglected majority in the LPA would not have arisen if it had been possible to design and produce the plan in an integrated fashion and with population specifications such as those found in chapter 5. As this did not happen, chapter 12 on women and development must be viewed as a necessary element in the plan, highlighting and to some extent correcting the plan's shortcomings. African leaders recognized this in the introductory paragraphs to the chapter, stressing that:

> The importance of giving special attention to women in the analysis of the reported situation and to measures to be taken in each of these sectors (industry, agriculture and trade, etc.) which have been previously considered, is acknowledged. The steps to be taken to solve the problems of African women should not be marginal and separate from the question of over-all development.[7]

In this light the rest of the chapter emphasizes that, apart from legislative, administrative, and institutional measures, action should be taken in relevant priority sectors with respect to education and training, employment, health, nutrition and family life, communications and media, and research and data collection.

When the ECA secretariat issued guidelines for the implementation of the LPA it was fully cognizant of the central role that women must play in achieving the plan's objectives.

> The full development and utilization of women as a large component of the natural human resources potential for industrial entrepreneurship, management, production, marketing, distribution, research and experimental development, institu-

> tional services (such as banking, insurance, shipping, civil aviation, business consultancy, tourism, and so on) is a necessary condition of the implementation of the Lagos Plan of Action and its successors.[8]

Within the secretariat itself the relocation of the ATRCW from the Social Development Division to the Cabinet Office of the Executive Secretary in 1983 gave it greater stature and emphasized the need for the redefinition of women's issues even in structural terms. The center is thus in a position to coordinate its activities more closely and undertake joint projects with the divisions of Agriculture, Industry, Natural Resources, Population, Public Administration, Management and Manpower, and Socio-Economic Research and Planning. Since 1981 the center has tried to organize its activities and report on its performance in the framework of the LPA in order to enhance the focus on women in the plan.[9]

Other measures have also been attempted by African women to correct the imbalances that exist in development plans and women's roles. The subregional committees and the Africa Regional Coordinating Committee have already been mentioned as key organs whose deliberations and recommendations should have a direct bearing on their counterpart policy organs, namely, the MULPOC Councils of Ministers and the ECA Conference of Ministers, respectively. The results achieved in the last four years are highly commendable, and the last meeting of the Lusaka Council of Ministers held at Addis Ababa in April 1984, for example, considered their women's program the most successful within the whole MULPOC system. However, there is room for improvement. Above all, there is need for the women on the committees and their supporting secretariats to ensure that the deliberations and recommendations made are really incorporated into the various sectors examined by the ministers and their experts, just as is requested in the LPA. This is a major challenge.

OBSTACLES AND PROBLEMS

The position of women in the implementation of the LPA and the UN Decade for Women was reviewed and appraised by women and men representing African governments, national liberation movements, and NGOs at the Arusha Regional Conference in October 1984. There was consensus that the UN Decade and the first four years of the Lagos Plan had seen great progress in the increase of women's visibility in society and their awareness of themselves. African women have gained the confidence to bring the subterranean inequalities and prejudices against them to the surface, whether these derive from structural weaknesses and rigidities in the socio-economic systems of their countries, scarcity of resources, or social and cultural values. As the Nigerian delegation emphasized, the new awareness has forced governments to accept that inequalities and prejudices exist and that they must adopt appropriate measures to combat them; it has also forced women into some self-assessment to see where they have contributed, however inadvertently, to their present condition through their own passivity or by teaching such prejudices to their children.[10] Several obstacles and problems yet remain.

Significant progress was reported also in the field of education for girls. At the primary school level there was near parity with boys; the secondary level showed an average of one-third female enrollment, with the exception of Mauritius and Swaziland, which had near parity, and of Botswana, Lesotho, and Seychelles, where girls outnumbered boys.[11] At the university and tertiary levels, progress was slight and the pattern of sex-segregated schools with unequal facilities and stereotyped curricula led to girls over-concentrating in liberal arts subjects with limited employment opportunities. Tanzania reported a remarkable increase in female enrollment at the university, from 9.7 percent in 1977 to 24 percent in 1982, as a result of the national policy of exempting girls from postsecondary national service. Nigeria also reported a positive change in that measures were being taken to give girls preferential access to science and technology educations. The indications are that at the initial stages some positive discrimination in women's favor might be necessary to redress inequities in many fields.

Reported changes in formal employment rates were generally modest. For instance, the percentage of women in wage/salary employment in Tanzania rose only from 6 percent in 1966 to 15.6 percent in 1983. Large numbers of working women in Africa are still found in low-status, low-paid, unskilled manufacturing jobs or in the nonmechanized, fluctuating, informal sector with poor working conditions and little or no trade union participation or worker benefits. While equitable participation of women in the industrialization process is essential to overall, self-reliant development, this will be difficult to achieve under conditions of surplus industrial capacity, surplus unskilled labor, and capital-intensive industrial policies. The few women currently in management or professional positions were slow to receive promotions and had limited opportunities for training.

Although women's representation has increased on high decision-making bodies such as parliaments, cabinets, and central and executive committees of political parties in several countries, it cannot be said that there is yet coresponsibility of women and men in the determination of or accountability for Africa's future. Often one or two women placed in high positions or the bureaus for women are expected to take care of "the women's problem" while their male counterparts deal with the "real" and "serious" issues of development.

Finally, the capacities for change, creativity, and inventiveness of the majority of women, especially in the rural areas, have not been galvanized for solving the central problems of African economic and social development. Women in the rural areas should have the greatest motivation for combating the harsh realities of drought, famine, hunger, disease, and poverty that haunt them and their families daily. There is evidence that such motivation is high, especially among the growing numbers of female heads of households. But they need technical and material assistance provided through participatory mechanisms that stress their self-motivation, self-reliance, and self-realization. In other words, there is a need for dynamic rural transformation and development where the inhabitants themselves assume responsibility in the formulation, planning, implementation, and monitoring of programs and projects. It is only when the "trickle down" approach to development is reversed that the majority of Africa's human resource capital can be placed in the center of the implementation of the *LPA*.

Major efforts are called for on two levels to surmount fundamental obstacles. The first must occur on the conceptual level and the second on the planning, implementation, and monitoring level. Conceptually, these are two separate yet related issues:

1. Is the notion of "integrating women in development" valid?

2. Is the pattern and structure of development into which they are to be integrated acceptable?

There is mounting evidence from research by many agencies, including ECA, ILO, the World Bank, and the International Research and Training Institute for the Advancement of Women (INSTRAW), as well as donor agencies, that poor perceptions of women's roles and work have led to the present inadequate concepts and measurements used in development planning. Women's work in the Third World is generally unrecognized and undervalued economically or is taken for granted as part of women's normal social and domestic functions. To combat such erroneous perceptions, vigorous campaigns were undertaken under the Mexico World Plan of Action for the "full integration of women in development" at the legislative, administrative, educational, and practical levels.

In Africa, however, the concept is inadequate and misleading. We cannot ask the majority of African women for fuller participation because they already work from dawn to dusk, and the sexual division of labor has made their tasks at home, in the farms and marketplace more tedious, time-consuming, and drudgery-filled than those of their male partners in development. According to ILO, young African girls start working at an earlier age (from 10 years of age) and old women (over 65 years of age) continue to work longer than their age groups anywhere else in the world. But the quality and efficiency of their participation are constrained by lack of technical and resource inputs and by lack of power.

Policy-makers and development planners, men and women, need to develop new concepts of economic activity and new measurements for the social and economic contributions to development of different classes and groups in society, as well as their equitable share of the responsibility, decision-making, and control over the course and products of that development. In particular there must be an end to the social and intellectual isolation of women in development policy, planning, and implementation. Their historic economic role, characteristic resourcefulness, and their accumulated experience should be recognized as some of the necessary inputs for a new type of development.

Care must be taken in the new framework of analysis to overcome the weaknesses in present approaches that isolate women as a single analytic category without due regard to class, social and cultural organization, environmental situation, etc. From Dakar to Bangui, from Tripoli and Kampala to Soweto, from the markets of Lagos to the Turkana nomadic communities of Kenya, African women present a mosaic of human resources, life-styles, and problems. Some women are endowed with major development resources, information and power; others, the majority, as already noted, are disadvantaged in marginal urban suburbs, poor rural areas, or drought-afflicted settlements. This reality makes women's issues and women's roles a complex set of concerns based on interrelated variables and requiring different levels of analysis and types of solutions within a holistic perspective of development.

The second conceptual problem relates to the pattern and structure of development itself. The integrationist view of women's issues implies an acceptance of the existing order, which in Africa before the Lagos Plan and to some extent even now means international dependency, emphasis on economic growth but not social equity, modernization on a large scale, and development from above with faith in the "trickle down" effect. How can women, properly defined as actors in development and agents of change, struggle to integrate into this order that has failed Africa? How can women seek equality in deepening poverty? Traditionally classified as social welfare "beneficiaries" of a system that does not adequately benefit anyone, the majority of women and their children have borne the brunt of Africa's poverty, as President Nyerere emphasized at the Arusha Conference.

WOMEN AND ALTERNATIVE APPROACHES TO IMPLEMENTING THE LAGOS PLAN OF ACTION

There is need to strengthen the focus on human beings as the center of development. This has been restated recently by Professor Adebayo Adedeji, Executive Secretary of ECA, who affirmed that:

> development is about people....To understand Africa's problems and to plan for their solution requires a knowledge of its population: how many people there are and the size of each age group, where they live, the extent and pace of migration. Such information makes it possible to allocate resources effectively.[12]

This was also the central theme in the discussions of a group of African and non-African experts, men and women, working in the region who met in October 1984 at Arusha, Tanzania, to deliberate on forward-looking strategies for the advancement of African women beyond the UN Decade. Their proposals were submitted to the Regional Intergovernmental Meeting, which amended and adopted them as the Arusha Strategies for the Advancement of African Women to the Year 2000. The overall message of these strategies is that it is now time to incorporate women into the solution of Africa's development problems, and that it is imperative for policy-makers and planners to recognize "that talent is not distributed by sex and that any policy that closes off from full development and uses the larger part of the national pool of talents is suicidal."[13]

In implementing the LPA from now to the year 2000, at least three important dimensions concerning women should be at the forefront of all considerations. The first is the demographic dimension. Estimates for 1980 showed there were 237 million women in Africa, giving a female to male ratio of 1.2 to 1. In the potentially economically active age range of 15 to 64 years there are more women than men, which has implications for labor force inputs into development. According to ILO estimates, most of the females in the African labor force are between 25 and 44 years of age; this is also the prime age group for childbearing. Moreover, African women have the highest rate of young marriage, below the age of 20, in the world --44 percent compared with the world average of 30 percent and 8 percent for the developed countries. The relatively high fertility rate--6.4 percent compared with the developing world average of 4.4 percent--and a declining infant mortality rate have combined to produce a young population and a high dependency ratio on the continent. By 1980, 44 percent of the total population was under the age of 15 years, and for every 100 active persons, there were 92 nonactive dependents.[14] In the existing unequal sexual division of labor in households, women bear the major responsibility for the care and welfare of Africa's large young population, and poor rural women work hardest to meet this responsibility. The inclusion of demographic variables in development planning will make possible family planning policies allowing women to control their fertility and bring better living conditions to themselves and their families.

The socio-economic dimension is the second area for consideration. While Africa's educational expansion between 1950 and 1980 surpassed that of all other regions in the world, UNESCO predictions indicate that by the year 2000 the disparity in secondary and postsecondary education between the sexes in groups 12-17 years of age and 18-23 years of age will increase. This reflects the persistent high dropout rate for girls, which is due largely to social and economic pressures. For those girls who do stay in school, there are limited opportunities for the scientific and technical training that would enable them to deal with their environment and compete with boys for jobs in the formal sector. For the nonschooled population, literacy (which now averages 25 percent among women) is increasing, but not fast enough to reach parity with men by the year 2000. The fear is that as the economic situation deteriorates so the existing gender-based factors working against the education and employment of women and girls will grow stronger.

The crucial role that women can play as agents of change in the much-needed rural transformation of Africa is severely constrained by their meager share of the means for production (land, capital, credit, technology, and training); insufficient supply and access to water (women are the principal water gatherers) for home consumption, irrigation, and transformation activities; heavy dependence on fuel sources with low grade energy conversion and high rates of energy loss (such as fuelwood, charcoal, crop residues, and animal dung), which only allows most women to undertake activities mainly for the maintenance and reproduction of life. While more women are migrating to cities, the majority of the projected 472 million urban dwellers in Africa by the year 2008 will be males.[15] The labor and social burdens of women left in the villages will be very great.

The Arusha strategies highlight a third dimension, namely, the environment of peace necessary for development. The sections on issues of peace, apartheid, and the question of refugees and displaced persons are more explicit than in the <u>LPA</u> in drawing attention to global tensions, the arms race, colonial and foreign domination, and racial discrimination, which have led African countries to divert scarce resources to security when resources should be channelled into economic development. Moreover, internal political instability, ethnic conflicts, and intolerance in many states, aggravated by scarcity of economic resources and natural disasters, have pushed hundreds of thousands of citizens across their national borders to live as refugees and displaced persons. Women and children are the worst victims as they represent the majority of the over three million refugees and ten million displaced persons officially recognized as such in 1983.[16] A proposal was in fact made at the Arusha conference that a women's component under a senior program officer should be established in the UN Center for the African Crisis to ensure that discussions and solutions to the crisis would adequately reflect the interests of the large numbers of women affected.

The present adverse situation of the majority of women in Africa is not irreversible. Other futures are possible. This has been shown in the report on "Women in Africa to the Year 2000" presented to the Arusha conference. The study of this question complements the ECA study, <u>ECA</u>

and African Development, 1983-2008, using the same outline and a similar scenario methodology. The report addressed the interrelationships of multiple variables such as the orientation and patterns of development itself, specific women-oriented policies and strategies, and a comprehensive, integrated strategy in which women's rights and duties would be conditioned neither by sex nor by elitism. A schema of the scenarios, variants, and trends is given in figure 12.1.

Figure 12.1

Alternative scenarios for the year 2000

Development trends

Women's trends	Scenario 1 Export-oriented development	Scenario 2 Transitional development	Scenario 3 Self-reliant and self-sustained development
No explicit plans or programs addressed to women	S1 Variant A Lack of policies oriented at integrating women within a dependent development pattern.	S2 Variant A Slow move to a different development pattern. No plans to palliate conflicting social demands.	S3 Variant A Structural change towards self-reliant development. Women's participation is not planned on integral basis.
Explicit plans and programs addressed to women	S1 Variant B Partial and fragmentary projects, geared from outside, oriented to integrate women within a dependent development.	S2 Variant B Improvements of women's spheres of participation remains fragmentary within a context of low economic growth.	S3 Variant B Participatory and democratic programs are launched to equalize women's condition within a self-reliant development.

It is not enough, however, to imagine alternatives for the future. It is necessary to adopt and implement plans to orient the present to what is seen as a better future. Some of the overall measures proposed in the Arusha strategies are summarized here.

1. Development planning should incorporate a definite awareness of the needs to improve the conditions of women and to involve women in the planning and decision-making processes and structures.

2. Feasibility studies, appraisals, and prospective evaluation of all projects should identify and anticipate their likely impact on women. Implementing bodies should assign proper responsibilities and mechanisms for accountability.

3. There is a need for institutional arrangements capable of monitoring changes in the situation of women in a sustained and consistent manner at various levels in order to assess what progress is being made and what problems are being encountered at the practical level.

4. In view of the centrality of women in development, planning ministries should establish a framework for incorporating women's needs and issues in development plans and strategies and for monitoring progress in their implementation in close collaboration with the national machineries for the promotion of women. In this regard interministerial collaboration and coordination is recommended.

5. National machineries should work in collaboration with judicial systems to initiate legislative changes in areas where discrimination still exists in legislation and practices.

6. As a long-term policy, schools and training institutions, centers, and adult education programs should incorporate leadership training in their curricula with emphasis on the part both men and women should play in decision-making. Suitable teaching materials should be revised or devised to meet this requirement.

7. In order to ensure the effective implementation of the overall development strategy, short-term and long-term arrangements should be made for increasing the representation of women, especially those in the rural areas and at the grass-root level, in policy-making bodies. There should be a definite system of distribution of responsibility and maintenance of accountability.

With respect to the sectors of development, the Arusha strategies highlighted agriculture and rural development, industry, and human resource development as some of the basic priority sectors that with proper handling can induce positive changes with multiplier effects within the economy and society. There is need for mobilization and development of domestic resources and factor inputs; the assurance of adequate water and energy for household consumption and agricultural and industrial transformations; research on development impacts; new technologies and methods of work; speedy dissemination of technical information through all media including local languages; and training and awareness-raising campaigns at various levels to emphasize the coresponsibility of men and women for policy formulation and decision-making, as well as the management of development.

Where women have deficiencies in capabilities in any of these respects, as well as in their productive and reproductive functions, programs should be designed within the overall development strategy and implemented by relevant technical ministries to overcome the obstacles and empower the women.

THE ROLE OF INTERNATIONAL ASSISTANCE AND COOPERATION

There is an important need for international understanding, assistance, and cooperation for the advancement of African women within a revitalized overall implementation program to achieve the goals of the LPA. The urgency of this cooperation in the overall program has been stated by African governments in the Special Memorandum by the ECA Conference of Ministers on Africa's Economic and Social Crisis submitted to the July 1984 Second Regular Session of ECOSOC.

Although a certain degree of sensitization remains to be undertaken among men and women, institutions and agencies, the major effort now for women, as for the LPA itself, is implementation. African women, men, and governments bear the major responsibility. But donor assistance is required for building domestic capabilities, especially of women, in project preparation, development, management, monitoring, and evaluation. Capacity needs to be developed to ensure that African men and women individually and in groups are continuously responsible and accountable for the translation into action of programs and projects intended to incorporate women into development. Research capabilities and methodologies also need to be developed or strengthened to ensure adequate assessments of the needs of rural and poor urban women, essential sex-aggregated data collection, development of appropriate statistical indicators, socio-economic analysis of women's situations, and, most importantly, approaches to incorporating women's concerns in major development projects.

Training opportunities, fellowships, and educational tours for the above purposes, within Africa and the Third World where possible, and in the developed world as necessary, would be a major contribution of the international community. In this respect, universities in the developed world with area interests and focus on Africa, such as Dalhousie University, can be of great assistance.

Communications networks and information dissemination channels and modes are a major area that can benefit from international assistance. Many governments, national machineries, and the ECA itself have a growing need to disseminate information effectively to men and women development agents and users especially in the rural areas. Efficient and innovative methods combining written and audio-visual materials in all operational languages in Africa are much needed.

The Arusha strategies strongly urge the involvement of women in donor roundtables, country programming exercises, and other negotiations for assistance to ensure that key areas of concern, such as the present drought, agriculture, water, energy, credit, industry, and rural development and education, include women as major actors for change as well as beneficiaries in an integrated development approach. In this regard, donor agencies should not only coordinate their programs at national, subregional, and regional levels with attention to women's participation but should ensure the involvement of women in determining quantitative targets in development assistance.

As the problems are huge and no single agency can render the necessary support alone, principles and practices of cost-sharing and trust funds can help to maximize the impact of international development assistance. In this respect the United Nations Trust Fund for African Development (UNTFAD), administered at the ECA, can be an important channel to provide assistance to development programs and projects that must be designed to have a definite positive impact on women.

CONCLUSION

A review of the situation of African women in development plans before and after the LPA shows that important progress has been made in awareness and some concrete programs. This chapter has concentrated, however, on only certain conceptual and implementation problems in development, showing that certain deficiencies exist that lead to the neglect of the central economic and social roles of women or to fragmented and tangential efforts to assist them. There are many reasons for adopting a new, holistic approach, which nevertheless pays attention to the demographic and socio-economic characteristics of women. Women are the majority of Africa's human resource; most of them lack basic resources and most of them are now very seriously affected economically and socially by the deepening crisis.

New strategies are required, and some are indicated in the *Arusha Strategies for the Advancement of African Women to the Year 2000*, which expand the areas and methods of intervention and implementation originally mapped out in the LPA. African women, men, and governments are aware of their primary responsibility for change, but clear understanding, cooperation, and assistance from the international community will strengthen their efforts to relieve the poverty of the majority of their people.

NOTES

1. *Women at Work* vol. 1 (Geneva: International Labour Organization, 1980), pp. 9-10.
2. President Nyerere's Speech to the African Regional Intergovernmental Preparatory Meeting for the World Conference of the UN Decade for Women, Arusha, Tanzania, October 1984, pp. 1-3.
3. Marie Angélique Savané, "Le Plan de Lagos et Les Femmes," CODESRIA/IDEP/ECA Seminar (Addis Ababa, March 1984), p. 11.
4. See *Special Memorandum by the ECA Conference of Ministers on Africa's Economic and Social Crisis* (E/ECA/CM.10/37/Rev.2), 1984, pp. 6-8, passim.
5. OAU, *Lagos Plan of Action for the Economic Development of Africa, 1980-2000* (Geneva: International Institute and Labor Studies, 1981), p. 17, para. 38.
6. *Ibid.*, p. 51, paras. 137-140; p. 59, para. 169; p. 69, paras, 196-197;
7. *Ibid.*, p. 111, para 296.
8. *Implementation of the Lagos Plan of Action* (Economic Consumer for Africa, ST/ECA/PSD.2/12, E/CN.14/TPCW.11/18/Rev. 1), Addis Ababa, 1982.
9. See "The African Training and Research Center for Women and Assistance to Member States in Implementing the Lagos Plan of Action"

(ATRCW/ARCC/82/WD/2), report submitted to ARCC II meeting, Douala, Cameroon, March 1982.

10. Report of Nigerian Delegation to Arusha Conference, October 1984.

11. See World Bank, World Development Report 1984 (Washington: World Bank, 1984) table 5, pp. 198-199 for 1981 statistics for these countries, also reports of delegations of Mauritius, Tanzania and Seychelles to Arusha Conference.

12. Adebayo Adedeji, Foreword to African Population (Addis Ababa: ECA, July 1984).

13. Report of the Regional Intergovernmental Preparatory Meeting for the World Conference (E/ECA/RCIWD/OAU/14), Arusha, Tanzania, October 1984.

14. See ECA, ECA and Africa's Development, 1983-2008: A Preliminary Perspective Study (Addis Ababa: ECA, April 1983), pp. 7-8; and "Women in Africa to the Year 2000" (E/ECA/RCIWD/OAU/10), report based on a study by an ECA/ATRCW consultant submitted to Arusha Conference. This section of the chapter is based mainly on this conference document.

15. ECA and Africa's Development, 1983-2008, p. 21 and "Women in Africa to the Year 2000."

16. "Refugee and Displaced Women in Independent African States" (E/ECA/RCWID/OAU/8), "Women and Apartheid in South Africa and Namibia" (E/ECA/RCWID/OAU/7), presented to Arusha Conference. ECA estimates that 150 million people have been adversely affected by the present crisis. See Adebayo Adedeji, The African Economic and Social Crisis: An Agenda for Action by Africa and the International Community (Addis Ababa: ECA, 1984), pp. 3-5.

George M. Kimani

13 Industry in Africa: Continental Cooperation and the Industrial Development Decade

This chapter is divided into two main parts. In the first part, the background and the meaning of the Lagos Plan of Action are reviewed, focusing on the plan's recommendations for industrial development and how industry can serve as a basis for international cooperation. Recent progress towards the implementation of the preparatory phase of the Industrial Development Decade is then discussed, and the impact of the African socio-economic crisis is assessed. The role of indigenous enterprise is underscored, and short-term and long-term priority areas for cooperation are identified in the context of the strategy of self-reliance and self-sustainment. In the second part, possible modalities of, as well as constraints on, industrial cooperation with different regions of the world are addressed, beginning with cooperation among African countries themselves.

IMPLEMENTATION OF THE INDUSTRY CHAPTER OF THE LAGOS PLAN

The starting point of Africa's dependent consumption and production patterns may be traced to the metropolitan economies that first used African markets to dispose of their surplus of manufactures. These economies also sought new types of raw materials to meet the expanding needs of home industry. In order to ensure exchange, it was necessary to identify some tropical products that met the consumption and raw materials needs of the industrial countries and for which there was no domestic supply. All these factors determined the volume of production and the form in which African products were marketed in metropolitan economies.

For every product, external demand determined the volume of production at any given time. The inelasticity of demand, the high volume of marketed output exported by many developing countries to a limited number of metropolitan markets, and the cyclical recessions in these economies led to frequent contraction of demand, persistent decline in terms of trade for primary commodities, and the introduction of export quota systems. The consequence is well known: control of the level of production in primary producing countries, especially in Africa, which slowed growth in those sectors producing export commodities. The impact of these external shocks on Africa has been most devastating, primarily as a result of the vulnerability of its economy; Africa is "uncommonly open" and hence more dependent on exports of primary products than any other region.

For products where some local processing was permitted, the degree of processing and volume of output were also bottlenecks: the more the raw material was processed the higher the tariffs assessed by metropolitan markets. This restriction hampered local processing and forward integration in production from raw materials to final goods. Not only did this policy limit the amount of the local value-added, it eliminated the introduction at local levels of more production activities that would generate the need for high level skills and technological growth. Finally, the frequent oscillation of external demand slowed down growth in the volume of output and hence in the number of people employed in industry at the time of a rapidly increasing potential labor force in Africa.

In the meantime, promotion of imports of surplus manufactures into Africa continued. The imitation of new consumption patterns, especially by the middle and higher strata in African society, was only a logical affirmation of the dependency syndrome. African values were destroyed, and there emerged the dependent person, alienated, shorn of self-respect and self-confidence, the peripherial or marginal person who was both mentally and economically dependent and incapable of self-reliance. "Economic dependence means political, social, and psychological subservience--whatever the rhetoric to the contrary may be. We all know full well that subservience saps initiative, vitality and creativity and results in loss of self-respect. Worse still it perpetuates the exploitation of the 'dependent' by the 'master'. A dependent economy having lost its self-respect commands no respect from the developed ones. Its people and leaders are despised at the same time as their economies are squeezed and exploited."[1]

Faced with mounting imports of new consumer goods and falling or stagnant exports earnings, import substitution was proposed as a cure for foreign exchange scarcities and as a means of creating jobs. The choice was clear: invite foreign investors to produce industrial goods locally. But since most of the companies who so invested were actually trading rather than investing companies, production of consumer goods in Africa was a good reason for maximizing exports to African countries in the form of intermediate inputs, parts, and raw materials. Under the circumstances, backward integration to natural resources did not and could not arise, so another major gap and a new form of structural dependency emerged.

The persistence of mass poverty, unemployment, pervasive malnutrition, rising food imports, declining terms of trade, deficits on the balance of payments, the growing debt service burden, and the increased underutilization of industrial productive capacities became commonplace. The dependence process was self-reinforcing: increasing external deficits called for more external orientation of production to meet rising foreign exchange commitments. The debilitating social and economic consequences of colonization are well known. "The impact of colonization remains more enduring in Sub-Saharan Africa than elsewhere, not only as regards the economic production and consumption structures, but also, and much more deeply, as regards the political and social structures."[2]

It was against this background that African leaders adopted the Lagos Plan as a strategy for self-sustaining economic development and individual and collective self-reliance. In the same context, the Industrial Development Decade for Africa was designed as the means of implementing the industrial chapter of the Lagos Plan. The objective of the decade program is to lay a solid foundation for a self-sustaining industrial sector, strong and dynamic enough to exert its influence and play its role in the economy as one of the main engines of growth and development, together with the food and agriculture sector. The industrial sector should not only provide its own inputs, but should also provide inputs for the food and agriculture, energy and transport, and communication sectors.

The Lagos Plan treats industrialization not as an end in itself but as a means to meeting inter alia the following ends within the framework of an integrated economy: (1) the satisfaction of the basic needs of the population, especially food, clothing, energy, and building materials; (2) exploitation of local natural resources; (3) the creation of jobs; (4) the establishment of a base for developing other economic sectors; (5) the creation of bases for accumulating and promoting technological progress; and (6) the modernization of industrial and other infrastructures. Furthermore, member states set for themselves targets of 1.4 percent and 2 percent of world industrial production by 1990 and the year 2000, respectively, against the 0.9 percent attained by 1980.[3]

In order to achieve the long-term and permanent goals of development and industrialization, members chose the strategy of self-sustaining industrialization and collective self-reliance. They proceeded to identify specific priority products and areas as a means of implementing this strategy. These include (1) development of human resources to ensure full mobilization for the industrial development process; (2) production in sufficient quantitites of agricultural inputs such as fertilizers, pesticides, agricultural tools, and machineries; (3) production in sufficient quantities of building materials for construction of decent urban and rural housing for the continent's growing population; (4) development of intermediate and capital goods industries, particularly those intended to support industries and infrastructures; (5) on-the-spot processing and upgrading of an increasingly large portion of the continent's raw materials; (6) satisfaction of energy needs by developing the different forms of energy available in the continent; and (7) satisfaction of textile requirements.

The Lagos Plan is therefore not merely an economic program; it is the crystalization of a historical process that began many years ago. The first President of Ghana, Kwame Nkrumah, referred to this process when he wrote of the African personality; the first President of Senegal, Leopold Senghor, expressed it in his writings and spoke of the empathetic African spirit; and President Julius Nyerere of Tanzania had this in mind when he popularized the idea and value of self-reliance. Particularly important, this process is the driving force in the African struggle for political independence. The struggle for total psychological, social, political and economic liberation and redefinition of the African person culminated in the Lagos Plan. Thus, the Lagos Plan is simultaneously several things: (1) it is an expression of the spirit of the new African self-appreciation; (2) it is also a statement of African aspirations as well as objectives and needs; and (3) it is an expression of the only appropriate means for attaining African social and economic goals: self-reliance and self-sustaining economic and social development.

Self-sustaining economic and social development means that the immediate needs of the majority of the people, not external demands, shall be the primary determinants in the allocation of resources and development efforts. And self-reliance means the commitment by the new African to use individual capacities and resources to meet personal and collective objectives and needs.

But the Lagos Plan fully recognizes the importance of possible contributions through economic and industrial cooperation at different levels. The plan recognizes that industrial cooperation could enable individual African countries to attain their objectives quickly. Such cooperation could strengthen the growth of the national capability for self-reliance in the industrial sector. But cooperation must be mutually advantageous and based on mutual respect for the objectives, needs, and interests of all parties concerned, especially regarding the sovereignty of African countries over their natural resources.

Since the industrial sector as an integral part of the economy is the dynamic force that must provide inputs not only for itself but also for other sectors, the ranking of priorities for industrial cooperation at different levels can only effectively be achieved by African countries as a group rather than in isolation. This must be the strategy for laying the foundation for self-sustainment and self-reliance in the industrial sector. Therefore the priorities for cooperation to bring about a minimum degree of self-sustaining industrial development were adopted by the African ministers of industry in Kigali, Rwanda, in March 1984. Within this strategy, some of the major activities to be undertaken at the national level were highlighted; these remain the basis and justification for industrial cooperation at all levels.

Before proceeding to identify the priorities for industrial cooperation it may be useful to summarize the progress made so far. This is important for two reasons: first, because the period from 1980 to 1984 was declared by African governments through their ministers of industry as the preparatory phase in the implementation of the Industrial Development Decade for Africa. The declaration of the decade 1980 to 1990 as the Industrial Development Decade was conceived as the principal measure for the implementation of the industrial chapter of the Lagos Plan.[4] And second, the review will ensure that priority areas and projects for cooperation fully take into account some of the problems and issues that have arisen as a result of the social and economic crisis that has gripped the African economies within the last few years.

THE IMPLEMENTATION OF THE PROGRAM FOR THE INDUSTRIAL DEVELOPMENT DECADE

The periods 1980 to 1984 and 1985 to 1990 were designated by African governments as the preparatory and implementation phases of the Industrial Development Decade, respectively. Unfortunately, the preparatory phase coincided with the worst deterioration in African economies in recent decades, arising from the deepening world recession.

This preparatory phase began at the regional level with the preparation and subsequent adoption by the African ministers of industry in November 1981 of a program for the Industrial Development Decade. The program identifies projects for all the major industrial branches and points to some alternative approaches to their development and implementation, depending on local resource endowments and levels of industrial development. It also underlines the broad, positive functions of key institutions at national levels, such as chambers of commerce and industry. It also underscores the role of the agents of production: indigenous, private, public, and cooperative, as well as foreign investors. While primary emphasis is accorded to actions to be taken at the national level, the significance of collective self-reliance at subregional, regional, and international levels is also highlighted.

Subsequently, guidelines prepared for initiating implementation actions at the national level were adopted and published in 1983. These guidelines define, for example, the concepts of resource-based and engineering cores and specify criteria for selecting national and multinational projects on the basis of the strategy agreed upon at Kigali in 1983. In the meantime, a campaign to publicize the decade was initiated, starting with a meeting of news media experts in 1982; posters were also printed and distributed in different parts of Africa.

The incorporation of the concepts, objectives, and priorities of the program into national industrial development plans was considered as one of the first actions to be undertaken by African governments. During the period 1982-84 many of the concepts were incorporated into the industrial policies and strategies of new regional organizations such as the PTA and ECCAS. During the seventh meeting of the ministers of industry, at which time individual countries reported on actions taken at the national level, an increasing number of countries pointed out that they had incorporated the objectives of the decade program into development plans under preparation. Some countries also reported that they had established the national focal points, as called for in the program, for coordinating the decades, activities, while others had assigned this task to appropriate existing national institutions. At the continental level, the establishment of the Federation of African Chambers of Commerce in September 1984, with its headquarters in Egypt, was another positive contribution.

By the end of 1983, the first set of project proposals that met the criteria for priority projects had been presented by governments and regional organizations. These proposals were subsequently considered at regional intergovernmental meetings and accepted for inclusion in the decade's projects. In this connection, representatives of African countries during the seventh meeting held in March 1984 called for the intensification of efforts for cooperation and joint actions in the following areas: fertilizers, iron and steel, pharmaceuticals, tractors and agricultural implements, and energy equipment. Attention was drawn to the example of the collaborative fertilizer project with Cameroon, India, Nigeria, Senegal and the African Refining Company participating.

The worsening of the global economic crisis has seriously impeded the implementation of the program. Attention was drawn to this problem in March 1984 at the meeting of ministers by a number of representatives who indicated that the efforts of their countries had been shifted to meet the immediate crisis, focusing on industrial rehabilitation, diversification, utilization of installed capacity, and reduction in raw material imports for industry. Others, especially from the Sahel and Southern Africa, reported that their countries had been unable to take any positive actions either because of the drought or political difficulties.

This situation of decreasing ability to import intermediate goods, raw materials, and spare parts because of declining foreign exchange receipts revealed the inflexibility and external dependency of the African industrial sector. The resulting underutilization of productive capacity in manufacturing is evidenced by the decrease in the rate of value-added during the period 1980-82 compared with its relatively high performance during the 1970s. Since the severity of the crisis increased further during 1983-84, it may be expected that the deceleration in industrial production is now actually much higher.

Table 13.1

Growth of manufacturing value-added (MVA) by subregions of Africa (in percentages)

Subregion	Share of MVA in GDP (%)		Annual average		
	1970-77	1977-82	1970-77	1977-82	1981-82
North Africa	12.5	12.8	6.6	6.5	4.4
West Africa	6.7	7.8	7.8	3.5	-1.7
East Africa	11.1	11.3	3.8	2.0	-2.8
Central Africa	8.0	7.9	3.4	1.6	0.6
	9.9	10.6	6.1	4.6	1.5

Source: ECA Statistics Division.

These aggregate subregional growth figures obscure wide differentials among countries in each region, particularly since a number of countries in each region experienced negative growth of value-added during the period 1980-82, as shown in table 13.2. On a subregional basis West and East Africa, which had registered impressive growth rates in the 1970s almost equal to or above the 8 percent target required in the Lima Declaration, saw their growth rates decline into the negative. Table 13.2 shows those countries that experienced a rate of growth of manufacturing value-added of 8 percent or more during the period 1970-77 and contrasts this with their recent performances.

During the period 1970-77, the following countries registered negative growth rates of their manufacturing value-added: Angola, the Central African Republic, Equatorial Guinea, the Gambia, Ghana, Mozambique, Togo, and Uganda. Angola, Central African Republic, Equatorial Guinea, the Gambia, and Uganda registered positive growth of the manufacturing value-added during 1980-82, while the decline continued in Ghana, Mozambique, and Togo.

Table 13.2

Countries that achieved or exceeded the minimum MVA growth rate of 8 percent during 1970-77 and changes in their growth rates during 1977-82 (in percentages)

Country	1970-77	1977-82	1980-82
Algeria	11.09	5.48	2.57
Botswana	14.94	6.68	16.56
Congo	15.20	9.35	4.95
Egypt	4.96	8.91	6.61
Gabon	28.65	- 1.18	0.09
Ivory Coast	9.65	5.09	-1.25
Kenya	8.89	6.43	3.86
Libyan Arab Jamahiriya	21.22	0.32	-8.40
Mauritania	10.95	3.48	0.78
Mauritius	14.41	2.85	8.39
Nigeria	15.78	6.49	0.57
Swaziland	19.56	6.58	7.17
Tanzania	7.16	-15.25	-5.87
Tunisia	12.74	11.50	7.89
Zambia	6.70	0.53	-5.87
Zimbabwe	3.42	6.04	4.51

Source: ECA Statistics Division.

Table 13.3 shows the declining trends in terms of trade and in export volumes of the African region. During the period 1980-81, falling export volumes are matched by declines in terms of trade and this in turn is reflected in sharp falls in manufacturing value-added.

The relevance of the foreign exchange constraint derives from the fact that the African manufacturing sector is not a foreign exchange generator but rather a spender of the foreign exchange surplus derived from commodity exports. Hence the collapse in commodity trade has had a profound impact on the performance of the manufacturing sector.

Table 13.3

Changes in terms of trade and export volumes: African oil importers and exporters, 1960-81 (percent per annum)

Group	Purchasing power of exports			Export volume			
	1960-70	1970-79	1979-81	1960-70	1970-79	1980	1981
Oil importer[a]	7.6	-2.7	-9.4	4.7	-1.5	-17.3	- 4.6
Oil exporter[b]	7.7	12.6	-3.2	7.2	-2.0	-11.7	-29.1

Source: William F. Steel and Jonathan W. Evans, "World Bank Industrialization Experience in Sub-Sahara Africa: Objectives, Strategy, Results and Issues," High-level Industrial Policies Seminar for Africa, April 1984, table 3.

[a]Sub-Saharan Africa for 1960-79; all developing Africa for 1979-81.

[b]Nigeria, Angola, and Congo for 1960-79 figures; Nigeria, Algeria, and Libya for 1979-81.

THE STRATEGY FOR SELF-SUSTAINED INDUSTRIAL DEVELOPMENT

The main objective of the Industrial Development Decade is to lay a solid foundation for self-sustaining industrial development through individual and collective self-reliance. On the one hand this means purposive creation of an indigenously managed and controlled integrated productive capacity flexible enough to satisfy changing domestic demand for basic needs including food, clothing, health, shelter, education, and cheap transport. It also means deliberate, selective creation of an increasingly competitive productive capability within the overall capacity, which, as it matures, will enable each country to become a solvent participant in the international division of labor through trade.

The rational way to approach this gigantic task is to identify the minimum necessary elements, their functional characteristics, and the possibilities of effective linkages among them so that they can form a solid foundation. As regards resources, the strategy depends less on the quantum of resources and more on the quality and structural complementarity among the critical elements. In order to start building the minimum integrated productive capacity, it is necessary to single out that subsector of industry that is self-reproductive, the engineering subsector; it produces relatively small types of equipment and forms a subsystem in itself. The manufacturing of small components has been identified as the core of the engineering subsector. Its functions include foundry work, forging, heat treatment, metal coating, machining and manufacturing tools and related equipment. The well-known peculiar feature of the engineering core is that it performs two major functions in industry. First, it reproduces itself; that is, the production of machine tools and related elements uses the same equipment and raw materials. And second, the engineering core is the one primarily used to produce other capital goods and various types of equipment; it is therefore also the main means for bringing technology to equipment. The strategy is to use the engineering subsector as the centerpiece for the development of productive capacity to meet the major requirements for inputs for food and agriculture, for essential consumer goods, and for equipment needed to build up a minimum integrated, resource-based subsector.

The engineering[5] core also is the main producer of spare parts and components. Available information indicates that the manufacturing of spare parts and components is idle in Africa due to inadequate maintenance of equipment and large demands for imported spare parts. In light of the diminishing supply of scarce resources, every effort has to be made to lengthen the life of available equipment, increase equipment runs, and reduce the demand for imported replacements as much as possible. It must be recognized, however, that maximum exploitation of this opportunity depends on the degree of standardization of equipment.

For the purpose of the strategy, a resource-based core subsector is a subsector able to develop a product group that can be generated from the utilization of a local natural resource, chosen on the basis of domestic demand, with a potential for export, provided price and quality are competitive. Second, a core subsector must, as in the case of the engineering core, allow for an indigenous skills capability to be built around the exploitation of the resource to initiate domestic production of intermediate and final products.

Concentrating on a resource-based core initiates vertical integration of production in one priority sector. The choice of a resource-based core (or cores) arises from recognition that relatively weak African countries faced with strong international competition cannot expect their manufactured goods to be competitive in world trade if they diffuse their efforts over a wide range of products. However, they can achieve some measure of competitiveness by concentrating resources in limited target areas until they achieve a breakthrough. This would enable them to convert their natural resource advantage into a technical advantage. In this connection, both the domestic and subregional or regional markets can serve as testing grounds for resource-based core products.

In addition, investment in a resource-based engineering core affords each country an opportunity to develop the production of capital goods, technological adaptation, and skilled manpower and opens an important avenue for cooperation with other countries. The choice also offers a starting point for systematic vertical integration among plants and therefore the possibility for reducing the unit cost of production, ensuring a stable supply of raw materials and maximizing value-added and employment.[6]

The increase in the demand for food and agricultural products in response to population growth can drive this kind of system if the food consumption basket is expanded. The techniques for doing this are available. Such expansion would serve two important purposes: first, it would increase the nutritional content of food consumed, and second, it would have the effect of creating employment by increasing domestic specialization in the production of various food items and hence stimulate domestic trade and widen and integrate the national markets.

An increase in the demand for food and agricultural products can also stimulate, inter alia, the demand for agricultural inputs, tools, implements, irrigation and energy equipment, as well as transportation, storage, fertilizers, and pesticides.[7] Supply of these inputs, depending on the level of the industrial development of the country in question, would be met by national and subregional production. However, the supply of these inputs to food and agriculture would no longer be treated as an end in itself; rather, it would be profitably utilized and managed through standardization and similar measures as a precious instrument for the integration of the economy on the one hand and, on the other, as a source of dynamic pressure to stimulate the growth of the engineering core industry and the engineering industry in general.

Similarly, increases in demand for the final products of the resource-based core subsector (e.g., a subgroup in leather, wood, textiles, etc.) would make possible the domestic production of the equipment required to produce intermediate and final products, the pace of the progress no doubt depending on the level of the industrial development of each country. Here, too, is another area for cooperation, especially for the countries whose resource cores are similar. This, too, would further the growth of the engineering core and related areas with technology and skill-generating opportunities. These streams of intersectoral flows and mutual interactions would increase as the development process proceeds.

The final major linkages would derive from rises in incomes of agricultural populations and employees of the resource-based sector and from the increased demand for manufactures of basic need goods and consumer durables. This demand would further generate demand for capital goods.

Another outcome of the development of the engineering core[8] is that it would enable a country gradually to develop domestic capability, to convert its own domestic savings into real capital goods without having to go through foreign trade.

It is evident that for African countries with relatively small domestic markets (almost all African countries) this strategy depends on effective subregional industrial cooperation in order to secure stable supplies of intermediate goods, such as iron and steel, related metals, fertilizers and pesticides, basic chemicals and agricultural implements, whose unit costs depend on economies of scale. Indeed, industrial and, more broadly, economic cooperation is an integral part of the strategy for the implementation of the Lagos Plan and the Industrial Development Decade.

Reference must also be made to the scale and the choice of technology. The scale of manufacturing will be dominated by small- and medium-sized industries, depending on the volume of domestic demand in each country. However, with regard to the production of intermediate inputs, raw materials, and some types of farm equipment, as well as fertilizers and pesticides, which are required to meet the demand of several countries in economic groupings, large-scale production is imperative.

Considering the choice of techniques, initially preference would be given to labor-intensive technology with a view to utilizing the abundant labor force. But this approach cannot and need not be dogmatically adhered to in light of changing circumstances and productive capacities and bearing in mind the importance of the deliberate creation of indigenous skills and technology, which can only grow through participation in actual production activities.

The attitudes, behavior, and the capability of the agents of production and distribution, who have the primary responsibility for the implementation of the strategy outlined above, are of the utmost importance. In the African region, which suffers more than the others from the paucity of indigenous enterprise, no significant advance may be expected in self-sustaining industrialization without the leadership of a strong and flexible, commercially operating public enterprise. In the absence of such a strong public sector, its place will, even in the future, be taken not by indigenous private enterprise but by foreign enterprise. And under such circumstances, the strategy of self-sustaining industrialization will not materialize.

With regard to the adaptation and development of technology (see chapter 14), it is indigenous enterprise that is free and willing to undertake R&D and significant product adaptation; foreign enterprise is more interested in the licensing of its technology rather than in its adaptation to suit local resource endowments. Foreign enterprise R&D is generally centrally organized and carried out at its parent company. Adaptation of technology by indigenous enterprises[10] can be enhanced through the formulation and implementation of a generous incentive scheme.

Under the existing conditions of socio-political change with the accompanying economic and political risks, foreign enterprise can hardly be expected to make large or long-term investments in most African countries. But African development needs cannot stop and wait. Equally important is the use of corporate gross savings. Frequently, foreign enterprises prefer to pay dividends out of profit instead of ploughing back gross savings and repatriating their depreciation funds. An indigenous enterprise would be likely to reinvest and thereby enhance self-sustainment of the industrial sector.

PRIORITY AREAS FOR INDUSTRIAL COOPERATION

In view of the serious industrial disruptions arising from the current socio-economic crisis, which have led to major reductions in industrial production, and taking into account the unpredictable recurrence of drought, certain areas of cooperation merit urgent short- and medium-term actions.

The frequent recurrence of drought in the African region increases food imports and continues to reduce the capabilities of the African countries to use available export receipts for investment in the industrial sector. It thereby retards implementation of the industrial program adopted in Lagos. In order to remedy the absolute dependency on rainfed agricultural production techniques, the following areas constitute priorities for industrial cooperation: (1) development of industries for production of small-scale irrigation equipment; and (2) development of industrial productive capacity for the utilization of renewable sources of energy, especially biomass and solar energy.

The other major short-term priority for industrial cooperation is the rehabilitation and upgrading of existing plants in Africa to facilitate fuller utilization of available industrial production capacity. From the preceding, it is clear that lack of adequate and stable supplies of spare parts and maintenance has been and will continue to be one of the major causes of idle industrial productive capacity. One of the urgent priorities is, therefore, the rehabilitation and upgrading of plant equipment through the supply of spare parts and components and of intermediate imports and raw materials. In order to put the demand for and the supply of spare parts in its proper perspective, it is necessary to note that the cost of producing a given product goes beyond the price of the specific equipment. It includes the costs of skilled manpower and managers, fuel, intermediate inputs and raw materials, spare parts and components, as well as maintenance costs. In developing African economies, almost all elements required to ensure the continuous utilization of industrial equipment have to be imported.

Currently, the major import demand for spare parts and components is concentrated in the transport and communications sector, including railways, motor vehicles, electronics, telecommunication equipment, agricultural equipment and machinery, and industrial machinery. Table 13.4 is indicative of the magnitude of import requirements of spare parts and components, showing the average annual rates of growth, even though only a few categories are covered by the data. Nevertheless, the table does show the importance of the underlying problem and its urgency. Between 1971 and 1978, the annual average rate of growth of imports ranged between 28 percent for Egypt and 2.7 percent for Tanzania. During the period from 1979 to 1980, Kenya and Libya registered high rates of import growth, while in Egypt, Tanzania, and Tunisia imports declined considerably.

While suppliers of equipment are required to provide their clients with spare parts for periods ranging up to 10 years, the longer the piece of equipment lasts, the better it is for foreign exchange-starved African countries. But due to actual and planned obsolescence, spare parts are not readily available after the expiration of supply contracts. At the expiration of such supply agreements, the supplier of spare parts may dictate the price; delays in supply become inevitable; and equipment setup costs raise the unit cost considerably. Difficulties arising from foreign exchange scarcity are often compounded by the actual unavailability of supplies. The net result from such a situation is to replace the equipment by importing newer equipment when the economies can least afford to do so.

The severity of the problem of shortages of spare parts in African economies is not a new one, but it has been aggravated by the current African socio-economic crisis. It highlights the urgency of implementing the industrial chapter of the Lagos Plan. Indeed, as early as the mid-1970s it was noted that in Zambia, for example, it was difficult to find one village in the more developed areas of the country without some tractors made useless by lack of spare parts and maintenance.[11] The first ILO study on employment in Kenya revealed that about half of the tractors and other agricultural machinery were out of order at any one time due to a lack of skilled operators, repair, maintenance, and, inevitably, spare parts.[12] In general, the demand for spare parts and maintenance increases in proportion to capital accumulation, especially of engineering equipment and machinery.

The significance of a stable supply of spare parts and components and adequate maintenance is that it increases the life of the equipment and arrests replacement demands, while ensuring continuity in productive utilization of the equipment in the short term.[13] Like any other industrial investment, domestic production of spare parts and components has to be put in the contexts of long-term economic development, the development of an indigenous capital goods industry, technological acquisition, and adaptation of engineering design. It also has to be placed in the context of the accumulation of engineering capital equipment and, in particular, equipment for specific resource-based products, agricultural implements, equipment for transport and communication, and energy generation and transmission equipment.

With regard to the demand for spare parts and components, one of the most pressing needs in most countries is for the integration of the domestic markets badly segmented by product differentiation through legislation to establish national standards. National standards and a "national standard model" for mass transport equipment and agricultural implements and machinery are urgently required; these would be changed only over long periods of time when the economy had developed all-round productive and engineering capability to set higher national standard models. This task is by no means easy; to implement it, African governments and communities have to resist the pressure of marketeers. It is preferable, of course, to have subregional standard models as a basis for cooperation at different levels in order to reduce the cost of production of spare parts by increasing the size of the market. Equally important is the necessity for each country to establish a public enterprise to spearhead the development of spare parts, which would also support and upgrade workshops, especially those in the informal sector both in the urban and rural areas, through arrangements such as subcontracts and coproduction.

It is now possible to summarize the areas identified above as priorities for industrial cooperation. These include the following:

1. resource-based industries that may not require very large markets;
2. resource-based industries requiring large markets and large financial investment;
3. energy generating and transmitting equipment;
4. agricultural tools, implements, and machines, and irrigation equipment, as well as transport and communications equipment;
5. the engineering core industry subsector;
6. equipment and machinery for production of basic needs manufactures;
7. spare parts and components and maintenance of plants and equipment;
8. trade;
9. financial resources; and
10. development of indigenous skills, technological capacities, and managerial ability.

The first package of multicountry projects in some of these areas has already been identified by individual countries and intergovernmental organizations. These multinational projects will be promoted by the governments through subregional economic groupings such as ECOWAS, MRU, ECCAS, PTA, and SADCC (see chapters 4 and 5).

There is no doubt that the scope and means for cooperation in the above areas will vary from subsector to subsector and from one product group to another and will depend on the conjunction of interests, objectives, and capacities of the parties concerned. These projects should serve as the initial practical bases for international cooperation.

INTERNATIONAL INDUSTRIAL COOPERATION IN THE IMPLEMENTATION OF THE INDUSTRIAL DEVELOPMENT DECADE

Priority Measures for Intra-African Industrial Cooperation

One of the options available to developing countries is outward orientation, specialization, and integration into the world economy.[14] For African countries, the only viable alternative is intra-African economic cooperation and integration. But the record of economic cooperation, particularly among common markets and free trade areas, has not been conspicuously successful; and such arrangements can be costly and trade-diverting. However, African governments and their peoples consider collective self-reliance among themselves through cooperation at subregional and regional levels to be the main instrument for the extension of individual national self-reliance. It is also the only dependable bedrock for their mutual survival and development in a not too hospitable international environment. The importance that African countries attach to this matter is revealed by the recent resurgence of initiatives in this area in different parts of the continent. It is also now evident that failures in this field in the past have been largely due to the inappropriateness of objectives, ineffective modalities, and the use of wrong instruments[15] for implementing cooperation arrangements.

Since for mutual survival and development there is no real alternative to cooperation among weak African countries, cooperation must take new forms. In the past, efforts in this area have been based on a model borrowed from developed market economies that required the existence of developed productive capacities and indigenous, competitive entrepreneurs. Some African countries do not have either. This model foundered because of unequal distribution of benefits. In the co-operation ventures established on the borrowed model, the stronger economies or those more favored by foreign investors were able to reap unduly disproportionate benefits at the expense of weaker partners. This cannot be the basis for cooperation, but rather cooperation must be based on mutual self-protection, preservation, and achievement of national objectives for all concerned.

Two recent developments have prepared a new basis for more sound forms of cooperation. First, during the import-substitution phase, benefits were not only small but were also location specific; they were limited to those arising from the last stage of production. In the absence of production of intermediate inputs and raw materials, a mechanism for generating and spreading benefits across various firms, industrial branches, and hence across countries became conspicuously lacking. And second, the import-substitution strategy--by creating in each African economy enormous, though often fragmented, domestic demand for intermediate goods and raw materials, whose production requires complementarity in natural resources, energy, investment, and economies of scale--has now opened up more options for mutually beneficial industrial cooperation among African countries than ever before. These new opportunities provide an impetus to the implementation of the Lagos Plan. This strategy has also created the long-sought practical opportunities for linking Africa's natural resources with basic needs.

Another favorable recent development is the emergence of indigenous public and, to a lesser extent, private enterprises, which can serve as more reliable and efficient instruments for implementing industrial cooperation arrangements among African countries than foreign MNCs, whose corporate goals in such ventures generally diverge from the goals of participating countries. The greatest gains in this regard have been made in the fields of banking, insurance, construction, and industry. In some national and regional economic groupings, clauses on the rules of origin have been passed to underline the primary role of indigenous enterprises in cooperative, mutual development.

Given the large scope for cooperation, new arrangements differ from previous ones in several respects: in objectives, in instruments, and in patterns for the distribution of dynamic gains. The new objectives are to create and increase indigenous resources including finance, capital, skilled manpower, technology, entrepreneurship, institutions, corporate structures, and effective sovereignty over natural resources. The instruments are to be primarily indigenous.

Different measures are to be devised to ensure fair distribution of gains. Industrial cooperation will, for relatively small African countries, play the crucial role of ensuring the initiation of self-sustaining, industrial development. One such measure consists of setting aside an agreed share of a specific product group from the enlarged market to serve as the export base for each country in connection with resource-based core industries. By producing for their own national and subregional markets with some competition, the countries will create export bases, upgrade the quality of their products, and reduce unit costs, as a preparation for entry into the world market. Different forms of cooperation will also be required to create a solid engineering core in each country, particularly because of differences among countries in levels of development in this sector. This sector will provide a wide scope for mutual technical assistance among African countries.

Reference has already been made to cooperation as indispensable in the implementation of national industrial objectives involving products needed for integrated and self-sustaining industrialization, which require economies of scale and high investment costs. Accordingly, high priority has been given to cooperation in the production of intermediate inputs such as iron and steel, copper, aluminium, zinc products, lead and energy-coal, hydropower, natural gas, and basic chemicals including ammonia, sulphuric acid, chlorine, caustic soda, and ethylene. Equally high priority has been given cooperation in the production of final inputs and equipment, required for food and agricultural production and the development of the rural areas, including agricultural implements and equipment, energy generating and transmission equipment, irrigation equipment, transport and communication equipment, fertilizers, and pesticides. The need for industrial cooperation also extends, with equal urgency, to the production of basic needs manufactured goods for the mass of the population including clothing, building materials, furniture, and other household essentials. Such cooperation is particularly important for the least developed countries.

The heavy burden of dependence on imported intermediate inputs and raw materials at a time of shrinking foreign exchange resources is revealed in table 13.5. For example, in 1982, in Kenya, the Ivory Coast, and Zambia, the imports of intermediate goods was more than the sum of imported consumer and capital goods combined. Cooperation in the production of intermediate goods and spare parts is therefore an area that constitutes a high priority.

Another area of the highest priority for cooperation is in the production of spare parts and components. This not only because importing spare parts constitutes an insatiable drain on the meager foreign exchange resources available to African countries, but also because, on average, demand for imported spare parts grows faster than for other imports. More significantly, the lack of spare parts renders useless equipment costing much more than the parts. Coproduction of spare parts would address the issues of economies of scale, differences in technological capacities and need for bulk procurement of materials, among the countries in each subregion. Cooperation would entail subcontracting and R&D of new materials among countries.

Besides collaboration in the production of general spare parts and components, joint production of parts could be based on standard models agreed upon by a number of countries, for example, a transport vehicle, "a "poor man's vehicle," and selected agricultural machinery. These models would allow for ongoing production of spare parts and components, as well as for facilitating the acquisition of technology and production techniques. They would also constitute the foundation for eventual production of the equipment. This possibility seems to hold a great deal of promise if it includes joint ventures with other developing countries that are at a higher level of development than those in Africa. For example, each of the African subregions may agree on standard models for a motor vehicle, a tractor, and some types of agricultural machinery. Each participating country would then be allocated the right to produce specific parts for sale to all other countries.

Taking into account the primary responsibilities of indigenous industrial enterprises (public and private) for the implementation of the Lagos Plan, the modalities for cooperation being promoted by the ECA include the exchange of information, joint mobilization of finance for agreed projects, subcontracting, buy-back and long-term purchase agreements, joint ventures, and equity shares in national projects. With a view to facilitating such collaboration among indigenous enterprises, efforts must be made to strengthen these enterprises and establish regular contacts among them. The Federation of the African Chambers of Commerce, as well as corresponding subregional federations currently organizing in West and Southeastern Africa, will increase contacts and at the same time serve to strengthen the capacity of the indigenous industrial sector. As indicated earlier, steps have also been taken to lay the foundation for appropriate policy frameworks for industrial cooperation in new regional economic groupings.

Development of skills and technological capacity, as well as R&D, management training, and mobilization of industrial investment finance, offer a wide scope for industrial cooperation among African countries. Among these priority areas, special attention needs to be paid to the advantage offered by cooperative development of indigenous skills and technology to supplement national efforts. It is probable that phenomena such as rising unemployment among graduates and brain drain derive, to a large extent, from a mismatch between skills required in industry and skills taught by education and training institutions. This raises the traditional issue of supply and demand serving as a basis for development. Given scarce resources for investment in human resources development, faced with a highly competitive international economic environment, and in view of the emerging waste of human resources through unemployment,

Table 13.4

Imports of some types of parts and components in selected African countries, 1971-80
(at 1970 constant market prices in thousand U.S. dollars)

Country	1971	1972	1973	1974	1975	1976	1977	1978	1979	1980	Average annual rates of growth in % over	
											1971-78	1979-80
Algeria	46706	62193	88752	65964	94674	95570	103896	125883			15.2	
Congo	2530	3064	3694	2446	2889	2519	2254	2384	2028		- 0.8	
Egypt	25986	22608	16883	36767	65733	83010	117722	153129	70617	35492	28.8	-49.7
Ivory Coast	12464	12390	19652	17705	15501	22549	28550	30807			13.8	
Kenya	11852	9677	7833	9542	8556	8821	11184	16137	11481	14072	4.5	22.6
Libya	44125	65737	68617	53360	128633	112501	117870	168279	164264	186793	21.1	13.7
Nigeria	64747	53653	43797	41302	86986	127638	149503	155119	124820		13.3	
Tanzania	12765	11250	11066	14584	15295	9008	10033	15391	10066	5212	2.7	-48.2
Tunisia	10676	13174	12970	20257	31511	25861	35486	39801	39645	29534	20.7	-25.5

Source: International Trade Yearbooks, 1972 to 1981, in current prices deflated with ECA sectoral deflators (1970 = 100).

Note: Values include in average 52% of Standard International Trade Classification (SITC) 7199 referring to machine parts and accessories and 48% of SITC 7328 referring to motor vehicle parts.

Table 13.5

Distribution of imports by end use in selected countries, 1960s to 1978/82
(percentages of total imports)

Country/Years	Consumer goods			Intermediate goods			Capital goods			
	1960s	1972	1978-82	1960s	1972	1978-82	1960s	1972	1974-75	1978-82
Ethiopia (1967, 1971, 1981/82)	29	33	24[c]	30	33	40[c]	40	34	16[c]	35[c]
Ghana (1962, 1972, 1979)	48	25	18	34	51	53	18	25	20	29
Ivory Coast (1960, 1972, 1979)	56	49	26	22	26	53	22	25	28	21
Kenya (1964, 1972, 1982)	27	20	6	55	56	68	15	20	30	26
Nigeria (1960, 1972, 1978)	61	36	28	17	26	24	22	37	42	49
Tanzania (1963, 1966, 1970, 1972, 1974, 1978, 1979)[b]	49	29	20		40[a]	35[a]	25	35	24	47
Zambia (1968, 1972, 1981)	26	31	20	48	40	57	18	25	20	29

Source: William F. Steel and Jonathan W. Evans, "World Bank Industrialization Experience in Sub-Sahara Africa: Objectives, Strategy, Results and Issues," High Level Industrial Policies Seminar for Africa, April 1984, table 12 (unpublished).

Note: Columns may fail to add up to 100 percent because of unclassified imports and because of rounding.

[a]Different source from consumer goods data.

[b]Machinery and transport equipment only.

[c]Drought relief imports have been excluded.

the supply and demand approach to skills development seems the more rational one for Africa.

Industrial Cooperation Among African and Other Developing Countries

The basis for cooperation among developing countries is the recognition that their growth and development is limited by continued dependence on the advanced countries. Dependence does not favor the balanced and harmonious growth of developing countries. Recent recognition of this fact has made obvious the need for developing countries to promote international cooperation based on the principles of national and collective self-reliance. In essence this involves economic and technical cooperation among developing countries. This kind of cooperation brings together countries with similar needs and similar constraints.

Such joint efforts are expected to foster faster growth and development. These cooperative efforts are to be pursued vigorously by African countries, while at the same time they expand their traditional economic relations with the developed countries. Over the past several years, regular consultations by the Group of 77 have yielded a number of priority areas for cooperation among developing countries. Among the areas accorded high priority in the industrial sector for South-South cooperation are production of essential inputs for food production, expansion of exports and their diversification, location of new industrial productive capacities in processing industries, technology, improvement of human skills, energy, and various forms of technical cooperation. The specific areas singled out for cooperation include raw materials, fisheries, agriculture and agro-industries, mining and mineral processing, petrochemicals, chemicals, fertilizers and pharmaceuticals, intermediate and capital goods, textiles, forest-based industries, building materials, and energy generation.[16]

Table 13.6

Annual average growth rates of exports from developing countries to the world (in percentages)

From developing countries	World	Developed market economy countries	Developing countries
1955/56 - 1960/61	2.5	2.3	1.0
1960/61 - 1965/66	6.1	6.5	5.0
1965/66 - 1970/71	9.0	9.3	8.3
1970/71 - 1976/77	29.0	28.5	31.3

Source: UNCTAD, (TD/B/C.7/36/Add.l), table 102.

The steadily rising rate of growth in trade among developing countries during the 1970s indicates the existence of a large potential not only for trade but also for investment, financial flows, and mutual training and technical assistance. But one of the preconditions for the expansion of trade and investment is the exchange of information on the capacity of developing countries and the potential areas for mutual cooperation. In this connection, a number of positive developments have taken place in recent years that have laid the foundation for other forms of cooperation. One of these is the increase of technical cooperation among developing countries (TCDC). Examples of this trend include increasing technical cooperation among Third World countries such as Brazil and African countries including Angola, Gabon, Mozambique and Nigeria, while Cuba, Mozambique and Tanzania have established similar relations. Similar technical cooperation arrangements are growing among African and Asian countries, notably among China, India, North Korea, Pakistan, and South Korea on one hand and Benin, Kenya, Mozambique, Nigeria, Sierra Leone, Tanzania, Togo, Zambia, and Zimbabwe on the other, to mention only a few. Similar relations are emerging among Arab and African countries.

Reinforcing these technical cooperation arrangements is the slow but steady flow of investment finance among African and other developing countries. These flows are reflected in the financing of national African projects by the Bank for Arab Development in Africa (BADEA), the direct cofinancing of projects by Saudi and Kuwait development funds, as well as the recent participation of developing countries as nonregionals in the expanded program of the African Development Bank (ADB).

Some positive progress has also been made in joint ventures in the industrial sector. India is perhaps the country that has made the greatest effort in this area. Joint ventures of African countries and India include a paper and pulp mill in Kenya, a machine tools project in Nigeria, and a fertilizer project in Senegal, with Cameroon and Nigeria also participating. India has also supported regional technological projects including the grant of equipment to the African Regional Center for Engineering Design and Manufacturing located in Ibadan, Nigeria.

Practically all the priority areas identified above for implementation of the Lagos Plan of Action lead Africa to cooperation with other developing countries bilaterally or multilaterally through relevant intergovernmental organizations. For example, production of spare parts and components for transport equipment, agricultural machinery, and industrial plants, and production of a multipurpose "poor people's car," basic chemicals, fertilizers, pesticides, pharmaceuticals, iron and steel, copper, and agricultural equipment and machinery are areas where there exists adequate technological capability in some of the more developed of the developing countries that could be brought to joint ventures involving an African subregion and several developing countries outside the region.

Perhaps one of the highest priority areas for joint ventures, which is bound to generate large direct and indirect mutual benefits for African and other developing countries, is investment in the production of intermediate inputs and raw materials, as identified above. The import-substitution strategy has generated enormous effective demand for intermediate goods and raw materials in all developing countries, some of which may not be as well endowed with natural resources as the African countries. Still others may wish to diversify their sources of raw materials. Joint ventures in which countries would agree to purchase output on a long-term basis would guarantee both the commercial viability of products and the advantages of economies of scale.

Developing countries in different parts of the world as well as in Africa, thanks to the reduction of transport costs, can establish joint ventures by borrowing from the experience of TNCs and producing the parts and components of a complex final product at various locations in the (Third) World. Under this type of scheme, developing countries at similar levels of industrialization may agree to produce a piece of equipment, such as a poor people's car, using mass production of components by affiliated or associated indigenous industrial companies. The components would then be traded among these same companies for assembly at national locations. Such a scheme would also provide training and technical support to the weaker partners of the joint enterprise to help them establish national engineering core industries and to share with them the benefits of an indigenous industry. Besides increasingly mutual trade among developing countries, such collaboration would also serve to diffuse standard skills and technologies.

In the specific area of upgrading industrial management and technological capability, the African region, as the least industrialized among developing regions, stands to benefit from entering into planned short-term management agreements on production and marketing among African countries and the more industrialized of the developing countries with a view to upgrading the capability of public industrial enterprises and consultancy companies. Lump-sum technology purchases and transfer agreements also offer other dimensions for cooperation.

In order to expand industrial cooperation between the African regions and other developing countries, a number of constraints have to be addressed. First, trade is more likely to expand through the creation of new productive capacities, since most of the existing plants were established by TNCs to promote trade among vertically integrated subsidiaries and to produce intermediate products, which do not enter the open markets. Second, indigenous public enterprises are, at the present stage of development, the most suitable instruments and channels for pioneering and developing coproduction joint ventures and trade among developing countries since, by virtue of their long corporate lives and governmental guarantees, they are better placed than indigenous private enterprises to enter into long-term purchase agreements. Third, the matching of product and consumption structures offers the greatest potential for mutually beneficial industrial cooperation. This is the case since, unlike a situation of wide differentiation, similarity of structures ensures that the markets of the participating economies are "open" to other countries, whereas in the case of a wide differentiation, as between developing and developed countries, only part of the mutual markets are open while large segments are "closed" because of differences in tastes and levels of productive capabilities. Another constraint is the lack of information exchanged regarding capacities for undertaking production activities and areas in which cooperation is desirable. Equally restrictive is the general absence of adequate distribution channels and after-sales services among developing countries.

In order to remedy some of these constraints, a number of measures need to be taken: organization of regular meetings of the chambers of commerce and industry of developing countries, greater utilization of public enterprises as instruments for cooperation; establishment as appropriate of joint ventures with host countries for distribution and after-sales companies;

and creation of information banks and focal points at the national level indicating potential areas for industrial cooperation with different developing countries with reference to areas of current and future national interest.

Prospects for Industrial Cooperation with Developed Market Economies

Due to historical factors, the external economic relations of the African region are dominated by relations with developed market economies in all areas including trade, official development assistance, and direct foreign investment. Indeed, relations with developed market economies have been further strengthened through agreements signed regularly by the ACP countries and the EEC.

Over the years, concessionary aid to the African region for socio-economic development (besides export credits) has been made available to governments and through IFC to the private sector with grants totaling at least 25 percent to finance a wide range of projects. A significant proportion of total concessionary resources for developing countries has gone to the African countries, since most satisfy the criteria for eligibility, namely, countries with per capita incomes under US$370 and middle income countries with per capita incomes between US$371 and US$680. As shown in table 13.7, the flow of this type of aid grew steadily over the years, as reflected in the difference between US$6.8 billion in 1975 and US$10.8 billion in 1981 (see chapters 6, 8 and 9).

Table 13.7

Flow of resources to Africa, 1975-81
(in billions of US dollars)

	1975	1980	1981
Concessional	6.859	10.50	10.8
Nonconcessional	6.168	9.70	8.6

Source: ECA, Survey of Economic and Social Conditions in Africa, 1978-1979, 1982-1983, (E/CN.14/743 and E/ECA/CM.10/4) March 1980 and April 1984, respectively.

However, in recent years concessional aid in real terms has been declining, partly because of the economic recession in the advanced countries and partly due to the disenchantment of aid donors with Africa's pattern of resource utilization. This attitude has been reflected both in policies to decrease ODA and in the hardening of conditionalities and policies accompanying such aid. Some of these new donor policies and attitudes relate to what they regard as defective policies, i.e., inadequate policies regarding price incentives and population control; increasing levels of public sector expenditures; lack of realistic national priorities and efficient resource allocations for projects; poor location criteria; neglect of maintenance of existing plants and physical infrastructures; increasing bias for new projects; poor national coordination of aid; and the belief that managerial capacities of the African countries have reached the limit for absorbing aid (see chapter 8).

Although the actual percentage of total ODA that goes to the industrial sector is not known, it is estimated to be relatively small. Any decline in this assistance would no doubt lead to a reduction of domestic resources from industry, which could be used to finance investments in other sectors not met by ODA. Since ODA is "provided under conditions that seek to influence the policies of the recipients and/or the allocation of their resources, and in many cases is combined with technical assistance,"[18] some of the problems may derive from divergences between donor policies and those perceived as good by African governments themselves. This in turn raises questions as to whether the implementation of the industrial chapter of the _Lagos Plan_ is consistent with the policies of the donor countries for the African region (see chapter 6).

Direct foreign investment to Africa in all economic sectors is dominated by the developed market economies; in 1967-77 the U.S. alone accounted for 21 percent of all foreign investment in Africa, the U.K. 30 percent and France 26 percent. About 30 percent of all this investment was in petroleum and 20 percent in mining. The percentage of foreign investment that actually went into manufacturing was about 12 percent.[19] In Nigeria, which accounts for about 15-20 percent of investment and gross domestic product in Africa South of the Sahara, market economies accounted for 88 percent of total investment in the country in 1965 (U.K. 50 percent; U.S. 16 percent; and Western Europe 22 percent), although it dropped slightly to 84 percent by 1976.[20]

Using Nigeria as an example, it appears that the sectoral preferences of direct foreign investment in African countries are the mining and trading sectors, which together accounted for 67 percent of the total foreign investment in 1965 and which dropped only slightly to 66.2 percent by 1976, as compared to 19.2 percent and 23.6 percent respectively for the same years for the manufacturing sector. Moreover, while it is difficult to collect information on the distribution of direct foreign investment between resource-based and general import-substitution industries, there are many reasons to assume that most foreign investment has gone to the import-substitution subsector. First, this has been the dominant and fastest growing subsector. Second, investment in it meets with one of the principal corporate objectives of TNCs, namely, to capture market shares in developing regions. It is also known that most foreign industrial investors, including the TNCs, are disinterested in the development and utilization of local raw materials on account of poor quality, limited size of natural resources, and because such an investment may conflict with existing capacities and interests elsewhere in the world. This may also serve to explain new investments being made in plants involved in the final stages of manufacturing and the growth of excess capacities in this area of African industry. It may also indicate why most African governments in the past have followed relatively passive and unselective strategies with regard to the direction of foreign investment.

Table 13.8

Outflow of profits from developing countries and territories, 1965-73
(in US$ mn) and (Index 1965 = 100)

Regions	1965		1967		1969		1971		1973	
	Value	Index	Value	Index	Value	Index	Value	Index	Value	Index
All non-oil exporting countries	821.0	100.0	1,212.0	147.6	1,554.2	189.3	1,335.1	162.6	1,853.0	225.7
Western Hemisphere	674.0	100.0	1,014.0	150.4	1,314.1	195.0	1,104.4	163.9	1,515.2	224.8
Middle East	31.0	100.0	30.0	96.8	55.2	178.1	40.0	129.0	39.8	128.4
Asia	41.0	100.0	88.0	243.9	85.7	209.0	65.4	159.5	92.3	225.0
Africa	75.0	100.0	80.0	106.7	99.2	132.2	124.7	166.3	205.7	274.3

Source: Peter Richter, "Capital Transfer: Are the Developing Countries in Reality Exporters of Capital?" _Intereconomics_ (July/August 1979), table 3.

The situation concerning the outflow of profits from developing countries is shown in table 13.8 for the period 1965 to 1973. In addition to resource outflows from developing countries through the repatriation of funds, other channels of resource outflow, excluding interest or royalty payments, include the underpricing of exports and overpricing of imports. The magnitude of these outflows are shown in table 13.9.

Table 13.9

Estimated losses of the developing countries from clandestine profit transfers by the MNCs, 1965-73 (in millions of US dollars)

Source of loss	1965	1967	1968	1971	1973
Underpricing of exports	6.4	7.0	8.6	10.1	17.7
Overpricing of exports	1.7	1.9	2.3	2.9	4.5
Royalty payments	0.9			2.6	3.7
Total	9.0	8.9	10.9	15.6	25.9

Source: As in table 13.9, tables 4 and 5.

Note: Developing countries excluding oil-producing countries.

Taking all the above factors into consideration, in what ways could developed market economies cooperate with African countries in the implementation of the industry component of the Lagos Plan? To help answer this question, let us look at the balance sheet for the 1980s.

1. African countries have and continue to register persistent deficits in their current accounts: US$3 billion in 1976 had jumped to US$9 billion in 1982.[21]
2. The debt service ratio of the African countries is rising to dangerous levels, and an increasing number of them are negotiating continuously to reschedule their debts.
3. In the industrial sector, African countries are saddled with a production structure with large foreign equity, which depends for its growth on imports of intermediate goods, raw materials and spare parts, and which is a foreign exchange user.
4. African countries are losing increasing amounts of resources through clandestine profit transfers.

In what ways then can the developed economies of the North support the decade program? They can lend their support as follows:

1. increase ODA to African countries;
2. increase concessionary loans and direct foreign investment to the export-oriented manufacturing subsector to generate additional resources for the implementation of the overall decade program;
3. encourage direct foreign investment in joint ventures and provide financial and technological resources for the production of intermediate goods and raw materials and spare parts, engineering and resource-based cores, with a view to reducing import dependence in manufacturing;
4. grant access of commodity exports from the African countries to the developing economy markets; and
5. write-off debts in cases where countries are incapable of paying debts even after rescheduling.

The possibilities for expansion of manufactured exports through indigenous and direct foreign investment seems attractive. Yet opinions are divided on the prospects, in spite of the GSP, the Lomé Conventions, and the success of the so-called gang of four NICs (Hong Kong, Korea, Singapore, and Taiwan) in the exportation of manufactures. Protectionism against developing countries' exports is on the rise in the advanced countries. For example, after examining the different options available to developing countries in exporting manufactured goods, some experts find only one alternative: export goods through vertically-integrated TNCs in order to circumvent protections[22] by interfacing TNC and national interests. The Lomé Conventions seem to close and open the door at the same time by stipulating a limit of 40 percent of the value of the finished product of imported materials from Third World countries to be admitted to the EEC market. "Stipulating high levels of domestic value-added negates the possibility, for if they could add 150 percent to the value of a wide range of imported materials, then they could hardly be described as among the less industrialized/nonindustrial developing countries."[23] The picture is not reassuring.

Prospects for Industrial Cooperation Among African and Socialist Countries

Economic and, in particular, industrial cooperation among most African countries and the developed socialist countries is of recent historical origin, having been established only soon after African independence in the 1960s. This relation offers the two parties new options and dimensions for international cooperation in the industrial sector that are unique both in substance and in style. In spite of the absence of long-established institutional machinery for promoting cooperation between the two groups of countries, substantial progress has been achieved in recent years especially in the trade and industry sectors. Experience gained thus far can now form the foundation for broad-based, long-term industrial cooperation in the implementation of the industrial priorities of the <u>Lagos Plan</u>. This optimism is supported by the growth of trade between developing countries as a whole and the centrally planned economies as reflected in table 13.10 below.

Table 13.10

Annual average growth rates of exports from developing countries to the world and the socialist countries (in percentages)

From developing countries	World	Socialist countries
1955/56 - 1960/61	2.5	22.3
1960/61 - 1965/66	6.1	11.4
1965/66 - 1970/71	9.0	7.3
1970/71 - 1976/77	29.0	23.5

Source: UNCTAD, "A Global System of Trade Preferences Among Developing Countries" (28 March 1980), table 202.

As might be expected, the composition of exports from African countries is dominated by commodities, while imports consist mainly of manufactures, as can be seen in table 13.11. This trade structure is therefore similar to the one prevailing among Africa and the developed market economies. It should also be noted that during the period 1977-82 trade among Africa and the socialist countries stagnated.

Table 13.11

The structure of trade between Africa and socialist countries (millions of US dollars)

	1976			
	Imports		Exports	
	World	Socialist countries	World	Socialist countries
Africa totals	38,486.2	1,751.0	41,527.3	1,787.0
Fuels	2,882.3	841.0	25,871.2	201.1
Commodities	9,930.8	554.3	9,660.0	1,281.1
Manufactures	25,550.9	1,032.0	887.9	284.7

Source: As in table 13.10, tables 202 and 203.

A review of the detailed trade data reveals that trade with socialist countries was at first limited to a few African countries, which in the 1970s included Algeria, Egypt, Ghana, Morocco, Nigeria, Somalia, the Sudan, and Tanzania. Over the years, this list of countries has expanded considerably to include the majority of African countries by the 1980s.

Recent industrial cooperation in production activities among African and socialist countries has been dominated by engineering industries and what is referred to in the decade program as multi-country resource-based industries. These include[24] the Helwan iron and steel complex in Egypt, producing 1.5 million tons per year, and the Algerian El-Khodja steel complex, which is expected to produce 2.0 million tons of steel per year when the second unit is completed. Also in the same field of metallurgical industries is the iron and steel complex currently under construction in Nigeria, which when completed will produce 1.3 million tons of steel per year. In Ethiopia, Ghana, and Zambia, the socialist countries are supporting the implementation of projects for production of agricultural implements and machinery, which are in accord with the high priority given to food and agricultural production in the Lagos Plan. The same countries are also increasing their support to regional institutions, including the African Regional Center for Engineering Design and Manufacturing.

There exists great potential for further cooperation among socialist and African countries in the above areas. A number of priority multi-country projects in the metallurgical subsector and involving agricultural implements and machinery have already been identified for implementation during the Industrial Development Decade within the context of the PTA, ECOWAS and, MRU, to mention only a few. By cooperating in these projects, socialist and African countries will improve their economic relations to their mutual benefit.

CONCLUSION

The review of the possibilities and modalities for international cooperation among African countries themselves and among African countries and other regions reveals that there exists an enormous unexploited potential for industrial cooperation, as well as some constraints.

Given the current policies of different groups, the potentiality for industrial cooperation is by far greatest among the African countries themselves and then among developing countries. The exploitation of the potentiality for cooperation with the socialist countries, while apparently limited in terms of trade, is substantial in the development of intermediate goods industries. While beneficial, short-term cooperative arrangements continue, intensification of industrial collaboration with the advanced market economies requires a basic reassessment of relations in order to come up with approaches that are viable in the long-term.

NOTES

1. Statement by Dr. Adebayo Adedeji, Executive Secretary, Economic Commission for Africa on the occasion of the celebration of the Twenty-first Anniversary of the Commission on 28 April 1979 in Addis Ababa.

2. OECD, Interfutures, Facing the Future, Mastering the Probable and Managing the Upredictable (Paris, 1979).

3. UN, A Program for the Industrial Development Decade for Africa (Document ID/287), 1982.

4. OAU, Lagos Plan of Action for the Economic Development of Africa, 1980-2000 (Geneva: International Institute for Labor Studies, 1981), para. 52, p. 19.

5. It has been estimated that the demand for engineering goods in a developing economy increases faster than per capita income, at least one and a half to two times faster, with income elasticity of demand ranging between 1.5 and 2.0; see for example, Economic Commission for Europe, The Role and Place of Engineering Industries in National and World Economies (ENGIN/R.1/Add.6), January 1973.

6. Lack of systematic integration among firms, as well as shortages of raw materials and spare parts, which lead to persistent balance of payments problems, are also among the factors that restrict the growth and competitiveness of potential exports of manufactures for development countries. For a treatment of this subject, see Atsushi Murakami, "Export Base and Infant Export Industries," Kobe University Economic Review 12 (1965).

7. There exists an enormous amount of literature on the link between industry and food and agriculture; see for example, John W. Mellor, The New Economics of Growth: A Strategy for India and the Developing World (Ithaca: Cornell University Press for Twentieth Century Fund, 1976); John Sigurdson, "Rural Industrialization in China, Approaches and Results," World Development 3 (7 and 8), (1975): 527-538 and Michael Lipton, "The New Economics of Growth: A Review," World Development 5 (3), (1977): 267-270.

8. The engineering industry is the sector of technological innovation par excellence. Through it, new products lead to new production processes, which, in turn, lead to retooling and related investment. For more discussion on this, see UN, Economic Commission for Europe, The Role and Place of Engineering Industries in National and World Economies (ECE/ENGIN/8), December 1976.

9. For more discussion on this aspect, see Lynn Krieger Mytelka, "Licensing and Technological Dependence in the Andean Group," World Development 6 (1978): 447-459.

10. It has been suggested that, whatever benefits a country may reap from the international division of labor and specialization in those activities that by their nature maximize learning by doing, such comparative advantages must always be weighed against the potential loss of the less obvious but perhaps very fundamental gains that a country acquires from widespread participation by its people in the design, manufacture, and repair of new types of equipment; see for example, Thomas G. Rawski, "Problems of Technological Absorption in Chinese Industry," "American Economic Review 65 (2), (May 1975): 383-388.

11. Elliot, Charles, ed., Constraints on the Economic Development of Zambia (Nairobi and Lusaka: Oxford University Press, 1971), pp. 284-286.

12. International Labor Office, *Employment, Incomes and Equality in Kenya* (Geneva: International Labor Office, 1972).

13. For a full discussion on this subject, see, for example, George C. Bitros, "A Statistical Theory of Expenditures in Capital Maintenance and Repair," *Journal of Political Economy* 84 (5), (October 1978).

14. D. Winfried Von Urff, "The Integration of the Developing Countries into an Unstable World Economy--Problems, Chances and Dangers," *The German Economic Review* 14 (1) (1976): 76-82.

15. See for example C.V. Vaitsos, "The Role of Transnational Enterprise in Latin American Integration Efforts: Who Integrates with Whom, Now, and for Whose Benefits," *Report for UNCTAD Secretariat* (Lima, May 1978).

16. UN, *Development and International Co-operation*, Caracas Program of Action, May 1981 (A/36/333), 26 June 1981.

17. Arthur W. Lewis, "The Slowing Down of the Engine of Growth," *The American Economic Review*, 70 (4) (1980).

18. For a full discussion of the issue of concessional aid, see for example, Raymond F. Mikesell, *The Economics of Foreign Aid and Self-Sustaining Development* (Boulder: Westview Press, 1983).

19. OECD Statistics, *Development Co-operation Review, 1976-78*, (Paris: OECD, 1978) and Carl Widstrand, ed., *Multinational Firms in Africa* (Uppsala: Scandinavian Institute for African Studies, 1975).

20. Martin Fransman, ed., *Industry and Accumulation in Africa* (London: Heinemann, 1982).

21. Excluding the oil exporting countries: Algeria, Libya, Nigeria and also Egypt. IMF, *Direction of Trade Statistics Yearbook, 1983* (Washington, 1983).

22. G.K. Helleiner, "Manufactures Exports from Less-Developed Countries and Multinational Firms," *The Economic Journal* 83 (329) (March 1973): 21-47.

23. Matthew McQueen, "Lomé: Rules of Origin--the Need for Reform," *Lomé Briefing* 10 (1983).

24. U. Ushakova, "Industrial Co-operation between the Council for Mutual Economic Assistance and Developing Countries," *Industry and Development* (UN Sales No.: E.84.II.B.2 007008), 1984.

D. Babatunde Thomas

14 Technology and Industrial Development in Africa

Out of the multitude of socio-economic problems confronting African countries, the technological underdevelopment of the region stands out as a multifaceted source of many of Africa's other problems. Technological progress is an inevitable part of the industrial development process, though it has been a latent agent in the industrial development of the African region. (There is a common saying that the development of a new technology takes 5 percent inspiration and 95 percent perspiration.) Technology and industry are vital agents to be mobilized through appropriate policies and strategies for diversification of economic activity and overall resource mobilization, and for efficient tackling of the long-term problems of unemployment and poverty and the immediate problems of food, shelter, and energy, which confront the region's large rural population and rapidly growing urban population.

Technology and industry offer excellent prospects for the fulfillment of African countries' socio-economic development aspirations, but at the same time they constitute barriers to effective participation in the world economy. The goals of rapid growth in building up technological and industrial capacities with enhanced opportunities for mutually beneficial international cooperation and entry into the world market have not materialized for African countries (as they have for a number in Asia and Latin America); furthermore, they are not likely to materialize without serious attempts to fulfill two conditions. These are (1) a major reorientation of national policies and strategies by African countries to anticipate and respond effectively to the dynamics of the international economic environment, and (2) a major restructuring of the growing dominant-dependent relationship between the other regions of the world and the African region. This chapter is an assessment of the prospects for the fulfillment of these two conditions. In making this assessment, attention has been focused on (1) the industrial and technological underdevelopment of the region and the inefficacy of national policy responses; (2) regional and international responses; (3) approaches to and frameworks for international cooperation; and (4) trends in the international technological environment and their implications for Africa's industrial and technological development.

INDUSTRIAL AND TECHNOLOGICAL UNDERDEVELOPMENT

In spite of increases in national outputs of African countries, there has been limited technological transformation and slow growth in industrial capacities. Technological infrastructures, including institutions and human resources and indigenous capacities to develop and apply science and technology to promote development, remain relatively weak. Although postindependence industrialization policies have endeavored to reverse this pattern, achievement levels by individual countries in the drive to industrialize have varied and are generally low compared to other regions. Differences in levels of achievement have been influenced by numerous factors, including degrees of national commitment, efficacy of national policies and programs, and responsiveness of policies and strategies to the dynamics of the international economic environment.

In general, national policy responses to industrial and technological underdevelopment have tended to focus mainly on transitory, short-term rather than long-term solutions. The typical response is the importation of the products of technological innovations--primarily capital goods or complete "turnkey" plants and equipment and the requisite foreign technical manpower. Normally, the technologies embodied in imported plants and equipment and the associated know-how can be acquired by the local work force through training and "learning by doing." But the presence of external impediments to the effective acquisition of embodied technologies precludes their internalization. These impediments are usually manifested in typical modes of supplying technology; for example, through licensing and joint-venture agreements, with protection for the embodied technologies through patents and industrial property rights. Furthermore, and more importantly, the absence of a critical mass of the relevant and active scientific and technological capabilities locally also constitutes an impediment to the internalization of the imported technologies. Consequently, technological know-how, particularly in industry, remains largely in the hands of expatriate technicians and managers, without whom most established industrial facilities could not operate uninterrupted for an extended period. Thus the consequences include an increasing drain on foreign exchange reserves occasioned by rising import bills for capital goods and foreign manpower and a growing rather than a diminishing dependence on external sources of technology.

As recently as 1982, less than 4 percent of technologies in application in African countries were indigenous, and these were largely upgraded traditional technologies in the agro-industries. The technological constraints to industrialization occasioned by an underdeveloped technological infrastructure and a monopoly by foreign suppliers of technology have tended to render the potential mainspring of industrialization--namely, the modern manufacturing sector--merely assembly operations for import-substitution of consumer goods with limited or no opportunities for backward and forward linkages and limited possibilities for the internalization of the embodied technology in the associated imported capital goods. Furthermore, the products of these assemblies, in particular consumer goods such as radios, televisions, and passenger cars, are often protected from competition through quotas and tariffs.

Protection of import-substituting consumer goods industries through quotas, exclusion of imports, or high tariffs is usually designed as temporary relief to enable the establishment to develop the capacity to compete effectively. However, the tendency is for such protection to be protracted and to breed monopoly conditions, excess capacity and inefficiency, low quality products at relatively high prices at the expense of export-oriented and capital goods industries.[1] This pattern is characteristic of passenger vehicle assembly plants throughout the region. Thus, given limited manufacturing capabilities, protection of such assembly operations tends to perpetuate technological dependence.

Technological underdevelopment has also been a constraining factor on attempts, through import-substitution, to extend the application of the industrialization process to increase value-added in production and processing of traditional export products and raw materials and for the development of local capacity for capital goods production.

Typically, the subsector producing capital goods offers opportunities for high value-added and for the acquisition of capabilities for production technology, but this subsector is relatively underdeveloped. Hence there exists virtually complete dependence on imported capital goods, as well as intermediate goods and raw materials. Consequently, associated with import-substitution of consumer goods is import-expansion of intermediate and capital goods. Ordinarily, expansion of capital investment in manufacturing and the application of the embodied technology should be accompanied by increased productivity and growth in value-added, but this has not been the norm in the manufacturing sector of African countries, largely because of the orientation of national policies responses that usually consist of (1) science and technology policy; and (2) industrialization policy. From the foregoing, the importance of national policies on industrial and technological development is apparent.

NATIONAL SCIENCE AND TECHNOLOGY POLICY

A major prerequisite in the formulation of policy is information. Typically, relevant information for the formulation of science and technology policy is obtained through policy studies on how science and technology could be mobilized for socio-economic development. Thus, mobilization of scientific and technological capacity is a political process and a managerial exercise; and formulation of efficacious policies requires a delineation of objectives and the design of appropriate strategies and instruments for policy implementation, monitoring, and performance evaluation. In such circumstances, national efforts on scientific and technological development address the major multisectoral issues of (1) identifying requisite technologies based on ordered national development priorities; (2) ensuring regular access to the requisite technologies; (3) deciding whether to pursue national or collective regional approaches to technology development; (4) strengthening bargaining capacities for appropriate choices of technologies and improved favorable terms and conditions on imported technologies; (5) upgrading local traditional technologies and reducing dependence on imported technologies; and (6) determining what should be the rates of substitution of locally developed technologies for imported technologies over time.

While science and technology policies of African countries duly recognize virtually all the foregoing issues, lack of coherence has tended to render them inefficacious. In general, policies are oriented in the short- and intermediate-term to the importation of foreign technology for applications mostly in the manufacturing sector and in the long-term to incoherent attempts at the development of indigenous capacity. These are manifested in the tendency of policies to ignore the vital linkage between science and modern industry by encouraging, directly and indirectly, scientific research that has limited or no direct application to national problems in industry but provides individuals recognition in the form of financial remuneration, promotion, or study leave. Basic science is important to modern industry as the source of its deductive thought, as its eye on the future, and as its impetus for industrial innovation.[2]

Furthermore, existing national policies on the development of capacity to make and implement decisions and exercise control to reduce technological dependence tend to focus on regulatory activities. However, regulation without local efforts to develop substitutes in regulated technologies and sectors is likely to leave an undesirable vacuum and thus be self-defeating. To render existing policies effective they should be reoriented to enhance the capacity to make technological decisions by developing information on alternative sources of technology and thus promote greater awareness in the acquisition of technology, enhance the capacity to make appropriate choices of technology, and avoid buying technologies in the public domain (as most African countries currently do).

INDUSTRIALIZATION POLICY

Recent trends show that the manufacturing sector has been the primary focus of industrialization policies and programs, and the strategy for its development has been mainly import-substitution, which is a reaction to adverse external impacts. A major defect in import-substitution policy is its failure to address constraints to industrialization such as (1) the small size of local markets for manufactured products and very limited external markets; (2) the absence of local control of industrial enterprises; and (3) the limited opportunities for intrasectoral and intersectoral linkages. These constraints are addressed below.

Size of Markets

Limited size of internal markets and limited opportunities for external markets, and hence for scale-economies in manufacturing, have encouraged the establishment of small, uneconomical plants, limited technological possibilities, slowed down productivity growth, made the cost of industries excessive, and necessitated recourse to high tariffs.[3] Consequently, limited size of markets precludes real opportunities for successful import-substitution and self-sustaining growth in the manufacturing sector. The limited access to external markets through protective measures in potential markets also constitutes an impediment to successful export-oriented industrialization.

Table 14.1

Distribution of manufacturing value-added (MVA) by sector in selected African countries, 1960-71 (in percentages)

Country	1960			1971		
	Mainly consumer nondurables[a]	Mainly intermediate goods[b]	Mainly capital goods (including consumer durables)[c]	Mainly consumer nondurables[a]	Mainly intermediate goods[b]	Mainly capital goods (including consumer durables)[c]
Angola	79.4	16.5	4.1	71.3	24.1	4.6
Ghana	87.4	5.2	7.4	84.0	7.8	8.2
Ivory Coast	53.0	17.0	30.0	51.0	17.0	32.0
Kenya	58.0	16.5	25.5	57.3	16.6	26.1
Malawi	83.9	8.9	7.2	79.5	12.5	8.0
Mauritius	79.8	10.4	9.8	78.2	11.7	10.1
Mozambique	79.3	13.8	6.9	73.6	18.7	7.7
Namibia	78.9	4.4	16.7	73.2	5.4	21.4
Nigeria	75.1	14.5	10.4	73.3	18.1	8.6
Senegal	80.4	9.3	10.3	73.7	9.9	16.4
Tanzania	96.5	1.3	2.2	95.4	1.4	3.2
Uganda	81.8	8.8	9.4	74.8	14.4	10.8
Zaire	34.3	8.2	57.5	41.3	11.2	47.5
Zambia	57.1	20.0	22.9	55.9	24.0	20.1

Source: UNIDO, Industry in a Changing World (New York: UN), pp. 18-19.

[a]ISIC 31, 32, 33, 342, 385, and 390.

[b]ISIC 341, 35, and 36.

[c]ISIC 37 and 381-384.

[d]1960-70.

Table 14.2

Distribution of manufacturing value-added (MVA) in selected African countries
(in percentages, 1975 prices)

	Food and agriculture	Textiles and clothing	Machinery and transport equipment	Chemicals	Other Manufactures	Value-added in manufacturing (millions of 1975 US dollars)	
	1981	1981	1981	1981	1981	1970	1981
Cameroon	41		2	7	50	199	477
Central Af. R.	66	21		2	11	44	29
Chad	49	34			17	37	21
Ethiopia	27	27		2	44	236	349
Ghana	28				72	591	505
Ivory Coast						398	706
Kenya	24	10	33	6	27	167	531
Lesotho						3	10
Madagascar	27	39	2	10	22	295	272
Malawi	54	10			36	44	81
Nigeria	33	18	12	11	26	1,191	4,000
Senegal	43	15		8	34	276	298
Sierra Leone						25	37
Tanzania						190	202
Togo	50	28			22	30	14
Uganda	54	25			21	222	87
Upper Volta	74	7		11	8	67	96
Zaire						186	163
Zambia	16	22	10	14	38	319	444
Zimbabwe	19	19	10	11	41	564	969

Source: World Bank, World Development Report, 1984 (Washington: World Bank, 1984), p. 230.

For the African region, subregional and regional economic integration and expansion of markets are preconditions for a successful industrialization policy and program. However, the checkered history of attempts at regional cooperation and integration does not constitute a hopeful sign. In this respect, the Lagos Plan, to be examined in detail below, takes on great importance to the region's collective approach to industrialization.

Ownership and Control of Enterprises

The manufacturing sector is usually composed of both traditional, cottage-type industries and crafts and modern industries. The actual extent of activities in traditional industries and crafts is significant but highly dispersed. Consequently, it has always been difficult to measure accurately the volume of its activity. Historically, there has been a high concentration of foreign ownership in modern manufacturing, and the structures of production and marketing tend to be oligopolistic. The small number of firms encourages barriers to entry and a high degree of sellers' concentration in essential manufacturing activities. Apart from the oligopolistic structure, the extent of participation by local entrepreneurs in modern manufacturing has been constrained by their preference for risk that tends to favor short-term profits associated with distributive trade. The absence of a critical mass of entrepreneurial manpower with the motivation to make long-term investments to build up national productive capacities, rather than short-term profitmaking in distribution, has necessitated growth of public sector participation in manufacturing through the establishment of public enterprises and "parastatals."

Thus, an essential aspect of the impediments to a viable and self-sustaining industrialization process is the limited extent of participation by private entrepreneurs in the manufacturing sector. Increases in local private ownership and control through a judicious indigenization of foreign industrial enterprises and reduction of the role of public enterprises are essential for broader participation in the industrialization process, improved efficiency, and improved opportunities for skill formation, particularly technical and managerial skills.

Intrasectoral and Intersectoral Linkages

Among the primary objectives of any industrialization policy is the promotion of intrasectoral linkages through "vertical balance" in the manufacturing of consumer, intermediate, and capital goods. Among the compelling economic reasons for vertical balance are (1) the limited impact of a consumer goods oriented, import-substitution strategy due to weak intrasectoral and intersectoral linkages, low value-added and employment and (2) the possibilities for linkage effects through intermediate and capital goods production. Areas where opportunities clearly exist for vertical balance include oil and chemicals. However, for a successful vertical balance, it is necessary to build up trade in manufactured exports. Recent trends in the manufacturing sector of African countries indicate serious vertical imbalances. Between 1960 and 1971 the production of nondurable consumer goods dominated the manufacturing sector (see table 14.1). This pattern has continued into the 1980s as shown in table 14.2. The growth observed in value-added in capital goods production was due largely to assembly operations, but a number of countries experienced a decline, notably Nigeria, Zaire, and Zambia.

While the manufacturing sector has a strong natural linkage to other sectors of the economy, a vital missing link--namely, the capital goods subsector--seriously constrains the extent of the technological possibilities for effective intersectoral linkages, particularly between manufacturing and agriculture (see chapter 13). The success of any efforts to promote intersectoral linkages, by relating industrialization to a local natural resource base and linking the agricultural sector with the manufacturing sector through the promotion of agro-industries, will depend on building requisite capabilities for capital goods production and giving major programmatic considerations to the development of processing capabilities at the source. The effectiveness of intrasectoral and intersectoral linkages will tend to depend on the appropriateness of choices and the mix of industries and technologies. Therefore any reorientation of industrialization policies would need to take account of the pattern of development in the manufacturing sector and design appropriate instruments to correct existing dysfunctional shifts between the output of the manufacturing sector and those of the other sectors through the promotion of intersectoral linkages.

The mammoth task of formulating and executing coherent national science and technology and industrialization policies is only accomplished when there is some form of national philosophy with a long-term commitment to a set of ordered national priorities. For the purposes of a direct and effective impact on local technological and industrial capacity-building, it is essential that the formulation and execution of industrialization policies are made integral parts of national science and technology policies and not independent activities. With this precondition, the formulation and execution of industrialization policy, as well as those of other sectoral development policies, can each be considered subsets of national science and technology policy formulation and execution and hence subject to the same conditions.

Recent Trends in the Manufacturing Sector

In spite of the growth in local industries, the pace of industrialization measured in terms of growth in the share of manufacturing in gross domestic product (GDP) has been slow. Compared to other developing regions where the share of manufacturing rose from 16.0 percent in 1960 to 21.2 percent in 1980, the increase experienced by the African region was from 7.1 to 9.7 percent over the same period.[4] Furthermore, the structure of manufacturing activities has been characterized by weak backward linkages, high import content of manufactured goods, and low value-added relative to the cost of raw materials (mostly imported) and the value of total production. Typical products for import-substitution include textiles, apparel, beverages, and industrial raw materials such as wood, cement, chemicals, and rubber products. Since the 1970s, manufacturing activities have included the assembly of durable consumer goods, such as radios and television from imported components, and passenger cars from imported, completely knocked down (CKD) parts.

The African region accounts for only about 1.0 percent of developing countries' share of world manufacturing value-added (WMVA), and the rate of growth in this share has also been slow. Between 1963 and 1982, Africa's share of developing countries' (excluding China) WMVA at constant prices rose from 0.77 to 1.11 percent (see table 14.3). A rise in the share of manufacturing in GDP was also observed in a number of African countries, notably Ghana, Ivory Coast and Nigeria, but a closer examination of the sectoral components of the GDP suggests that the increases were largely achieved at the expense of the agriculture sector. For the same period, Latin America's share of WMVA rose from 4.17 percent to 5.68 percent, and South and East Asia's share rose from 2.13 percent to 3.43 percent. Overall, the developing countries' share of the world manufacturing value-added rose between 1963 and 1982 from 8.1 percent to 11 percent. It is worth noting that in 1982, while the developing regions accounted for 11 percent of the WMVA, they constituted 66 percent of the world's population. Furthermore, over the same two-decade period, only 10 developing countries accounted for about 72 percent of the manufacturing value-added of all developing countries, and not a single one of these 10 countries is in Sub-Saharan Africa (excluding South Africa). It is instructive to note that during the same period, the centrally planned economies experienced a decline in their share from 77.3 to 64 percent.

Table 14.3

Share of developing regions in world MVA, 1963-82
(in percentages)

Year	Africa	South and East Asia	Latin America
1963	0.77	2.13	4.71
1964	0.79	2.11	4.88
1965	0.79	2.07	4.86
1966	0.78	1.98	4.86
1967	0.75	2.02	4.84
1968	0.77	2.05	4.89
1969	0.78	2.09	4.92
1970	0.83	2.18	5.15
1971	0.84	2.23	5.40
1972	0.81	2.28	5.48
1973	0.81	2.33	5.50
1974	0.83	2.44	5.74
1975	0.88	2.60	5.87
1976	0.84	2.75	5.74
1977	0.85	2.85	5.64
1978	0.87	3.04	5.65
1979	0.91	3.15	5.75
1980	0.97	3.14	6.14
1981[a]	1.02	3.26	5.82
1982[b]	1.11	3.43	5.68

Source: UNIDO, Industry in a Changing World, (New York: UN), p. 36.

Notes: At constant 1975 prices.
South and East Asia excludes China.
[a]Preliminary figures.
[b]Estimates.

The inefficacy of existing science and technology and industrialization policies in their impact on key internal factors in the socio-economic development of African countries constitutes an impediment to any major growth in Africa's share of WMVA or any viable and self-sustaining industrialization. In sum, it is apparent from this background that existing policies, though broad in scope, lack the policy instruments for affecting policy objectives. These shortcomings in national policies are reflected in the industrialization process and particularly in the performance of the manufacturing sector. The impact of the various policies on the build up of technological capabilities has also been weak, and any significant improvement would require the harmonization of the various policies. It is against this backdrop of the limitation of national responses that both international and regional responses to the promotion of Africa's industrial and technological development should be gauged, reoriented, as appropriate, and reinforced.

RESPONSES TO THE PROMOTION OF AFRICA'S TECHNOLOGICAL AND INDUSTRIAL DEVELOPMENT

A review of national responses to promoting industrial and technological development and recent trends indicates that the limited national capacities have not been fully and efficiently mobilized. As a result, the monumental task of improving economic conditions in African countries under the prevailing international economic environment dominated by modern industry and advanced technologies is going to prove to be more and more difficult for the national capacities of most countries. For these reasons, existing international and regional responses for improving the region's economic conditions should be reexamined and viable international cooperative responses evolved to fully and efficiently mobilize national capacities.

International Responses: Aid and Technical Assistance

Various agenda and official declarations have sought to promote socio-economic development in the African region, but virtually all have gone unfulfilled. For example, major attempts through multilateral assistance by the international community to redress the technological backwardness of developing countries date back to the 1960s with the UN resolution on the Development Decade, which set 5 percent as a target minimum annual growth rate of national income for these countries. In 1963, a conference on the application of science and technology for the benefit of the developing countries gave much hope for redressing their technological underdevelopment. This was followed by various other international conferences and declarations, notably the "Declaration and Action Program on the Establishment of a New International Economic Order" (May 1974) and the UN Conference on Science and Technology for Development and the Vienna Program of Action (August 1979). However, in the two decades since 1963, the technological gap between the advanced industrial countries and African countries has been widened rather than abridged, and the disparities in wealth and income distribution have also worsened. The declarations and the laudable agenda for action thus remain unfulfilled.

Another problem area has been international bilateral aid and technical assistance, where the aid giver and the recipient rarely have shared experiences. The nature of development problems has been seen largely through the eyes and understanding of foreign experts rather than through those of (indigenous) nationals. Assistance provided in these circumstances constitutes imported, packaged solutions often unrelated to national experiences or priorities of recipients and tends to promote a distorted perspective of what should be the true nature of international relations. Furthermore, the priorities of donors tend to shift without consideration for the priorities of potential recipients. A primary aim of aid, most of which is usually tied, is to promote export markets for the donor, and the consequences for recipients are seemingly perpetual dependence and weakening of local incentives.

For most African countries, past approaches to improving economic conditions have emphasized external solutions such as aid, technical assistance, and trade. The resulting increased dependence has left most economies in varying degrees of crises with increasing food imports, growing external debts, and balance of payment deficits. This dependence in turn reinforces the tendency to treat aid as a permanent feature of national planning and budgeting, rather than as a supplementary and transitory component.

In spite of the massive flow of bilateral and multilateral assistance to the region, failure to coordinate these efforts at the international and national levels, relate them to national priorities, and harmonize them with national efforts has left most efforts highly diffused and dysfunctional. Consequently, performances of economies have not been commensurate with the volume of aid. Hence, there is an urgent need to reexamine international responses in order to develop viable approaches to international cooperation through aid for the mutual benefit of all concerned.[5]

Regional Responses: The Monrovia Strategy and the Lagos Plan of Action

Regional responses to the task of improving economic conditions in African countries changed dramatically in 1979 with the adoption of the Monrovia Strategy. This marked a major change of direction away from a primary national focus to a regional focus in the search for solutions to socio-economic problems. The Lagos Plan of Action for the implementation of the Monrovia Strategy also constituted a milestone in the mobilization of political will and determination for a regional focus and collective approach to development.[6]

Through the strategy and the Plan, African governments committed themselves to the development of indigenous entrepreneurial and technological manpower, as well as the technological capacities that will enable the African people to assume greater responsibility in the attainment of rapid industrialization. They represent an admission of national responsibilities and a demonstration of collective will to mobilize and expand the region's industrial and technological capacities for socio-economic development. The Lagos Plan accorded industry and science and technology, in its Chapters II and V, respectively, paramount roles in "mobilizing the region's resources through industrialization, in view of ... potential impact on meeting the basic needs of the population, ensuring the integration of the economy and the modernization of society," and promoted the application of "science and technology in the service of development by reinforcing the autonomous capacity of African countries in this field."[7] Industry is viewed as the major supplier of input requirements for the agriculture sector, in particular agro-based industries for food production, processing, preservation, storage, and distribution, as well as for other key sectors such as mining, energy, and communications.

The Lagos Plan remains basically a summary of objectives and a framework for the types of actions required at national, subregional, and regional levels. The next task is for the various goals, including the various targets, to be translated into operational and bankable project activities in the short, medium, and long terms, at the national, subregional, and regional levels. The successful implementation of the Plan will depend on (1) access to and successful application of existing technologies in industry and agriculture to solve the immediate problems of the food deficit and energy crisis in the short and medium term; and (2) the successful build-up of endogenous technological capabilities to tackle the long-term problems of unemployment and poverty.

The Industrial Development Decade for Africa

The vital role accorded to industry in the structural transformation of African economies has also been reinforced by the Program on the Industrial Development Decade for Africa (IDDA).[8] To this end, production capacities are to be expanded in agro-industries, building, energy, steel, and chemicals in the short term such that the region attains a target of 1.0 percent of world industrial production by 1985. For the medium term (i.e., by 1990), the target has been set at 1.4 percent, based on the expectation of significant progress in increasing the local processing of raw materials. On the basis of recent trends, these targets are unlikely to be attained. In 1982, Africa's share of the world manufacturing value-added was only 0.1 percent. Furthermore, in order for the targets to be meaningful they would need to be translated into national targets.

Clearly, the IDDA offers an initial major opportunity to translate the goals and objectives concerned with industry, as well as science and technology, into concrete operational activities and bankable projects. Although, unlike the Lagos Plan, the IDDA contains concrete operational activities at the national, subregional, and regional levels, it also provides a broad framework and a set of guidelines for the implementation of program activities. The recent approach to IDDA notwithstanding, the current lack of major commitments and financial support for the programs of IDDA is likely to leave them unfulfilled. The proposal at the recent fourth conference of UNIDO for a modest $200 million program for IDDA to be funded through voluntary contributions further leaves its future in doubt. Admittedly, one of the aims of IDDA is to establish a firm foundation for attaining self-reliance to sustain the region's industrial development in accordance with the goals and objectives of the Lagos Plan. However, rather than lapse into the previous approach of seeking voluntary aid to fulfill this objective, mutually beneficial international cooperation on specific project activities in the IDDA program should be intensified.

APPROACHES TO VIABLE INTERNATIONAL COOPERATION

The current primary approach to international cooperation involves technical assistance and aid, which constitutes a transitory or stop gap response, rather than providing the effective means for self-sustaining collaboration based on shared experience.[9] Productive capacity can be built and sustained not primarily through aid, but through trade and other modalities of mutually beneficial cooperation.

Is it often argued that the world economy is characterized by interdependence and that growth in world trade is a manifestation of growth in international economic cooperation and interdependence. However, relations between less developed and advanced industrialized countries in industry and technology are characterized by the dependence of the former on the latter: and there is no region or group of countries where this is more evident than in Africa. In 1978, African countries had imports equivalent to 25 percent of their combined GDP and exports totalling less than 1.0 percent of total world trade. This state of affairs, which is also representative of recent trends, means a high degree of dependence and hence vulnerability to the vicissitudes of the international economic environment.[10] Although industrialized countries depend on a number of African countries for primary resources, this dependence tends to be transitory as substitutes for industrial raw materials are successfully developed; and the trend in the development of advanced technologies is likely to accelerate the rate of replacement of intermediate as well as primary resources. On the other hand, the dependence of African countries on industrially advanced countries for manufactured (consumer and capital) goods, technology, and managerial know-how tends to be expanding.

In view of the current framework's inability to respond adequately to the divergent goals of the advanced countries and African countries, there is a need for a new form of partnership in development coordination--a teleological partnership based on mutual goal-seeking to reconcile divergent interests, establish convergent economic, social, and political goals, and establish mutually acceptable rules for mutually beneficial international cooperation. An essential consideration in such an approach is a mutually beneficial international division of labor based not solely on comparative advantages, but also on political and social considerations affecting policies of trade, investment, and technology flows and on an understanding of the decision-making process in cooperating countries.

In order to be mutually beneficial, cooperation should be preceded by established sets of national priorities, explicit and realistic goals and expectations, ample capacity to negotiate mutually beneficial terms and conditions, and an established framework for monitoring and evaluating outcomes. Other essential requirements include (1) a clear understanding of the criteria for the distribution of gains from cooperative activities and (2) increases in gains from cooperation under conditions of positive-sum-games, in which the gains by one protagonist are not necessarily losses for another.

Science and technology development are universal pursuits. In order to be sustained, national scientific and technological activities require effective linkages with the international scientific and technological community for regular interactive flow of information. Given that imported technology will continue to play a prominent role for some time to come, fostering international cooperation for the facile flow of technology (for example, through a reexamination of the existing framework on patents and industrial property that reposes virtually all technologies in the advanced countries, and increased access by African countries to the results of publicly funded research and development activities in the advanced countries) is a matter of utmost urgency. "The sharing of technology is a world-wide concern, since all countries have much to learn from others. But clearly it is most important to the developing countries; and it can even be argued that their principal weakness is the lack of access to technology, or of command of it. The acquisition of technology is crucial, not only to growth, but to the capacity to grow."[11]

International cooperation in scientific and technological research offers opportunities for the sharing of technology. Cooperative joint-research and development programs involving African institutions and their counterparts in the advanced countries offer opportunities for the enhancement of the problem-solving capacity of local African researchers and institutions, and through the cooperating institutions from the advanced countries, enhance opportunities for the productive exchange of information and for trade. A major viable approach for international scientific and technological cooperation, and hence cooperation for industrial development, is direct bilateral or multinational joint research and development programs.

Joint R&D activities envisaged in this framework may entail the participation of a number of institutions in two countries, one developed and the other developing (or more than one country from both groups of countries) in a research and development program of common interest and international importance with each institution using a different approach and sharing the experience. This requires a developed infrastructure for direct communication. Among the modalities for such joint activities are networking and twinning. The former would be suitable for multinational cooperative programs and the latter for bilateral cooperation on a joint research program that may entail a division of labor among the institutions concerned. A vital requirement of both modalities is the accessibility to relevant, usable, and up-to-date information.

The areas of food and energy are of high priority and offer many opportunities for bilateral and multinational joint R&D programs. Currently joint R&D work is ongoing in the area of food technology at the International Institute of Tropical Agriculture (Ibadan) and Institut de Technologie Alimentaire (Dakar). One aspect of joint R&D requiring intensification is the application of existing technologies in the short term for food processing, storage, preservation, distribution, and marketing to reduce postharvest food losses, improve in the long term farming and agricultural techniques for higher yields, develop new crops with resistance to the vicissitudes of the environment, increase nutritional food value of products, and enhance appeal for locally produced products (see chapters 10 and 11).

Another target of opportunity for bilateral and multinational joint R&D programs is the capital goods subsector (see chapter 13). There is an urgent necessity to expand the assembly and manufacture of capital goods and industrial machinery, given their critical roles in the industrial and technological development of African countries and in order to reduce dependence on imports. The priority areas are, at one level, machine-tool manufacturing of metal cutting tools, lathes, foundries, precision instruments, electrical parts, and machine tool accessories, and at another, higher level, agricultural machinery and electrical power and transport equipment. Machine tooling offers opportunities for development of machine operating, maintenance, and repairing skills, and agricultural, electrical, and transport machinery and equipment offer opportunities for the acquisition of specialized, high technology skills. However, international cooperation in these areas would require vigorous effort in view of competition among existing capital goods producers and the proprietary nature of the technology involved. Nonetheless, collaboration agreements with other regions of the world offer many possibilities for the development of capital goods production in African countries. In order to collaborate effectively and ensure mutual benefits, the role of local consulting engineering and design organizations would need to be strengthened to optimize the use of imported drawings and designs and facilitate the absorption of capital goods production technologies.

Virtually all these areas of opportunities for joint R&D programs on food and capital goods production correspond to program elements in the Lagos Plan of Action. However, to implement these programs, concrete projects need to be developed, based on a judicious choice of priorities for the region.

CONCLUSION

The critical issues and challenges to the technological and industrial development of the African region in the 1980s and the 1990s are how to enhance capabilities to make appropriate choices and mixes of industry and technology; increase access to relevant and usable technological information; develop coherent industrial and technology policies and strategies, bargaining capacities, and effective policy instruments; strengthen linkages between the local suppliers and local users of technology; and avoid a major loss of industrial capacity. Access to technologies from advanced countries is not likely to improve significantly, as the flow of technology becomes restricted in reaction to the perceived threat of competition of manufactured goods from developing countries. Although African countries pose no such threat as yet, the consequences of the trends likely to emerge--for example, higher prices and difficult access to requisite technologies that cannot be readily developed locally--could have long-term adverse effects on technological development in the region. Therefore, international cooperation on the basis of mutual benefits is a vital and indispensable instrument for meeting the technological requirements of industrialization. This has been duly recognized in the Lagos Plan and should be incorporated in its implementation.

Major leaps in technological development in the advanced countries and associated significant reductions in production costs (in particular labor costs) pose serious problems and point to the eventual loss of the advantage of low labor costs, which in the 1960s shifted production plants to developing regions. The greatest beneficiary of this shift in production plants has been Asia. Advanced and frontier technologies, namely in microelectronics (microcomputing technology, fiber optics, lasers), genetic engineering and biotechnology, robotics, and weapons technology, portend a shift of production plants back to the advanced countries, thus causing a major reversal in the existing international division of labor.[12] All these technological advances are inextricably linked. The semiconductor makes possible the semiconductor laser, which makes possible fiber optics, which in turn makes possible light-wave communication systems.[13] Thus, the possibilities for the application of modern technology are not only constrained by their proprietary characteristics but by their complex interrelationships.

The existing policy and strategy of import-substituting industrialization under conditions of virtually complete dependence on foreign sources of technology offer limited opportunities for relieving technological underdevelopment in the African region. In addition to reorienting existing policies and strategies for improving the industrial and technological state of affairs in the African region, efforts to implement the Lagos Plan would need to be intensified by developing bankable projects from the program elements of the plan. For this purpose, major commitments of resources are required to enhance capacity-building in indigenous technology development, through the build-up of indigenous research and development (R&D) manpower, promotion of local R&D activities as an integral part of economic activity in the productive sector, and the establishment of complementary relationships between imported and indigenously developed technologies through the conduct of R&D, including reverse engineering activities.

Implications of trends in the international technological environment are clear. In order to move from a dependent to an interdependent relationship with the rest of the world, first it is essential that African countries rapidly develop the capacity to feed their populations, and this requires a genuine national commitment and resolute action at the national and regional levels regarding industrial and technology development.

While international and regional dispersion of industry is a plausible proposition in order to reduce industrial congestion, avoid possible economic decline in the advanced countries, stimulate development in the African region as well as in other developing regions, and promote reduction of unequal income distribution, ongoing major technological advances and the changing character of industries in the advanced countries are likely to delay such dispersion indefinitely. Therefore, such a proposition does not offer any good prospects for the industrial development of the African region in the foreseeable future.

Possible shifts in manufacturing plants back to the advanced countries in response to ongoing technological advances would create a vacuum that could be filled either through local entrepreneurs or more likely, as the recently emerging pattern suggests, by the NICs, such as Brazil, South Korea, and India. If current trends in the orientation of local entrepreneurs prevail, the former option could lead to dying industries as the flow of investment slows, and without possibilities for international competition, export earnings decline. The latter option involving the NICs would require a close examination of the opportunities it offers for harmonization of interests and for mutually beneficial cooperation in technological and industrial development.

In addition to the necessity of applying and upgrading traditional technologies to solve basic problems of food, shelter, and energy, major efforts are required simultaneously on the selective development of modern technologies and the judicious application of these to all sorts of socio-economic development problems, in particular, for increased food production, reduction of postharvest food losses, and capital goods production. There already exists a vast body of technological knowledge both within and outside the African region that is potentially and actually applicable in meeting the technological requirements of the region, especially in the agro-industries and small- to medium-scale manufacturing. However, most of the technologies are not readily available for direct application; consequently, the need arises for increased access to relevant technological information, for appropriate unpackaging, repackaging, and adaptation, including any necessary upgrading or downgrading of these technologies based on local requirements. To meet these needs would require strengthening the scientific and technological infrastructure, in particular the human resources industry, to render it capable of conceiving, designing, installing, and managing productive enterprises successfully.

NOTES

1. See Paul Prebisch, *Towards a New Trade Policy for Development: Report of the Secretary General of UNCTAD* (Geneva, 1964), pp. 21-22.
2. Allan Crawford, "Science and Industry," *Science* 213 (4 September 1981): 1976.
3. Prebisch, *Towards a New Trade Policy for Development.*
4. See UNIDO, *Industry in a Changing World* (New York: United Nations).
5. See The Brandt Commission, *Report of the Independent Commission on International Development Issues, North-South: A Programme for Survival* (London: Pan Books, 1980), chap. 3.
6. OAU, *Lagos Plan of Action for the Economic Development of Africa, 1980-2000* (Geneva: International Institute for Labour Studies, 1981).
7. *Ibid.*
8. See ECA, OAU and UNIDO, *A Program for the Industrial Development Decade for Africa* (New York: United Nations, 1982).
9. See ARCT/UNFSSTD, "The Report of the Joint Meeting on International Cooperation for African Technological Development" (Dakar, December 1983).
10. World Bank, *World Development Report 1981* (Washington: World Bank, 1981), p. 19.
11. *The Brandt Report*, pp. 193 and 194.
12. Inger Krugmann-Randolf, "The Technological Hitch: Editorial," *Development and Co-operation* 4 (Bonn, July/August 1984).
13. Colette Dowling, *The Techno/Peasant Survival Manual* (New York: Bantam Books, 1980), p. 312.

Timothy M. Shaw

Conclusion: African Development and the New International Division of Labor

> The future that emerges from the historical trends scenario... is horrendous. To imagine that the African region will be more dependent on other regions in all critical areas is a cause for alarm...riots, crimes and misery would be the order of 2008 if present trends continue without conscious change. With the weak and fragile socio-political systems, the sovereignty of African states will, then, be at stake. As such, self-reliance and independence will, to the generation of 2008, sound like slogans of the past...another future must be designed. Hence, the normative development scenario...of self-determination, self-confidence, collective self-reliance and self-sustainment. This "willed future" [consists of] a will to establish, today, a genuine development process.
>
> Adebayo Adedeji, Introduction to ECA and Africa's Development, 1983-2008[1]

> The only true resolution of the contradictions that increasingly characterise the societies of the periphery is a national and popular one. This is the only way in which these societies can avoid the disintegration that has already begun--a disintegration that bears witness both to the local ruling classes' inability to impose a re-sharing of world surplus value to their advantage, and demonstrates the absence of an immediate revolutionary challenge.
>
> Samir Amin, "Crisis, Nationalism and Socialism"[2]

The joint ECA-Dalhousie Conference coincided with the centenary of the Berlin Conference on the division of Africa and took place during the contemporary UN debate on "the critical economic situation in Africa."[3] These seemingly disparate events are, in fact, quite closely related: Berlin's "balkanization" of the continent provides the background to the current crisis. If the Berlin Conference of the colonial powers constitutes one cause of Africa's underdevelopment--from precolonial to imperial rule--then the UN debate signals another stage in Africa's troubled history: its marginalization in the new international division of labor. Lomé III, the formal restatement of EurAfrican relations,[4] was signed just after the UN debate ended with a unanimous resolution on Africa's crisis. The continuing crisis marks, then, the transition from a colonial and neocolonial situation to a postcolonial one, in which the basis of power has shifted away from colonial commodities to new resources, facilities, and relations. So the current condition is not merely a short-term disaster of drought, debt, refugees, and decline; rather it is the stark early warning of a long-term movement toward peripheralization and impoverishment: Africa's apparent lot in the new international division of labor. And this new position, whether involuntary or not, has distinctive impacts on and implications for different countries and classes and for the social causes and consequences of the Lagos Plan, as indicated in the preceding chapters.

INHERITANCE

Notwithstanding such challenges and responses, Africa has yet to adjust fully its perceptions and policies to a transformed world system in which ubiquitous neocolonial connections have been superceded by deliberate and discrete deals among calculating countries, corporations, and classes in the industrialized world and a selection of African commodity dealers, centers, and compradors. The new scramble for Africa is neither so frantic nor so final as a hundred years ago because the new division of labor is based on technologies rather than commodities and on communications rather than colonies (see chapter 14). While at the level of diplomacy, Africa and the nonaligned world still seek a NIEO, in reality, a new system is already being forged. But the postindustrial, high-technology division of labor involves regions of the world and production sectors unfamiliar to Africa: the Pacific Rim as well as Europe and microchips as well as primary products. It is for this postimperial world that Africa has proposed the Lagos Plan of Action. A response to disappointments in both development theories and development results, the Lagos Plan is also a preliminary attempt to define the continent's place in the emerging postindustrial, postneocolonial world.

So the contemporary African condition[5] of crisis has been brought about both by inheritance of the colonial imperative to incorporate Africa into the world system and by subsequent changes in the world economic order that have rendered Africa more peripheral than ever. The shocks that swept through the global political economy of the 1970s--from the floating U.S. dollar and expensive energy to middle power emergence and superpower confrontation--have had a massive impact on established patterns of African dependence and underdevelopment. The idealistic myths central to PanAfricanism--that all African states are essentially similar and equally free to develop--have been replaced by a new realism verging on pessimism: states are diverging exponentially, with only a minority likely to experience sustained growth.[6] In terms of politics, psychology, diplomacy, and security, realpolitik poses a dramatic, almost awesome, set of problems for the continent, hence the Lagos Plan of Action.

This preliminary yet promising redirection of the continent's political economy gives, on the one hand, an indication of the intensity of the crisis and, on the other hand, acts as a measure of the limits of radicalism, given institutional and ideological constraints. Yet, as a restatement of collective nationalism and as a redefinition of consensual needs, it does offer a framework for transcending inherited difficulties: a possible, yet not definite, new beginning for economic orientation and development. Hardly radical yet clearly not orthodox--an African version of internationalist social democracy à la Keynes and Brandt[7]--the Lagos Plan at least offers one escape--a "willed future"[8]--from continual crisis and projected decline. To this extent, the ECA secretariat, despite its international "civil service" style, has advanced a relatively innovative position that goes beyond both conservatism and reformation as indicated by the breadth of this collection. Its mix of nationalist, populist, and continentalist views embodies dependencia and ecological and enlightened values, as projected through the rather bourgeois and synthetic lenses of an international organization.

Nevertheless, the Lagos Plan, by contrast to both World Bank and other futures studies for Africa[9] does offer a considered and coherent indigenous alternative to further marginalization and impoverishment: an indigenous attempt to anticipate and moderate changes in the international division of labor. As such, its intellectual and ideological roots, as well as its political and economic genesis, are deserving of empathetic yet not uncritical treatment by both policy analysts and policy-makers.

INNOVATION

The agitation and advocacy that led to the articulation of the Lagos Plan have their roots, as suggested in the first part of this volume, in a number of factors, which came together in the mid-1970s.[10] First, at the global level, the combination of (1) fluctuating exchange rates, (2) inter-imperial rivalries, and (3) energy crises marked the end of the postwar Bretton Woods period and the beginning of a new, postindustrial global order. Second, at the continental level, a series of challenges led to a renewed willingness to abandon old prescriptions: (1) the obvious development demise and the incidence of decline and decay; (2) unpromising, even threatening, projections for the immediate future; and (3) the revisionism apparent in development theory and policy everywhere, including Africa, with the redefinition of development, reconsideration of human rights, and new concerns for basic human needs, along with those for renewable resources and appropriate technologies. And third, at the institutional level, the accession of Professor Adebayo Adedeji to head the ECA and the latter's renewed willingness to collaborate with a more mature and modest OAU. The ECA thereby began to transcend its status of institutional insignificance within both UN and African systems and to bring itself to the conceptual and political cutting edge:[11] the ECLA of the 1980s.

The Lagos Plan thus constitutes a relatively bold initiative-cum-response at global, continental, and institutional levels. And at all three levels, it represents a dramatic contrast with the more orthodox and conservative World Bank response given in its Agenda for Action. While the

Lagos Plan advocates self-reliance as the only orientation for a continent in crisis, the World Bank has revived extroverted commodity production as a panacea.[12] The latter denies any transformation in the global economy and so seeks to revive Africa's traditional place in the colonial division of labor, whereas the former begins to acknowledge the nonreversibility of external changes and to consider alternative African responses to them.

The contours of the crisis are now quite familiar--Africa was the hardest hit of all regions in the 1970s--so that, a century after the Treaty of Berlin, the continent is now more economically marginal than ever, and Africa already contributes least to global trade and production in terms of both primary products and manufactured goods. According to estimates from the ECA and elsewhere, this general trend towards marginalization is likely to continue, while any growth will occur in just a few states, such as Algeria, Ivory Coast, Kenya, Nigeria, and Zimbabwe. And within these political economies, of course, it is the relatively rich social classes that suffer least. As Adedeji himself has warned:

> Not only are the forecasts for the immediate future gloomy, but the perspectives of development and economic growth in Africa up to the end of this millennium are heart-rending and continue to give cause for increasing uneasiness. Very bleak prospects are foreseen for Africa in global projections... the 1960s and the 1970s may by the end of the century appear in retrospect to have been a golden age for Africa.
>
> Projections by the ECA indicate that unless the orientation of the African economy changes, there is a danger that poverty and the attendant problems of political and social instability will become considerably worse in Africa in the next two decades.[13]

Adedeji hopes, however, that something positive can yet come out of such an unpromising scenario: an African cultural and economic revolution as a creative response to the emerging international division of labor as has been discussed in this book.

> Given these portentous prognostications, what can Africans and their governments do to avert the impending doom?... Africa has the capacity and capability to change the tide of her economic fortune in her favor and to emerge from her present economic doldrums and lay the foundation of an internally-generated, self-sustaining and self-reliant process of development.[14]

Notwithstanding either the prophecies of economic decline or the potentials of economic renewal, Africa's consensual response has been both cautious and controversial, a reflection of the significance and newness of transformations in the postindustrial global economy.

The urgent debate over alternative strategies poses challenges not only to African interests but also for extraAfrican actors; the latter are also edging toward responses to both global transitions and continental tensions. If either dependent development, the IBRD preference, or collective self-reliance, the OAU's proposal, becomes the motif for Africa up to the year 2000, then demands on and implications for external trade, aid, and financial interests vary widely. And vice versa, restructuring in Africa would impact, however marginally, on international institutions and interactions. Ironically, the present wave of protectionist pressures in the North may be more compatible with the nationalist orientation of Africa than with the internationalist advocates such as multinational corporations and the World Bank. The reformist and globalist inclinations of the Brandt Report may now be under attack from nationalists in both the North ("mercantilists") and the South ("independentistas"): the African crisis is having worldwide impact.

This conclusion reviews the African debate and examines implications for both Africa and the North: Which regimes and classes on the continent are likely to favor continued dependence rather than disengagement? Which African and Northern interests advocate increased external interaction rather than increased intraregional exchange? What coalitions or coincidences of interest may arise based on "monetarism" or "managerialism"?

The concern here is, then, with a set of interests and issues--other than any definition of or debate over alternative economic systems and development strategies, that both produce and reproduce the continental crisis in the global reordering. First, Africa is increasingly divided into a minority of semiperipheral and a majority of truly peripheral--Fourth World--states. These groups tend to prefer different development orientations: outward- or inward-looking, respectively. Second, the continent, as indicated in the second section of this book, is divided regarding different levels of emphases for pursuing self-reliance--national, regional and/or continental levels--in part related to divergent perceptions of the continent's future. Third, internal inequalities within African political economies have begun to lead to distinct, dominant coalitions, usually under the hegemony of particular bourgeois elements, such as national, comprador, bureaucratic, or military fractions. And finally, fourth, intra-African differences are intensified through interimperial rivalries: Which Northern (Eastern and Western) countries and their corporations favor extroversion or introversion? And which Northern classes--metropolitan national, bureaucratic, or military fractions--favor increased or reduced transnational linkages with elements in African social formations? In short, the attempt is made to identify the forces and features that are being discarded or rearranged as the post-industrial international economy is established.

The character of the African crisis has become increasingly clear as relentless and exponential setbacks have hit most countries on the continent over the last decade or so: the first waves generated by the global restructuring. As a recent IBRD <u>World Development Report</u> indicates:

> Low income countries in Africa, being more dependent on primary commodity exports, have suffered badly from the world recession. Their per capita income has continued to fall, and there is a real possibility that it will be lower by the end of the 1980s than it was in 1960.[15]

In response, as in <u>Agenda for Action</u>,[16] the World Bank advocates "policy reforms by many African governments, a recovery of commodity prices, and a large expansion of international aid to the region,"[17] i.e., old panaceas for new problems, which serve only to extend not resolve the crisis.

If the 1960s were hardly easy years for postindependence regimes, the 1970s and 1980s have been much harder, particularly the past decade.[18] In response to (1) the demise of any real prospect of an effective North-South dialogue, (2) the perpetuation of international recession and competition, and (3) the prospect of a new international division of labor rather than a NIEO, African states since 1980 have been debating the merits of the two contrasting continental diagnoses and prescriptions--the OAU Lagos Plan and the IBRD Agenda for Action--recognizing their almost diametrical (dialectical?) characters. In general, African states favor the former over the latter; as an early assessment by the combined OAU, ECA, and ADB secretariats suggested, "it is quite clear that the total effect of the [World Bank] recommendations addressed to African governments could very well make Africa more dependent and less self-reliant."[19] However, as I suggest, certain regimes and classes may yet identify with the IBRD's Agenda, while still others may go beyond the reformist self-reliance proposed in the OAU's Lagos Plan. Moreover, reactions to these alternative proposals are still fluid and may yet be affected by any revival of international trade or any pressure from international interests and institutions: the vagaries of exchange and the "conditionality" of the IMF.[20] Yet, the Lagos summit and declaration do still represent one definition of the collective interest of Africa's leadership, the basis of a response to the new division of labor that condemns the continent to the periphery.

INTEREST

At a rather abstract level, the Lagos Plan can be seen to reflect the common interest and ideology of Africa's ruling classes as well as of certain petit-bourgeois and nonbourgeois fractions. Given the continent's inherited and intensified marginality in the global system, the Lagos Plan attempts to transcend and transform such underdevelopment in terms of policy, ideology, and relationship. So although some leaders and regimes may have rather serious reservations about certain aspects of the plan--and so may be less than intent on implementing it in its totality[21]--they are all apprehensive about the political consequences of further stagnation or decline. Common fears of civil strife, social disorder, and military intervention[22] underlay the shift towards consensus of policy apparent in the late 1970s, notwithstanding the emergence of a set of supposedly radical regimes in southern Africa. The dialectic between economic reality and political response became quite apparent in the inevitable acceptance of South Africa's terms for an end to regional "destabilization" against impoverished neighbors.

So despite the apparent divergence of diplomacy between a growing "radical" coalition within the OAU and an established "conservative" bloc--the basis of disagreements over Chad, the Horn, the Sahara, and the abortive 1982 Libya summits--regarding development policy there is a surprising degree of agreement or at least a common apprehension, as reflected in the Lagos conference. There may yet be differences of opinion over continuing strategic situations but with regard to underlying structural conditions, recognizing how these do differ in incidence and impact throughout the continent, there is a distinct common interest centered around the challenge shared by disaffected nonbourgeois classes. Hence class coalitions designed to limit contradictions and secure their participants' property and status have appeared, along with the limits on radicalism as embodied in and expressed by the Lagos Plan. Yet the opinions of the really conservative class constellations--especially those representing extra- as well as intra-

African interests--are reflected in the Agenda with its orthodox, laissez faire tone, which contrasts the self-consciously "radical chic" tone of the Lagos Plan.

The motif of the collective indigenous response to the crisis--as indicated in the Lagos statements and in the earlier deliberations at the Monrovia symposium[23]--is "rapid self-reliance and self-sustaining development."[24] By contrast the IBRD Agenda advocates a "growth-orientated programme: i) more suitable trade and exchange rate policies; ii) increased efficiency of resource use in the public sector; and iii) improvement in agricultural policies."[25] While the Lagos Plan calls on Africa to use the crisis productively to utilize its own resources and to "cultivate the virtue of self-reliance,"[26] the Agenda advocates a return to agricultural production for export; these constitute contrary responses to the new international division of labor. Not that self-reliance means autarky; rather, it is an assertion of "Africa first" in economic as well as in strategic and diplomatic matters: "outside contributions should only supplement our own effort: they should not be the mainstay of our development."[27] It may also constitute a reluctant recognition that in the new order, Africa cannot really count on external attention or generosity, especially if recurrent emergencies absorb all energies and resources.

In an attempt to mediate apparent ECA-IBRD divergencies and disagreements over strategy, as well as to reassure skeptical conservative regimes on and off the continent, Adedeji and the World Bank have moved towards a middle ground without agreeing on a single solution involving introversion, industrialization, and indigenization. Instead of a radical definition of self-reliance--public rather than private sector, industry rather than commodities, and intracontinental rather than extracontinental exchange--Adedeji has come personally to advocate a shift in emphasis, as indicated in his landmark speech to the Western group for Cooperation for Development in Africa:

> Our requirements are at two levels. We need massive transfer of resources from the developed countries to Africa. But no less important, we need your understanding, your appreciation and your acceptance of our perception of the kind of development that we need in Africa....[28]

Nevertheless, while moderating Africa's economic demands somewhat, Adedeji has continued to emphasize the psychological aspect of the Lagos Plan: "If Africa is to develop the necessary self-confidence to pull its economy out of the shadows of backwardness and underdevelopment, it is essential that our partners-in-development respect our priorities, perceptions, goals and strategies."[29] Such psychological as well as physical preparation is imperative for facing any new order.

Agreement on the Lagos Plan at the first continental economic summit remains a singular achievement, given Africa's historical, ideological, and development diversities: a tribute to the tenaciousness of ECA diplomacy and the persuasiveness (and moderateness?) of the Monrovia Strategy, as well as an indication of the seriousness of the economic crisis. It is also suggestive of a belated awareness that a new, post-Bretton Woods order was in formation. The continent had already moved towards forms of regional self-reliance through a variety of integration schemes such as the ill-fated EAC and the fragile ECOWAS (see chapters 4 and 5), but national and continental arrangements were and are more controversial: will there be an African economic community by the year 2000?[30]

At the national level, self-reliance had by the 1980s been adopted as strategy by a group of more radical and peripheral states--Angola, Benin, Mali, Somalia, and Tanzania, for example. It has been avoided assiduously by those countries and regimes at the semiperiphery that still hope to benefit from continued incorporation in the world system--Algeria, Egypt, Ivory Coast, Kenya, and Nigeria, for example. Many others are both ideologically and structurally ambivalent--e.g., Malawi, Senegal, Sudan, and Zambia. And still others, in many ways, have lost whatever they had of a national economy--Chad, Gambia, Ghana, and Uganda, for instance--because of the combination of black market, smuggling, and foreign exchange difficulties.[31] Indeed, the withdrawal of commodities, including labor, from these national economies and the return of self-sufficient subsistence constitutes a dramatic, if uncoordinated, form of intranational self-reliance, not one which most regimes would want to encourage. Not all forms of self-reliance are compatible, then, as many of the chapters in this volume indicate; internal, national, regional, and continental strategies need to be carefully coordinated and integrated to avoid conflicts and contradictions in the future. Support for national self-reliance at the periphery and regional dominance at the semiperiphery, let alone alternative definitions of regions and assorted attempts at continental leadership,[32] pose considerable difficulties for any serious implementation of the *Lagos Plan*. But such deficiencies in ECA resources must be balanced by the recognition that doing nothing is not an option.

If the more radical and peripheral regimes can identify most readily with the *Lagos Plan* then the less radical, semiperipheral regimes may do so the least. Notwithstanding the pressures for African consensus, the latter still retain some confidence in orthodox developmentalist approaches because they have experienced rapid growth rates themselves thus far. So the semiperiphery has served not only as a market for OECD capital and technolgoical exports but also, at least until 1980, as an example of "successful" orthodox growth policies. Even if the majority of people in, say, Kenya or the Ivory Coast or Nigeria have not benefited from high rates of growth, at least their ruling classes have kept their confidence in established assumptions. As the retainers of faith in and linkages with OECD interests, such semiperipheral regimes can come to exert a regional dominance akin to the global hegemony of OECD countries and corporations, which perhaps makes for a very distinctive form of collective self-reliance. Yet even countries and classes in the semiperiphery may be marginalized as the new order is established, especially if structural adjustment produces deflation or stagnation there too, thereby creating a further reason for the revival of PanAfricanism.

This group displays most ambivalence about the *Lagos Plan*, supporting its regional and industrial development provisions while downplaying its disengagement and agricultural goals. Moreover, as their economic position and projection are already relatively assured--even if their regional dominance is a function of African underdevelopment rather than an indication of their equivalence to NICs like Brazil and South Korea[33]--they can afford to be generous, i.e., provide support or at least show disinterest while retaining close transnational linkages. Further, the more national fractions of such indigenous bourgeoisie may themselves use at least the rhetoric of the *Lagos Plan*--self-reliance, not socialism--to bolster their claims vis-à-vis more comprador elements.[34] So notwithstanding selective country and class interests who at the semiperiphery are concerned with maintaining linkages with the metropole, the OAU membership as a whole, augmented by widespread national bourgeois interests, has espoused the values of the Lagos Plan: Africa's reaction to and protection from any new and nonempathetic division of labor.

In part, the advocacy of self-reliance and the satisfaction of basic human needs and wants makes good political sense in the short as well as long term: African leaders are not interested in encouraging antagonistic contradictions that might lead to their downfall. Moreover, even the so-called success stories, such as the Ivory Coast and Kenya (and now perhaps Zimbabwe), face structural constraints that the plan, especially its regionalist elements, might help to transcend. For the developmentalist doctrine of the 1960s has run into difficulties in the 1980s even in the semiperiphery, as the Agenda indicates:

> Import substitution can be a sound policy and most industrialisation has started on that basis. But in many African countries it has been badly implemented....For countries that have nearly completed the first stages of import substitution, such as Kenya, Ivory Coast and Tanzania, few import substitution opportunities exist based on the internal market.[35]

The real reason for IBRD reservations about import substitution may have to do, of course, with new protectionist pressures for reindustrialization in the North. Industrialization, as the Lagos Plan recognizes, is the sine qua non of development--hence the designation of the years 1980 to 1990 as the Industrial Development Decade in Africa (see chapter 12)[36]--so any hasty acceptance of the Agenda's priority of agriculture may serve to perpetuate dependence as well as exclude other sectors forever. Conversely, the logic of laissez faire is based upon differentiation: the successful (in the semiperiphery) expand, albeit modestly, while those without resources (i.e., the periphery) are allowed to decline. The growth of inequalities both within and among African states threatens national and continental order, hence the interest reflected in the Lagos Plan for a form of Keynesian welfarism--"international managerialism"--at the African level. The continent's unity is already sufficiently fragile; structural as well as strategic and diplomatic divergence might shatter any remaining cohesion. By contrast, the implication of the Agenda is for renewed differentiation: those with agricultural and mineral exports would survive, while those with neither would be abandoned to triage. OECD interests lie with the Third rather than Fourth World; ECA is attempting to camouflage and compensate for such an unequal division of labor.

Although the Lagos Plan and the Agenda are both responses to the present continental crisis, the former would seem to offer an enhanced prospect of development by contrast with the latter. Both of them are reflective of current intellectual and ideological conditions and of established modes of analysis and praxis.[37] While the Agenda adopts an essentially revisionist developmentalist perspective within the modernization genre, the Lagos Plan falls within the dependencia tradition. Notwithstanding considerable evidence to the contrary, the IBRD report still proposes outward-looking growth based on agricultural exports--a viable option in a world of protection and deflation?--with minimal regional cooperation, whereas the

OAU strategy advocates inward-looking development based on integrated sectors, especially industry, with substantial regional and continental integration: an African Economic Community by the end of this century.[38]

The two plans are not only antithetical in intellectual association and policy direction; they are also advocated by two exclusive coalitions, themselves reflective of the old politics. The more nationalist or "Africanist" coalition of the OAU/ECA under the leadership of Adedeji consists of indigenous and progressive academics, advisers, and leaders (many of whom participated in the Dalhousie conference in late 1984), whereas the more "internationalist" IBRD group is less cohesive, more conservative, and less indigenous, consisting of bankers, bureaucrats, and economists. The former is clearly a more radical coalition than the latter. And both are now articulating and refining their assumptions, conditions, and expectations as indicated by the present collection, as the African caucus challenges the World Bank's *Agenda*: the *Lagos Plan* "is conceived on the basis of individual state and multi-state collective self-reliance based on internal resources. On the other hand, the World Bank report broadly favors the African trade *status quo*; thus, by implication, unduly tying African economies to extra-African influences."[39]

The basic distinctions between the two strategies are (1) the degree of African incorporation within the world system and (2) the major sector of emphasis for development with its consequences for any new division of labor. The *Lagos Plan* advocates development through collective (regional and continental) self-reliance; whereas, the *Agenda* still espouses growth through further integration into the global economy. The latter proposes more agricultural investment, production, and exportation through the private sector, and the former prefers an industrial concentration in the public sector. So the latter still advances outward-looking growth despite (1) its history of failure and (2) protectionist pressures among advanced industrialized states; the former, attempting to learn from past mistakes and to anticipate future difficulties, advocates a break with past policies to relieve present problems. These constitute strikingly different, essentially dialectical, views of the continent's prospects based on divergent explanations of the causes of Africa's unenviable condition and on divergent expectations of any new global economic order.

The World Bank asserts that internal rather than external factors were the causes of underdevelopment:

> When the Sub-Saharan states won independence some 20 years ago, they faced formidable constraints to development. These included under-developed human resources, political fragility, insecurely rooted and ill-suited institutions, a climate and geography hostile to development, and rapid population growth. And while the governments have scored considerable achievements, the legacy of history and the facts of geography continue to hamper African progress.[40]

Such a revisionist perspective is compatible with established developmentalist assumptions, whereas the *Plan* adopts a more radical approach compatible with *dependencia* analyses:

> Africa, despite all efforts made by its leaders, remains the least developed continent....Indeed, Africa was directly exploited during the colonial period and for the past two decades; this exploitation has been carried out through neo-colonialistic external forces which seek to influence the economic policies and directions of African states....
>
> We view, with disquiet, the over-dependence of the economy of our continent on the export of basic raw materials and minerals. This phenomenon has made African economies highly susceptible to external developments and with detrimental effects on the interests of the continent.[41]

So the Lagos Plan sees disengagement as a prerequisite for development; whereas, the Agenda still argues that "trickle-down" will, eventually, generate growth. Ironically, the former blames external conditions and advances an internal solution--a continental common market--whereas the latter situates the causes of underdevelopment internally, as the result of inappropriate policies and processes, yet advocates an external solution. Moreover, the World Bank is concerned with individual African states in the world system and with exchange rather than production, i.e., with superstructure. By contrast, the OAU deals with the collectivity of African states in the global economy and with production not just trade, i.e., with substructure. Finally, the Bank prefers the privatization of economic relations; whereas, the OAU strategy is compatible with state control over the means of production. Both solutions are products of a period of economic instability and intellectual uncertainty. Both need to be revised to be relevant to any new world economy, hence ECA and Africa's Development and the World Bank's Joint Program of Action.

Notwithstanding all the evidence of declining terms of trade and the outflow of capital undermining Africa's development, the World Bank still offers an essentially simplistic and contradictory explanation for Africa's negative balances of trade and growth: "external forces were not the chief factor behind growing deficits: for the oil-importing African nations as a group, poor export performance was more significant."[42] The OAU coalition rejects such outmoded analysis and argues that acceptance of the Agenda will merely perpetuate Africa's dependence on external values and factors:

> We are...concerned about the general tone of the [IBRD] report which tends to suggest that the region's problems are entirely of its own making and that unless the outsiders are allowed to come in with aid and new policies, the crisis would get out of hand and the result will be catastrophic.[43]

The African coalition's insistence, as reflected in this collection, on self-reliance, industrialization as well as agriculture, the public sector, and meeting basic human needs constitutes a turning point in the OAU's collective foreign policy. In an era in which only Namibia and South Africa remain unfree, PanAfricanism has become an ideology of economic decolonization, rather than one of political nationalism, more appropriate to a postapartheid, post-Bretton Woods order. The 1980 Lagos summit constituted "...an agonizing but frank reappraisal of the present situation and the future prospects of African economic conditions....Our success in exploiting our political unity should encourage us to exploit the strength inherent in our economic unity."[44]

In essence, then, the OAU and IBRD perspectives and prescriptions are quite incompatible, although the Agenda claims that it "accepts the long-term objectives of African development as expressed by the...Lagos Plan of Action."[45] It asserts that it "builds on the Lagos Plan of Action." This report deals with short- to medium-term responses to Africa's current economic difficulties. It focuses on how growth can be accelerated and how the resources to achieve the long-term objectives set by the African governments can be generated, with the support of the international community.[46] As such externally oriented vulnerability is exactly what the OAU seeks to escape, the African coalition rejects most of the World Bank's assumptions, analyses, and prescriptions, as indicated consistently, if carefully, throughout this collection:

> The goals, objectives and characteristics of the strategy contained in the Report are in many ways inconsistent with those of the Lagos Plan of Action....
>
> The implication of the recommended approach is to make Africa more dependent on external markets for its agricultural and mineral products and for its essential factor inputs. This is contrary to the principles of self-reliant and self-sustaining development of the Lagos Plan of Action.[47]

The African attack on the IBRD Agenda was reinforced by a critique from the very group that had requested the study from the World Bank: the African governors. In early March 1982, they too (1) rejected its focus on domestic factors, (2) opposed its concentration on agriculture rather than industry, and (3) expressed skepticism about whether it would deliver the envisaged finance.[48] They also lamented its disinterest in regionalism and its dissatisfaction with the public and parastatal sectors. But their major complaint was about its focus--the attempt to blame Africa for its own condition--which they asserted placed insufficient importance on external, global conditions. Instead, Africa imports many of its problems:

> Certain questions have not been dealt with in the World Bank Report: problems such as the soaring of interest rates in the international financial markets, global negotiations with a view to establishing a new international economic order, and stabilization of commodity prices.[49]

With the receding prospect of a consensual NIEO being created to replace the Bretton Woods system--reflective of IBRD inattention to global rather than continental conditions--African leaders have, then, a collective interest in designing an alternative to another North-dominated international division of labor. Aside from the apparent trend towards increasing repression and depoliticization--an attempt to contain the results of underdevelopment--the Lagos Plan is one major aspect of the continuing quest by Africa'a ruling classes to secure (or, in a few cases, to recapture) high degrees of development and order. The realization of these objectives would enhance their prospects of surplus production and accumulation. If most projections of insufficient growth materialize, then African leaders would be faced with massive marginalization and opposition, as the first opening citation speculates.[50]

The reformist and welfarist elements of the Lagos Plan reflect, then, the common interest of all of Africa's ruling classes in retaining power. For not only have African states become less equal since the independence period, African classes have become more established and antagonistic. Given prevailing global, regional, and national conditions--the African crisis--the ability of regimes to meet basic human needs has decreased. The threat of anarchy and the withdrawal of peasants from the commodity and cash crop sectors, let alone massive unemployment and underemployment, are all the results of declining real personal incomes and living standards. They acted as catalysts for the Lagos summit.

If the initial African assertion of its collective self-reliance was a response by the continent's ruling class to Northern protectionism, then the subsequent African reaction to World Bank subversion of its self-reliant orientation was a rejection of Northern paternalism. In addition, Africa is dubious about whether the West has the resources or readiness any longer, given the impact of the world recession on it, too, to implement any of its schemes; the new international division of labor is characterized by self-interest, not disinterest, as indicated by difficulties in funding IDA and the World Bank's new African fund. Mahbub ul Haq expressed this widespread fear--the inability of the World Bank to deliver any accelerated assistance as indicated in its Agenda for Action--on his resignation from the World Bank because of his opposition to its move away from a real concern for poverty, the retreat from McNamara's BHN to Claussen's (or Berg's) GNP:

> The major danger is that the Report may well be used to lecture to Africa about its internal policy reforms without providing an increase in financial assistance. It will be very unfortunate if the foreign assistance recommendations of the Report fall through, which looks likely at the moment, and all that remains are generalizations and homilies about Africa's domestic problems.[51]

Notwithstanding such a possibility, and notwithstanding the general preference of the OAU coalition for the Lagos Plan over the Agenda, certain states and fractions both inside and outside the continent may well still identify with the World Bank perspective. Indeed, the Bank not only has moderated its harsh opinion, it has also provided significant supplementary assistance to Africa. Despite IMF conditions and U.S. reservations, the IBRD has increased its support for and involvement in Africa in the 1980s. In turn, the ECA has toned down its antagonism towards the World Bank group, and at its Twenty-fifth Jubilee celebration called for a "willed future" rather than an unplanned successor to Bretton Woods.

IDEOLOGY

Self-reliance in the 1980s can be seen to constitute a continental motif of PanAfricanism as did the concepts "we are all Africans" and "try Africa first" in the previous decades. In a certain sense, it represents a higher, collective form of economic nationalism than other forms developed and articulated in prior periods. Moreover, as a consensual, synthetic ideology, it embodies some novel elements. First, its emphasis on the continent's intellectual as well as material resources is related to the imperative of psychological, as well as legal or political, liberation. Second, its concern for ecology and sustainability is related to the general global issue of renewable resources and basic human needs. And third, its emphasis on local production is compatible with the rise, not so much of African socialism as of national capitalism, being particularly compatible with the nascent interests of an indigenous bourgeoisie. To this extent, the Lagos Plan is a masterful mix of African populism, international socialism, and national capitalism. It may constitute, at one level, a blueprint of the continent's preferences for a successor to Bretton Woods; a redefinition of its external economic linkages.[52] It may also emphasize some interests over others within indigenous political economies, hence the unevenness of implementation.

As indicated in the Introduction, our interest in and support for the LPA derives from an appreciation (1) of the lack of choice for the continent and (2) of the imperative of rendering short- and long-term responses compatible. The crisis has concentrated attention; it may yet concentrate strategy, so that Africa two hundred years after the Berlin Conference may be better placed to satisfy BHN and be more judicious in its choice of partners and priorities. In short, the Lagos Plan has the potential, not yet guaranteed, to stimulate a renaissance: a truly new Africa by the year 2000. Given the current rate of decline, the old Africa may not be in existence by then in any case: a reconstituted continent must perforce rise Phoenix-like from the ashes, or dust, of the old. As the UN "Declaration on the Critical Economic Situation in Africa" cautions:

> Africa, despite its enormous potential, remains the least developed of all continents....According to all projections, prospects for recovery, growth and development remain very dim unless the efforts currently under way in African countries are fully supported by the international community.[53]

NOTES

1. Adebayo Adedeji, "Introduction" to ECA and Africa's Development, 1983-2008: A Preliminary Perspective Study (Addis Ababa: ECA, 1983), p. 2.

2. Samir Amin, "Crisis, nationalism, and socialism," in Samir Amin et al., Dynamics of Global Crisis (London: Macmillan, 1982), p. 198.

3. See UN, Secretariat, "Critical Economic Situation in Africa. Review of the Emergency Rehabilitation and Reconstruction Situation in Food-Aid and Drought-Affected Countries," Thirty-ninth Session, (Agenda item 139. A/39/594), 23 October 1984.

4. See Robert Boardman et al., eds., Africa, Europe and Lomé III, Dalhousie African Studies Series (Washington: University Press of America, 1985).

5. For a distinctively unorthodox yet unradical perspective see Ali A. Mazrui, The African Condition: A Political Diagnosis (London: Heinemann, 1980).

6. For an overview of this transition see Timothy M. Shaw, Africa's International Affairs: An Analysis and Bibliography (Halifax: Center for Foreign Policy Studies, 1983).

7. See Timothy M. Shaw, "Debates about Africa's Future: the Brandt, World Bank, and Lagos Plan Blueprints," Third World Quarterly 5 (2) (April 1983): 330-344.

8. See ECA and Africa's Development, pp. 93-103.

9. For an overview of these see Timothy M. Shaw, ed., Alternative Futures for Africa (Boulder: Westview, 1982).

10. See inter alia Timothy M. Shaw, Towards an International Political Economy for the 1980s: from Dependence to (Inter)dependence (Halifax: Center for Foreign Policy Studies, 1980) and Amin et al., Dynamics of Global Crisis.

11. On this transition see Timothy M. Shaw, "Conclusion" in Towards a Political Economy for Africa: The Dialectics of Dependence (London: Macmillan, 1985) and Isebill V. Gruhn, "The Economic Commission for Africa" in African Regional Organizations, ed. Domenico Mazzeo (Cambridge: Cambridge University Press, 1984), pp. 27-48.

12. For orthodox analyses and comparisons see Christine A. Bogdanowicz-Bindert, "Sub-Saharan Africa: An Agenda for Action," Journal of World Trade Law 16 (4) (July-August 1982) and Carol Lancaster "Africa's Economic Crisis," Foreign Policy 52 (Fall 1983): 149-166.

13. Adebayo Adedeji, "Africa: Permanent Underdog?" International Perspectives 17 (March-April 1981).

14. Ibid., p. 17. On the human dimensions and rights involved as well as the politico-economic difficulties see Richard Sandbrook "Is There Hope for Africa?" International Perspectives (January-February 1983), pp. 3-8.

15. World Bank, World Development Report, 1983 (Washington: World Bank, 1983), p. 2.

16. See World Bank, Accelerated Development in Sub-Saharan Africa: An Agenda for Action (Washington: World Bank, 1981).

17. World Development Report, 1983, p. 2.

18. See J.F. Ade Ajayi, "Expectations of Independence," Daedalus 3 (2) (Spring 1982): 1-9.

19. "Accelerated Development in Sub-Saharan Africa: An Assessment by OAU, ECA and ADB Secretariats," (CM 1177 (XXVIII) Annex 1), Council of Ministers, Thirty-ninth Ordinary Session, Addis Ababa, 22 February to 1 March 1982, p. 29.

20. See Gerald K. Helleiner, "The IMF and Africa in the 1980s," Canadian Journal of African Studies 17 (11) (1983): 17-33. See also Thomas M. Callaghy, "Africa's Debt Crisis," Journal of International Affairs 38 (1) (Summer 1984): 61-80.

21. See ECA, "Implementation of the Lagos Plan of Action," (E/CN.14/TPCW.II/18/Rev.2) Addis Ababa, April 1982.

22. On popular pressures and people's coups see Alan Cowell, "Africa's Angry Young Men," New York Times Magazine, 19 December 1982, pp. 39-40, 68-72 and 106 and Tetteh A. Kofi, "Black Africa: Bleak Prospects and Rising Interest," Business Week, 1 November 1982, p. 122.

23. On this "non-official" continental gathering see "Africa Towards the Year 2000: Final Report on the Joint OAU/ECA Symposium on the Future Development of Africa," appendix C in Alternative Futures for Africa, ed. Shaw, pp. 329-340.

24. OAU, Lagos Plan of Action, p. 5.

25. World Bank, Accelerated Development in Sub-Saharan Africa, p. 5.

26. OAU, Lagos Plan of Action, p. 8.

27. Ibid.

28. Adebayo Adedeji, Address at the formal opening of the annual policy meeting of the Cooperation for Development in Africa Conference, Washington, 26 October 1982, p. 14.

29. Ibid.

30. See "Annex 1: Final Act of Lagos" in Lagos Plan of Action, p. 128.

31. On the latter group and the associated problems of political and economic decay see Timothy M. Shaw, "Beyond Underdevelopment: The Anarchic State in Africa," African Studies Association, Washington, D.C. (November 1982).

32. See Timothy M. Shaw, "The Future of the Great Powers in Africa: Towards a Political Economy of Intervention," Journal of Modern African Studies 21 (4) (December 1983): 555-586.

33. On the differences as well as similarities between, say, Brazil and Nigeria, see Peter Evans, Dependent Development: the Alliance of Multinational, State, and Local Capital in Brazil (Princeton: Princeton University Press, 1979), pp. 308-314. And in terms of the relevance of Bill Warren's thesis to Africa see Alain Lipietz, "Towards Global Fordism?" and "Marx or Rostow?" New Left Review 132 (March- April 1982): 33-58.

34. On the national bourgeoisie in Nigeria and Zambia see Timothy M. Shaw, "Nigeria in World Politics: Contemporary Calculations and Constraints," in Nigerian Foreign Policy: Alternative Perceptions and Projections, eds. Timothy M. Shaw and Olajide Aluko (London: Macmillan, 1983), pp. 23-24 and with Jane L. Parpart, "Contradiction and Coalition: Class Fractions in Zambia, 1964-1984," Africa Today 30 (3) (Third Quarter 1983): 23-50.

35. World Bank, Accelerated Development in Sub-Saharan Africa, p. 93.

36. OAU, Lagos Plan of Action, p. 19. See also A Program for the Industrial Development Decade for Africa, prepared jointly by ECA, OAU and UNIDO (New York: United Nations, 1982).

37. For comparisons between development strategies see inter alia, A.M. Babu, "Development Strategy--Revolutionary Style" in his African Socialism or Socialist Africa? (London: Zed, 1981), pp. 144-164 and Timothy M. Shaw, "From Dependence to Self-reliance: Africa's Prospects for the Next Twenty Years," International Journal 35 (4) (Autumn 1980), pp. 821-844.

38. See OAU, Lagos Plan of Action, p. 128.

39. OAU, "Report of the Secretary-General on the World Bank Report," (CM/1177 (XXXVIII) appendix II) (Council of Ministers Thirty-eighth Ordinary Session, Addis Ababa, 23 February to 1 March 1982, p. 3.

40. World Bank, Accelerated Development in Sub-Saharan Africa, p. 9.

41. OAU, Lagos Plan of Action, p. 7.

42. World Bank, Accelerated Development in Sub-Saharan Africa, p. 17.

43. OAU, "Report of the Secretary-General on the World Bank Report," appendix II, p. 1.

44. OAU, Lagos Plan of Action, p. 8. On the polemics of Third World unity see Timothy M. Shaw, "Dependence to (Inter)Dependence: Review of Debate on the New International Economic Order," Alternatives 4 (4) (March 1979): 557-578 and "The Political Economy of Non-Alignment: From Dependence to Self-reliance," International Studies 19 (3) (July-September 1980): 476-502. See also A. Benachenhou, "South-South Cooperation, the Lagos Plan of Action and Africa's Independence," Africa Development 8 (4) (1983): 5-19.

45. World Bank, _Accelerated Development in Sub-Saharan Africa_, p. v.

46. _Ibid._

47. "Accelerated Development in Sub-Saharan Africa: An Assessment by OAU, ECA and ADB Secretariats," annex I, pp. 44-45; see the rejoinder by IBRD President, Alden Claussen, "Looking Towards a Brighter Future," _West Africa_ 3378 (3 May 1982): 1194-1199.

48. See "What the World Bank Didn't Say," _Africa News_ 18 (19) (10 May 1982): 3 and 11.

49. "World Economy: Africans Respond to World Bank Study," p. 2.

50. See John Ravenhill, ed., _Africa in Economic Crisis: Problems and Strategies_ (London: Macmillan, 1985).

51. "World Bank 'Stagnant and Confused' Says Former Director," _Africa Now_ 13 (May 1982): 89. But note the positive public relations tone--"... greater involvement will demand a new era of more intense partnership between the people of Africa and the Bank." (p. 1194)--set by Alden Claussen in his address at the Nigerian Institute of International Affairs, "Looking Towards a Brighter Future." See also the revised and moderated successor to Berg, "Sub-Saharan Africa: Progress Report on Development Prospects and Programs," (Washington: World Bank, September 1983); selections in Luke & Shaw, eds., _Continental Crisis_, pp. 205-223.

52. On Africa's dilemmas, particularly the inappropriateness of IMF "medicine" and the need for a new Bretton Woods, see Norman Girvan "Adjustment via Austerity: Is There an Alternative?" _IFDA Dossier_ 45 (January/February 1985): 45-54.

53. UN "Declaration on the Critical Economic Situation in Africa" (A/RES/32/79) 7 December 1984, p. 2.

Appendix: Participants at the ECA-Dalhousie Conference, November 1984

Adebayo Adedeji

Agnes Akosua Aidoo

J. Olu Aiyegbusi

S.K.B. Asante

Bolanle Awe

Negussay Ayele

Robert S. Browne

G.P.O. Chikelu

Adel Cortas

Cyril Kofie Daddieh

Ibrahim H. El-Issawy

Amir Jamal

A.R. Jiagge

George Kimani

G.E.A. Lardner

David Fasholé Luke

Maurice W. Makramalla

L.A. Odero-Ogwel

H.M.A. Onitiri

E.P. Pallangyo

Jane L. Parpart

N.A. Rweyemamu

Philip M. Saunders

Gilbert A. Sekgoma

Timothy M. Shaw

D. Babatunde Thomas

Peter Underwood

Bibliography

Adedeji, Adebayo. "Africa's Economy in 1984: Crisis upon Crisis." West Africa 3516, 14 January 1985, 52-53.
Adedeji, Adebayo. "The African Development Problematique." Addis Ababa: ECA, March 1985.
Adedeji, Adebayo. "The Evolution of the Monrovia Strategy and the Lagos Plan of Action: A Regional Approach to Economic Decolonisation." Addis Ababa: ECA, 1983.
"Africa: The Land is Growing Old. What Will the Children Inherit?" UNICEF News 120, 1984, 1-35.
"Africa's Population Alert." Development Forum 12(5), June 1984, iv.
African Development Bank & Economic Commission for Africa Economic Report on Africa, 1985. Abidjan and Addis Ababa, March 1985.
"African Food Crisis Series-3: A Background Dossier." Development Forum 12, November-December 1984, 11 and 16.
"Agricultural Special: Seeking Food Self-Sufficiency." West Africa 3520, 22 April 1985, 783-796.
Benachenhou, A. "South-South Cooperation, the Lagos Plan of Action and Africa's Independence." Africa Development 8(4), 1983, 5-19.
Bogdanowicz-Bindert, Christine A. "Sub-Saharan Africa: An Agenda for Action." Journal of World Trade Law 16(4), July-August 1982.
Browne, Robert S. "Africa and the IMF Conditionality: A New Form of Colonialism?" Africa Report 29(5), September-October 1984, 14-18.
Browne, Robert S. and Robert J. Cummings. The Lagos Plan of Action Vs The Berg Report: Contemporary Issues in African Development. Washington: Howard University Press, 1984.
Callaghy, Thomas M. "Africa's Debt Crisis." Journal of International Affairs 38(1), Summer 1984, 61-80.

Carlsson, Jerker ed. Recession in Africa. Uppsala: Scandinavian Institute of African Studies, 1983.

Chikelu, G.P.O., G.A. Sekgoma and G. Tanwo. Implementation of the Lagos Plan of Action: Africa, Nigeria and Sierra Leone. Halifax: Dalhousie African Studies Working Paper No. 6, May 1985.

Clausen, A.W. "Address to the World Bank Board of Governors." Washington, D.C.: World Bank, September 1984.

Commonwealth. The Debt Crisis and the World Economy. Report by a Commonwealth Group of Experts. London: Commonwealth Secretariat, 1984.

Diallo, Alio S. "Note on the Lagos Plan of Action." African Administrative Studies 22, 1983, 3-6.

D'sa, Rose M. "The Lagos Plan of Action - Legal Mechanisms for Cooperation Between the OAU and the UNECA." Journal of African Law 27(1), Spring 1983, 4-21.

ECA. Annual Report, May 1983-May 1984. New York: United Nations, 1984, E/ECA/CM.10/38.

ECA. ECA and Africa's Development, 1983-2008: A Preliminary Perspective Study. Addis Ababa: ECA, 1983.

ECA. "Progress Report on the Implementation of the Lagos Plan of Action by the ECA Secretariat." E/ECA/CM.11/74, April 1985.

ECA. "Proposals for Food and Agriculture Development 1986-1990." E/ECA/CM.11.39, February 1985.

ECA. "Response of the UN System to the General Assembly Declaration on the Critical Economic Situation in Africa and Their Proposed Contributions to the Long-Term Aspects of the Critical Economic Situation." E/ECA/CM.11/75, April 1985.

ECA. "Review of the Progress Made in the Taking Into Account of the Objectives and Directives of the LPA into the Development Policies of the African Countries." E/ECA/CM.11/73, April 1985.

ECA. "Special Memorandum by the ECA Conference of Ministers on Africa's Economic and Social Crisis." 1984 E/ECA/CM.10/37/Rev.

ECA. Survey of Economic and Social Conditions in Africa 1978-1979, 1982-1983 and 1983-1984. Addis Ababa, 1980, 1984 and 1985, E/CN.14/743, E/ECA/CM.10/4, and E/ECA/CM.11/16.

ECA. The Establishment of an African Monetary Fund: Structure and Mechanism. A Technical Feasibility Study. Addis Ababa, January 1985.

ECA, OAU and UNIDO. A Program for the Industrial Development Decade for Africa. New York, 1982.

Girvan, Norman P. "Adjustment via Austerity: Is There an Alternative?" IFDA Dossier 45, January-February 1985, 45-54.

Helleiner, Gerald K. "The IMF and Africa in the 1980s." Canadian Journal of African Studies 17(11), 1983, 17-33.

Hyden, Goran. No Short-Cuts to Progress: African Development Management in Perspective. Berkeley: University of California Press, 1983.

Industrial Development Decade for Africa. Bulletin. Vienna: UNIDO, occasionally from 1985 onwards.

Lancaster, Carol. "Africa's Economic Crisis." Foreign Policy. 52 Fall 1983, 149-166.

Lancaster, Carol. "Africa's Development Challenges." Current History 84 (501), April 1985, 145-149, 183 and 186.

Luke, David Fasholé and Timothy M. Shaw eds. Continental Crisis: The Lagos Plan of Action and Africa's Future. Washington: University Press of America, 1984.

Mtei, E.I.M. "Africa and the IMF: An Evolving Relationship." Africa Report 29 (5), September-October 1984, 19-21.

Nyerere, Julius K. "Address to the OAU Summit Meeting at Addis Ababa, November 1984 when Accepting Chairmanship." Dar es Salaam: State House, 1984.

Nyerere, Julius K. "Is Africa Responsible?" Dar es Salaam: State House, March 1985.

Nyerere, Julius K. "Speech at UN Emergency Conference on Africa, March 1985." Dar es Salaam: State House, March 1975.

Nyerere, Julius K. "Speeches in United Kingdom, March 1985." Dar es Salaam: State House, March 1985.

Obasanjo, Olusegun. "Africa's Needs." Foreign Policy 57, Winter 1984-85, 80-91.

ODI. "Africa's Economic Crisis." Briefing Paper. May 1982.

ODI. "Africa's Food Crisis." Briefing Paper. May 1984.

OAU. Democratisation of National Development in Africa. Proceedings of a Symposium, Dakar, March 1982. Geneva: International Institute for Labour Studies, 1983.

OAU. Food Self-sufficiency, Technological Autonomy and Social Progress in Africa: Research Guide. Geneva: International Institute for Labour Studies, 1984.

OAU. Lagos Plan of Action for the Economic Development of Africa, 1980-2000. Geneva: International Institute for Labour Studies, 1981.

OAU. Monrovia Strategy for the Development of Africa and the Declaration of Commitment. Monrovia, July 1979.

OAU. What Kind of Africa by the Year 2000? Addis Ababa, May 1979.

Poats, Rutherford M. "Crisis and Response in Africa." OECD Review 131, November 1984, 26-29.

Ravenhill, John ed. Africa in Economic Crisis: Problems and Strategies. London: Macmillan, 1985.

Relly, G.W.H. "Economic Development in Africa: Performance, Problems and Prospects." Optima 32(2), July 1984, 56-63.

Sandbrook, Richard. "Is There Hope For Africa?" International Perspectives. January-February 1983, 3-8.

Saunders, Phil & Cyril Kofie Daddieh. Oceans and Coastal Development in West Africa: Regional and National Potentials. Halifax: Dalhousie University African Studies Working Paper No. 8, forthcoming.

Shaw, Timothy M. ed. Alternative Futures for Africa. Boulder: Westview, 1982.

Shaw, Timothy M. "The African Crisis: Alternative Development Strategies for the Continent." Alternatives 9(1) 1983, 111-127.

Shaw, Timothy M. "Debates About Africa's Future: the Brandt, World Bank, and Lagos Plan Blueprints." Third World Quarterly 5(2), April 1983, 330-344.

Shaw, Timothy M. "South Africa's Role in Southern Africa in the Year 2000" in Olajide Aluko & Timothy M. Shaw eds. Southern Africa in the 1980s. London: George Allen & Unwin, 1985, 294-318.

Shaw, Timothy M. and Olajide Aluko eds. Africa Projected: From Recession to Renaissance by the Year 2000? London: Macmillan, 1985.

Shepherd, Jack. "When Foreign Aid Fails." *Atlantic Monthly*. April 1985, 41-46.

Thahane, Timothy T. "Africa and the World Bank: The Development Challenges Ahead." *Africa Report* 29(5), September-October, 1984, 48-52.

"Toward Sustained Development: A Joint Program of Action for Sub-Saharan Africa." *Finance and Development* 21(4), December 1984, 29-30.

UN. "Critical Economic Situation in Africa. Review of the Emergency Rehabilitation and Reconstruction Situation in Food-Aid and Drought-Affected Countries." Report of the Secretary-General (23 October 1984) and General Assembly Resolution 39/29, 7 December 1984, A/39/594 and A/RES/39/29.

UN/FAO. "Regional Food Plan for Africa." *Tenth FAO Regional Conference for Africa*. Arusha, Tanzania, September 1978.

UN/OAU/ECA. *Documents on the African Crisis*. Halifax: Dalhousie University African Studies Working Paper No. 7, June 1985.

UN. Office for Emergency Operations in Africa. *Africa Emergency*. New York, monthly from May 1985 onwards.

USDA. *Food Problems and Prospects in Sub-Saharan Africa*. Washington, 1981.

Wangwe, S.M. "Sub-Saharan Africa: Which Economic Strategy?" *Third World Quarterly* 6(4), October 1984, 1033-1059.

Wheeler, David. "Sources of Stagnation in Sub-Saharan Africa." *World Development* 12(1), January 1984, 1-23.

World Bank. *Accelerated Development in Sub-Saharan Africa: An Agenda for Action*. Washington, D.C., 1981.

World Bank. *World Development Report, 1982, 1983, 1984*. Oxford: Oxford University Press, annually.

World Bank. *Sub-Saharan Africa: Progress Report on Development Prospects and Programs*. Washington, D.C., 1983.

World Bank. *Toward Sustained Development in Sub-Saharan Africa: A Joint Program of Action*. Washington, D.C., 1984.